The Modern Language Review

OCTOBER 2014   VOLUME 109   PART 4

General Editor
Professor Derek Connon

English Editor
Professor Andrew Hiscock

French Editor
Dr Alison Williams

Italian Editor
Professor Jane Everson

Hispanic Editor
Professor Derek Flitter

Germanic Editor
Professor Robert Vilain

Slavonic Editor
Dr Katharine Hodgson

Assistant Editor
Dr John Waś

MODERN HUMANITIES RESEARCH ASSOCIATION

The Modern Humanities Research Association

was founded in Cambridge in 1918 and has become an international organization with members in all parts of the world. It is a registered charity number 1064670, and a company limited by guarantee, registered in England number 3446016. Its main object is to encourage advanced study and research in modern and medieval European languages, literatures, and cultures by its publication of journals, book series, and its Style Guide.

Further information about the activities of the Association and individual membership may be obtained from the Hon. Secretary, Dr Barbara Burns, School of Modern Languages and Cultures, University of Glasgow, Glasgow G12 8RS, UK, email membership@mhra.org.uk, or from the website at www.mhra.org.uk

The Association's publications, including most back volumes, are available in print or electronically. Full details are available from www.mhra.org.uk

The Modern Language Review

The *Modern Language Review* is one of five journals available to members of the Modern Humanities Research Association in return for a composite membership subscription payable in advance through the Assistant Treasurer. (Associate membership is open to graduates for four years after their first degree, and postgraduate membership is also available.) Some other publications of the MHRA are available to members at special rates.

The *Modern Language Review* and other journals published by the MHRA may be ordered from JSTOR (http://about.jstor.org/csp).

ISSN 0026–7937 (Print)
ISSN 2222–4319 (Online)

© 2014 The Modern Humanities Research Association

All rights reserved. No part of this publication may be reproduced in any material form (including photocopying or storing it in any medium by electronic means) without the prior written permission of the copyright owner, except in accordance with the provisions of the Copyright, Designs and Patents Act 1988, or under the terms of a licence permitting restricted copying issued in the UK by the Copyright Licensing Agency Ltd, Saffron House, 6–10 Kirby Street, London EC1N 8TS, England, or in the USA by the Copyright Clearance Center, 222 Rosewood Drive, Danvers, Mass. 01923. Application for the written permission of the copyright owner to reproduce any part of this publication must be made to the General Editor.

DISCLAIMER

Statements of fact and opinion in the content of the *Modern Language Review* are those of the respective authors and contributors and not of the journal editors or of the Modern Humanities Research Association (MHRA). MHRA makes no representation, express or implied, in respect of the accuracy of the material in this journal and cannot accept any legal responsibility or liability for any errors or omissions that may be made.

TYPESET BY JOHN WAŚ, OXFORD

Guidelines for Contributors to *MLR*

The *Modern Language Review* publishes articles and book reviews in English on any aspect of modern and medieval European (including English and Latin American) languages, literatures, and cultures (including cinema). The journal does not publish correspondence. We are glad to receive general and comparative articles as well as those on language-specific topics. We encourage submissions from postgraduates. Articles should be submitted to the appropriate section editor in one typescript copy together with an identical electronic copy sent as an email attachment. Articles should conform precisely to the conventions of the *MHRA Style Guide*, 3rd edn, 2013 (ISBN 978-1-78188-009-8), obtainable from www.style.mhra.org.uk, price £6.50, US$13, €8; an online version of the *Guide* is also available from the same address. Authors should provide an abstract of their articles with keywords highlighted in bold type. This abstract should not exceed 100 words. At the end of articles and reviews contributors should include, in this order, their affiliation or location; name as it is to be printed; name and postal address for correspondence; and email address. Simple references should be incorporated into the text (see *MHRA Style Guide*, 10.2). Double spacing should be used throughout, including quotations and footnotes, which should be in the same large size of type as the rest of the article. Articles are typically about 8000 words in length including footnotes, but longer and shorter ones are also welcome. Quotations and references should be carefully checked. Quotations from languages covered by the journal, and from Latin and Greek, should be given in the original language. Latin and Greek passages should normally be translated or at least paraphrased; usually this is not required in the case of modern languages, though it may be helpful where dialects or early forms of the language are cited. However, since the journal has a broad readership, please provide translations or paraphrases of quotations within comparative or general articles (except for modern French). If in doubt, consult the appropriate section editor.

The *Modern Language Review* regrets that it must charge contributors for the cost of corrections in proof which the Editor in his or her discretion thinks excessive. Contributors should keep a copy of their typescript. Typescripts not accepted for publication will not normally be returned. If your article is accepted, you will be asked to supply a definitive version of it both in hard copy and as an email attachment. Authors should ensure that there is no discrepancy between the computer file and the printout.

It is a condition of publication in this journal that authors of articles and reviews assign copyright, including electronic copyright, to the MHRA. *Inter alia*, this allows the General Editor to deal efficiently and consistently with requests from third parties for permission to reproduce material. The journal has been published simultaneously in printed and electronic form since January 2001. Permission, without fee, for authors to use their own material in other publications, after a reasonable period of time has elapsed, is not normally withheld. Authors may republish contributions on a personal website or in an academic institution's digital repository without seeking further permission from the Association, but no earlier than 24 months after publication by the MHRA.

On publication of each issue of the journal authors will receive, by email, the finalized PDF of their contribution as it appears in the printed volume. Physical offprints are not supplied. Authors of articles will also receive a complimentary copy of the printed issue in which the article appears.

Articles and books for review should be sent to the Editor concerned:

General and Comparative. Professor Derek Connon, Department of French, Swansea University, Swansea, SA2 8PP (d.f.connon@swansea.ac.uk).
English and American. Professor Andrew Hiscock, School of English, Bangor University, Bangor, LL57 2DG (mhraassistant@bangor.ac.uk)
French. Dr Alison Williams, Department of French, Swansea University, Swansea, SA2 8PP (a.j.williams@swansea.ac.uk).
Italian. Professor Guido Bonsaver, Pembroke College, Oxford OX1 1DW (guido.bonsaver@pmb.ox.ac.uk).
Hispanic. Professor Derek Flitter, School of Modern Languages, Queen's Building, University of Exeter, Exeter EX4 4QH (d.w.flitter@exeter.ac.uk).
German, Dutch, and Scandinavian. Professor Robert Vilain, School of Modern Languages, University of Bristol, 17 Woodland Road, Bristol, BS8 1TE (robert.vilain@bristol.ac.uk).
Slavonic and Eastern European. Dr Katharine Hodgson, School of Modern Languages, Queen's Building, University of Exeter, Exeter EX4 4QH (k.m.hodgson@exeter.ac.uk).

CONTENTS

ARTICLES PAGE

The Disenchantment/Re-enchantment of the World: Aesthetics, Secularization, and the Gods of Greece from Friedrich Schiller to Walter Pater
By SARA LYONS 873

Problematic Realisms: German Poetic Realism and Michel Butor's *Portrait de l'artiste en jeune singe*
By MICHAEL J. WHITE 896

Science in Three Dimensions: Werner Herzog's *Cave of Forgotten Dreams*
By CHRISTOPHER JOHNSON 915

Gower *Agonistes* and Chaucer on Ovid (and Virgil)
By DAVID R. CARLSON 931

Royal Self-Assertion and the Revision of Chivalry: *The Entertainment at Kenilworth* (1575), Jonson's *Masque of Owls* (1624), and *The King's Entertainment at Welbeck* (1633)
By LESLEY MICKEL 953

'Il n'y a presque pas de ces génies grandioses qui étonnent le monde': Unveiling Genius in David d'Angers's *Paganini*
By VIVIENNE SUVINI-HAND 977

Maupassant's *Bel-Ami* and the Secrets of *Actualité*
By EDMUND BIRCH 996

Gil y Zárate and *Carlos II el hechizado*
By JORGE AVILÉS DIZ 1013

Home and Homelessness in Works by Novalis, Dorothea Schlegel, and Tieck
By CHARLOTTE LEE 1030

REVIEWS

Terry Eagleton, *How to Read Literature* (ADAM WATT) 1048
Verena O. Lobsien, *Jenseitsästhetik: Literarische Räume letzter Dinge* (THEODORE ZIOLKOWSKI) 1049
Philologie et théâtre: traduire, commenter, interpréter le théâtre antique en Europe (XVe–XVIIIe siècle), ed. by Véronique Lochert and Zoé Schweitzer (EDWARD FORMAN) . 1052
Naghmeh Sohrabi, *Taken for Wonder: Nineteenth-Century Travel Accounts from Iran to Europe* (REBECCA BUTLER) 1053
Gothic Topographies: Language, Nation Building and 'Race', ed. by P. M. Mehtonen and Matti Savolainen (SARAH ILOTT) 1054
Capital Crimes: Crime Fiction in the City, ed. by Lucy Andrew and Catherine Phelps (KATHARINA HALL) 1056
Constantin V. Ponomareff, *The Time before Death: Twentieth-Century Memoirs* (SCOTT FREER) 1057
The Poetics of the Margins: Mapping Europe from the Interstices, ed. by Rossella M. Riccobono (SILVIA ROSS) 1059
Simone Heller-Andrist, *The Friction of the Frame: Derrida's 'Parergon' in Literature* (K. M. NEWTON) 1061

Roger D. Sell, *Communicational Criticism: Studies in Literature as Dialogue* (Jonathan Baldo) 1062
Nicole D. Smith, *Sartorial Strategies: Outfitting Aristocrats and Fashioning Conduct in Late Medieval Literature* (Sarah L. Peverley) 1065
Nan Goodman, *Banished: Common Law and the Rhetoric of Social Exclusion in Early New England* (Philip Major) 1066
Manushag N. Powell, *Performing Authorship in Eighteenth-Century English Periodicals* (Daniel Cook) 1068
Jonathan H. Grossman, *Charles Dickens's Networks: Public Transport and the Novel* (Paul Young) 1069
Alexandra Socarides, *Dickinson Unbound: Paper, Process, Poetics* (Páraic Finnerty) 1070
The Politics and Poetics of Displacement: Modernism off the Beaten Track, ed. by Massimo Bacigalupo and Luisa Villa (Paul Poplawski) 1072
Genevieve Abravanel, *Americanizing Britain: The Rise of Modernism in the Age of the Entertainment Empire* (Arin Keeble) 1074
Jennifer Margaret Fraser, *Be a Good Soldier: Children's Grief in English Modernist Novels* (Aneesh Barai) 1075
The Letters of Samuel Beckett 1941–1956, ed. by George Craig and others (Derval Tubridy) 1076
Theodore F. Sheckels, *The Political in Margaret Atwood's Fiction: The Writing on the Wall of the Tent* (Kiriaki Massoura) 1078
John Flower, *Historical Dictionary of French Literature* (Nicholas Hammond) .. 1080
Shaping Courtliness in Medieval France: Essays in Honor of Matilda Tomaryn Bruckner, ed. by Daniel E. O'Sullivan and Laurie Shepard (Catherine Leglu) 1081
Olivier Delsaux, *Manuscrits et pratiques autographes chez les écrivains français de la fin du moyen âge: l'exemple de Christine de Pizan* (Angus J. Kennedy) 1082
Marianne Legault, *Female Intimacies in Seventeenth-Century French Literature* (Emilia Wilton-Godberfforde) 1083
Maria C. Scott, *Stendhal's Less-Loved Heroines: Fiction, Freedom, and the Female* (Susannah Wilson) 1084
Charles Lafont and Charles Desnoyer, *Le Tremblement de Terre de la Martinique: drame en cinq actes, suivi de documents inédits*, ed. by Barbara T. Cooper (M. Lynn Weiss) 1086
Nicholas White, *French Divorce Fiction from the Revolution to the First World War* (Phoebe Maltz Bovy) 1086
Anna Freadman, *The Livres-Souvenirs of Colette: Genre and the Telling of Time* (Kathleen Antonioli) 1088
Helen Tattam, *Time in the Philosophy of Gabriel Marcel* (Geoffrey Karabin) ... 1089
Christopher Fynsk, *Last Steps: Maurice Blanchot's Exilic Writing* (Mauro Di Lullo) 1090
'D'un parlar ne l'altro': aspetti dell'enunciazione dal romanzo arturiano alla 'Gerusalemme liberata', ed. by Annalisa Izzo (Mark Davie) 1092
Fabian Alfie, *Dante's 'tenzone' with Forese Donati: The Reprehension of Vice* (John Took) 1093
Matteo Maria Boiardo, *Pastoralia. Carmina. Epigrammata*, ed. by Stefano Carrai and Francesco Tissoni; *'Amico del Boiardo', Canzoniere Costabili*, ed. by Gabriele Baldassari (Carlo Caruso) 1094
Bernardo Rucellai, *De bello Italico. La guerra d'Italia*, ed. by Donatella Coppini (Carlo Caruso) 1096
Lyric Poetry by Women of the Italian Renaissance, ed. by Virginia Cox (Maria Galli Stampino) 1098
'Eunuco': un volgarizzamento anonimo in terza rima, ed. by Matteo Favaretto (Diego Zancani) 1099

Contents

Barbara Torelli Benedetti, *'Partenia': A Pastoral Play*, ed. and trans. by Lisa Sampson and Barbara Burgess-Van Aken (RICHARD ANDREWS) 1101

Florinda Nardi, *Comico e modernità nel 'Discorso del riso' di Basilio Paravicino* (MATTEO FAVARETTO) 1102

John Champagne, *Aesthetic Modernism and Masculinity in Fascist Italy* (CHARLOTTE ROSS) 1104

William Jervis Jones, *German Colour Terms: A Study in their Historical Evolution from Earliest Times to the Present* (HOWARD JONES) 1106

Diskurslinguistik im Spannungsfeld von Deskription und Kritik, ed. by Ulrike Hanna Meinhof and others (SYLVIA JAWORSKA) 1110

The Faustian Century: German Literature and Culture in the Age of Luther and Faustus, ed. by J. M. van der Laan and Andrew Weeks (JOHN L. FLOOD) 1113

Friedemann Stengel, *Aufklärung bis zum Himmel: Emanuel Swedenborg im Kontext der Theologie des 18. Jahrhunderts* (PAUL BISHOP) 1116

Sven-Aage Jørgensen, *Querdenker der Aufklärung: Studien zu Johann Georg Hamann* (DAVID BARRY) 1118

Hugh Barr Nisbet, *Gotthold Ephraim Lessing: His Life, Works, and Thought* (THOMAS MARTINEC) 1119

William J. McGrath, *German Freedom and the Greek Ideal: The Cultural Legacy from Goethe to Mann*, ed. by Celia Applegate and others (RITCHIE ROBERTSON) . . . 1121

Pamela Currie, *Goethe's Visual World* (CHARLOTTE LEE) 1122

May Mergenthaler, *Zwischen Eros und Mitteilung: Die Frühromantik im Symposion der 'Athenaeums-Fragmente'*; Friedrich Schlegel, *Alarcos: Ein Trauerspiel. Historisch-kritische Edition mit Dokumenten*, ed. by Mark-Georg Dehrmann with Nils Gelker (ROGER PAULIN) 1124

Anita-Mathilde Schrumpf, *Sprechzeiten: Rhythmus und Takt in Hölderlins Elegien* (IAN COOPER) 1126

Dietmar Pravida, *Brentano in Wien: Clemens Brentano, die Poesie und die Zeitgeschichte 1813/14* (CLAUDIA NITSCHKE) 1127

Korrespondenzen und Transformationen: Neue Perspektiven auf Adalbert von Chamisso, ed. by Marie-Theres Federhofer and Jutta Weber (JOANNA NEILLY) 1128

Eckhard Höffner, *Geschichte und Wesen des Urheberrechts*, vol. I, rev. edn (ROGER PAULIN) 1130

Realism and Romanticism in German Literature/Realismus und Romantik in der deutschsprachigen Literatur, ed. by Dirk Göttsche and Nicholas Saul (ROGER PAULIN) 1132

John B. Lyon, *Out of Place: German Realism, Displacement and Modernity* (MICHAEL J. WHITE) 1134

Caroline Pross, *Dekadenz: Studien zu einer großen Erzählung der frühen Moderne* (THEODORE ZIOLKOWSKI) 1135

Walter Benjamins anthropologisches Denken, ed. by Carolin Duttlinger and others (WILFRIED VAN DER WILL) 1137

Ernst Jünger, *Letzte Worte*, ed. by Jörg Magenau; Ernst Jünger, *Atlantische Fahrt: 'Rio: Residenz des Weltgeistes'*, ed. by Detlev Schöttker; Ernst Jünger, *Feldpostbriefe an die Familie: 1915–1918; mit ausgewählten Antwortbriefen der Eltern und Friedrich Georg Jüngers*, ed. by Heimo Schwilk (CHRISTOPHE FRICKER) 1141

Elaine Morley, *Iris Murdoch and Elias Canetti: Intellectual Allies* (DAGMAR C. G. LORENZ) 1142

Áine McMurtry, *Crisis and Form in the Later Writing of Ingeborg Bachmann: An Aesthetic Examination of the Poetic Drafts of the 1960s* (RÜDIGER GÖRNER) . . . 1144

German Text Crimes: Writers Accused, from the 1950s to the 2000s, ed. by Tom Cheesman (FLORIAN KROBB) 1145

Stuart Taberner, *Aging and Old-Age Style in Günter Grass, Ruth Klüger, Christa Wolf, and Martin Walser: The Mannerism of a Late Period* (ALEXANDRA LLOYD) . . . 1147
Rainald Goetz, ed. by Heinz Ludwig Arnold and others; *Medialität der Kunst: Rolf Dieter Brinkmann in der Moderne*, ed. by Markus Fauser (REBECCA BRAUN) . . . 1149
Ilija Trojanow, ed. by Julian Preece (STUART TABERNER) 1151
Sinéad Crowe, *Religion in Contemporary German Drama* (GILLIAN PYE) 1152
Michael Minden, *Modern German Literature* (BEN HUTCHINSON) 1154
J. A. E. Curtis, *The Englishman From Lebedian'—A Life of Evgeny Zamiatin (1884–1937)* (ROGER COCKRELL) 1156
Miriam Neirick, *When Pigs Could Fly and Bears Could Dance: A History of the Soviet Circus* (RACHEL S. PLATONOV) 1157
Kristin Roth-Ey, *Moscow Prime Time: How the Soviet Union Built the Media Empire that Lost the Cultural Cold War* (NATASHA RULYOVA) 1159

Abstracts of Articles, Vol. 109, Part 4 (October 2014) 1162

THE DISENCHANTMENT/RE-ENCHANTMENT OF THE WORLD: AESTHETICS, SECULARIZATION, AND THE GODS OF GREECE FROM FRIEDRICH SCHILLER TO WALTER PATER

Max Weber's oracular phrase 'Entzauberung der Welt' ('disenchantment of the world'), from his 1918 lecture 'Wissenschaft als Beruf' ('Science as a Vocation'), is often invoked as a shorthand for a particular narrative of Western secularization.[1] This narrative has acquired a proverbial status, and has a powerful imaginative appeal as a secularized version of the myth of the Fall and the expulsion from Eden: it accounts for the woes of the modern condition even as it hints that our fall into the secular might be understood as a *felix culpa*, necessary for our redemption as enlightened subjects.[2] It can be summarized thus: the rise of science and modern capitalism, coupled with the destruction of traditional forms of community, leached the world of its mystery and, by extension, its meaning. God dwindled, or disappeared, or died. Nature lost its visionary gleams and was exposed as a purposeless mechanism. Human life was reduced to calculable, material forces, and the cost was a pervasive sense of alienation, nihilism, and ennui.[3]

For several decades historians, sociologists, philosophers, and literary critics have been contesting and recasting the terms of what is now often characterized as the 'standard' or 'crude' secularization thesis: that is, the theory that the conditions of modernity inevitably—or at least irreversibly—relegate religion to the margins of social life and lead to a general decay of belief in traditional theologies, or in the supernatural broadly construed.[4]

---

[1] Originally delivered at Munich University in 1918 and published in 1919 by Duncker & Humbolt, Munich.

[2] The imaginative link between the 'disenchantment' narrative of secularization and the myth of the fall is often remarked. See e.g. Jane Bennett, *The Enchantment of Modern Life: Attachments, Crossings, and Ethics* (Princeton: Princeton University Press, 2011), p. 84; and Jonathan Sheehan, 'When was Disenchantment? History and the Secular Age', in *Varieties of Secularism in a Secular Age*, ed. by Michael Warner and others (Cambridge, MA: Harvard University Press, 2010), pp. 217–42 (pp. 217–19). The notion that secularization is desolating yet ultimately salutary—a kind of *felix culpa*, or fortunate fall—is central to Weber's work. As Jeffrey C. Alexander writes, for Weber 'rationalization is at once enervating disenchantment and enlightening empowerment [. . . It] is at once a terrible condition, the worst evil, and the only human path for liberation' ('The Dialectic of Individuation and Domination: Weber's Rationalization Theory and Beyond', in *Max Weber: Rationality and Modernity*, ed. by Sam Whimster and Scott Lash (London: Allen & Unwin, 1987), pp. 185–206 (p. 187)).

[3] My summary here is extrapolated from Weber's argument, but as Bennett notes, his is only the most famous 'disenchantment tale' of secularization; for a more wide-ranging discussion see *The Enchantment of Modern Life*, pp. 56–90.

[4] The literature on this topic is vast and rapidly expanding. For a recent review essay which gives an

Although critiques of the secularization thesis are diverse in their motivations and theoretical commitments, they are generally united by a suspicion of what Dominic Erdozain describes as its 'nomothetic hubris':[5] the thesis seems to confer a dogmatic authority upon a phenomenon it affects only to name and analyse. Perhaps surprisingly, however, Weber's disenchantment paradigm remains compelling for some important critics of the thesis, apparently because it constructs secularization in such grandly pessimistic terms. Most notably, the Catholic philosopher Charles Taylor makes Weberian disenchantment key to his sweeping and influential rewriting of the secularization narrative, *A Secular Age* (2007). Although Taylor aims to problematize the equation between modernity and the decline of religion, he nonetheless draws upon Weber to clarify the distinction between premodern religiosity and modern secularity. Taylor distinguishes between a porous, premodern self, which was open to 'enchantment'—that is, to 'spirits, demons, cosmic forces'[6]—and, by extension, to religious faith, and the 'buffered' or 'disenchanted' nature of modern subjectivity, which encloses itself within an 'immanent frame' and is thus largely impervious to religious possibility (though Taylor emphasizes that many people remain committed or at least receptive to such possibility).[7]

Meanwhile, a flurry of recent books have sought to revise the secularization thesis not by challenging the idea that modernity is fatal to religion, but by contesting Weber's identification of modernity with disenchantment. Unlike Taylor, these critics are not concerned to rethink the relationship between religion and modernity, but to argue for the value and plenitude of thoroughly secular forms of enchantment. Jane Bennett, Simon During, Joshua Landy, George Levine, and Michael Saler have suggested in various ways that modernity does not disenchant so much as yield new, often paradoxical, and perhaps superior varieties of enchantment, ones which inspire an 'excited affirmation of things of this world',[8] in Levine's phrase; motivate ethical and political engagement, in Bennett's account; or, in During's and Saler's similar models, are compatible with secular

---

illuminating account of the current debate in the fields of history and sociology see Dominic Erdozain, '"Cause is not quite what it ued to be": The Return of Secularization', *English Historical Review*, 127 (2012), 377–400. For recent analyses of the implications of challenges to the secularization thesis for the study of nineteenth-century literature see Colin Jager, 'Romanticism/Secularization/Secularism', *Literature Compass*, 5 (2008), 791–806; and Charles LaPorte, 'Victorian Literature, Religion, and Secularization', *Literature Compass*, 10 (2013), 277–87.

[5] *The Problem of Pleasure: Sport, Recreation, and the Crisis of Victorian Religion* (Woodbridge: Boydell & Brewer, 2010), p. 199.

[6] *A Secular Age* (Cambridge, MA: Harvard University Press, 2007), p. 38.

[7] For Taylor's discussion of 'enchantment' see *A Secular Age*, pp. 25–27, 29–43; for his concept of a 'closed' immanent frame see pp. 542–57.

[8] Levine, 'Introduction', in *The Joy of Secularism: 11 Essays for How We Live Now*, ed. by George Levine (Princeton: Princeton University Press, 2011), p. 22.

assumptions in so far as they reconstruct the supernatural as an aesthetic experience.⁹

This essay aims to clarify some of the ambiguities inscribed within the 'disenchantment' paradigm as it was formulated by Weber, and as it circulated as a theme in the Romantic literary tradition he was drawing upon. I trace the theme to its origin in Friedrich Schiller's 1788 poem 'Die Götter Griechenlands' ('The Gods of Greece'), through Heinrich Heine's 1827 poem of the same title as well as his prose work *Les Dieux en exil* (1853), both of which respond to Schiller's poem, before performing an extended reading of Walter Pater's imaginary portrait 'Denys l'Auxerrois' (1887), which responds in turn to Heine's *Les Dieux en exil*. I argue that the disenchantment theme, rather than being a conclusive and melancholic diagnosis of secularization, often served as a means of articulating a paradoxical impression of the extent to which Western culture was undergoing such a process, and of sustaining a carefully ironized ambivalence about the implications of the possibility. Charting some of the complex literary genealogy of Weber's disenchantment diagnosis also illuminates the extent to which the categories of the 'pagan' and the 'aesthetic' often both enable and destabilize secularization narratives. Weber's disenchantment paradigm was partly a gloss on the Romantic investment in the legacy of ancient Greece: specifically, on the topos of the displacement and/or return of the ancient Greek gods. The fact that the classical gods could be treated as purely imaginative constructs provided Romantic writers with potential scope for an oblique form of literary secularism, one that implicitly casts conceptions of divinity in ironic terms or gestures at a possible analogy between the demise of ancient Greek religion and the fate of religion in modernity.¹⁰ However, this Romantic recourse to the classical gods only makes secularization representable in unstable, relativist terms: the gods operate as a *tertium quid* that confounds distinctions between the religious and the secular, and thereby keeps the character of secularization enigmatic.¹¹

---

⁹ See Bennett, *The Enchantment of Modern Life*; During, *Modern Enchantments: The Cultural Power of Secular Magic* (Cambridge, MA: Harvard University Press, 2002); Levine, *Darwin Loves You: Natural Selection and the Re-enchantment of the World* (Princeton: Princeton University Press, 2008); Saler, *As If: Modern Enchantment and the Literary Prehistory of Virtual History* (Oxford: Oxford University Press, 2011); and Saler and Landy, 'Introduction', in *The Re-enchantment of the World: Secular Magic in a Rational Age*, ed. by Saler and Landy (Palo Alto: Stanford University Press, 2009), pp. 1–14.

¹⁰ Martin Priestman suggests that Romantic poets sometimes pressed the classical gods into the service of an implicit secularizing agenda: see *Romantic Atheism: Poetry and Freethought, 1780–1830* (Cambridge: Cambridge University Press, 1999), pp. 44–45.

¹¹ For convenience, I am here classifying Pater as a 'Romantic' writer, though his literary career belongs to the late Victorian period (he was actively publishing from 1866 until his death in 1894). He is often read as a 'late Romantic': see e.g. Catherine Maxwell, *Second Sight: The Visionary Imagination in Late Victorian Literature* (Manchester: Manchester University Press, 2009), pp. 68–113.

Weber

Although Weber's claim about the 'disenchantment of the world' is often treated as a synonym for Western secularization, for Weber there was in fact no simple correlation between the two processes. Firstly, as is clear from *Die protestantische Ethik und der Geist des Kapitalismus* (*The Protestant Ethic and the Spirit of Capitalism*, 1905), Weber thought that Christianity, at least in the form of Protestantism, was a key matrix of modern disenchantment: Weber believed that Protestantism had been extraordinarily successful at ridding the world of pagan magic, spirits, and demons, and that science only took over the ascetic, rationalizing work that Protestantism had begun. Secondly, Weber's elaboration of the 'disenchantment' paradigm in 'Wissenschaft als Beruf' often turns upon convoluted references to the ancient Greek gods, which, while perhaps partly intended as rhetorical flourishes, also exemplify how the concept of the 'pagan' often both underpins and complicates secularization narratives.

In 'Wissenschaft als Beruf' Weber persistently constructs modern conflicts between science and religion as struggles between ancient gods. In particular, he suggests that modern culture, in so far as it is constituted by a plurality of value systems, resembles the polytheistic culture of ancient Greece:

> Es ist wie in der alten, noch nicht von ihren Göttern und Dämonen entzauberten Welt, nur in anderem Sinne: wie der Hellene einmal der Aphrodite opferte, und dann dem Apollon und vor allem jeder den Göttern seiner Stadt, so ist es, entzaubert und entkleidet der mythischen, aber innerlich wahren Plastik jenes Verhaltens, noch heute.[12]

> We live as did the ancients when their world was not yet disenchanted of its gods and demons, only we live in a different sense. As Hellenic man at times sacrificed to Aphrodite and at other times to Apollo, and, above all, as everybody sacrificed to the gods of his city, so do we still nowadays, only the bearing of man has been disenchanted and denuded of its mystical but inwardly genuine plasticity.[13]

In other words, the modern world is defined by relativism; we no longer repose in the ideal of a 'letzte[ ] Stellungnahme' ('ultimate standpoint', WaB, p. 28 = trans., p. 148) as we did when our habits of thought were grounded in monotheistic religion, but are instead confronted by a multitude of competing truth systems, just as the ancient Greeks worshipped a variety of gods. However, Weber draws this comparison only to emphasize the vast gulf between an enchanted world of polytheism and the modern age. We still make apparently irrational sacrifices to forces that exceed our control and comprehension (Weber is thinking principally of the vocation of science, which he suggests

---

[12] Max Weber, 'Wissenschaft als Beruf' (Berlin: Duncker & Humblot, 1967), pp. 5–37 (pp. 27–28). All subsequent references to this edition are identified by the abbreviation WaB.

[13] Max Weber, 'Science as a Vocation', in *From Max Weber: Essays in Sociology*, ed. by H. H. Gerth and C. Wright Mills (London: Routledge, 2009), pp. 129–56 (pp. 147–48). All subsequent English translations refer to this edition.

demands a quasi-religious kind of dedication despite being unable to satisfy a religious desire for ultimate meaning). However, where the ancient Greeks enjoyed many varieties of spiritual fulfilment and moved fluidly from one cult to another, modern people are afflicted by a sense of an 'unlösliche[r] Kampf' ('irreconcilable conflict', WaB, p. 27 = trans., p. 147). Commenting on this passage, Fredric Jameson observes:

> The metaphorical language of pantheism [...] underscores the way in which for Weber the religious phenomenon is the very hypostasis of value in general, value seen from the outside by the man who no longer believes in any values and for whom such living belief has thus become a kind of mystery [...]. In this Weber takes his place in that modern tradition of an aesthetic valorization of religion.[14]

The extent to which Weber's vision of secularization is underwritten by a distinctive and highly self-conscious aesthetic sensibility is also suggested by how frequently this lecture—ostensibly about the vocation of science—digresses into reflections on literature, the obvious source of his baroque secularization metaphors. Weber clearly thinks that the disenchantment of the world produces what we tend to identify as 'decadence' in the realm of aesthetics: modern art, epitomized for him by Baudelaire's poetry and, he suggests, most incisively theorized by Nietzsche, has not only prised apart the theological identification of beauty with goodness, but revived the apparently pagan insight that 'etwas heilig sein kann nicht nur: obwohl es nicht schön ist, sondern: weil und insofern es nicht schön ist' ('something can be sacred not only in spite of its not being beautiful, but rather because and in so far as it is not beautiful', WaB. p. 27 = trans., pp. 47–48). Like other spheres of modern life, then, art is disenchanted in so far as it bears witness to a fragmentation of values; and yet, Weber suggests, this same fragmentation might also be construed as a rebound to a pagan imaginary, and perhaps thus as a form of—*re*-enchantment. Weber's oscillation between two poetic figures for the modern fragmentation and secularization of values—on the one hand, it is a disenchantment of the world; on the other, it is a return of the pagan gods—seems to enact the very relativism that he seeks to describe.

Weber goes on to extend his polytheism metaphor, and again the effect is disorienting, since, although he seems to be drawing an analogy between the ancient and the modern, he does so less in the interests of revealing similarity than of revealing difference—and of sharpening our awareness of the distinction between enchantment and disenchantment:

> Der großartige Rationalismus der ethisch-methodischen Lebensführung, der aus jeder religiösen Prophetie quillt, hatte diese Vielgötterei entthront zugunsten des 'Einen, das not tut' — und hatte dann, angesichts der Realitäten des äußeren und inneren Lebens,

---

[14] 'The Vanishing Mediator: Narrative Structure in Max Weber', *New German Critique*, 1 (1973), 52–89 (p. 62).

sich zu jenen Kompromissen und Relativierungen genötigt gesehen, die wir alle aus der Geschichte des Christentums kennen. Heute aber ist es religiöser 'Alltag'. Die alten vielen Götter, entzaubert und daher in Gestalt unpersönlicher Mächte, entsteigen ihren Gräbern, streben nach Gewalt über unser Leben und beginnen untereinander wieder ihren ewigen Kampf. (WaB, p. 28)

The grandiose rationalism of an ethical and methodical conduct of life which flows from every religious prophecy has dethroned this polytheism in favour of 'the one thing that is needful'. Faced with the realities of outer and inner life, Christianity has deemed it necessary to make those compromises and relative judgments, which we all know from its history. Today the routines of everyday life challenge religion. Many old gods ascend from their graves; they are disenchanted and hence take the form of impersonal forces. They strive to gain power over our lives and again they resume their eternal struggle with one another. (pp. 148–49)

Modernity, then, marks both a return of paganism—old gods ascend from their graves—*and* a disenchantment of the world; no sooner do the gods return than they are stripped of their divinity and consigned to the status of impersonal forces (although, even in this rationalized form, they seem to participate in some kind of mythic struggle). Weber invokes the pagan gods in order to underscore the extent to which an apparently secular modernity is pervaded by thoroughly worldly forms of irrationalism; he was keen to stress that the process of rationalization is not, as Johannes Weiss puts it, 'a zero-sum game of "rationality versus irrationality": rather, it is a matter of recognizing conflicting developments, including frequent reversals'.[15] Nevertheless, Weber's insistence upon the disenchanted nature of the gods raises the question of why he is determined to use the metaphor at all—he seems to mobilize it only in order to underline its awkwardness, its basic incommensurability with the cultural conditions he seeks to anatomize. The fact that the classical gods are at once summoned and banished when Weber seeks to describe a process of secularization, or to articulate the nature of the conflict between science and religion, perhaps partly attests to his sense of tact.[16] In the passage quoted above he segues from a discussion of modern Christianity into an invocation of ancient polytheism, which was perhaps intended to soften his depiction of Christianity as a beleaguered force—though it also produces the strange suggestion that Christianity's efforts to answer modern challenges have the effect of resurrecting pagan gods. Weber's classical metaphors may also be understood as part of the wearily erudite and often ironic tone of the lecture, and to reflect his keen awareness of the extent to which differences between Christian and pagan forms of spirituality were often elided within

---

[15] Weiss, 'On the Irreversibility of Western Rationalization and Max Weber's Alleged Fatalism', in *Max Weber*, ed. by Whimster and Lash, pp. 154–63 (p. 155).

[16] As Bruce Robbins notes, Weber's focus on the concept of pagan magic 'whether for reasons of diplomacy or not [. . .] certainly takes the emphasis off divinity' ('Enchantment? No, Thank You!', in *The Joy of Secularism*, ed. by Levine, pp. 74–94 (p. 75)).

the tradition of German Romanticism: he makes a number of mordant references to the youth of Germany who shrink from the rigours of scientific reason and crave other, perhaps Christian, perhaps vaguely Romantic or pagan, modes of '"Erlebnis"' ('personal experience', WaB, p. 12=trans., p. 137). Yet Weber's suggestion that modernity is defined by the return of the pagan gods in disenchanted guises also simply reflects the fact that he borrowed his concept of 'disenchantment' from a Romantic poem: Schiller's 'Die Götter Griechenlands'.[17]

Schiller

In English the word 'disenchantment' sounds as if it refers to an affective state—a disillusionment, disappointment, or embitterment—and the phrase 'disenchantment of the world' is often used to gesture broadly at modernity and its discontents, especially the notion that the loss of religious frameworks confronts modern people with a stark and unprecedented crisis of meaning. Certainly, in 'Wissenschaft als Beruf' Weber suggests that modernity empties out traditional sources of meaning, and his concept of 'disenchantment' is part of his pessimistic vision of modern life as a rationalized 'stahlhartes Gehäuse' ('iron cage').[18] Yet the German word *Entzauberung* more precisely suggests the de-magification of the world, and Weber apparently extrapolated it from a moment in Schiller's 'Die Götter Griechenlands' that refers to the un-godding or de-divinization of nature ('Die entgötterte Natur' (SGG, l. 112)).[19] Schiller's poem does not identify the un-godding of nature with the decline of Christianity or with the waning of religion more broadly; he is specifically referring to the demise of a pagan, or animistic, apprehension of nature. Schiller's poem is an elegy for the Greek gods and for the sense of harmonious relationship between the human and the natural that Greek polytheism supposedly fostered. The Greeks, according to Schiller, perceived the cosmos as holistic and magical, suffused with divinity, and this enabled them to experience the pleasures of the body without guilt and to be insouciant in the face of death. Like Weber, Schiller attributes the disenchantment of the world to both Christianity and modern science: Christianity purged the Greek pantheon in the interests of concentrating worship on a single, tran-

---

[17] See Gerth and Wright's 'Introduction' to *Essays in Sociology*, pp. 3–74 (p. 51).

[18] Weber, *Die Protestantische Ethik und der Geist des Kapitalismus*, ed. by Dirk Kaesler (Munich: Beck, 2004), p. 204.

[19] All German references are to the second, amended version of the poem in *Sämtliche Werke*, ed. by Gerhard Fricke and Herbert Göpfert, 5 vols (Munich: Hanser, 1965), I, 169–73, identified by the abbreviation SGG; for the first, longer version see pp. 163–69 in the same volume. All English translations refer to Edgar Alfred Bowring's translation in *Complete Poems of Schiller*, ed. by Henry D. Wireman (Philadelphia: Kohler, 1879), pp. 64–69; for Wireman's translation of the first version of the poem see pp. 69–75 in the same volume.

scendent God, while Newtonian physics reduced nature to a 'tote[r] Schlag der Pendeluhr' ('pendule-clock's dead, hollow tone', SGG, l. 110). However, Schiller's disenchantment narrative concludes with an optimistic flourish: he suggests that what has been lost as pagan religious experience can be recuperated as modern aesthetic experience. Art can save the pagan from the 'Zeitflut' ('Time-flood', SGG, l. 125); while a sense of nature's divinity may have perished as a belief, it retains an immortal life in song or in poetry ('unsterblich im Gesang soll leben', SGG, l. 127), and the gods live on at least as fertile poetic conceits. This logic bestows an equivocal status upon the category of poetry, or of the aesthetic, in Schiller's vision of a disenchanted world. On the one hand, the aesthetic seems like an agent of re-enchantment, compensating (however inadequately) for the pagan magic that has been lost. On the other, there is the possibility that the aesthetic, no less than science or Christianity, colludes in modern disenchantment: it seems to require the death of the gods to consummate itself: 'Was unsterblich im Gesang soll leben, | Muß im Leben untergehn' ('All that is to live in endless song, | Must in Life-Time first be drown'd!', SGG, ll. 127–28). Moreover, the fact that Schiller characterizes the bygone age of enchantment as a fundamentally poetic phenomenon—it was when 'der Dichtung zauberische Hülle | Sich noch lieblich um die Wahrheit wand' ('the magic veil of Poesy | Still round Truth entwin'd its loving chain', SGG, ll. 9–10)—renders the poem's lament circular: what has been irrevocably lost is a poetic vision of the world; now only poetry, which thrives by loss, can compensate us for the loss of that poetic vision.

Schiller's poem caused a scandal upon publication. Most notably, he was attacked by a fellow poet, Friedrich Leopold Graf zu Stolberg, who suspected that his elegy for pagan enchantment was really a covert form of atheism: he accused Schiller of espousing 'the sad relation of the naturalist to the deity'.[20] As Jeffrey L. High observes, Stolberg's attack marks only the beginning of a long 'ideological struggle for Schiller's *Geist* (the appropriately ambiguous German term for soul, spirit, mind, and intellect)': Schiller's reception history is fissured by controversies over the nature of his religious belief, or his lack of it.[21] I am not concerned here with the truth of Stolberg's accusation—certainly Schiller denied the charge, and amended the poem in response to it[22]—but it is worth noting that the poem's lament for an enchanted world in which divinity was fully immanent in nature could resonate among his contemporaries not as a complaint about the secularized nature of modernity, as Charles Taylor suggests in a recent essay on the concept of enchantment, but as the

---

[20] Quoted in Jeffrey L. High, 'Judex! Blasphemy! and Posthumous Conversion: Schiller and (No) Religion', *Goethe Yearbook*, 19 (2012), 143–64 (p. 153).

[21] Ibid., p. 145.

[22] For an account of the controversy and Schiller's response see Lesley Sharpe, *Friedrich Schiller: Drama, Thought and Politics* (Cambridge: Cambridge University Press, 1991), pp. 97–106.

very opposite: a thinly veiled celebration of atheism.[23] The reasons for this interpretative instability are complex, but may be suggested briefly here. As Taylor himself has shown, and as some of the essays in Levine's collection *The Joy of Secularism* bear out, modern secularism often constructs itself as a bid to dispense with theistic models of transcendence and affirm *this* world as the locus of 'enchantment', which is used as a poetic term for a sense of wonder or well-being.[24] With this logic in mind, Schiller's poem can be read as a celebration of a 'pagan' secularism that affirms the fulfilments of this world, and which apparently prevailed before Christian concepts of transcendence alienated us from nature and from ourselves; in this reading the classical gods are ciphers for a subversive, secularizing message. At the same time Taylor characterizes the perception of an immanently enchanted world (albeit one that also points beyond itself to a higher, theistic reality) as the originary religious experience that the process of secularization has eclipsed. From this perspective Schiller's poem reads as a sincere lament for a sacralized vision of the cosmos, teeming with divinity and spirits, which obtained before modern reason alienated us from nature and from ourselves; the classical gods are metaphors for an authentic religious experience, desired despite its apparently anachronistic status. The fact that Schiller's poem divides the blame for modern disenchantment between religion and reason seems designed to allow and to destabilize both readings. Schiller uses the disenchantment theme at once to announce that secularization has occurred—there has been an irreparable rupture between the epoch of enchantment and rationalized modernity—and to render its stakes uncertain: what has been lost is a mysteriously 'pagan' way of being which does not answer to conventional distinctions between the religious and the secular (though it perhaps answers to that other ambiguous concept, the 'aesthetic').

Heine

Weber's paradoxical vision of secularization as the disenchanted return of the gods in 'Wissenschaft als Beruf' is one way of condensing the ambiguities of Schiller's 'Die Götter Griechenlands'. Another is Heinrich Heine's poem of the same title, from his 1827 collection *Buch der Lieder* ('Book of Songs'). Heine partly reprises Schiller's elegiac tone and his image of ancient Greek religion as luminous, sensual, and life-affirming—his speaker imagines

---

[23] 'Disenchantment-Reenchantment', in *The Joy of Secularism*, ed. by Levine, pp. 57–73 (pp. 62–63).

[24] For Taylor's analysis of the tendency of modern secularism to frame itself as an effort to affirm the world see *A Secular Age*, pp. 546–48, 606–07. In Levine's volume see especially Paolo Costa's 'A Secular Wonder', pp. 134–54, and Rebecca Stott's 'The Wetfooted Understory: Darwinian Immersions', pp. 205–24.

a time when the gods 'freudig die Welt beherrschten' ('joyously ruled the world', HGG, l. 11)[25]—but the poem pivots upon one of his signature ruptures of mood, known as *Stimmungsbrechung*,[26] and unfolds into a critique of Schiller's disenchantment narrative. Heine suggests that Schiller's exaltation of Greek religion springs less from an earnest desire for a vibrant pagan spirituality than from a perverse impulse to mourn whatever is irrevocably lost. His poem challenges the Romantic logic that reflexively idealizes lost causes, defunct religions, and vanished cultures without interrogating the nature of what is being idealized: the Greek gods, Heine points out, would have disdained such sympathy with history's losers, and Romantic repining after ancient Greek religion thus essentially falsifies what it purports to mourn.[27] In contrast, Heine's speaker flaunts his own cynicism; he is willing to adopt a supplicatory attitude towards the Greek gods only because such supplication is transparently an empty gesture, except as an act of irreverence towards Christianity. After expressing a mournful piety towards the classical gods, he abruptly announces that he actually finds ancient Greek religion as odious as Christianity, and is willing to pay homage to the former only out of spite:

> Ich hab euch niemals geliebt, ihr Götter!
> Denn widerwärtig sind mir die Griechen,
> Und gar die Römer sind mir verhaßt.
> Doch heilges Erbarmen und schauriges Mitleid
> Durchströmt mein Herz,
> Wenn ich Euch jetzt da droben schaue,
> Verlassene Götter,
> Tote, nachtwandelnde Schatten,
> Nebelschwache, die der Wind verscheucht —
> Und wenn ich bedenke, wie feig und windig
> Die Götter sind, die Euch besiegten,
> Die neuen, herrschenden, tristen Götter,
> Die Schadenfrohen im Schafspelz der Demut —

[25] Heine, 'The Gods of Greece', in *The Complete Poems of Heinrich Heine: A Modern English Version*, trans. by Hal Draper (Boston: Suhrkamp/Insel, 1982), pp. 152–54; all subsequent English references are to this edition. See also Heine, 'Die Götter Griechenlands', in *Buch der Lieder* (Hamburg: Hoffmann und Campe, 1827), pp. 358–62; all subsequent German references to the poem are to this edition, identified by the abbreviation HGG.

[26] Susan Youens defines Heine's characteristic technique of *Stimmungsbrechung* (literally 'breaking the tone') as follows: 'at the ends of poems, he swerves abruptly in another direction, addresses someone or something other than the audience had thought was there all along, and alters the verb tenses, thereby changing poetic time zones' (*Heinrich Heine and the Lied* (Cambridge: Cambridge University Press, 2007), p. 32).

[27] As E. M Butler notes, Heine's poem is a 'slashing criticism' not only of Schiller's 'Die Götter Griechenlands' but of 'Homer's pantheon of gods as interpreted by Winckelmann, Herder, [and] Goethe' and of the 'tyranny of Greece' over the German literary imagination (*The Tyranny of Greece over Germany: A Study of the Influence Exercised by Greek Art and Poetry over the Great German Writers of the Eighteenth, Nineteenth and Twentieth Centuries* (Cambridge: Cambridge University Press, 1935), p. 257).

> O, da faßt mich ein düsterer Groll,
> Und brechen möcht ich die neuen Tempel,
> Und kämpfen für Euch, ihr alten Götter,
> Für Euch und Eur gutes, ambrosisches Recht,
> [...]
> Denn immerhin, Ihr alten Götter,
> Habt Ihr's auch eh'mals, in Kämpfen der Menschen,
> Stets mit der Partei der Sieger gehalten,
> So ist doch der Mensch großmüth'ger als ihr,
> Und in Götterkämpfen halt ich es jetzt
> Mit der Partei der besiegten Götter.
>
> Also sprach ich, und sichtbar erröteten
> Droben die blassen Wolkengestalten,
> Und schauten mich an wie Sterbende,
> Schmerzenverklärt, und schwanden plötzlich.
> (HGG, ll. 64–80, 85–94)

> I have never loved you, you ancient gods!
> For the Greeks are repulsive to me
> And even the Romans are hateful.
> But holy compassion and terrible pity
> Flow through my heart
> Now when I see you up there,
> Forsaken godheads,
> Dead night-wandering shadows,
> Feeble as mist that flees from the wind,
> And when I consider how craven and hollow
> The gods are that conquered you,
> The new, sad gods that rule in your places,
> That gloat over woe, in sheep's clothing of meekness—
> Oh, then black rancour seizes my soul,
> And then I would smash the new-raised temples
> And fight for you, you gods of old,
> And for your good old ambrosial cause,
> [...]
> For though it is true, you ancient gods,
> That in the battles of men, of old
> You have always taken the side of the victor,
> Yet man is more generous than you,
> And now in the battles of the gods I take
> The side of the gods that were vanquished.
>
> Thus did I speak, and they visibly reddened,
> Those pallid cloud-figures floating above me,
> And gazed at me with a dying air,
> Transfigured with pain, and suddenly vanished.

Heine points out that we now adopt the same attitude of amused superiority towards the Greek gods that they famously adopted towards humanity. In effect, he asks, who's laughing now?—'Das unauslöschliche Göttergelächter' ('the inextinguishable laughter of the gods', HGG, l. 63)[28] has long been silenced, or at best reduced to a Homeric allusion. At the same time, the allusion to Homer underscores the way in which the 'inextinguishable laughter of the gods' was always already reduced to a literary trope; the fact that imagining humanity as the plaything of the gods is a poetic cliché with an ancient origin paradoxically confirms that the gods were always the playthings of the poets. In this way, Heine's poem celebrates its own bad faith and implicitly accuses Schiller's poem of being in bad faith, too: he suggests that Schiller does not sincerely lament the inaccessibility of pagan enchantment but actually revels in the complexities of his own disenchanted posture; he pretends to regret the death of paganism but really affirms that it was well lost because, once lost, it can achieve its true vitality as an object of nostalgia (and as a sly weapon against Christianity).

We are perhaps meant to perceive that it is a Christian compassion for the weak and outcast that disposes Heine's speaker to ally himself, however flippantly, with the vanquished gods: his vision of the gods as dying and 'Schmerzenverklärt' ('transfigured by pain', HGG, l. 94) jarringly confounds the demise of ancient Greek religion with the Crucifixion of Christ. The ironies of this Romantic tendency to invest the Greek gods with Christian pathos are also key to Heine's prose work on the same theme, *Les Dieux en exil*, first published (in French) in 1853. Heine, born to a Jewish family, had converted to Christianity two years before he wrote 'Die Götter Griechenlands', though it is plain that this was a conversion of convenience, not conviction.[29] The precise date of composition for *Les Dieux en exil* is uncertain, though the year of publication would seem to indicate it was written after the watershed of 1848.[30] After this time, illness confined Heine to his famous 'mattress grave', and, repudiating the atheistic tendencies of his earlier work, he turned towards God. The nature of Heine's second conversion—whether it was a turn, or return, to Judaism, to Christianity, to a less definable and more idiosyncratic faith, or only the last of his mordant ironies—is a matter of interpretative controversy, and not only because of Heine's mercurial, relentlessly self-reflexive style.[31] No less than in the case of Schiller (or in the case of Pater, as discussed

[28] The 'inextinguishable laughter' of the gods is a common rendering of the phrase *asbestos gelōs* from Book i, l. 771 of the *Iliad*; see Homer, *The Iliad*, trans. by Alexander Pope (London: W. Bowyer, for Bernard Lintott, 1715), p. 36.

[29] On Heine's 'insincere' conversion to Christianity see Robert C. Holub, 'Troubled Apostate: Heine's Conversion and its Consequences', in *A Companion to the Works of Heinrich Heine*, ed. by Roger F. Cook (Rochester, NY: Camden House, 2002), pp. 229–50 (p. 230).

[30] Jeffrey Sammons writes, 'I suspect [*Les Dieux en exil*] may have been conceived around [1846], especially as the commitment to pagan sensualism and its irreligious affect are stronger than they became after 1848. However, the actual writing may have been done in 1853' (*Heinrich Heine: A Modern Biography* (Manchester: Carcanet New Press, 1979), p. 319).

[31] For an account of the ambiguities of Heine's second conversion see Joseph A. Kruse, 'Late

below), the reception history of Heine's work is a struggle for the 'Geist' of a writer who used the legacy of ancient Greece to construct contradictory fables of modern secularization which programmatically destabilize distinctions between the religious and the secular. As Willi Goetschel observes, Heine 'casts secularization as a process that sheds light on the complicities and hidden affinities between a fully emancipated rationalism and its other, that is, religion, tradition, even superstition'.[32]

Les Dieux en exil is an extended *jeu d'esprit* that pivots on the conceit that the Greek gods were entirely real and have endured, not in a transcendent realm impervious to mortals, but in the secret places of the world or as apparently ordinary citizens of modern Europe. Heine here constructs the pagan gods as objects of pity because they have been displaced and vilified by Christianity. Yet, as is the case in his 'Die Götter Griechenlands', this fantasy has a paradoxical logic: the fact that Christianity has triumphed over paganism means that the gods have assumed a Christlike status as suffering gods; their persecution within Christian civilization partially humanizes them and means that they share in Christ's paradoxical status as a deity who comes down to earth and experiences human suffering. Thus Heine invites us to sympathize with the gods as 'ces émigrés olympiens, qui n'avaient plus ni asile ni ambroisie, [qui] durent avoir recours à un honnête métier terrestre pour gagner au moins de quoi vivre'.[33] If the Greek gods in their humbled, sorrowful condition vaguely resemble Christ, their experience of exile and dispersal across Europe also clearly parallels the Jewish diaspora. The fact that Heine's exiled gods invite a range of conflicting allegorical interpretations— they resonate by turns as Jewish, Christian, and secularized—seems to encode his sense of Western culture as a comedy of failed supersessions, with each new dispensation—Hellenic, Judaic, Christian, secular—uncannily inhabited by all it has sought to pass beyond. Heine also uses the notion of the gods in exile to allegorize a shift from the traditional enchantments of the romance genre to the secularizing conventions of modern realism: once glorious pagan gods are now forced to 'travailler comme simples journaliers chez nous [. . .], et de boire de la bière au lieu de nectar' (*DE*, p. 241). He parodies the literal-mindedness underpinning realist conventions by literalizing the idea that paganism has in some sense survived within modern culture; here what

Thoughts: Reconsiderations from the "Matratzengruft"', in *A Companion to the Works of Heinrich Heine*, ed. by Cook, pp. 315-38. As Sammons notes, Heine's 'refusal to keep a straight face or a solemn tone when discussing his religious "regression", as he put it, has made it difficult for many people to believe that any substantial transformation took place' (*Heinrich Heine: The Elusive Poet* (New Haven: Yale University Press, 1969), p. 353).

[32] 'Heine's Critical Secularism', *boundary 2*, 31.2 (2004), 149–71 (p. 152).

[33] Heine, *Les Dieux en exil*, in *Historisch-kritische Gesamtausgabe der Werke*, vol. IX, ed. by Manfred Windfuhr (Hamburg: Hoffmann und Campe, 1987), p. 241. All subsequent references are to this edition, identified by the abbreviation *DE*.

survives of the pagan is no mere cultural legacy or archaic residue within modern consciousness, but reified forms of the apparently fabulous objects of ancient religious belief, which continue to intervene in human affairs despite belief in them having long passed away. More broadly, Heine's suggestion that the Greek gods lived on and people simply failed to notice may be read as a satire on the metaphysical blindness of a modern, secular rationalism, which occludes the divine by reducing it to anthropological or empirical forces, or by exiling it to the realm of the imagination. Heine lampoons this tendency in his preface to the tale, where he suggests that the Enlightenment campaign against gods, beliefs, and traditions ('dieux, croyances et traditions', *DE*, p. 227) has been so remorseless that belief in the existence of the moon has come to be despised as a superstition in some parts of the world. At the same time Heine's suggestion that the gods have been subject to a humiliating process of secularization seems to confirm the secular view that their status is entirely contingent upon human perception.

Crucially, the fates of Heine's Greek gods are diverse—some meet realistic fates and appear to have been utterly secularized; others seem to be responsible for the continuing vitality of enchantment within modern, Christian civilization, as well as for outbreaks of superstition and Gothic violence. For example, Apollo, who takes up employment as a shepherd in Austria, has his real, pagan identity exposed by a monk and is delivered over to the ecclesiastical courts (*DE*, p. 241). Heine here draws attention to the ambivalent status of art within the modern, Christian imagination: Apollo plays his lyre so enchantingly that he causes his audience to weep; and yet this aesthetic rapture also induces fear and hatred, and leads the community to transfix him with a stake as a vampire (*DE*, p. 241). Meanwhile, Dionysus integrates himself seamlessly into the Church: he is the superior of a Franciscan monastery who is noted as a skilled exorcist and practitioner of corporal punishment (*DE*, pp. 245–46). The suggestion that paganism persisted within Christianity under various disguises, some prosaic, others retaining a magical potency, has complex implications. On the one hand, Heine invites us to relish the notion that Christianity was always inhabited by an antithetical force—wild, sensual, joyous, and magical—that subverted it from within. On the other, he implies that many of the Greek gods adapted themselves so fully to the contours of modern, Christian civilization as to be entirely indiscernible within it; their very success at concealment suggests that in some respects there no longer exists any meaningful distinction between the Christian and the pagan. Heine has it both ways: he implies both the vital, subversive presence of the pagan within the Christian *and* that the Christian has diffused and diluted the pagan to the point of neutralizing it. For Heine as for Weber, Christianity has and has not vanquished the pagan gods, and modernity is both thoroughly disenchanted and yet still enchanted after all.[34]

In the opening of the essay Heine playfully legitimates his gods-in-exile conceit by reference to Christianity. He points out that historically, Christianity did not simply debunk the pagan deities but reinterpreted them as evil spirits (DE, p. 230). Christianity thus preserved paganism by investing it with real, malign power. At the same time, however, Heine calls attention to the extent to which the disturbing power of paganism within the Christian imagination has become secularized and turned into a banal literary trope. In the middle of the essay he suddenly accosts the reader, who is presumed to be a decadent sophisticate, too inured to the modern fetishization of all things Greek to be truly receptive to pagan enchantment:

Mais, cher lecteur, j'oublie que vous avez fait vos classes et que vous êtes parfaitement instruit; vous avez donc compris dès les premières lignes qu'il est question ici d'une bacchanale, d'une fête de Dionysos. Sur des bas-reliefs ou dans des gravures d'ouvrages archéologiques, vous avez vu assez souvent le pompeux cortège qui suit ce dieu païen. Versé comme vous l'êtes dans l'antiquité classique, vous ne seriez pas trop effrayé, si à minuit, au milieu de la solitude d'une forêt, la magnifique et fantasque apparition d'une marche triomphale de Bacchus se présentait tout à coup à vos regards, et que vous entendissiez le vacarme de cette cohue de spectres en goguettes. Tout au plus éprouveriez-vous une espèce de saisissement voluptueux, un frisson esthétique, à l'aspect de ces gracieux fantômes sortis de leurs sarcophages séculaires et de dessous les ruines de leurs temples pour célébrer encore une fois les saints mystères du culte des plaisirs! Oui, c'est une orgie posthume: ces revenants gaillards, encore une fois, veulent fêter par des jeux et des chants la bienheureuse venue du fils de Sémélé, le rédempteur de la joie; encore une fois, ils veulent danser les danses des anciens temps, la polka du paganisme, le cancan de l'antiquité, ces danses riantes qu'on dansait sans jupon hypocrite, sans le contrôle d'un sergent de ville de la vertu. (DE, p. 244)

Heine's critique here is two-pronged and unstable. Most obviously, he is mocking the modern reader who fails to recognize the real wildness of the Dionysian revels and fancies that paganism is no more than a source of conventionalized aesthetic pleasure. He goes on to suggest that the believing Christian has a more profound insight into the nature of ancient Greek culture

[34] Robert Button has provided an insightful analysis of Heine's 'proto-Weberian sensibility', particularly his anticipation of Weber's disenchantment paradigm. However, his reading of Les Dieux en exil emphasizes that the gods are fully assimilated into 'routinized, disenchanted, rational modernity', and suggests that whatever vestiges of magic they retain attest only to the negative enchantments of modern capitalism. While I agree that this aspect of Heine's tale anticipates Weber, I emphasize that the disenchantment concept in both writers is also an effort to convey the 'polytheism' of modern life, that is, its pluralism and relativism; the fact that some of Heine's gods, such as Apollo, remain authentically 'other' and disturbing to the social order conveys Heine's equally 'Weberian' view of secularization as an ambiguous and variegated process, not simply a rationalized 'iron cage'. See Button, 'A Note on Thematic Affinities in Max Weber and Heinrich Heine: Disenchantment, Devaluing Reversal, and the Demonic', Max Weber Studies, 12 (2012), 95–119 (pp. 114, 111).

than does the secular intellectual: where the latter merely derives a mild aesthetic thrill from the notion of Dionysian ecstasy, the Christian who believes his soul is in danger is properly alive to its power (*DE*, p. 245). Where Schiller claims that poetry remains in contact with the pagan and can therefore redeem the disenchantments of both modern science and Christianity, Heine highlights the extent to which modern literary culture conventionalizes all bids at pagan re-enchantment and reduces them to a set of high-culture affectations. At the same time, Heine appears to ironize a critique of Christianity he had often ventured in his earlier work: namely, that it drove sensual, pagan gaiety out of the world and entrenched a life-denying moral code. Arguably, Heine ventriloquizes this point of view with such gusto that it seems to exceed irony: he hints that such critiques of Christianity and efforts to rehabilitate the pagan have authentic substance, even if articulations of this position have become stale.[35] Ultimately, however, *Les Dieux en exil* ventures no coherent critique or position—Heine mocks both the Christian morality that demonizes paganism and the more secular literary sensibility that valorizes it as an alternative to Christianity. For Heine, we err in taking the gods seriously, and we err in failing to take them seriously. The discrepant fates of the Greek gods in modernity allegorize not just the fissured, partly Judaeo-Christian, partly pagan character of Western culture, but the extent to which irony and authentic desire, aesthetic and religious experience, are often hard to distinguish in an unevenly secularized age. Heine claims that while modern sailors will laugh at a pantomime Neptune, they never really doubt the existence of the god and often pray to him in extremity (*DE*, p. 251). Likewise, Heine self-consciously pivots between reverence and irreverence towards the legacy of ancient Greece, and articulates hope for a pagan re-enchantment of modernity even as he punctures such hopes. The mixed generic mode of *Les Dieux en exil* also attempts to capture this disorienting co-implication of scepticism and belief, enchantment and disenchantment: Heine's text is at once a fable and a critical essay; at once a full-blown exercise in, and a trenchant critique of, Romantic Hellenism.

Pater

It is well known that Walter Pater's *Imaginary Portraits* were partly inspired by Heine's *Les Dieux en exil*.[36] Pater appropriates not only Heine's return-of-the-

---

[35] As Paul Reitter writes, Heine's early work had called, 'at times ironically, yet often ardently, for the gods' rehabilitation'. Noting the absence of Venus from *Les Dieux en exil*, Reitter argues that the tale attests to Heine's growing pessimism about the extent to which Hellenism could promote an emancipatory sensualism in the modern world. See Reitter, 'Heinrich Heine and the Discourse of Mythology', in *A Companion to the Works of Heinrich Heine*, ed. by Cook, pp. 201–26 (pp. 213, 214–24).

[36] The importance of Heine's gods-in-exile theme to Pater's entire œuvre has been a critical

gods conceit but his rich conjunction of fictional and non-fictional literary modes: Pater writes four essayistic fables which at once analyse a moment of historical rupture and suggest the resurgence of mythic or pagan forces, or even the ancient gods themselves, in ostensibly Christian and modern contexts. Yet critics often suggest that Pater adopts Heine's theme while dispensing with his satirical bite and freewheeling ironies. For instance, Jeffrey Wallen remarks: 'there is no evidence of a sense of humor in Pater, which makes his great appreciation for Heine [. . .] all the more striking'.[37] There is good reason for perceiving a serious intent behind Pater's handling of the myth of the returning gods in his *Imaginary Portraits*. From the late 1870s Pater had been composing essays such as 'A Study of Dionysus' (1876) and 'The Myth of Demeter and Persephone' (1876), which would later be collected in the posthumously published volume *Greek Studies* (1895), and which address the subject of ancient Greek religion in a tone of wistful solemnity. Yet Pater absorbed more of Heine's ironic spirit than is often recognized. In particular, he inherits and extends Heine's tendency to foreground and ironize the interplay between the Christian, the pagan, and the secular in modernity. Like Heine, Pater was notorious for having espoused a neo-pagan form of religious scepticism, though his *Imaginary Portraits* were composed during a period when he appears to have been contemplating a return to religion.[38] The extent to which Pater re-embraced Christianity in his later work is an intricate question, and here I wish to note only that, like Heine before him, Pater invokes the Romantic disenchantment theme—that is, the gods-in-exile theme—in order at once to posit a process of secularization and to render its terms equivocal.

Pater's *Imaginary Portraits* focuses not simply on moments of dramatic cultural change, but more specifically on moments that seem to mark a transition from a religious to a secular imaginary. 'Denys l'Auxerrois' is in a sense an anomaly in the volume: it dramatizes not a culture on the cusp of modernity or the collision between Enlightenment ideals of reason and progress and older, mythic and religious modes of consciousness, but the return of the god Dionysus to the French town of Auxerre in the late Middle Ages. Unlike 'The Duke of Rosenmold', which may be considered the companion piece in the collection, this tale focuses on a confrontation between Christianity and ancient Greek religion proper, rather than upon a modern, secularized effort

---

commonplace since John Smith Harrison's article 'Pater, Heine, and the Old Gods of Greece', *PMLA*, 39 (1924), 655–86.

[37] 'Alive in the Grave: Walter Pater's Renaissance', *ELH*, 66 (1999), 1033–51 (p. 1048).

[38] For an overview of Pater's early scepticism and later, more sympathetic attitude to Christianity see Gerald Monsman, *Walter Pater* (Boston: Hall, 1977), pp. 17–47, 102–04. Lesley Higgins gives a subtle account of Pater's later stance towards Christianity in 'Doubting Pater: Religious Discourse and "the conditions of modern life"', *English Literature in Transition*, 38 (1995), 285–303.

to recuperate ancient Greece for aesthetic purposes. Although all four of the *Imaginary Portraits* contain fairy-tale elements and sometimes suggest parallels between their protagonists and ancient Greek deities, 'Denys l'Auxerrois' is much more overtly a fable than the other tales, and, like Heine's *Les Dieux en exil*, it literalizes the notion that the pagan persists within the Christian by imagining the return of the god Dionysus.[39]

'Denys l'Auxerrois' embeds its return-of-the-gods theme within a modern frame narrative. The narrator, like that of Heine's *Les Dieux en exil*, is an aesthete with a taste for the esoteric and recherché aspects of history. At the opening of the tale he is a tourist in search of historical curiosities in modern Auxerre, and he duly finds himself beguiled by two medieval art objects: a fragment of stained glass and some tapestries.[40] Both objects originally formed part of the decorations of the town cathedral, but the narrator is struck by the fact that they seem to depict a lurid and profoundly un-Christian scene, which he identifies as a Dionysian revel. The embedded narrative consists of the narrator's fanciful attempt to account for this incongruous presence of the Dionysian within officially Christian art: he imagines that medieval Auxerre witnessed not just a cultural efflorescence of paganism that insinuated itself into local customs and religious practices, but the return of the god Dionysus himself. Like Heine, Pater both affirms and ironizes the notion that Christianity has always been inhabited by antithetical, pagan energies, which periodically overwhelm its ascetic ideal and liberate a repressed sensuality. Although the embedded tale vividly pursues the implications of this idea, the presence of the frame narrative draws attention to the extent to which it constitutes a modern fantasy, the wish-fulfilment of a particular type of Romantic antiquarianism that prizes the pagan as a source of non- or anti-Christian varieties of enchantment. The story is thus a self-reflexive fantasy, one which does not simply temper its imagination of ancient paganism with irony, but reveals how such an ironic posture itself gives rise to distinctive kinds of fantasy.

The paradoxical implications of the gods-in-exile theme in Heine's handling—the pagan is posited both as an alien, subversive element within Christian culture and as a phenomenon that is difficult, even impossible, to distinguish from it—are also central to Pater's story. 'Denys l'Auxerrois' is ostensibly about the return of Dionysus to a medieval Christian town in the form of a mysterious and charismatic young man named Denys. However, as

[39] For an analysis of the mythic resonances of the *Imaginary Portraits*, especially Pater's creative use of the Dionysus/Apollo opposition, see Gerald Monsman, *Pater's Portraits: Mythic Pattern in the Fiction of Walter Pater* (Baltimore: Johns Hopkins University Press, 1967); and Anna Budziak, *Text, Body, and Indeterminacy: Doppelgänger Selves in Pater and Wilde* (Newcastle: Cambridge Scholars, 2008).

[40] Pater, *Imaginary Portraits* (London: Macmillan, 1887), pp. 56–60. All subsequent references are to this edition, identified by the abbreviation *IP*.

Stefano Evangelista's and Ellis Hanson's suggestive readings both imply, Pater constructs the narrative so that it may also be read with the key elements transposed: that is, as a fable about the return of Christ to a medieval pagan town.[41] As he does in 'A Study of Dionysus', Pater accentuates the parallels between Dionysus and Christ, dwelling upon their shared status as gods who suffer and who undergo death and resurrection, as well as upon the wine symbolism associated with both figures.[42] While Denys obviously brings a Bacchanalian spirit to Auxerre, unleashing an ecstatic sense of community, new social freedoms, and a new identification of the sacred with the sensual and the earthly, he clearly triggers a Christian revival at the same time. Crucially, the arrival of a Dionysian spirit in Auxerre does not undermine but actually enhances Christian worship in the town, which is underscored by the fact that Denys bolsters community enthusiasm for the decoration and completion of a great cathedral (*IP*, pp. 79–80). What is more, Denys displays the moral qualities that are often thought to mark off the Christian from the pagan: he demonstrates a special compassion for the sick and unfortunate, as well as a particular sympathy with children. Ironically, it is these, his most Christ-like attributes, that ultimately lead the people of Auxerre to turn on him and suspect him of witchcraft. In other words, the apparently Christian townspeople respond ecstatically to what seems distinctly pagan about Denys, but demonize what seems more distinctly Christian about him (*IP*, pp. 70–71). Pater further spells out the Christian aspects of the apparently Dionysian Denys by having him undergo a period of religious repentance and join a monastery towards the end of the story (*IP*, p. 79). In a further irony, it is only after Denys has repented of his apparently Dionysian powers that he becomes the victim of a Bacchanalian frenzy, and is torn limb from limb by the community in the middle of a pageant. Pater means us to notice that the initial justification for this pageant was a Christian ceremony, and that Denys, now in a monk's habit, resembles the crucified Christ or at least a martyred saint as much as he does Dionysus (*IP*, pp. 86–89). Yet these ironies are all unstable: while, by the end of the tale, the god Dionysus certainly seems more authentically Christian than the members of the medieval Christian community, the overall effect is dizzying, with each new detail and event in the story charged with both Christian and Dionysian significance.

At precisely the point where the tale reaches its gruesome climax, Pater abruptly returns us to the frame narrative. We remember that the tale is a kind

[41] Stefano Evangelista, 'A Revolting Mistake: Walter Pater's Iconography of Dionysus', *Victorian Review*, 34.2 (2008), 200–18 (pp. 211–13); and Ellis Hanson, *Decadence and Catholicism* (Cambridge, MA: Harvard University Press, 1997), p. 222.

[42] For a discussion of Pater's emphasis upon the parallels between Christ and Dionysus in 'A Study of Dionysus' see John Coates, *The Rhetorical Use of Provocation as a Means of Persuasion in the Writings of Walter Pater* (New York: Mellen, 2011), p. 182. See also Evangelista, 'A Revolting Mistake', pp. 211–13.

of hallucinatory exercise in ekphrasis: the notion that Dionysian ecstasy inevitably descends into decadence and barbarism is itself part of the narrator's daydream. Pater's tale does not simply expose the limits of modern fantasies about pagan enchantment by revealing, as he puts it, the 'dark or antipathetic' side of the Dionysian (*IP*, p. 75). Rather, he underscores the extent to which this revelation of darkness is intrinsic to such fantasies. The narrator is initially captivated by the tapestries and the stained glass not simply because they depict scenes of gaiety and sensual abandon, but because they include an image of a 'tortured figure' (*IP*, p. 60) amid the revelry, and thereby suggest a kind of primordial nexus between ecstatic pleasure and suffering (which is also, we are clearly meant to infer, the submerged point of contact between the Christian and the Dionysian). The notion that the medieval and/or pagan past discloses the real agonies of the human condition—as well as the real savagery of human nature—compels the narrator at least as much as the vision of a golden age (indeed, he says that he relishes not only the 'quaint dreams' of the Middle Ages, but its 'quaint nightmare[s]' as well: *IP*, p. 54). The word 'quaint' here is telling: the narrator allows himself to feel the temptations of the pagan and the medieval—and even suggests that they represent the deepest truths of human experience—only to affirm his enlightened distance from them. The tale actually begins with his assertion that modern people cannot earnestly desire a return to a more primitive phase of culture—they can entertain this idea only in a self-consciously ironic spirit. Pater raises the possibility that it is this very modern self-consciousness that introduces a decadent quality to the narrator's imagination of the past:

> Almost every people, as we know, has had its legend of a 'golden age' and of its return—legends which will hardly be forgotten, however prosaic the world may become, while man himself remains the aspiring, not quite contented being he is. And yet in truth, since we are no longer children, we might well question the advantage of the return to us of a condition of life in which, by the nature of the case, the value of things would, so to speak, lie wholly on their surfaces, unless we could regain also the childish consciousness, or rather unconsciousness, in ourselves, to take all that adroitly and with the appropriate lightness of heart. (*IP*, p. 51)

As is the case with *Les Dieux en exil*, an ironic, decadent enjoyment of the notion of the pagan is, to an ambiguous extent, itself an object of irony here. Pater leaves open the possibility that the story is actually a provocation to take the notion of premodern enchantment in general, and the entanglement of the Christian and the Dionysian in particular, more seriously than the narrator does. Arguably, by the end of the story the narrator's own fantasy of the past has overmastered him, and the medieval artefacts that he initially contemplated in an ironic spirit have taken possession of his imagination. Certainly the tale ends with the narrator confessing that on 'days of a certain atmosphere, when the trace of the Middle Age comes out, like old marks in the stones in rainy weather, I seemed actually to have seen the tortured figure there—to have met Denys l'Auxerrois in the streets' (*IP*, p. 88).

However, Pater's tale is organized around an irony that undermines the distinction between the enchanted, premodern past and a 'prosaic' modernity established in the frame narrative. His narrator is partly fascinated by ancient Greek religion and by medieval Christianity because he imagines that both cultures enabled a more exalted perception of the powers of art. He is intrigued by the tapestries and the stained glass because they depict scenes of music inducing communal rapture, and he ascribes a pagan identity to the figure of the organ-builder to account for this apparently magical effect (*IP*, pp. 59–60). And yet the fable he constructs to satisfy his own curiosity about this convergence of the pagan and the Christian, the religious and the aesthetic, the spiritual and the sensual, only partially affirms that the premodern past enabled any such ideal experience of reconciliation. As M. F. Moran observes, medieval Auxerre itself seems 'marked by a secularized consciousness'; 'despite the grand churches and elaborate religious liturgy [. . .] there is little sense of the transcendent'.[43] This is surely because the medieval inhabitants of Auxerre are as obsessed with excavating the past as the narrator himself—the story repeatedly shows them exhuming graves and searching for relics in an apparently desperate effort to come into contact with the sacred. Pater means us to notice the parallel between the narrator's own fetishization of the remnants of the pagan and the medieval, and the medieval Christian veneration of relics, which, within the logic of the story, mirrors or even encodes a pagan reverence for the material, the sensual, and the chthonic.[44] Pater lays heavy emphasis upon these continuities: the ceremonial exhumation of a saint's body inspires 'a wonderful curiosity' in Denys which recalls the modern narrator's curiosity about historical artefacts (*IP*, p. 85). The exhumation of the saint also inspires Denys to exhume his mother's body and rebury it in consecrated ground, an act which seems to symbolize the fluid conversion of pagan impulses into Christian ones, and vice versa (*IP*, p. 85). Pater suggests the morbidity of this transhistorical preoccupation with disinterring the past by lingering over the grotesqueness of the disinterred saint's body, and the sensual grandeur of the exhumation ceremony (*IP*, p. 78). He also dramatically underscores the extent to which the enchantments of the premodern past have more than a residue of barbarity: the exhumation of the

---

[43] 'Pater's Mythic Fiction: Gods in a Gilded Age', in *Pater in the 1990s*, ed. by Laurel Brake and Ian Small (Greensboro: ELT Press, 1991), pp. 169–88 (p. 177).

[44] Critics often remark upon what might be termed Pater's 'chthonic imagination'—that is, his preoccupation with graves, relics, and the materiality of the earth. See Linda Dowling, 'Walter Pater and Archaeology: The Reconciliation with Earth', *Victorian Studies*, 31 (1988), 209–23; and Angela Leighton, *On Form: Poetry, Aestheticism, and the Legacy of a Word* (Oxford: Oxford University Press, 2007), pp. 93–98.

saint's body is paralleled by the accidental discovery of a skeleton under a bridge—apparently the remains of a child who had been buried there alive to ward off evil spirits (*IP*, p. 83). Pater's tale thus seems to critique Romantic nostalgia for a premodern enchantment—whether it takes the form of a longing for ancient Greece, or for medieval Christianity—on two different grounds. Most obviously, the tale dwells upon the dark side of premodern enchantment, its proximity to superstition and its more macabre energies. At the same time, Pater emphasizes that enchantment is always imagined as a lost or buried object: even at the height of the at once Christian and pagan golden age of Denys, the community at Auxerre—as well as Denys himself—is gripped by a compulsion to disinter the past. This makes the fantasy of the golden age of Auxerre appear spurious not simply because it culminates in horror, but because the fantasy implies an infinite regress, with every apparent golden age striving to retrieve a prior golden age through artefacts and relics. Disenchantment, and the desire for re-enchantment through an encounter with a historical object, turns out to be an ancient and medieval phenomenon as much as a modern one. And yet these threads of critique are compromised by the fact that they emerge only from the logic of the narrator's fantasy.

Conclusion

Weber's suggestion that modernity witnesses the return of pagan gods in disenchanted form is in some sense an inspired reading of a Romantic literary tradition that fantasizes about the persistence or return of paganism within modernity while gesturing self-consciously at the artificiality, literariness, or darker implications of this fantasy. As I noted in my introduction, Michael Saler has recently contested the Weberian identification of secular modernity with disenchantment by celebrating the vitality of the ironic imagination in modern literature, which he defines as a provisional, 'as if' form of imagining that enables writers to reconcile rationality with a sense of the magical or marvellous.[45] In her book *The Enchantment of Modern Life* Jane Bennett also secularizes and aestheticizes the concept of 'enchantment' in order to dispute Weber's thesis. She notes that: 'the word *enchant* is linked to the French verb *to sing: chanter*. To "en-chant": to surround with song or incantation; hence, to cast a spell with sounds, to make fall under the sway of a magical refrain, to carry away on a sonorous stream.'[46] Bennett makes a passionate case for the tenability of modern, secular forms of enchantment, and even characterizes these as 'perhaps neo-pagan [. . .] enchantment[s]'.[47] Yet Bennett's very attachment to the word 'enchantment' leaves her open to the common charge

---

[45] *As If*, pp. 8–13.
[46] *The Enchantment of Modern Life*, p. 6.
[47] Ibid., p. 40.

that secularity is a parasitic condition, one that prospers only by dissimulating its debts to the older, religious forms of consciousness it disavows.[48] Although the possibility of a purely aesthetic experience—of a song sung, or a refrain repeated, just for its own pleasing sake, rather than to conjure spirits or work supernatural effects—is embedded, even at an etymological level, in the concept of 'enchantment', the appeal of the secularized interpretation of the term surely relies on the magical aura which hovers around it as a connotation. Bennett's impulse to label these secular-but-enchanted experiences 'pagan' only returns us to the ambiguities of Weber's thesis and of Schiller's seminal poem.

Heine and Pater certainly frame their explorations of the notion that paganism maintains a potent life in modernity with ironic detachment—but this irony often seems to return upon itself, so that a sceptical, merely aesthetic enjoyment of the enchantments of paganism becomes the object of critique. The notion that the Greek gods were real and continue to exert influence in subterranean ways enables Heine and Pater to articulate dissatisfaction with a modern tendency to gloss the supernatural in purely aesthetic terms, or to treat the West's classical inheritance as merely an archive of beguiling poetic conceits. And yet the apparent implication of this critique—that the enchantments of the pagan are more than figurative, and that they remain both viable and desirable—is ventured only equivocally, from within the protection of an ironic frame. Like Weber, Heine and Pater invoke the gods of Greece to underscore the thoroughly 'prosaic' and disenchanted nature of modernity *and* to suggest that this is not the whole story—that there is perhaps some enchanted remainder after all. The status of this remainder—how far it affirms the survival of the pagan or a sense of magic in modernity, and how far it just attests, as in Schiller's poem, to the immortality of a metaphor—is no clearer in Pater's and Heine's work than it is in Weber's.

UNIVERSITY OF KENT   SARA LYONS

[48] The claim that modern secularism imitates or remains captive to the religious frameworks it apparently rejects is at the centre of debates about secularization. For a subtle discussion of this subject see Vincent Pecora, *Secularization and Cultural Criticism: Religion, Nation and Modernity* (Chicago: University of Chicago Press, 2006), pp. 1–61.

PROBLEMATIC REALISMS: GERMAN POETIC REALISM AND MICHEL BUTOR'S *PORTRAIT DE L'ARTISTE EN JEUNE SINGE*

I

Realism is, according to J. P. Stern, a perennial mode of literature.[1] Poetic Realism, it could also be argued, constitutes a perennial problem for German literary history: the German brand of Realism remains as yet poorly integrated into German and European narratives of literary development, and decades of critical enquiry appear, on the surface at least, to have done little to alter the fact that German Realism's defining characteristics are often seen as its shortcomings.[2] This article takes a different approach. Reading Michel Butor's autobiographical caprice of 1967, *Portrait de l'artiste en jeune singe*, through the interpretative lens of German Realist poetics, the analysis explores the long-term European relevance of German Realist poetics and argues that many of the particularities of German Realism may be seen to foreshadow formal innovation in mid-twentieth-century narrative.

Set in Bavaria in the period immediately after the Second World War, Butor's *Portrait* is in large measure a document that reveals and explores the author's deep engagement with the German language and German literary culture. Indeed, this 'fête littéraire' abounds in references to German literature, from medieval works on alchemy to Thomas Mann.[3] It is a highly complex work and, perhaps because of its uncertain status as a *capriccio*, there is relatively little scholarship on its formal structure.[4] Research to date has tended to focus rather on the text's use of alchemical symbolism and on tracing its setting.[5] Here it will be argued that reading the text from the perspective

---

[1] J. P. Stern, *On Realism* (London: Routledge & Kegan Paul, 1973), p. 168.

[2] For the purposes of this essay, German Realism and Poetic Realism will be used interchangeably, referring to the German nineteenth-century Realist tradition in German-speaking countries, as is usual in German literary scholarship. However, the terms are not entirely synonymous, as the term Poetic Realism can also refer to movements in other literatures, such as Scandinavian literature, for example. See Clifford Albrecht Bernd, *German Poetic Realism* (Boston: Twayne, 1981), for German Realism within this context, and the same author's *Poetic Realism in Scandinavia and Central Europe* (Columbia, SC: Camden House, 1995), for an analysis of the movement outside Germany.

[3] David Meakin, 'Michel Butor and the Thomas Mann Connection', *Forum for Modern Language Studies*, 26 (1990), 109–26 (p. 109).

[4] See most recently two articles in a special edition of *nord*: Jean Duffy, 'Curiosité, collection et culture dans *Portrait de l'artiste en jeune singe*', *nord*', 62 (2013), 87–96, and Michael White, 'L'Allemagne de Michel Butor', *nord*', ibid., pp. 77–85. For the *capriccio* form see Reinhold Grimm, 'From Callot to Butor: E. T. A. Hoffmann and the Tradition of the Capriccio', *Modern Language Notes*, 93 (1978), 399–415.

[5] Mary Lyndon, *Perpetuum Mobile: A Study of the Novels and Aesthetics of Michel Butor* (Edmonton: University of Alberta Press, 1980); Wolfgang Hübner, *Michel Butor auf der Harburg: Untersuchungen zu 'Portrait de l'artiste en jeune singe'* (Munich: Vögel, 1987).

of Poetic Realism reveals hitherto unseen patterns of narrative coherence in the work, principally in the form of recurrent centre–periphery structures. Conversely, the close correspondence between Butor's highly reflective and exploratory text and the typical features of German Realist writing indicate that, however historically determined the aesthetic choices of the Realists might have been, they engaged with literary questions in a manner comparable to even the most innovative of twentieth-century authors. I shall begin by reviewing the reputation of German Realism, considering its principal characteristics, which are often seen as its problems. I shall then use these same characteristics as an interpretative framework for the analysis of Butor's *Portrait*.

II

As Martin Swales observed in 'The Problem of German Realism' (1986), 'German prose writing may need an apologist, but we do not need to be apologetic about it.'[6] By this Swales means that, while the quality of German Realist writing can readily be demonstrated, there remains a need to make the case for the specificities of the German brand of Realism when making comparisons with texts from other periods or cultures. For despite decades now of re-evaluations of the writing produced in German-speaking countries between 1840 and 1900, there appears to have been little change in the overall view of Realism's place within the German canon, or in its perceived value when compared with French or English equivalents. What is perhaps most surprising is the tenacity of these value judgements. Todd Kontje begins his *Companion to German Realism* (2002) with the observation that Realism suffers from a 'bad reputation'.[7] In 2005 Lilian Furst's presentation of German Realism in the context of European culture repeats the argument that, after Goethe, German literature dropped from the European stage, re-emerging only at the end of the century.[8] Her analysis, which appears in a standard introduction to nineteenth-century German literature and can be seen as a summary of critical opinion as well as an individual assessment, characterizes Realist writing with loaded terms such as 'limitation', 'withdrawal', and 'inward[ness]'.[9] Nor are such value judgements the preserve of broad historical

[6] Martin Swales, 'The Problem of German Realism', in *Realism in European Literature: Essays in Honour of J. P. Stern*, ed. by Nicholas Boyle and Martin Swales (Cambridge: Cambridge University Press, 1986), pp. 68–84 (p. 69).

[7] Todd Kontje, 'Introduction: Reawakening German Realism', in *A Companion to German Realism, 1848–1900*, ed. by Todd Kontje (Rochester, NY: Camden House, 2002), pp. 1–28 (p. 1).

[8] Lilian Furst, 'Parallels and Disparities: German Literature in the Context of European Culture', in *German Literature of the Nineteenth Century, 1832–1899*, ed. by Clayton Koelb and Eric Downing (Rochester, NY: Camden House, 2005), pp. 45–60 (p. 55).

[9] Ibid., pp. 53–55.

introductions. In a monograph study, again called the 'Problem of German Realism' (2009), Ingo Meyer goes further, stressing the ultimate bankruptcy and discreteness of Realism as a movement, concluding 'vom Realismus führt kein Weg zur Moderne!' ('no road leads from Realism to Modernism!').[10]

There are of course recent positive evaluations, too. John Walker's monograph *The Truth of Realism* (2011) is a case in point, positioning itself specifically as a reassessment. Walker develops Swales's analyses from the 1980s, responding to the assertion that German Realism is socially uncritical because it is dominated by *Innerlichkeit* ('inwardness'), a consequence of philosophical Idealism. Walker's argument that Realism is a thoroughly critical form because it 'expresses a critique of [German society's] cultural self-representation' is sophisticated and persuasive,[11] as indeed was Swales's earlier, more general insight that German Realism offers a realism of 'idea and concept'.[12] Both of these analyses are also valuable in that they seek especially to redress the place of Realism within the history of nineteenth-century German fiction, in particular its relationship with the *Bildungsroman*.

Yet both of these positions are essentially about the realism of Realism, about whether it is justifiable to call German prose fiction of this period 'realist' at all. They leave intact the objections to specific features of Realist poetics, such as provincialism. Furthermore, Walker's aim is ultimately to demonstrate the uniqueness of German Realism; he argues that Realism creates a 'radically different image' of selfhood.[13] While this argument is certainly welcome, it perhaps consolidates rather than challenges the view of German Realism as an episode apart. It is worthwhile, therefore, to consider specifically how German Realism can be integrated into the narrative of European letters and to approach this problem by addressing the identifiable characteristics of Realist writing.

The first distinguishing feature of German Realism within the European context is its focus on topographical peripheries, its provincialism. Erich Auerbach, whose *Mimesis* set the tone for much subsequent criticism, makes the point with characteristic vigour:

If we consider that Jeremias Gotthelf (born 1797) was but two years older and Adalbert Stifter (1805) six years younger than Balzac, that the German contemporaries of Flaubert (1821) and Edmond de Goncourt (1822) are men like Freytag (1816), Storm (1817), Fontane, and Keller (both 1819) [. . .] these names alone are enough to show

[10] Ingo Meyer, '*Im Banne der Wirklichkeit*'? *Studien zum Problem des deutschen Realismus und seinen narrativ-symbolistischen Strategien* (Würzburg: Königshausen & Neumann, 2009), p. 584.

[11] John Walker, *The Truth of Realism: A Reassessment of the German Novel 1830–1900* (London: Legenda, 2011), p. 4.

[12] Martin Swales, '"Neglecting the weight of the elephant...": German Prose Fiction and European Realism', *MLR*, 83 (1988), 882–94 (p. 888).

[13] Walker, *The Truth of Realism*, pp. 2 and 6.

that in Germany life itself was much more provincial, much more old-fashioned, much less 'contemporary'.[14]

He continues: 'Those noteworthy German writers [. . .] all had one thing in common. They were all immersed in the traditional attitudes of the land in which they were rooted'.[15] Furst's observation of Realists' tendency to 'withdraw' into their home areas is more neutral, but the value judgement can still be heard.[16]

Undeniably, the location of the authors created regional specificities (Fontane in Berlin and Brandenburg, Storm in Schleswig-Holstein, Raabe in Braunschweig), but, more importantly, their works were knowingly provincial in setting too. Raabe's *Horacker* (1876) is typical:

> Wenn wir nun den höchsten Berg der Gegend—wenig mehr als achtzehnhundert Fuß über das Meer sich erhebend—besteigen, so begreifen wir mit einem Rundblick nicht nur den Horizont, sondern auch die Grenzlinie, über die er, Eckerbusch, nie hinauskam, abgerechnet die drei Jahre seiner Universitätszeit. Es ist eine Gegend, in der man schon mit erklecklichem Behagen geboren worden sein kann, eine recht schöne Gegend in der wirklichen Bedeutung des Wortes.[17]

> If we now climb the highest mountain in the region, which is only a little higher than 1800 feet above sea level, then, looking around, we perceive at once not only the horizon, but also the limit that he, Eckerbusch, never crossed, except for his three years at university. It is a region where one can be content indeed to have been born, a really beautiful region in the truest sense of the word.

However, recent research has demonstrated that the province–world relationships in Realism are characterized by a complexity and dynamism that cannot be properly accounted for by the traditional narrative of retreat or withdrawal.[18] Moreover, John Lyon's work on spatial representation in Realism analyses texts precisely in terms of their representations of modernity, suggesting that their settings are perhaps best seen as the poetic response to dehumanizing displacements, rather than necessary products of real-life limitations.[19] Indeed, even within the short quotation above, there is evidence of interaction with the wider world—the university—which indicates that the German focus on the province may be part of a deliberate cultivation of

---

[14] Erich Auerbach, *Mimesis: The Representation of Reality in Western Literature*, trans. by Willard R. Trask (Princeton: Princeton University Press, 1953), p. 516.
[15] Ibid.
[16] Furst, 'Parallels and Disparities', p. 53.
[17] Wilhelm Raabe, *Werke*, ed. by Karl Hoppe, 4 vols (Munich: Winkler, 1961–63), IV, 613.
[18] See e.g. *Metropole, Provinz und Welt: Raum und Mobilität in der Literatur des Realismus*, ed. by Roland Berbig and Dirk Göttsche (Berlin: de Gruyter, 2013).
[19] John B. Lyon, 'German Realism's Other: The Space of Modernity', in *Realism's Others*, ed. by Geoffrey Baker and Eva Aldea (Newcastle upon Tyne: Cambridge Scholars, 2010), pp. 91–106; John B. Lyon, *Out of Place: German Realism, Displacement and Modernity* (New York: Bloomsbury, 2013).

distance, but it is a distance that acknowledges and demands some interaction with life beyond narrow borders. Topographically German Realist writing involves not an ignorance of but a consistent steering away from centres of interest towards wayside, marginal spaces; importantly, this tendency is observable not only in the city–province relationship, but in smaller spatial relationships too, indicating that there is more at issue than the lack of a metropolitan centre, however significant that may be. Here Storm's famous poem of 1848, 'Abseits' ('Wayside'), is illuminating. Set in an isolated cottage, it encapsulates the sense of self-conscious distance that these peripheral locations evoke. Crucially, as with Raabe, the sound of the distant clock and the poem's ending point towards a perceived but unnamed centre of action:

> Kaum zittert durch die Mittagsruh
> Ein Schlag der Dorfuhr, der entfernten;
> Dem Alten fällt die Wimper zu,
> Er träumt von seinen Honigernten.
> —Kein Klang der aufgeregten Zeit
> Drang noch in diese Einsamkeit.[20]
>
> A far-off strike of the village clock
> Scarce trembles through the midday rest.
> The old man's head begins to rock,
> He's dreaming of his honey harvest.
> No sound of troubled days, nor rude,
> Had pierced yet this solitude.

The unexpected modernity of these last lines will become clear later.

Related to the world of topographical peripheries is the second characteristic feature of Realism, its interest in *das Nebensächliche*, i.e. peripheral or insignificant details.[21] At one level, German Realist texts manipulate the representation of artefacts to convey information to the reader about a character, a place, or a situation. The 'poetry of clutter',[22] or 'plénitude référentielle',[23] is a hallmark of Realism in general, but German Realism pays particular attention to the seemingly insignificant as part of a conscious inversion of values. As Raabe's narrator in *Die Gänse von Bützow* (*The Geese of Bützow*, 1869) observes: 'In Bützow an der Warnow ist mir allmählich das Kleinste zum Größesten geworden und das Größeste zum Kleinsten geworden' ('In

---

[20] Theodor Storm, *Sämtliche Werke*, ed. by Peter Goldammer, 4 vols (Berlin and Weimar: Aufbau, 1978), I, 110.

[21] See Peter Michelsen, '"Nebensächliches": Zu Theodor Fontanes *Stechlin*', in *Literarisches Doppelportrait: Theodor Fontane/Fritz Mauthner*, ed. by Uta Kutter (Stuttgart: Verein der Freunde der Akademie für gesprochenes Wort, 2000), pp. 61–80.

[22] Martin and Erika Swales, *Adalbert Stifter: A Critical Study* (Cambridge: Cambridge University Press, 1984), p. 40.

[23] Roland Barthes, 'L'effet du réel', in *Littérature et réalité*, ed. by Gérard Genette and Tzvetan Todorov (Paris: Seuil, 1982), pp. 81–90 (p. 90).

Bützow-an-der-Warnow the greatest things have gradually become the smallest for me, and the smallest, the greatest').[24] Or, as Fontane puts it more laconically in *Die Poggenpuhls* (*The Poggenpuhl Family*, 1896), 'Ich bin fürs Kleine' ('I'm for small things').[25]

Significantly, the inclination towards *das Nebensächliche* does not concern objects alone. It is the same tendency towards the inconspicuous that often leads secondary characters in Realist texts to be sources of unexpected insight, as Hoppenmarieken in Fontane's *Vor dem Sturm* (*Before the Storm*, 1878) asserts: 'De Dummen, so as wi ick, de sinn ümmer de Klöksten' ('It's the stupid ones like me who are always the cleverest').[26] Nor is this argument—that truth is to be found in small corners—merely the petty self-assertion of provincial pen-pushers. The capacity to perceive beauty and the truth of the world in the insignificant is at once the Realists' claim to scientific objectivity and a central tenet of their aesthetic project, as Paul Schlenther's review of Fontane's *Unwiederbringlich* (*No Way Back*, 1891) makes clear:

Es ist auf künstlerische Produktion übertragen, dasselbe, was einer der größten wissenschaftlichen Entdecker unseres Jahrhunderts, was schon Jakob Grimm als Forschertugend gepriesen hat: die Andacht zum Umbedeutenden. Wie bedeutend und bedeutsam auch das Unbedeutendste im Sehergeiste eines Künstlers werden kann, lehren Theodor Fontanes Romane auf jeder ihrer Seiten.[27]

The same quality has been transferred onto artistic production that one of the greatest scientific discoverers of our century, Jakob Grimm, praised as the virtue of the researcher: devotion to the insignificant. On each of their pages Fontane's novels teach us just how significant and signifying even the most insignificant thing can become in the visionary spirit of an artist.

Indeed, Realist art functions both to highlight and to explore the beauty and significance of small everyday things and occurrences, and to promote the appreciation of that meaning among readers by developing aesthetic understanding, and this is a constant that we can trace from 'das sanfte Gesetz' ('the gentle law') of Stifter's *Bunte Steine* (*Colourful Stones*, 1853) to Wüllersdorf's 'Hilfskonstruktionen' ('auxiliary structures') in *Effi Briest* (1895).[28]

This privileging of the wayside on the one hand and the steering towards the secondary on the other inevitably entail both avoidance of but implicit

---

[24] Raabe, *Werke*, IV, 134.
[25] Theodor Fontane, *Werke, Schriften und Briefe*, ed. by Walter Keitel and Helmuth Nürnberger, 20 vols in 4 sections (Munich: Hanser, 1962–97) [first published as *Sämtliche Werke*], sect. I, 4, 533. Cited hereafter as HA.
[26] Fontane, HA sect. I, 3, 659.
[27] Paul Schlenther, cited in Theodor Fontane, *Romane und Erzählungen*, ed. by Peter Goldammer and others, 8 vols (Berlin and Weimar: Aufbau, 1969), VI, 488.
[28] Adalbert Stifter, *Werke und Briefe: Historisch-kritische Gesamtausgabe*, ed. by Alfred Doppler and others, 10 sections (Stuttgart: Kohlhammer, 1978–), sect. II, 2, 12 (Preface to *Bunte Steine*); Fontane, HA sect. I, 4, 288; Theodor Fontane, *Effi Briest*, trans. by Hugh Rorrison and Helen Chambers (London: Angel, 1995), p. 216..

reference to unmentioned centres. Indeed, evasiveness or avoidance of big issues is the final hallmark of German Realism under consideration here, and one for which it has been and remains, perhaps, most widely taken to task.[29] We can observe the persistence of this criticism in literary histories, such as Peter Nusser's survey of 2012:

> Es ist dieses Beharren auf der 'Verklärung' der Verhältnisse, zu der sich Fontane noch in den 80er Jahren in seinen Briefen wiederholt bekannt hat, *das die deutschen Realisten den Anschluss an die Entwicklung des europäischen Romans nicht hat findenlassen.* [...] Selbst Wilhelm Raabe und Theodor Fontane, die ihre Romanhandlungen häufiger nach Berlin und seine Umgebung legten, *gingen an der industriell geprägten Großstadt und ihren sozialen Problemen eher vorbei. Gerade die Wahl der Schauplätze macht die Abkopplung der deutschen Erzählliteratur von der europäischen augenfällig.*[30]
>
> It is this stubborn commitment to the 'transfiguration' of circumstances, something which Fontane professes in his letters even in the 1880s, that prevented the German Realists from connecting with the development of the European novel. Even Wilhelm Raabe and Theodor Fontane who set the events of their novels more frequently in Berlin and its environs tended to pass over the industrialized city and its social problems. It is precisely this choice of setting that makes the dislocation of German narrative literature from that of Europe conspicuous.

Here Nusser highlights German Realists' unwillingness to represent and discuss social problems or industrialization explicitly in their prose, and it is an excellent example of how Realism's tendency to evasion and periphrasis causes German Realism to be seen as unworthy or incapable of being considered within the European canon.

To an extent, this criticism must be acknowledged. It is in part the result of Germany's specific historical situation and a corresponding aesthetic that eschews crudeness in favour of transfiguration; yet this discursive turning away is part of broader narrative and aesthetic practices and occurs in many guises. Famously, Fontane's old Dubslav Stechlin 'litt als Briefschreiber daran, gern bei Nebensächlichkeiten zu verweilen und gelegentlich über die Hauptsache wegzusehen' ('suffered as a letter-writer from a preference to dwell on trivial matters and occasionally to overlook the main point entirely').[31] This quotation affords us insight, for example, into the relationship between the idea and direction of perception in Realism on the one hand and the practice of writing on the other. For the tendency towards the peripheral and insignificant that occurs in focalized settings and in descriptions is also reflected stylistically: digressions and lengthy discussions are counterbalanced by preg-

---

[29] For a brief account of these criticisms see Lyon, *Out of Place*, pp. 12–13.
[30] Peter Nusser, *Deutsche Literatur: Eine Sozial- und Kulturgeschichte*, 2 vols (Darmstadt: Wissenschaftliche Buchgesellschaft, 2012), II, 419 (my emphasis).
[31] Fontane, HA sect. I, 5, 245.

nant silences, while key events in the plot, such as Effi's first night of adultery, or the death of Carsten Curator's son, are alluded to relatively obliquely.[32]

It is possible to see other criticisms of Realist writing in this vein too, such as the tendency towards sentimentality. Thus Storm's *Söhne des Senators* (*The Senator's Sons*, 1881), where two brothers apparently 'forget' their bitter feud, has been criticized for its 'Verharmlosung und Verdrängung' ('trivialization and suppression'), literally pushing a problem away,[33] but in so doing the *Novelle* in fact problematizes precisely the issue of turning away from difficult problems.[34] One might even consider the issue of genre as related: a study in 2012 of the *Novelle*, the predominant form of narrative in Germany in the nineteenth century, has argued that it should be seen as an 'anti-genre', outside the normal bounds of literature.[35]

In short, what we have in Realism, rather than a series of problems, is a coherent set of aesthetic choices, a number of varied but ultimately related textual structures which favour indirectness and obliqueness, periphrasis and localism, while eschewing directness, explicitness, and big issues. Now I shall proceed to demonstrate that rather than these aesthetic choices precluding entry into the European canon, it is these same structural patterns that correspond to twentieth-century literary developments.

III

Given the quantity of scholarship on Poetic Realism, studies of its legacy in the twentieth century are surprisingly few. This may be, as Keith Bullivant's *Realism Today* (1987) suggests, the result of a distinction between academic discourse, which historicizes the term *Realismus*, and non-academic discourses on realism and representation, which, in the twentieth century, make reference to the French tradition. Bullivant summarizes nineteenth-century discourses on Realism and presents the realism debates of the late 1960s and 1970s in this context, arguing that the tradition of nineteenth-century German prose is responsible for a problematic relationship with the concept of literary realism in Germany from the Second World War onwards.[36] Bullivant's work is important for present purposes, because it establishes that,

[32] In both cases the main characters collapse, interrupting the narrative. See Fontane, HA sect. I, 4, 162; Storm, III, 71.
[33] Georg Böllenbeck, *Theodor Storm: Eine Biographie* (Frankfurt a.M.: Insel, 1988), p. 200.
[34] See Michael White, 'Space and Ambiguous Sentimentality: Theodor Storm's Die Söhne des Senators', in *Raumlektüren: Der Spatial Turn und die Literatur der Moderne*, ed. by Tim Mehigan and Alan Corkhill (Bielefeld: Transcript, 2013), pp. 107–21 (pp. 116–18).
[35] Florentine Biere, *Das andere Erzählen: Zur Poetik der Novelle 1800/1900* (Würzburg: Königshausen & Neumann, 2012), p. 10.
[36] Keith Bullivant, *Realism Today: Aspects of the Contemporary West German Novel* (Leamington Spa: Berg, 1987), p. 16. Exceptions here are Fontane and Raabe, whom Bullivant sees as part of a separate tradition.

whether acknowledged or not, German Realism does have a legacy in the twentieth century. There are several problems that Bullivant's analysis appears to pose today, however. Firstly, his evaluation of the bulk of German Poetic Realism is essentially negative; Bullivant's comparison of nineteenth- and twentieth-century discourses is essentially founded on the notion that German nineteenth-century Realism is the inheritor of Idealism, and as such is anti-realist. The second issue that seems worthy of attention is the fact that the basis of the study lies precisely in discourses about literary realism. It does not address those peculiar attributes of Poetic Realism, such as provinciality, which are perhaps the real source of the interpretative problem. Finally, Bullivant's solution is to argue for German peculiarity: he argues that the heritage of anti-realism—which becomes canonical in the nineteenth century and continues to shape literary discussions about the possibilities of literary realism—is specific to Germany. The question as to the relevance of German Realism for twentieth-century writing beyond Germany thus remains unexplored.

As suggested above, a more recent strain of Realism research involves seeing German Realism as a realism of ideology, as a mode of representing critically society's own self-representations. Within the nineteenth century, this makes the German form of Realism unusual, even unique; when considered in the context of twentieth-century explorations of realism, however, it is this apparent uniqueness which arguably makes Poetic Realism relevant to more recent concerns. In particular, this preoccupation appears to foreshadow the 'nouveau réalisme' of France, a movement that eventually became known as the *Nouveau Roman*.[37] For here 'naïve realism [is] replaced by the subjective realism of the phenomenologists',[38] the 'visual dictation' of Balzac is succeeded by a realism that explores the 'representation of reality which a particular society possesses and assumes as "Reality"'.[39] In short, the exploration of literature's capacity to represent reality that takes place in France from the late 1940s onwards involves rejecting a model based on the objective reproduction of the real world and concentrating instead on the relationship between empirical reality and the contingent meanings ascribed to that reality by individuals in society, mirroring, to a certain extent, the nineteenth-century German realism of 'idea and concept'.

It is important, of course, not to overstate the case. Both the *Nouveaux Romanciers*' problematization of character in narrative and the overt theor-

[37] Alain Robbe-Grillet, *Pour un nouveau roman* (Paris: Gallimard, 1963), p. 13. For a brief list and discussion of the 'assortment of terms' that grew up around the movement see Stephen Heath, *The Nouveau Roman: A Study in the Practice of Writing* (London: Elite, 1972), pp. 40–41.

[38] John Sturrock, 'The Nouveau Roman', in *French Literature and its Background: The Twentieth Century*, ed. by John Cruickshank (Oxford: Oxford University Press, 1970), pp. 284–98 (p. 284).

[39] Heath, *The Nouveau Roman*, p. 20.

izations about how 'bourgeois ideology was to be subverted and eventually overturned by an attack on its representational use of language' are specific to their historical epochs, as are, conversely, the Poetic Realists' concerns with beauty and morality.[40] A full exploration of the relationship between the type of realism envisioned by the German Realists and the *Nouveaux Romanciers* lies outside the scope of this essay, whose concern is less the realism of Realism than the literary forms that Realist writing takes. However, the notion that a similarity may be observed between the critical discourses on these two movements is important because it lends substance to our assertion that there are parallels in their formal characteristics. To demonstrate this correspondence, Michel Butor's *Portrait de l'artiste en jeune singe* will be analysed in terms of the three hallmarks of German Realism discussed above: topographical peripheries, insignificant details, and evasion and circumlocution.

IV

The story of *Portrait de l'artiste en jeune singe* is very simple. Butor relates how at the end of his lycée years he becomes interested in philosophy and alchemy. His teacher recommends that he go and stay with a German count, the custodian of a large private library in a castle in Germany, who is looking to refresh his French. The young Butor agrees, and spends several weeks exploring the countryside and of course reading, so much so in fact that he leaves with a swollen eye. This brief recapitulation does nothing, however, to evoke the disrupted and confusing nature of the prose, the strange dreams about vampires that Butor weaves into the narrative, the lists of specialized terms and words that render much of the text difficult to read, nor indeed the magical enthusiasm for ideas and for reading that is so fresh and alive on nearly every page. On the surface, the *Portrait* does not appear to be a straightforward example of the *Nouveau Roman*. Certainly it is not one of the canonical works such as Robbe-Grillet's *Les Gommes* (1953) or Butor's own *La Modification* (1957). As a biographical *capriccio* it is not a novel at all, and published in 1967, it is arguably the product of an author who is already moving away from the movement.[41] And yet, with its emphasis on the necessary difficulty of reading, and its thematization of narrative through games, alchemy, and dreams, it does exemplify many of the core concerns of the New Novelists. Furthermore, as will be demonstrated, it can not only be read productively through the lens of Realist poetics: it also offers a discursive

---

[40] Celia Britton, *The Nouveau Roman: Fiction, Theory and Politics* (New York: St Martin's Press, 1992), p. 9.

[41] Butor's relationship to the *Nouveau Roman* group is complicated, but most scholars tend to balance acknowledging this complexity with the need to include Butor as highly significant. See e.g. Britton, *The Nouveau Roman*, p. 7.

examination of the issues of indirect representation which form the basis of that poetics.

Perhaps the most obvious point of correspondence between Butor's text and German Realism is the focus on topographical peripheries, that is, the province and wayside spaces. The narrative is set predominantly in 'H.', which refers to Harburg, a small Bavarian town.[42] Butor's description of the long journey from Paris, by train and on foot, underscores the remoteness of this location.[43] On his way, Butor's narrator bypasses the major local cities: he sees the black silhouette of Ulm Cathedral at night and changes at Augsburg station. These short references accentuate Harburg's provinciality but also introduce another key theme. Both Ulm and Augsburg were heavily bombed, and consequently the journey to the province also represents an escape from the dominant issue of the time, the war and its aftermath. This escape from a central concern is paralleled by an act of temporal decentring: the journey to Harburg appears to take Butor back to Germany before its unification in the nineteenth century, back to the divided world of the Holy Roman Empire.[44]

Within the microcosm of Harburg too, Butor's text continues to explore centre–periphery relationships. Butor's destination point is the castle, which is the geographical, political, and cultural centre of the town. As the narrator points out, however, the main life of Harburg is on the outskirts where the people live. Separated by its walls and high situation, the castle is isolated. These topographical ambiguities are mirrored linguistically: on the one hand, the narrator finds it hard to understand the dialect and to read the signs in Fraktur, and the greeting 'Grüß Gott' seems to him indicative of Harburg's provincial detachedness; on the other, the tradition of this place seems to connect Butor with a real Germany, and indeed what could be more centred or centring than the consistently evoked presence of God?

Paradoxically, Harburg, symbolically an 'anti-centre', is itself the organizing point of Butor's views of the landscape and his explorations. He views the countryside through the castle loopholes (p. 123), his afternoon walks take him 'en grandes spires autour du château' (p. 151), and he tours the surrounding towns on the railway system, which appear, in Butor's memory at least, 'comme une couronne de planètes autour de l'étoile qu'est H' (p. 183). Yet, what appears to be a neat centralized structure is misleading: recalling his visits to the town, Butor underlines the freedom of the narrative to move beyond predetermined networks: 'je saute de sphère en sphère' (p. 183). Furthermore,

---

[42] For a detailed analysis of the representation of Harburg see Hübner, *Butor auf der Harburg*.

[43] Michel Butor, *Portrait de l'artiste en jeune singe: capriccio* (Paris: Gallimard, 1967), pp. 56–58. Subsequent references are to this edition and will be cited in parentheses in the main body of the text.

[44] For an analysis of the symbolism of Germany and the Holy Roman Empire see White, 'L'Allemagne de Michel Butor'.

Harburg's function as an organizing point is not unique: these patterns are replicated in Butor's visits to other castles and towns in the surrounding areas (p. 125).

Like the representation of the town, that of the castle takes what is a circular structure with a centre (the walls and the well), and presents these in a way which creates, or rather uncovers, a sense of disorder. In reality, Harburg castle has a well at its centre and a relatively circular defensive wall, but this is not the impression that Butor's text gives us. Firstly, the young Butor is taken on a tour that follows the wall and 'chemin de ronde', resulting in a succession of towers, rooms, and impressions (pp. 95–101). More importantly, these rooms and towers contain alternative centres: whether that is centralized structures, in the form of the ceiling painting in the 'tour de la Salle des Chevaliers' (p. 100), or in a more abstract sense, in the discovery of other families living separate lives (p. 101). Furthermore, Butor's stylistic device of separating sentences and paragraphs across lines, although by this point in the narrative familiar to the reader, also serves to dislocate the castle's various elements from each other, creating a sense of ambiguity. In particular, the reference 'au centre le puits profond' could, were we not aware of the well's actual location, just as well refer to the centre of the garden in the preceding paragraph, rather than the centre of the castle (p. 101). Butor seems, at a representative level, to reflect what Derrida would argue about the centre losing its organizational priority in the structures of modernity; here the well is simply part of a succession.[45] At a textual, grammatical level, Butor seems to go further: the various prepositional references, 'à l'étage', 'à l'ombre', 'au centre', refer not to a stable point—there is no fixed point around which the narrative is oriented (p. 101)—but either to each other in a movable reciprocal relationship, or, in the case of the well, to nothing at all. The reader emerges as organizer, filling in the deictic gap 'du château' to create a sense of narrative and spatial coherence.

As we have seen, then, the *Portrait*'s setting in H. is not merely the product of an accident of biography. Nor is the text based on a simple centre–periphery antithetical structure. Rather, Butor's *Portrait* creates a fine balance of overlapping and complementary topographies and metaphors which involve centre–periphery relationships but also suggest the existence of alternative centres within pluricentred structures. This spatial strategy serves to place the organizing and interpretative function of narrative into relief.

As in German Realism, the discovery of the significant occurs in hidden corners. The castle tour we have just analysed occurs in the chapter 'Minéralogie' (pp. 93–110). This refers to an eighteenth-century mineral collection

---

[45] Jacques Derrida, 'La structure, le signe et le jeu dans le discours des sciences humaines', in *L'Écriture et la différence* (Paris: Seuil, 1967), pp. 409–28 (p. 411).

in one of the buildings. The collection is neglected in dusty disarray, and the stones are small, although some are apparently very precious (p. 97). After being shown the collection at the beginning of the chapter, the names of its objects run through the narrator's mind and are woven into the representation of the castle, evoking a sense of wonder produced precisely by the collection's confusing mass. A similar story of discovery takes place while the narrator is still in France. Butor's narrator reminisces about holidays at his grandmother's, where the books were divided across two buildings, the older, apparently unreadable ones being stored not in the main library but in a large piece of sacristy furniture in the grandmother's second house on the other side of an alley (p. 27). It is these unreadable but beautiful volumes that appeal to Butor. Rather like the mineral collection, it is in this neglected place that a discerning reader like Butor can find worth: for here are housed the tomes by Montesquieu and Rousseau (p. 27).

By this point, the analysis has moved away from peripheral locations and towards the second characteristic of Poetic Realism, the conscious homage to the insignificant, *das Nebensächliche*, and here it is essentially the library that is important. It is, after all, for the vast library at Harburg, that Butor has made the journey. Certainly the presence out in rural Bavaria of this precious private collection appears to imply that real value is to be found in unassuming places. Yet at the same time, this library is a symbol of the insignificant. As the count relates, it is the second largest private library in Germany, not the first, and most of the important volumes have already been sold off (p. 76). It is thus a secondary library of second-rate authors, a provincial monument to almost-greatness. It is also worth highlighting that the volumes cited as the most important are in fact French authors (Diderot, Rousseau, and Voltaire). This seems to classify the whole of Germany, and perhaps this narrative, as rather 'second-order'.

Furthermore, the immediate effect of the library on Butor appears to be one of distraction. Rather like the mineral collection interrupting the stream of consciousness during the castle description, here the library takes Butor's focus away from what is supposed to be the object of his attention. So absorbed is he in the books and dusty papers on his first visit alone that he not only forgets to turn off the alarm, but remains oblivious to the noise until it is extremely loud and a crowd has assembled outside (pp. 102–04). Thus the library is not only itself peripheral and second-rate, it actively leads Butor away from that which is important, pressing, and that which he is required to do, namely turn off the alarm. Butor's words of panic—'est-ce que la guerre, une autre guerre?'—when he eventually hears the noise are illuminating (p. 104). They indicate that it is this distracting aspect of Harburg which is important: it is an escape away from the dominant issue of the time, the war and its repercussions. It is in this context that the final line in Storm's 'Abseits' is particularly resonant: 'Kein Klang der aufgeregten Zeit | Drang noch in dieser Einsamkeit' ('no sound of troubled days, nor rude | had pierced yet that solitude').[46] If the period of war had been a time when all efforts were focused, here distraction, disorder, and evasion create spaces for other values. And it seems that like those German Realists, Butor too is aware of the fragility of these special places, and the need to enjoy them while they last:

> Après cela, je savais que le silence de la cellule était comme un fragile pont bâti sur un gouffre de hurlement. Ce château tout entier était une bulle de temps passé, miraculeusement épargné par les flammes, une île dans le temps, aux rives, aux enceintes battues par les mares, les laves d'aujourd'hui, une île qui avait recueilli tous ces rescapés d'une autre région du Saint-Empire, d'une autre bulle de temps passé qui, elle, avait expiré sous la fureur. (p. 105)

What emerges, then, is a spatial structure whereby H., or Harburg, is presented as an anti-centre, a place of disorder, of absences and of changeable structures; at the same time it offers an alternative centre, or indeed several layers of structures. This, it seems, is more than a plea for relativism, or the valuing of the seemingly valueless. Rather, it is the evocation of an experience which challenges patterns of thinking, and the way in which travel, cultural exploration, reading, and even silence offer alternative modes of orientation, and it is for this reason that Butor's experience in Harburg encourages him to go to Egypt (p. 124).

V

So far, this analysis has considered the parallels between German Realist poetics and Butor's *Portrait* via the first rubric, topographical peripheries, and it has gone on to consider the significance of peripheral and ostensibly unimportant objects, the second topic. Both of these, it has been argued, are traditionally seen not only as hallmarks of German Realism but also as its characteristic weaknesses; the discussion has demonstrated thus far that these two focal points provide us with productive channels of analysis for this most challenging of twentieth-century texts, suggesting that these facets of Realist poetics deserve to be re-evaluated. Before the *Portrait* is studied from the third aspect of the framework, evasion and circumlocution, it can be shown that Butor's text not only appears to bear formal correspondences with the typical forms of indirectness in Poetic Realism, but that it offers a critical reflection on the aesthetic value of indirectness, adding weight to the earlier proposition that the forms of German Realism have a relevance beyond their temporal and local limitations.

[46] Storm, I, 110.

Butor's *Portrait* is a hymn to the joys of reading, to beautiful books, but it is also about a young man discovering landscapes, seeing paintings; in short, it is about the value of aesthetic experience. Indeed, the reader is introduced to this theme in Chapter 1, 'la couleur des yeux', which is a fascinating essayistic exposé on perception, recall, and representation (pp. 13–18). The discussion prepares the reader for this autobiographical text: a creation that seeks to represent real occurrences (with the exception of the dreams), and real people, it is of course based on Butor's personal and, as he repeatedly reminds us, fallible memories (pp. 21, 60, 83). Butor's particular dramatization of 'the seeing eye' here surpasses typical *Nouveau Roman* strategies of perspective, for this introductory chapter makes the case for indirectness: it argues that real perception of what truly interests us can only occur as a glance, or when that which we wish to perceive is couched among insignificant details, like the valuable stones in the mineral collection.[47]

The opening sentence, 'je remarque très rarement la couleur des yeux', reveals the author's intention of exploring perception and aesthetics (p. 15). Butor introduces an apparent paradox: 'objets peut-être justement trop fascinants pour moi; ils m'attirent tellement que je ne puis en abstraire la couleur, surtout dans le souvenir' (p. 15). This is a statement of an aesthetic problem: how do we perceive, remember, and then represent the things which fascinate us? Butor uses the metaphor of eyes and their colour to explore the idea of representing an object which has a particular resonance, a 'source illuminant l'envers d'autrui, m'introduisant à son secret' (p. 16). Butor notes that the difficulty in recalling and thus reproducing eye colour can be the result of familiarity or of the fact that looking at someone's eyes means becoming oneself the object of observation, implying that he sees past the eyes and perceives the person, the human being. In short, a direct approach does not work.

The remedy to this paradox is itself seemingly paradoxical: perception is aided by apparent lack of focus or distraction: seeing objects in a crowd or not looking at someone well help to see the eye as an object in its own right: 'C'est lorsque je regarde mal quelqu'un, lorsque je ne le regarde pas comme quelqu'un, que je puis voir son œil tel un œil de verre, objet parmi les autres' (p. 16). Even for portrait artists, according to Butor, 'l'œil était la seule chose qu'il était impossible de peindre "d'après nature"'. They rely on the sitter changing his expression, so that they can paint the eye, not as it appears in the present, but reconstituted from memory (pp. 17–18).

To a certain extent, it can be argued that Butor is describing the aesthetic experience as theorized by many aestheticians, such as Clive Bell, and the

---

[47] See Ann Jefferson, *The Nouveau Roman and the Poetics of Fiction* (Cambridge: Cambridge University Press, 1980), p. 108. Jefferson regards the dramatization of perspective as an essential narrative strategy in the *Nouveau Roman*; she sees Henry James as 'the starting point of this kind of narrational realism' (p. 110).

discussion of memory in this preamble is not remarkable at the beginning of an autobiography.[48] Yet, Butor's insistence that significant matters can be perceived and represented only indirectly functions as an aesthetic statement in its own right, justifying the patterns of indirectness which give the text its particular structure. For example, Butor's suggestion that he can recall eye colour in a crowd indicates that detail in the text, while it appears gratuitous and distracting, is in fact playing a key role in facilitating true perception. Similarly, when Butor explains 'c'est lorsque je regarde mal quelqu'un' he justifies the various strategies of obscurity and of indirect reference that the text makes (p. 16). For present purposes too, this analytical exposition demonstrates the appropriateness of the aesthetic framework proposed and reads, for this reader at least, like a twentieth-century apology for German Realist practices.

There is thus a theoretical underpinning for the text's various strategies of evasion and circumlocution, the final topic in our interpretative framework. The avoidance of big issues has already been mentioned briefly: in Realism, this manifested itself in the elision of social problems. Butor's text functions similarly through its indirect reference to the war, as was noted when discussing Harburg's location, the cities of Ulm and Augsburg, and the library. Any reader of this text would be hard placed to reconstruct the physical reality of the immediate post-war era. Instead, the author has chosen to represent a world which the narrator and we the readers experience as a threatened idyll. In so doing, however, he poignantly creates a sense of fear about loss, and for a French readership, a sense of what has been lost in Germany. The count, for example, eventually ends up, as we find out at the end, working in a bank in Frankfurt (p. 227).

Perhaps more significantly for this text, however, is linguistic circumlocution. For language, particularly the German language, and reading both create and represent the indirectness and obscurity that Butor explores in his first chapter and that we have seen as part of an aesthetics of indirectness. The journey to Harburg is presented in part as a reading of German: 'je flairais ma voie à travers des poètes anciens, les pages des auteurs modernes' (p. 48). German is presented from the beginning as a language which permits its initiates to access knowledge. Germany is a 'terre des philosophes' (p. 48). Reflecting the indirect perception Butor praises in his introduction, the narrator's knowledge of German allows him to understand some of what he hears and reads, but this understanding is partial and difficult. This difficulty is linked in part to what Butor is reading: 'je déchiffrai péniblement à travers l'ancien allemand'; it is also the result of his unfamiliarity with Gothic type and, by implication, the local accent (p. 75). Various levels of distance,

[48] See Clive Bell, *Art* (London: Chatto and Windus, 1913).

then, geographical, temporal, and cultural, create the necessary environment for this opacity. Furthermore, Butor not only explicitly designates German as obscure, 'ah, comme ruisselaient pour moi les obscures eaux vives de la langue allemande!' (p. 48), he also correlates the particularities of the language and the topographical imagery seen earlier: his zig-zagging and nonchalant wandering around town is accompanied by his recitation of German declensions (p. 77). In short, Butor creates an impression of German as a strenuous *déchiffrage*, and just as Butor's descriptions of the landscape create shifting, destabilized topographies, so his representation of German, with its emphasis on either single words or partial understanding, creates a sense of enjoyable disorder in the land of grammatical clarity.

Like language in general, reading is presented as an indirect means of perception. This can be the result of specific graphemes which create obscurity, such as the 'palpitation délicieuse' in Butor's reading because of the similarity between 'u' and 'v' in old texts (p. 29). More often, books offer alternative frameworks of reference, leading the reader (Butor) to consider and create new centres of reference and constantly shifting the object of enquiry. Thus, as a result of this time in a German library, during which Butor reads Mann's *Joseph in Ägypten* (*Joseph in Egypt*) in translation, he decides to go to Egypt, which becomes a 'seconde terre natale' (p. 11). This idea of an alternative frame of reference is most strongly in evidence in the alchemical texts, which present alternative readings of reality, a parallel symbolism built on intertextuality. A final but important aspect of the reading practice in the text which is easily overlooked are Butor's reading habits. Rather than being armed with a systematic reading plan, he dips into books and samples the collections. Thus the readings are partial, both in terms of the text which is revealed and in terms of the understanding, and just like the impression created by the mineral collection, it is this wash of glimpses that creates interest and excitement.

VI

The purpose of this discussion has been to propose a re-evaluation of the German form of Realism, not based on an assessment of the realism of German Realism, but on a re-examination of the peculiar formal attributes of Realist texts in the context of later developments in European prose. I have argued that, however historically determined these features may be, they constitute a coherent aesthetic, consisting in a broad range of interrelated and connected literary strategies which promote indirectness. For the sake of clarity, these have been grouped under three headings: topographical peripheries, the insignificant, and circumlocution. It is typically argued that these features of German Realism are the specific products of the German cultural context in the nineteenth century. It would be fruitless to deny that these literary strategies are poetic responses to historical circumstances; both the pragmatism and resignation of the age can readily be traced in contemporary critical writing and personal correspondence. However, too narrow a focus on German Realism's peculiarity and a normative view of nineteenth-century narrative development have rendered German Realist prose an interpretative problem; rather than arguing for the uniqueness of German Realism, then, this essay has sought to demonstrate that the indirectness and evasiveness of German Realism is a form of writing which bears a marked resemblance both to twentieth-century explorations of literary representation and to writing beyond the German tradition.

Michel Butor's *Portrait de l'artiste en jeune singe*, as we have seen, sheds considerable light on this issue. Although a highly original piece, this text, through considerable formal innovation and an almost defiant thematic density, explores many of the patterns of indirectness which we have identified with German Realism. In the representation of provincial Harburg, Butor's narrative creates a complex web of overlapping centre–periphery structures. These create a sense of otherness, evoking a world which is at once distant from France and Paris, a place where the young Butor's willingness to lose himself in alchemical and historical intricacies is given free rein; at the same time they function reflexively as an appropriate expression of the mature author's explorations of narrative and textual organization. The peripheries in the text's represented topography mirror a tendency to find value in the insignificant, of which the mineral collection and the library are the most significant symbols. Harburg emerges as a place of alternative values and modes of thinking, a threatened idyll where traumatic experiences can, temporarily, be evaded, and space given to silence, reading, and reverence before humanist endeavours. Harburg's function as a place of evasion is complemented by the text's thematization of periphrasis: the portrayal of the German language as opaque parallels the young Butor's experience in this place of half-pierced mysteries; at the same time it thematizes the stylistic impediments which characterize the narrative, offering a reflexive discourse on the necessary difficulty that underlies transformative reading, as Butor argues in 'L'alchimie et son langage':

L'alchimiste considère cette difficulté d'accès comme essentielle, car il s'agit de transformer la mentalité du lecteur afin de le rendre capable de percevoir le sens des actes décrits. [. . .] Le lecteur, d'abord dérouté, s'habitue s'il persiste, et finit par trouver ce langage tout naturel.[49]

[49] Michel Butor, 'L'alchimie et son langage', in *Répertoire* (Paris: Minuit, 1960), pp. 12–19 (p. 17).

In short, reading Butor's text through the prism of Poetic Realism appears to indicate that the collection of attributes for which German Realist texts are often criticized do not necessarily constitute a unique aesthetic. Nor are they the necessary expression of old-fashioned provincials. Here, in this innovative text which explores some of the essential problems of representation in twentieth-century narrative, a similar aesthetic is discernible. Significantly, the literary explorations of indirectness which this analysis has identified appear supported by Butor's discussion of perception which precedes the narrative proper.

An analysis of a single text can, naturally, provide only a limited insight into the much larger problem posed by the legacy of Realism. It might also be countered that finding patterns of indirectness in literature is inevitable, as literature, and indeed all symbolic art, is indirect expression by its very nature. Certainly this is true. Yet it is precisely through the predominance of this literary mode that both German Realism and the text studied here achieve lasting value, for their explorations of the possibilities of literary representation are governed by an impulse to stay true to literature's own reality.

UNIVERSITY OF ST ANDREWS   MICHAEL J. WHITE

SCIENCE IN THREE DIMENSIONS: WERNER HERZOG'S *CAVE OF FORGOTTEN DREAMS*

One of the distinguishing features of Werner Herzog's *Cave of Forgotten Dreams*, noted by reviewers at the time of its release in 2010, was the fact that it had been filmed in 3-D.[1] While Herzog himself was critical of the use of 3-D in mainstream cinema, his decision to use the technology for this particular documentary was determined by its subject, the Palaeolithic paintings of Chauvet Cave in the Ardèche region of south-eastern France.[2] It is a well-known fact that prehistoric cave paintings are not normally flat, as our own traditions of two-dimensional representation might lead us to assume, but exploit the three-dimensionality of their support, the accidents and irregularities of the cavern walls themselves. In this sense Herzog's use of stereoscopic projection is scientifically correct, as it allows him to capture something of the objective reality of the paintings. It is also, in a wider sense, phenomenologically correct, to the extent that 3-D provides the viewer—who will never have direct access to Chauvet Cave—with a heightened sense of immersion in the total environment of which the paintings are an integral part. However, despite the effectiveness of the use of 3-D in *Cave of Forgotten Dreams*, it is not in my view the most interesting or compelling aspect of the film. In this respect, the 'three dimensions' of my title are more metaphorical than literal, referring not so much to Herzog's exploitation of the medium of 3-D as to his tendency to present science itself in three dimensions, to look at the subjects of science, those who make science, as well as the objects of science.

This, it could be argued, is what distinguishes *Cave of Forgotten Dreams* from more generically conventional documentaries on prehistoric culture. In common with these documentaries, Herzog's film fulfils the basic educational function of science communication, which is to present the facts of a given domain of knowledge and, ideally, to encourage further reflection on it. At the same time, the film's mode of composition—the closing credits indicate that it is 'Written, Directed and Narrated by Werner Herzog'—seems immediately to present us with a more reflexive perspective on its subject matter. In this sense it is very much the product of what is commonly referred to as Herzog's 'vision', and equally the product of what should here be referred to as his 'voice'. It would be a mistake, however, to reduce the film to some unique combination of vision and voice, to an expression of the personal

---

[1] *Cave of Forgotten Dreams*, dir. by Werner Herzog (Creative Differences Productions/History Films, USA, 2010); running time 87 minutes.

[2] Discovered in 1994, these paintings are the oldest representations of their kind, dated at approximately 32,000 years BP (Before Present). See *La Grotte Chauvet: l'art des origines*, ed. by Jean Clottes (Paris: Seuil, 2010).

and ultimately subjective meditations of the director Werner Herzog. More accurately, it could be said that Herzog's highly structured staging of the documentary and his strategic deployment of its protagonists create an additional dimension of objectivity, providing a fascinating insight into what the human science of prehistory has become in the twenty-first century, both in France and internationally. The following analysis will look in turn at the treatment of locations, institutions, and individuals in *Cave of Forgotten Dreams*, concluding with a consideration of how this remarkable film might help us to think in a more critical and more reflexive manner about 'humanness' or 'what it means to be human'.

The importance of location and landscape in Herzog's films is explicitly acknowledged by the director himself. As he comments in his interviews with Paul Cronin: 'I like to direct landscapes just as I like to direct actors and animals. [. . .] What I look for in landscapes in general is a humane spot for man, an area worthy of human beings. [. . .] The starting point for many of my films is a landscape.'[3] The striking opening scene of *Cave of Forgotten Dreams* is indeed a floating perspective of a landscape. Moving to the metre of Dutch composer Ernst Reijseger's soundtrack, the camera in sequence tracks a vineyard near to Chauvet Cave, rises abruptly to encompass the surrounding landscape, including the spectacular Pont d'Arc—the natural geological feature created by the Ardèche river—then descends to scan the cliffs leading to the cave entrance before cutting to its interior. This opening composition is completed by the voice-over of the director himself, situating the cave in terms of its geographical location, the history of its discovery, and its significance as the repository of the oldest known examples of prehistoric cave art. In addition to the factual contextualization provided by the director's voice, the visual movement of ascent–descent characterizing this opening sequence seems to constitute a kind of thought-process in itself, transiting from a human-engineered landscape (nature–culture) to a geologically transformed landscape (nature–nature) to the human–semiotic landscape of the cave itself (culture–nature). At the same time, Herzog's sequencing is convergent with the statistical evidence about sites such as Chauvet, which indicates that they are frequently found in geographical locations that are in one way or another visually remarkable.[4]

The cave named after Jean-Marie Chauvet, one of its three discoverers, is a sealed vault, sealed from public access and the atmospheric variations which would over time compromise the state of preservation of its contents. This was the hard lesson learnt from the example of Lascaux Cave, which from the time of its opening to the public in 1948 through to its closure in 1963 suffered

[3] *Herzog on Herzog*, ed. by Paul Cronin (London: Faber and Faber, 2002), pp. 81, 83.

[4] On the importance of landscape types in the location of Palaeolithic sites see Jean Clottes, *Pourquoi l'art préhistorique?* (Paris: Gallimard, 2011), pp. 161–65.

near-irreparable damage due to the carbon dioxide emitted by human visitors. The Chauvet Cave is therefore accessible only to scientists and researchers, at strictly regulated times of the year. Herzog and his small filming team were allowed access for four hours a day over a period of six days in 2010. The hypnotic attraction of the film, enhanced by Reijseger's soundtrack, resides for a large part in the way it initiates the viewer into the internal space of the cave, the 3-D camerawork of director of photography Peter Zeitlinger allowing us to experience, vicariously, the beauty of its mineral concretions, producing a more immediate sense of *inhabitation* than conventional two-dimensional projection. As the filming team moves through this enchanting environment, the narrator confesses at one point to an uncanny sense of being watched, as if the previous inhabitants of the cave were somehow still present—a feeling also experienced by certain scientists and the cave's discoverers. For myself, watching the carefully choreographed movements of the cave's visitors elicited the distinct sense of another presence, in this case the spirit of twentieth-century science as represented by the prehistorian André Leroi-Gourhan. The leading figure in his discipline in France until his death in 1986, Leroi-Gourhan campaigned extensively for the proper protection and preservation of archaeological sites such as Lascaux. In addition to the atmospheric degradation mentioned above, the other tragedy of Lascaux Cave was that precious archaeological evidence scattered on its floors had been destroyed in the construction of pathways for visitors to view the paintings.[5] The movements of the filming team in Herzog's documentary are therefore strictly controlled: wearing sterilized boots and under the supervision of the cave guards, they process along a 60 cm-wide metal walkway protecting the floors. It is forbidden to step off the walkway.

Over a period of more than thirty years, Leroi-Gourhan had visited virtually all of the decorated prehistoric sites in France, and came to use the term 'sanctuary' to describe the nature of these locations.[6] While this term, still current in the discourse of prehistorians, is not explicitly used in Herzog's film, it is easy to see that his audio-visual representation of the cave also follows this interpretation. The geographical location of Chauvet Cave, its internal structure and composition, its ambience and aura, compel the visitor to acknowledge this spiritual significance, even if the absolute loss of context means that it is impossible to determine its ultimate meaning for prehistoric humans. It is equally easy to see that Herzog's focus is also on how humans of the twenty-first century relate to the cave, how the scientific protection and preservation of the Chauvet site creates what is effectively a second degree or dimension of sanctification. The tracking shot at the start of the film is in this

[5] See André Leroi-Gourhan, *Les Racines du monde: entretiens avec Claude-Henri Rocquet* (Paris: Belfond, 1982), pp. 215–16.

[6] Leroi-Gourhan discusses his use of this term in *Les Racines du monde*, p. 218.

respect simple but significant: it follows the small group of researchers winding their way to the cave entrance, the narrator's commentary informing us of the periodicity of their visits to the site. The construction of this sequence, its representation of the seasonal convergence of a group of scientists—two of whom are carrying sticks—on the site of Chauvet, clearly communicates the sense of a pilgrimage, a recurrent theme in Herzog's films.[7] If the human context of the 'sanctuary' of Chauvet is irretrievably lost, what remains is the directly observable, living context of the community of researchers who create meaning around it.

Herzog's practice as a director is to extract different individuals from the scientific community at Chauvet, who in their turn comment on different aspects of the cave, in particular the paintings. While this mode of presentation is standard practice in the factual documentary, there is a clear gradation in the relative foregrounding of the film's protagonists, reflecting what one might briefly term the elective affinities of Werner Herzog. The selection of these protagonists seems at first sight to be a structural and hierarchical one. The archaeologists Dominique Baffier, Jean Clottes, and Jean-Michel Geneste are the elders of the community, those who act as the guardians and guides of the cave. In the credits at the end of the film they are listed first and separately from the rest of the Chauvet research team. Dominique Baffier is the curator of the cave—Herzog describes her as its 'custodian'—and she is the main guide in the first part of the documentary. Jean Clottes was the first director of the Chauvet research programme following the cave's discovery in 1994, and also accompanies the visitors in the opening sequences of the film. Jean-Michel Geneste is the current director at Chauvet, and is most present in the middle and closing sequences. These three protagonists together represent the generational authority that is necessary for the institutional organization and transmission of knowledge in a discipline such as prehistory. However, the director's presentation of these protagonists is not equally balanced, indicating a selective bias which may have something to do with language.

The research team at Chauvet is French and French-speaking—the discipline of prehistory has a long history in France, dating back to the middle of the nineteenth century, and the country is commonly described as *le berceau de la préhistoire*, the cradle of prehistory.[8] At the start of the twenty-first century, on the other hand, the language of international science has become, and remains, massively English. Werner Herzog's adoptive language, as an

---

[7] See Brad Prager, *The Cinema of Werner Herzog: Aesthetic Ecstasy and Truth* (London: Wallflower Press, 2007), pp. 127–35; Eric Ames, *Ferocious Reality: Documentary according to Werner Herzog* (Minneapolis: University of Minnesota Press, 2012), pp. 83–85.

[8] See René Joffroy's foreword to *La Préhistoire française*, ed. by Jean Guilaine and Henri de Lumley, 3 vols (Paris: Éditions du CNRS, 1976), II, p. ix.

international film-maker living in the US, is also English. Moreover, he confesses to a certain aversion to French as a language. It is not that he cannot speak the language, rather that he *refuses* to speak it, that he will only speak it if compelled by exceptional circumstances. In his interviews with Paul Cronin he attributes this linguistic prejudice to his inability to understand irony, which he describes as a specifically French cultural trait.[9] Whatever we might make of this explanation, Herzog's confession alerts us to the lines of linguistic demarcation that may separate different categories of protagonist in the film. Of the three protagonists we have considered so far, Baffier speaks in French, with an English-language voice-over, while Clottes and Geneste speak in English. Other members of the Chauvet research team—the palaeontologist Michel Philippe, archaeologists Carole Fritz and Gilles Tosello—also speak in French, again with voice-overs. The use of voice-over rather than subtitling can be frustrating for the bilingual viewer, as it tends to block out the original voices of the presenters.[10] But apart from this technical consideration, and perhaps more fundamentally, the division in the film between French- and English-speakers seems to correlate with the difference between fact and interpretation, between the objects of science and the subjects of science.

The scenes involving Baffier, Philippe, Fritz, and Tosello are the most straightforwardly factual and descriptive sequences in the film, and closest to the conventional form of the science documentary. Here we are presented with experts who explain to the audience the current state of scientific knowledge about the contents of the Chauvet Cave. Thus, in an extended tour of the cave Baffier guides us from the series of positive hand-markings to the Panther Panel, the Panel of the Horses, and finally the Panel of the Big Lions.[11] Fritz and Tosello comment on the chronology of clawmarks left on the walls by cave-dwelling bears and the different stages of composition of the Panel of the Horses. Philippe, the only palaeontologist represented in the film, reminds us of the importance of the fossil deposits on the cave floors, which provide evidence of relative frequentation by different animal species. The testimonies of these different experts provide the viewer with a selective but representative picture of current archaeological knowledge about the cave, and the carefully forensic approach of the scientific teams who study it. However, the director clearly does not approach these individuals in the same way that he approaches their English-speaking colleagues. With the latter, the

[9] Cronin, *Herzog on Herzog*, pp. 27–28.

[10] In the French version of the film, voice-overs are applied to the English-speaking protagonists, with a symmetrically problematic elision of their voices. This is compounded by the fact that the main narrator is no longer Werner Herzog, but fellow German film-maker Volker Schlöndorff. Herzog is of course the narrator in the film's German version, but voice-overs are applied throughout to both French- and English-speaking protagonists.

[11] See the general plan of Chauvet Cave in *La Grotte Chauvet*, ed. by Clottes, p. 13.

viewer senses that there is a background dialogue between director and actor beyond what is presented on screen, that we are in contact with the subjects of science as much as with the objects of science. Because their interventions are most clearly framed by the format of the interview, these individuals are not only communicating their knowledge but also responding to questions, and therefore seem to assume a more reflexive position with respect to the established facts of their science.

One of the most immediately engaging of Herzog's protagonists in this category is the young archaeologist Julien Monney. Throughout the documentary, Monney is interviewed not in the cave but in an office, next to a laptop computer and facing the director, who is out of view. Responding to the latter in an accented but very proficient English, he insists on the situated humanity of the scientist: 'I'm a scientist, but a human too.' He describes his own subjective experience of being in the cave as so powerful that he had found it difficult to sleep following his first contact with it. Replicating what is a thematic leitmotif in Herzog, who claims that he does not dream, Monney confesses to having had recurrent dreams of lions, both real and representational (the film's camera scans the famous Panel of the Big Lions, located in one of the deepest recesses of the cave), in which, like Daniel in the lions' den, he was not afraid. Prompted by the director's questioning, he reveals that he was once a circus performer, which seems to place him in a recognizable lineage of Herzogian characters who possess what might be termed a binary existence, who do not fit simply and squarely into the structures of professional identification imposed upon us by society.[12]

Despite his unusual past, and his willingness to speak of the human dimension of science, Monney nevertheless conforms to the institutionalized division of labour of his chosen discipline. As an archaeologist, his articulate responses on the cave do not deviate from the established norms of the discipline, and he is carefully circumspect in his interpretations. In this sense he and his French colleagues at Chauvet continue the research tradition established by Leroi-Gourhan, who was suspicious of speculations on the meaning and function of prehistoric artefacts which were not grounded in a meticulously assembled body of archaeological evidence. Leroi-Gourhan had criticized the unscientific nature of previous archaeological excavation practices, and distinguished between the authentically scientific imagination which creates the means for further discovery and a more intuitive form of scientific imagination based on unfounded extrapolation from the facts. In particular, he was critical of certain kinds of ethnographic comparatism, that is, interpreta-

---

[12] One thinks here of the protagonists of documentaries such as *The Great Ecstasy of Woodcarver Steiner* (1973), *The Dark Glow of the Mountains* (1984), and *Encounters at the End of the World* (2007).

tions of prehistoric culture based on what we know about contemporary, or historically recorded, traditional societies.[13]

If the sealed vault of Chauvet Cave and the narrow metal walkways that protect its floors can be seen as the material manifestation of this research tradition, its intellectual legacy can be observed in the collective behaviour of the research team at Chauvet. Indeed, what the director shows us in the first half of the film is a community dedicated mainly to the empirical analysis and description of the facts of Chauvet.[14] A particularly striking—and beautiful—image early in the film seems to summarize this attitude: it is a three-dimensional computer-generated topographical map of the cave based on the laser-scanning techniques of expert geometer Guy Perazio. The viewer moves through this virtual environment as if flying across a landscape, the narrator explaining that 'This map is the basis for all of the scientific projects being done here.' While Herzog's perspective in the film is not an anti-scientific one—he seems on the contrary to be fascinated by the array of analytical techniques available to the twenty-first-century archaeologist—his question to Monney immediately following this sequence crystallizes the viewer's own questions. The laser-scanned representation of the cave, he suggests, is like the Manhattan telephone directory; it is a total topographical description of the cave, but tells us nothing about its prehistoric visitors: 'Do they dream, do they cry at night, what are their hopes, what are their families?', he asks. Monney has already explained that this type of measurement is the starting point but not the goal of the Chauvet research project, which is to create 'stories' about Palaeolithic existence derived from the scientific evidence, but he cannot of course respond to Herzog's question. He describes the prehistoric past as irretrievable, and instead speaks to the existential question of how he or Herzog as human beings can relate to its remains. His own dreams of lions did not scare him at all, and gave him a deeper, non-scientific intuition of the nature of the cave: 'It was more a feeling of powerful things and deep things, a way to understand things which is not a direct way.'

Herzog's elicitation of the human dimension of science through his dialogue with Monney is only the starting point of the film's investigation of Chauvet. It does not exhaust the metaphysical impulse which is characteristic of Herzog as a director, but which is also the characteristic impulse of the audience he is mediating—a phenomenon such as Chauvet naturally generates a demand for meaning. As the film unfolds, this meaning is slowly introduced

[13] See e.g. the introduction to Leroi-Gourhan's *Les Religions de la préhistoire* (Paris: Presses Universitaires de France, 1964), pp. 1–9.

[14] Jean Clottes is critical of this tendency in post-war French prehistory, describing it as 'un empirisme trompeur et sans ambition' which prefers to 'laisser les faits parler par eux-mêmes'. If such research is able to establish the 'what?', 'when?', and 'how?' of prehistoric art, it fails to address the question of its 'why?', of its possible meanings (*Pourquoi l'art préhistorique?*, pp. 12, 18–19, 72–73).

through the guiding voice of its narrator, in dialogue with the voices of his English-speaking interlocutors—the presence of French-speaking specialists ends more or less literally with Dominique Baffier's guided tour of the cave, just short of the first half of the film. In order properly to understand Chauvet, it is necessary to look at the wider material culture in which the paintings at Chauvet participated. In the following sequence, Jean-Michel Geneste shows us two examples of portable art, replicas of a 'Venus' and a lion-headed male figure from Hohlenstein-Stadel in the Swabian Alps. Leaving France and transcending historically defined borders, the camera takes us to the Prehistoric Museum of Blaubeuren, also in southern Germany, where archaeologist Nicholas Conard demonstrates the Venus of Hohle Fels, the oldest example of Palaeolithic figurative art, which replicates part of the visual theme of a hybrid bison-woman representation found in Chauvet Cave.[15] The didactic content of these sequences is that there is a common cultural complex linking archaeological sites in modern-day France and Germany, but this is accompanied by what may be described as meta-empirical speculation on what these artefacts might tell us about the beings who made them. Thus Geneste asks whether the lion-headed figure represents the spirit of the lion in anthropomorphic form, a marriage of human and animal, or an entirely new being, while Conard proposes that such artefacts are clear evidence of 'a religious concept involving the transformation between humans and animals'. As the camera adopts a high aerial perspective, pointing north in a breathtaking vista along the Ardèche river towards south-western Germany, the narrator himself proposes that the art at Chauvet 'was not a primitive beginning, or a slow evolution, it rather burst onto the scene like a sudden explosive event. It is as if the modern human soul had awakened here.' He continues: 'Even more astonishing to consider is that at the time Neanderthal man still roamed this valley.'

It would be easy to dismiss this commentary as the first-person reflections of a metaphysically minded director, but in fact it replicates at least one side of the received wisdom among prehistorians on the origins of so-called 'modern' humanity. This particular interpretation of the archaeological evidence argues for a relatively rapid development in the cognitive and cultural capacities of *Homo sapiens* around the period of Chauvet, a phase of transition frequently described by specialists as an 'explosion'.[16] If they certainly would not use the term 'soul', these specialists nevertheless refer to the Palaeolithic 'mind' or Palaeolithic 'cognition' as the outstanding adaptive trait defining 'modern' humans. If it is difficult to accept Herzog's dramatized image of Neander-

---

[15] Apart from its effectiveness in the representation of the internal space of the cave, mentioned above, the haptic potential of 3-D also becomes evident in the sequences in which different specialists handle artefacts as they explain their significance or mode of construction.

[16] See e.g. Randall White, *Prehistoric Art: The Symbolic Journey of Humankind* (New York: Abrams, 2003), pp. 67–68.

thals 'roaming' a landscape inhabited by more civilized Cro-Magnons, his interpretation is subsequently reiterated and confirmed in scientific mode by the archaeologist Conard, who states quite categorically that Neanderthals, despite their 'sophistication', never possessed the kind of symbolic artefacts in evidence at Chauvet and the sites in southern Germany. This genetic discrimination, this need to distinguish between different categories of the human, reveals the metaphysical impulse at work within the discipline itself, the compulsion to address the fundamental questions of essence and of origin: who or what are we; when, where, and how did we begin? What makes us human? And therefore implicitly, by way of opposition: what is not (quite) human?

Through his scientific protagonists, Herzog carefully lays out the defining features of the (modern) human (soul). Chauvet has given us the example of sophisticated graphic representation, while the caves in Germany yield evidence of portable objects with symbolic significance. The German caves also contain evidence of what is defined as another essential feature of emergent human creativity: music. Here, Conard is the perfect ambassador for his discipline, reminding us that 'archaeology today is not a heroic adventure with spades and picks, but high-tech scientific work that's done with incredible detail'. He illustrates his point by asking fellow archaeologist Maria Malina to demonstrate how she reconstructed an ivory flute from tiny fragments of bone found dispersed in a cave located in the same region as Hohle Fels. But while the scientist reconstructs the flute, Herzog calls upon another protagonist, the experimental archaeologist Wulf Hein, to play it. It is here that the documentary appears to deviate somewhat from its hitherto predominant mode of science communication. Filmed next to the entrance of the cave at Geissenklösterle, Hein is dressed from head to toe in a costume made of reindeer skins; compared with the university-based archaeologists we have seen so far, his appearance is relatively unkempt. We as viewers know that Herzog as a director is intuitively drawn to this kind of character, and we recognize his type. His appearance injects a certain degree of levity into a film which until now has unfolded mainly in the registers of muted fascination and reverence. Hein plays 'The Star-Spangled Banner' on a replica Palaeolithic flute.

While Hein's performance is a pleasure to watch, it would be misleading simply to file him away under the category of the eccentric Herzogian character. As the self-description 'experimental archaeologist' suggests, his specialization is the attempted reconstruction of the behaviour of Palaeolithic humans, in particular aspects of their material culture. In a sense, it could be said that his function is to bring us down to earth, to the everyday existence that would have surrounded exceptional sites such as Chauvet, and to the outside world: the myth of cave-dwelling humans is an enduring one. His flute-playing demonstrates the cognitive continuum linking us to prehistoric humans—he is able to play 'The Star-Spangled Banner' on the flute because it is pentatonic. But equally significantly, his performance brings us a step closer to what up to this point has been a missing dimension of the film: the question of technology.[17] Hein may be slightly unkempt, but he is well dressed, and his reindeer suit is exquisitely tailored. As he explains, evoking with a sweep of his hand the glacier-filled landscape of the Upper Palaeolithic, the climate in this part of Europe would have been an exacting one, and the suit, like Inuit clothing, is the signifier of an advanced technical culture, perfectly adapted to its environment. Contrary to appearances, the para-institutional character of Hein does not therefore depart from the film's main scientific narrative, but provides it with an additional dimension.

Structurally, the film stages its return from Germany to France through the character of Maurice Maurin, a retired master perfumer who was for some years chair of the French Society of Perfumers: 'Back in France, near Chauvet Cave, explorers using more primal techniques in search of hidden underground chambers roam the landscape.' Maurin is filmed with his head close to the ground, smelling the rocks, then turns to face the camera. Even less than Wulf Hein does this character belong to the institutionalized structures in which the majority of the film's protagonists operate; it is difficult to imagine him as a participant in a more conventional documentary on Chauvet. But again, the inclusion of this character, immediately following that of Hein, has its own intrinsic logic. Speaking in French—this is the only voice-over in the second half of the film—Maurin correctly explains that explorers locate underground cave complexes by searching for tell-tale air currents emanating from the landscape.[18] The narrator then adds that 'There are plans to build a theme park for tourists with a precise replica of the cave a few miles from here. This replica may even contain a recreation of the odour of the prehistoric interior.' The character of Maurin therefore functions as a kind of poetic condensation of objective practice, that of the speleologists who discovered the cave and that of the experts who aim—doubtless exploiting the laser-scanning techniques presented earlier in the film—to reconstruct the total environment of Chauvet. But, echoing what Monney says about his dreams, he also seems to represent an alternative way of exploring Chauvet: 'It's a matter of trying to experience it in a different manner.' While specialists such as Conard demonstrate the 'high-tech scientific work' of archaeological reconstruction, Maurin, an individual who has spent a lifetime refining his sense of smell, and who, like Neanderthal man, *roams* the landscape, uses 'more primal tech-

---

[17] There is a very brief reference to flint tools just before Geneste's demonstration of the Venus and lion-headed figures.

[18] See Jean-Marie Chauvet, Éliette Brunel Deschamps, and Christian Hillaire, *La Grotte Chauvet à Vallon Pont-d'Arc* (Paris: Seuil, 1995), p. 16.

niques' of exploration. His research, predicated on one of the more viscerally immediate of the senses, extends our thinking about Chauvet beyond the instrument-mediated analysis of what has endured—flint, bone, decorated rock—reminding us of the more evanescent realities of a disappeared world.

The two relatively more eccentric characters in Herzog's film, Hein and Maurin, are presented in sequence and back to back. Structurally, they function as a point of transition, a signpost which points us in the direction of the film's conclusion. In line with Herzog's alternating dialectic between inside and outside, once more we enter the space of the cave, this time without the mediating guidance of the experts. It is at this point that the narrator refers to his team's sense of being watched, as if they were disturbing the Palaeolithic people in their work. The sanctuary of Chauvet elicits an ecstatic response—a number of scenes show different protagonists transfixed in contemplation—but it can also become oppressive: 'It was a relief to surface again above ground.' The concluding sequences of the film are mainly staged outside, in the landscape surrounding Chauvet, and could be said to constitute an argument, or perhaps more precisely a play of perspectives, in the manner of Flaubert. Appropriately, the metaphysical impulse that runs through the film is given its most focused expression in these closing sequences, as the principal English-speaking protagonists in their turn speak to the meaning of Chauvet.

The first sequence takes place in the vineyards of the film's opening scene. Here, Jean-Michel Geneste demonstrates the hunting techniques of Palaeolithic peoples. The camera focuses on his hands as he indicates the different points of articulation of a spear: its sharp point constructed from bone; the forked joint and tight binding which fix the point to a long shaft made of wood. In a gesture enhanced by 3-D projection, Geneste thrusts forward with the spear, demonstrating its effectiveness as an instrument made to kill. The demonstration, however, does not end here. Geneste points to the feathers at the base of the spear, designed to stabilize its flight when thrown. The tool then becomes a machine as he explains the principle of the spear-thrower, which when attached to the base of the spear, allows the thrower both to amplify the power of the throw and increase its precision. Geneste demonstrates this advanced projectile technology by launching the spear some distance into the rows of vines. Though his demonstration is gently mocked by the director, who presumes that the Palaeolithic hunter would have been more effective, the purpose of this sequence is clear. At this comparatively late stage in the film, like Wulf Hein's costumed re-enactment, it brings us closer to the total human fact of Chauvet Cave, to the material conditions of possibility of human aesthetic production, that is, advanced human technics. In anticipation of the following sequence, let us simply call this particular manifestation of the human *Homo technicus*.

Following another brief interlude in the cave, our next sequence is again filmed outside, with the other elder protagonist Jean Clottes. Unlike Geneste, Clottes is not demonstrating something—he is not, to paraphrase Leroi-Gourhan, combining gesture and speech.[19] He is simply talking, or rather, professing. Clottes speculates that like traditional peoples, humans of the Palaeolithic period would not have had the same rationalistic attitude as ourselves towards the material world. In an English whose formulations appear idiomatically French, he uses the concepts of *fluidity* and *permeability* to characterize Palaeolithic mentality. Fluidity refers to what would have been the relative lack of distinction between different categories of object or being. Thus the human can become animal or the animal human, the animal or human can become an object, and so on. Permeability refers to the abolition of boundaries between the material and spiritual worlds. A shaman, for example, is able to visit supernatural spirits in other worlds or receive visits from them. Together, these two concepts give us a sense of the radical difference between the lives of prehistoric peoples and our own. Clottes concludes that our self-characterization as *Homo sapiens* is not a valid one—'we don't know, we don't know much'—preferring the description *Homo spiritualis*. The director's footnote to this argument is the shot of a bear skull placed on a rock, pointing towards the cave entrance, commenting that it is the strongest evidence in the cave of human activities with a potentially spiritual signification: 'The staging seems deliberate.' However, he adds: 'What exactly took place here only the paintings can tell us.'

Jean Clottes's definition of *Homo spiritualis* is not specific to Herzog's film. It is part of a wider hypothesis about Palaeolithic culture which he has formulated over a number of years in collaboration with the South African archaeologist David Lewis-Williams. In their co-authored book *The Shamans of Prehistory*, originally published in French in 1996, Clottes and Lewis-Williams argue that prehistoric cave art needs to be understood in the context of shamanic practices specific to traditional hunter-gatherer societies. Adopting a neurophysiological and ethnographic-comparative perspective, they propose that the altered states of consciousness and out-of-body experiences of the shaman are human universals, with an identifiable structure and sequence across cultures. If one accepts the anatomical and neurological modernity of Palaeolithic humans, it follows that the shamanic experience would have been the same for them. It is therefore possible to argue that a certain number of representations found in prehistoric cave art are of shamanic origin,

---

[19] *Le Geste et la parole*, I: *Technique et langage*; II: *La Mémoire et les rythmes* (Paris: Michel, 1964–65).

the graphical expression of the geometric figures and animal-hybrid forms perceived at different stages of the hallucinatory experience.[20]

Clottes and Lewis-Williams's theory has been a controversial one, and it is not my intention here to comment on its coherence or its ultimate validity; my interest is rather in its place in the speculative economy of Herzog's film. On the one hand, it would seem that the voices of director and protagonist are convergent regarding the definition of *Homo spiritualis*; they combine in an attempt to answer the question of the metaphysical status of the paintings at Chauvet. The final intervention of Julien Monney following this sequence seems to confirm this interpretation, as he gives the comparative-ethnographic example of an Aboriginal wall-painter who insists that it is not he himself who is painting, but the hand of the 'spirit' who is painting through him. On the other hand, in terms of sequencing, this evaluation of what-makes-us-human is presented back to back with the demonstration of *Homo technicus* by Jean-Michel Geneste. This sequencing or staging could be read as dialectical, in the sense of *Homo spiritualis* representing both the antithesis and the sublation of *Homo technicus*, but it can also be read in a more Flaubertian sense, as a play of perspectives on the human. As always, everything is in the sequencing, and the staging seems deliberate. Significantly, the film does not conclude with Clottes's assertion of *Homo spiritualis*.

The final intervention is in fact made by Jean-Michel Geneste. Here, as in an early sequence of the film, Geneste is filmed outside, sitting with the Pont d'Arc behind him. In his inimitable voice, Herzog asks Geneste the most impossible question, the question concerning the origin and foundations of 'modern' humanity: 'Do you think that the paintings in Chauvet Cave were somehow the beginning of the modern human soul? What constitutes humanness?' Geneste does not respond to this question directly, or rather, he responds to the second element of the question, the question of 'humanness', discreetly leaving aside the question of the 'beginning' or the 'modern'. His response is first Darwinian and materialist. Humanness is an effective adaptation to landscape and the beings that inhabit the landscape, animals and other human groups. Humanness is also the capacity to communicate something, to 'inscribe' memory on specific things such as walls, wood, and bones. This, he proposes, is the *invention* of Cro-Magnon. On Herzog's prompting, he agrees that music and mythology are also specifically human attributes, but keeps firmly to the concepts of communication and memory, qualifying that the figuration of animals, of humans, and of things is a way of communicating between humans, using the future to evoke the past, to transmit information in a more stable form than oral communication.

[20] See Jean Clottes and David Lewis-Williams, *Les Chamanes de la préhistoire: transe et magie dans les grottes ornées* (Paris: Seuil, 2001). See also David Lewis-Williams, *The Mind in the Cave: Consciousness and the Origins of Art* (London: Thames and Hudson, 2002).

Geneste's Darwinian-materialist response is therefore also—and there is no contradiction in this sequence—a grammatological response. In a co-authored book on Lascaux, published in 2003, Geneste explores precisely this idea of Palaeolithic art as inscription, as a form of collective memory. Symptomatically, he and his co-authors are sceptical about the Clottes–Lewis-Williams hypothesis concerning the shamanic origins of some of the cave paintings: visions experienced in a state of trance, they argue, are an ephemeral phenomenon, whereas the animal figures at sites such as Lascaux are not dissociable and form complex ensembles linked to diverse aspects of social and individual experience.[21] The book questions the idea of a sudden and dramatic 'explosion' or 'revolution' in human development during the Upper Palaeolithic. While accepting that the graphic representations and signs that appear in the archaeological record between 40,000 and 35,000 years BP are indicative of a qualitative shift in human cognition, the authors prefer to situate the emergence of art within the incomparably longer duration of the evolution of technology. The appearance of human technics four million years ago was the material condition of possibility of an extended history of human thought conceived as successive stages in the formalization of memory.[22]

Taken together, the different appearances of Jean-Michel Geneste in Herzog's film seem to represent a cumulative demonstration of this argument, which functions as the virtual counterpoint of Jean Clottes's subordination of *Homo sapiens*–*Homo technicus* to *Homo spiritualis*.[23] From this perspective, the response to Clottes's assertion that 'we don't know, we don't know much' would be that we do know, that we in fact know more and more, and that this was already the case for the Palaeolithic humans who are the question mark of Herzog's documentary. The hunting instruments demonstrated by Geneste in the landscape next to Chauvet are clear evidence of the advanced state of technical development during the Upper Palaeolithic, a development which cannot be separated from evidence of behaviour of a more 'spiritual' nature: *Homo sapiens* is *Homo technicus* is *Homo spiritualis*.

In what is one of the more stylized moments of the film, Geneste concludes his definition of 'humanness' by pointing at the camera which is filming him: despite the temporal distance between them, the grammatological 'invention' of Cro-Magnon is structurally no different from our contemporary audio-visual recording technologies. At this point, the film cuts to the point-of-view of the miniature remote-controlled aircraft which has been filming, in three dimensions, the different aerial perspectives shown in the documentary. Whereas in previous scenes, including the captivating opening sequence,

---

[21] Jean-Michel Geneste, Tristan Hordé, and Chantal Tanet, *Lascaux: une œuvre de mémoire* (Périgueux: Fanlac, 2003), p. 113.

[22] Ibid., pp. 114–17.

[23] This subordination is most clearly stated in Clottes, *Pourquoi l'art préhistorique?*, pp. 54–57.

its flying perspective is accompanied by a narrative and musical soundtrack which evokes transcendence, here our suspension of perceptual disbelief is punctuated by the vulgar buzz of its motor as it heads towards the filming team. The director of photography David Zeitlinger catches the aircraft with both hands.

This surprising conclusion is not simply a cinematic statement of self-reflexivity; it is clearly continuous, both thematically and conceptually, with the archaeologist's argument concerning the technical artifice of communication. Earlier in the film, the director described the multiple depictions of a bison leg or rhino horn as a kind of 'proto-cinema', 'like frames in an animated film', while he and Geneste together comment on a scene from *Swing Time* (1936) depicting Fred Astaire dancing with his shadows, linking this twentieth-century example of visual *truquage* with prehistoric humans' manipulation of light and shadow in caves. A less explicit scene, unobtrusive in its banality but revealing in terms of what it shows us, depicts members of the French research team—some ten or so individuals—at work in a room near Chauvet. As the camera pans across the room, the surface narrative comments on how the intellectual division of labour between the scientists is counterbalanced by the collaborative and interdisciplinary nature of their work: 'Although they each have their special field, they compare and combine their findings.' However, the film's mediation of this twenty-first-century environment, in which the majority of the protagonists are seated, takes on a more salient meaning for the viewer as we see that it is entirely populated with screens. The two archaeologists that Herzog extracts from this seated community (Carole Fritz and Gilles Tosello, referred to above) are standing, visibly for the purposes of their presentation, next to an Apple Macintosh computer monitor. On one level, their demonstration is simply part of the didactic convention of the science documentary, that of the expert explaining to the public the detail of his or her specific area of research. On another level, we as viewers become aware of the abysmal nature of this scene, the fact that we are looking at a representation of a representation of a representation—the environmental punctuation, or framing, of the prehistoric painting sublated in the computer-generated framing of its composition sublated in the cinematic framing of the scene of scientific demonstration. From the long-durational perspective of human-technological evolution, these nested representations can be seen as simply variations on the technical theme of framing. What links us with Palaeolithic humans is our capacity and compulsion to window the world, to selectively project its features onto a suitably sanctified screen or space. What distinguishes us from them is our terminal existence, our predominantly sedentary and solitary postures as operators of the keyboard and computer.[24]

To conclude, we have shown how *Cave of Forgotten Dreams*, while remaining true to the objective standards of the science documentary, also manages to integrate the human dimension of the subjects of science, eliciting from its protagonists confessions of a more existential or metaphysical nature which combine with Herzog's own voice and vision to produce something which seems to be more than the sum of its constituent parts. In this respect, the film captures the epistemological ambivalence of the discipline of prehistory itself, which as one of the human *sciences* is bound to the most rigorous standards of objective verification, but which as a *human* science is in the final instance compelled to respond to the demand for meaning. The film's highly structured staging of its protagonists provides us with a multidimensional view of the discipline, from the careful empiricism of members of the research team at Chauvet to the more speculative testimonies of individuals such as Clottes and Geneste. Viewed as a kind of philosophical essay, it is not clear that the film reaches any definitive resting place in terms of explanation or argument; like the flying perspective that is a persistent theme in Herzog's films, it seems restlessly to visit the different polarities of our relationship to Chauvet.[25] The signature Herzogian 'postscript' to the film seems to confirm this relativity of perspective. In a quasi-science-fictional scenario, albino crocodiles in a tropical greenhouse barely twenty miles from Chauvet, their environment warmed by the excess heat from a nearby nuclear power station, are imagined reaching the flooded cave, the narrator's voice-over asking what *they* would make of the paintings. However, this is not the film's final image. As the credits proceed in time with Reijseger's music, the camera freezes on one of the many negative hand-markings found on the cave walls. Like the hundreds of abstract signs which accompany the paintings at Chauvet, these markings have not been mentioned in the film itself.[26] If we were to give any interpretation to this final image, it would have to be that it represents something like the analogical signature of the human, a signifier of the anatomical variation which, a long time before Cro-Magnon, first distinguished humans from the animals around them.

UNIVERSITY OF NOTTINGHAM   CHRISTOPHER JOHNSON

[24] In his interviews with Paul Cronin, Herzog expresses the sentiment that 'Humans are not made to sit at computer terminals or travel by aeroplane; destiny intended something different for us' (*Herzog on Herzog*, p. 280).

[25] On Herzog's documentaries as examples of the 'essay film' genre see Timothy Corrigan, 'The Pedestrian Ecstasies of Werner Herzog: On Experience, Intelligence, and the Essayistic', in *A Companion to Werner Herzog*, ed. by Brad Prager (Oxford: Wiley-Blackwell, 2012), pp. 80–98.

[26] The markings commented on in the first part of the film are *positive* imprints of the human hand.

GOWER *AGONISTES* AND
CHAUCER ON OVID (AND VIRGIL)

The English poets John Gower (c. 1330–1408) and Geoffrey Chaucer (c. 1340–1400) may have been friends in some sense of the term; however, the evidence for amity is not as extensive nor as explicit as is that for literary antagonism.[1] In writing, they were rivals. Evidence for anxious literary relations between them extends beyond the self-avowing passages, moreover, where each names the other: Gower's 'Chaucer greeting' in the one version of the *Confessio amantis* prologue;[2] Chaucer's censorious 'moral Gower' remark in *Troilus and Criseyde*, the stick with which Gower has ever since been beaten;[3] then Gower's expunction of the 'Chaucer greeting' from subsequent redactions of the *Confessio amantis*; finally, the properly derisive remarks about Gower's work ('so horrible a tale for to rede') of the Chaucerian 'Man of Law' in one version of the prefatory remarks to a tale in the unfinished *Canterbury Tales*,[4] possibly meant for comedy, though the textual evidence is that Chaucer was still sharpening these barbs when he died in 1400, before Gower. Further, in a series of inexplicit places, where neither names the other, each appears to reply to the other's work. A. S. Galloway has argued that the differences of the *Confessio amantis* and the *Canterbury Tales* amount to a quarrel between the two over 'a didactic solution' to the ethical problems of their common 'worldly, self-interested, and individualistic culture'.[5] In particular, the *Nun's Priest's Tale*, incorporating Chaucer's lone explicit remark on the 1381 Social Revolt, has been shown by S. Justice to be a derisive attack on Gower's *Visio Anglie* of the same events.[6] Likewise, Chaucer's *Manciple's Tale* has been said to deride Gower, who worked with the same matter for the *Confessio amantis*

---

[1] The most thorough analysis of the two poets' relations remains that of John Hurt Fisher, *John Gower: Moral Philosopher and Friend of Chaucer* (London: Methuen, 1965), pp. 26–34, 285–92; though on the shared tales see also Derek Pearsall, 'Gower's Narrative Art', *PMLA*, 81 (1966), 475–84 (esp. pp. 483–84).

[2] John Gower, *Confessio amantis*, VIII. 2952–55, ed. by Russell A. Peck with Latin translations by Andrew Galloway, TEAMS Middle English Texts Series, 3 vols (Kalamazoo: Western Michigan University Medieval Institute Publications, 2000–06), I, 218. Further references are given parenthetically in the text.

[3] Geoffrey Chaucer, *Troilus and Criseyde*, v. 1856, in *The Riverside Chaucer*, ed. by Larry D. Benson, 3rd edn (Boston: Houghton Mifflin, 1987), pp. 473–585 (p. 585). Subsequent references to Chaucer's writings are to the texts in this edition, given by means of the abbreviated titles it provides (p. 779).

[4] Chaucer, *MLT*, l. 84 (Benson, pp. 87–104 (p. 88)).

[5] Andrew Scott Galloway, 'Gower's Quarrel with Chaucer, and the Origins of Bourgeois Didacticism in Fourteenth-Century London Poetry', in *Calliope's Classroom: Studies in Didactic Poetry from Antiquity to the Renaissance*, ed. by Annette Harder and others (Leuven: Peeters, 2007), pp. 245–67 (p. 266).

[6] Steven Justice, *Writing and Rebellion: England in 1381* (Berkeley: University of California Press, 1994), pp. 211–18, citing *obiter dicta* of Ian Bishop, 'The Nun's Priest's Tale and the Liberal Arts', *Review of English Studies*, n.s., 30 (1979), 257–67 (pp. 263–64).

(III. 768–817), 'the butt of Chaucer's parody', 'as the chief purveyor of banal literary fare to the audience Chaucer wrote for'.[7] Gower's *Visio Anglie* included already clear condemnation of the kind of complicit mummery espoused in Chaucer's *Manciple's Tale*:

> My sone, ful ofte, for to muche speche
> Hath many a man been spilt, as clerkes teche,
> But for litel speche avysely
> Is no man shent, to speke generally.[8]

Gower had pointed out that the execution of the king's Lord Chancellor in 1381 was the work of many who, despite demurrals after, were all guilty in law:

> Iste iuuat quod et ille facit, consentit et alter,
>   Vt malus et peior pessimus inde forent.
> Iura volunt quod homo facinus qui mittit, et alter
>   Qui consentit ei, sint in agone pares.[9]
>
> One acts, another helps, a third consents,
>   So bad and worse develop into worst.
> The laws require that he who acts and he
>   Who goes along are equal in the crime.

In agone would be Gower's phrase for it, for he too participated in public literary contests. Gower's rivalry with Chaucer was only part of his manifold literary antagonism, however, encompassing not only a senior poet's rivalry with a junior, but also Gower's rivalry with an ancient author, whom Chaucer too used but Gower knew better, Ovid (43 BCE–17 CE). From French to Latin, then from Latin to English; also, from lyric to didactic satire, then from didactic satire to narrative, compound-complex narrative, moreover, involving stories within stories from narrators in dialogue: Gower's multiple developmental trajectories were not neatly linear, but were characterized by recursion and incorporative supersession. There can be no strict segregation in Gower's work of the didactic from the narrative, for example, nor of his work in one language from his work in another. In the development of Gower's relations with other writers, both modern and ancient, his progression (a traditional one) appears to have been from tyronian imitation, to adaptive emulation,

---

[7] Richard Hazelton, 'The *Manciple's Tale*: Parody and Critique', *Journal of English and Germanic Philology*, 62 (1963), 1–31 (pp. 23–25). Cf. William Cadbury, 'Manipulation of Sources and the Meaning of the *Manciple's Tale*', *Philological Quarterly*, 43 (1964), 538–48 (p. 543): 'It is interesting to speculate that Chaucer's version may thus be direct rebuttal of what he considered Gower's mistakes in interpretation.' Also, John P. McCall, *Chaucer among the Gods: The Poetics of Classical Myth* (University Park: Pennsylvania State University Press, 1979), pp. 129–31.

[8] Chaucer, *MancT*, ll. 318–62 (Benson, pp. 282–86 (p. 286)).

[9] Gower, *Visio Anglie*, ll. 1121–24, in *Poems on Contemporary Events: The 'Visio Anglie' (1381) and 'Cronica Tripertita' (1400)*, ed. by David Carlson, trans. by A. G. Rigg (Toronto: Pontifical Institute of Mediaeval Studies; Oxford: Bodleian Library, 2011), pp. 24–173 (pp. 104–05).

to mastership.¹⁰ However, whether Gower was writing in French or Latin or English, likewise whether he was working generically in lyric or satire or narrative, these kinds of relations he had with other writers recombine and recur, early and late. In addition to Chaucer and Ovid, the other writers he rivalled include his own younger self.

Gower and Ovidian Emulation

When in the *Confessio amantis* Gower returned yet again to the tale of Ceyx and Alcione—there are four instances, in three languages—he reduced description of the sea-storm to two lines, particularly effective lines, it must be said, exquisitely fashioned. In the wife's vision of her husband, 'Al this sche mette', Gower has it, 'and sih him dyen': 'The tempeste of the blake cloude, | The wode see, the wyndes loude' (IV. 3063-65). Odd enough to have elicited comment,¹¹ Gower's lines represent remarkable restraint, for in his source, Ovid's *Metamorphoses*, the sea-storm itself that separates Ceyx and Alcione, killing the one immediately and then the other by consequence, dominates disproportionately and grotesquely.¹² It exemplifies a propensity already observed in antiquity: Ovid did not know when to stop. 'nam et Ovidius nescit quod bene cessit relinquere' is the judgement of Seneca the Elder.¹³ Ovid himself says as much, in autobiographical remarks explaining his lifelong facility:

> at mihi iam puero caelestia sacra placebant,
>   inque suum furtim Musa trahebat opus.
> saepe pater dixit 'studium quid inutile temptas?
>   Maeonides nullas ipse reliquit opes'.
> motus eram dictis, totoque Helicone relicto
>   scribere temptabam uerba soluta modis.
> sponte sua carmen numeros ueniebat ad aptos,
>   et quod temptabam scribere uersus erat.
>   (*Trist.* IV. 10. 19-26)

---

¹⁰ David R. Carlson, 'Gower's Early Latin Poetry: Text-Genetic Hypotheses of an *Epistola ad regem* (c. 1377-1380), from the Evidence of John Bale', *Mediaeval Studies*, 65 (2003), 293-317 (esp. p. 308, n. 29).

¹¹ J. A. W. Bennett, *Middle English Literature*, ed. and completed by Douglas Gray (Oxford: Clarendon Press, 1986), p. 410; also, C. S. Lewis, *The Allegory of Love: A Study in Medieval Tradition* (Oxford: Clarendon Press, 1936), p. 207.

¹² *P. Ovidi Nasonis Metamorphoses*, ed. by R. J. Tarrant, Oxford Classical Texts (Oxford: Clarendon Press, 2004), XI. 410-748. Citations of other ancient texts are given parenthetically by means of the system of abbreviated references in *L'Année philologique*. Translations are authorial, except as indicated.

¹³ *Contr.* IX. 5. 17, though on the hermeneutic utility of this and related Senecan remarks see Richard Tarrant, 'Ovid and the Failure of Rhetoric', in *Ethics and Rhetoric: Classical Essays for Donald Russell on his Seventy-Fifth Birthday*, ed. by Doreen Innes and others (Oxford: Clarendon Press, 1995), pp. 63-74.

The Muse's heavenly rites delighted me, even as a child, and unbeknownst she was drawing me into her work. My dad kept asking, 'Why do you try such useless things? Homer himself left no one any riches'. I took his words to heart and, putting Parnassus aside, tried writing just plain prose. Poetry came out, though, and in fine form, as if it had a will of its own; whatever I tried to write turned out all verse.

The product in the present instance is the fabulous wind-and-wave war ensuing on Ceyx's departure from Alcione—'bella gerunt uenti fretaque indignantia miscent' (*Met.* XI. 491: 'the winds wage war and rouse the angry waves')—where Ovid's chief objective may have been to outdo his own preeminent contemporary, the older Virgil (70–19 BCE) (esp. *Aen.* I. 34–156), as well as other literary antecedents, Ovid being Ovid, and writing about writing rather than concentrating on his protagonist couple and their plight.[14] It has been felt that the yield in this instance is perverse comedy, 'full of Ovidian whimsy and ingenuity', 'bathetic silliness' of the kind that comes of overdoing things; so, here as in other instances where Ovid is caught up in the fecundity of his own fecundity, how many different ways can he find to say the same again?[15]

> ecce cadunt largi resolutis nubibus imbres,
> inque fretum credas totum descendere caelum
> inque plagas caeli tumefactum ascendere pontum.
> uela madent nimbis, et cum caelestibus undis
> aequoreae miscentur aquae. caret ignibus aether,
> caecaque nox premitur tenebris hiemisque suisque;
> discutiunt tamen has praebentque micantia lumen
> fulmina; fulmineis ardescunt ignibus ignes.
>   (*Met.* XI. 516–23)

Huge rains descend, lo!, from burst clouds; you'd think the whole heavens fall down into the straits, and welling seas mount up into the heavens' zone. The sails are soaked with rain, and in with the billows of the heavens the sea's waters mix. The sky lacks its usual lights, and the blinded night is overcome by its own darkness and that of the storm; the lightning yet tears the darkness asunder and flashes forth its illumination; the night's lights glow at the lightning's lightings.

In Gower's *Confessio amantis* the reduction of so much Ovid, so characteristic of Ovid's manner of excess, to bare 'The tempeste of the blake cloude, | The

---

[14] For analysis see esp. Brooks Otis, *Ovid as an Epic Poet*, 2nd edn (Cambridge: Cambridge University Press, 1970), pp. 238–46; the Graeco-Roman antecedents to which Ovid responds are analysed in M. P. O. Morford, *The Poet Lucan: Studies in Rhetorical Epic* (Oxford: Blackwell, 1967), pp. 20–36; see also E. de Saint-Denis, *Le Rôle de la mer dans la poésie latine* (Paris: Klincksieck, 1935), pp. 345–54.

[15] G. Karl Galinsky, *Ovid's 'Metamorphoses': An Introduction to the Basic Aspects* (Oxford: Blackwell, 1975), pp. 145–47, the quotation from p. 146; the other quotation is David W. Hiscoe, 'The Ovidian Comic Strategy of Gower's *Confessio amantis*', *Philological Quarterly*, 64 (1985), 367–85 (p. 373), though see too Elaine Fantham, 'Ovid's Ceyx and Alcyone: The Metamorphosis of a Myth', *Phoenix*, 33 (1979), 330–45 (p. 337, n. 32).

wode see, the wyndes loude', is emulous: what is not in Gower speaks out as loudly as what is, or more. However, such an instance of Gower's supersession of Ovid, by suppression, is itself imitative of the ancient *auctor*. This very way of dealing with poetic forebears was one that Ovid himself practised, extensively, pushing it characteristically to perverse limits and beyond. Virgil's Sibyl's dire admonition, on the difficulty of exiting the underworld for the still living who have yet found a way to enter in—'sed reuocare gradum superasque euadere ad auras, | hoc opus, hic labor est' (*Aen.* VI. 128-29: 'yet to come back again and escape to the breezes aloft, that is hard, that a labour')—transferred in Ovid to the problem of getting tolerably fucked without having first to pay—'hoc opus, hic labor est, primo sine munere iungi' (*Ars*, I. 453: 'that is hard, that a labour, without payment to get sex first')—may be the egregious instance, where Ovid's emulousness has spilled over into offensive poor taste. It is characteristic, nonetheless, of Ovid's dealings with Virgil's work: to detail what had been left out, as Ovid does with the immediately post-fall Trojan matter omitted from the *Aeneid*; also, to pass over what the other had already done; in any event, to be other than Virgil. Ovid practises similarly on himself: the two versions of the rape of Proserpina, probably written together, one in hexameters (*Met.* V. 341-661) and the other in elegiac distichs (*Fasti*, IV. 417-618), have been taken to represent Ovid's assertion of his own mastery over both pre-eminent kinds of Roman verse, where others earlier had mastered one or the other but not both.[16] *Referre aliter idem* is the acme of poetic achievement in this Ovidian oratorical aesthetics: one way and another, do the same thing but differently.[17]

Ovid in Gower's 'Visio Anglie'

Gower learnt so much—his thorough exploitable knowledge of such narrative matter as the *Metamorphoses* had to offer a later writer, as well as an apprehension of the Ovidian *referre aliter idem*—from what would appear to have been an intensive study of the corpus of Ovidian verse, 'the whole of Ovid', moreover, 'a poet whose work Gower knew better than any other'; though the corpus is extensive, Gower 'drew on every part of Ovid's work', as Bruce Harbert points out.[18] For in redoing differently for the late *Confessio amantis* the Ovidian sea-storm from the Ceyx and Alcione of the *Metamorphoses*, Gower

---

[16] For the comparison see now Stephen Hinds, *The Metamorphosis of Persephone: Ovid and the Self-Conscious Muse* (Cambridge: Cambridge University Press, 1987), pp. 99-134. On rewriting Virgil see Philip Hardie, 'Ovid's Theban History: The First "Anti-*Aeneid*"', *Classical Quarterly*, n.s., 40 (1990), 224-35.

[17] The phrase is adapted from *Ars*, II. 127-28, where the subject of the first verb is Calypso and *ille* refers to Ulysses: 'haec Troiae casus iterumque iterumque rogabat: | ille referre aliter saepe solebat idem.' See Galinsky, *Ovid's 'Metamorphoses'*, esp. pp. 4-5.

[18] Bruce Harbert, 'Lessons from the Great Clerk: Ovid and John Gower', in *Ovid Renewed:*

was redoing himself differently, too—again Ovid-like. Gower had once earlier reworked matter from the Ovidian Ceyx and Alcione, already masterfully, for his own different purposes, in a way that demonstrated the thoroughness of his knowledge of the ancient poet and his capacity to supersede by retelling differently.

A point of Gower's arrival at mastery (as opposed to imitation, strict and simple) occurred with the completion of the *Vox clamantis* by the addition of the poem known also as the *Visio Anglie* at its beginning: a nightmarish dream-vision of the invasion of Gower's own London in the Great Revolt of 1381, which Gower could not have written until after a six-book *Vox clamantis* had been already completed and published.[19] In the *Visio Anglie*, for recounting what was for him the crucial event of the revolt—that is, the revolutionary seizure of London for a period of three days, 13–15 June 1381—Gower uses three differing approaches to telling the same thing.[20] First, Gower has a historical-legendary version of it, as a re-enactment of the fall of Troy (ll. 879–1358). The poet's London, 'Troynovant', is overrun by ravening beasts, whose victims are then figured as Trojan spoil, most extendedly in the case of the chancellor Simon Sudbury (also archbishop of Canterbury), executed by the revolutionaries for treason by royal warrant on the morning of 14 June, whom Gower represents as a type of Priam's son, Cassandra's brother the augur and prophet Helenus:

> interpres diuum, qui numina Phoebi,
> qui tripodas Clarii et laurus, qui sidera sentis
> et uolucrum linguas et praepetis omina pennae.
> (*Aen.* III. 359–61)

the gods' own prophet, whose insight reaches even to the divine powers of Phoebus, the tripod and laurel of him of Claros, the stars, the tongues of birds, and the omens of prophetic wing.[21]

Ovidian Influences on Literature and Art from the Middle Ages to the Twentieth Century, ed. by Charles Martindale (Cambridge: Cambridge University Press, 1988), pp. 83–97 (p. 84); also, 'The Myth of Tereus in Ovid and Gower', *Medium Aevum*, 41 (1972), 208–14 (p. 214). Of special pertinence on this point is the work of Kathryn L. McKinley, including 'Manuscripts of Ovid in England 1100 to 1500', *English Manuscript Studies*, 7 (1998), 41–85; the fundamental analysis remains Pearsall, esp. pp. 478–81.

[19] For this scheme of the genesis of the *Vox clamantis* see esp. Maria Wickert, *Studien zu John Gower* (Cologne: Universitäts-Verlag, 1953), pp. 13–30 and 169–73; also Fisher, pp. 99–109, and A. G. Rigg, *A History of Anglo-Latin Literature 1066–1422* (Cambridge: Cambridge University Press, 1992), pp. 287–88, with additional particulars in *Poems on Contemporary Events*, ed. by Carlson, pp. 7–8.

[20] Wickert, p. 36.

[21] On the events and sources see George Kriehn, 'Studies in the Sources of the Social Revolt in 1381', *American Historical Review*, 7 (1902), 254–85 and 458–84 (pp. 279–84). On representation of the chancellor see Conrad Van Dijk, 'Simon Sudbury and Helenus in John Gower's *Vox clamantis*', *Medium Aevum*, 77 (2008), 313–18; and on the beast allegory, Eve Salisbury, 'Violence and the Sacred City: London, Gower, and the Rising of 1381', in '*A Great Effusion of Blood*'? *Interpreting*

Second, Gower retells the same events as an uncannily disorienting type of exile (ll. 1359-1592), where the chief source of the developed metaphor is, not the historical-legendary matter of Troy, but the post-relegation verse of Ovid, the *Tristia* and *Epistulae ex Ponto*. In Gower, 'dem sein Vaterland über alles ging' ('for whom the fatherland is more important than anything else'), the narrator remains at home but the changes worked on his London by its invaders render him *alienus*, even in his own home: without leaving, Gower is as if driven into exile.[22] Third, Gower develops the figure of a ship at sea beset by storm (ll. 1593-2012), and this is the point at which, for describing the storm itself, Gower takes up matter from *Metamorphoses* (XI. 410-748).

Gower's third version of the invasion of London has considerable allusive complexity to it; to begin with, however, for describing the storm that besets his metaphorical-allegorical ship at sea, Gower uses a deal of verbal matter directly from the excessive storm description in Ovid's Ceyx and Alcione. Ovid used nearly a hundred lines for describing the storm (*Met.* XI. 474-572), and Gower here quotes only from this portion of the Ovidian tale. Gower reuses twenty of the Ovidian lines complete. In ll. 1653-58, 1665-68, and 1673-74 he has all of *Met.* XI. 516-21 in the Ovidian order, though he interposes between his quotations of ll. 518 and 519-520 quotations of XI. 499 and XI. 501 as well (but reversed: l. 501 followed by l. 499). Italicized matter in the quotations below represents the lines and parts of lines, terms and parts of terms, that Gower took from Ovid; the bracketed numerals at the right tell the numbers of the lines from the *Metamorphoses*:

Ecce cadunt largi resolutis nubibus ymbres,	[XI. 516]
Aeris et medio fulminis ira tonat;	
Inque fretum credas totum descendere celum,	[XI. 517]
Terruit et terras Iris vbique minis;	
*Inque plagas celi tumefactus scand*it et equor,	[XI. 518]
Vt si de proprio vellet abire loco.	
Sternitur interdum spumisque sonantibus albet,	[XI. 501]
Et redit in subtus quod fuit ante super;	

Medieval Violence, ed. by Mark D. Meyerson and others (Toronto: University of Toronto Press, 2004), pp. 79-97, and 'Violence and the Sacrificial Poet: Gower, the *Vox*, and the Critics', in *On John Gower: Essays at the Millenium*, ed. by Robert F. Yeager (Kalamazoo: Medieval Institute Publications, 2007), pp. 124-43; also, Carlson, 'Gower's Beast Allegories in the 1381 *Visio Anglie*', *Philological Quarterly*, 87 (2008), 257-75.

[22] Oscar Eberhard, *Der Bauernaufstand vom Jahre 1381 in der englischen Poesie*, Anglistische Forschungen, 51 (Heidelberg: Winter, 1917), p. 38. On the exile topic see Yoshiko Kobayashi, 'The Voice of an Exile: From Ovidian Lament to Prophecy in Book I of John Gower's *Vox clamantis*', in *Through a Classical Eye: Transcultural and Transhistorical Visions in Medieval English, Italian, and Latin Literature in Honour of Winthrop Wetherbee*, ed. by Andrew Galloway and R. F. Yeager (Toronto: University of Toronto Press, 2009), pp. 339-62 (esp. pp. 349-53); also, Carlson, 'A Fourteenth-Century Anglo-Latin Ovidian: The *liber exulis* in John Gower's 1381 *Visio Anglie* (*Vox clamantis* I. 1359-1592)', *Classica et Mediaevalia*, 61 (2010), 293-335.

> *Et modo cum fuluas ex ymo vertit arenas,*   [XI. 499
>   Tincta superficies fulua patebat aquis.
> [. . .]
> *Equoree miscentur aque celestibus* auris,   [XI. 520
>   Mixtaque cum pluuia salsa tumescit aqua.
> *Vela madent nimbis,* tegumenta nec vlla iuuabant,   [XI. 519
>   Vnus vt in sicco contegat inde capud.
> [. . .]
> *Tetraque nox premitur, tenebrisque* micancia lumen   [XI. 521
>   Fulmina fulmineis ignibus ipsa dabant.
>   (ll. 1653–62, 1665–68, and 1673–74)[23]

> From opened clouds great streams of rain pour down
> And in the air the thunder's wrath resounds;
> You'd think all heaven fell upon the strait;
> The rainbow threatened earth on every side;
> Amazed, it spread across the sky and sea,
> As if it would depart its proper place.
> It's sometimes flattened, white with hissing foam,
> And what was once above returns below;
> Now, as it stirred the yellow sands beneath,
> Its surface, wave-stained yellow, showed to view.
> [. . .]
> Sea's waters now are mixed with heaven's winds
> And salty water swells when mixed with rain.
> Our sails grew wet; no covering availed
> For anyone to keep his head quite dry.
> [. . .]
> Dark night is quashed; the flashing thunderbolts
> Themselves lent light to darkness of the storm.

In this instance, Gower's Ovidian quotations are distributed over a greater number of lines because, in adapting the Ovidian hexametric verse for his own elegiac distich, Gower has regularly interposed pentameters of his own invention between the hexameters he quotes from Ovid. In ll. 1675–91, more compactly, though again in the Ovidian order, Gower uses almost all of *Met.* XI. 480–95.[24] Here, however, Gower makes pentameters by reworking the uncharacteristically epical hexameters of Ovid's even-numbered lines, so that Gower makes Ovid's work back into the elegiacs more to be associated with the antique poet's work, as if to remake Ovid as proper Ovid:

> *Cum mare sub noctem tumidis albescere cepit*   [XI. 480
>   Fluctibus, et preceps Eurus ad arma furit.
> '*Ardua iam dudum dimittite cornua* nauis',   [XI. 482
>   *Clamat;* '*et ad velum* currite', *rector* ait.   [XI. 483

---

[23] The chief Ovidian lines that Gower altered here are quoted properly above.
[24] Only omitting 481, 490, and 493–94 (for reasons that do not occur to me).

> *Hic iubet. Impediunt aduerse iussa procelle,* [XI. 484
>   Nec fragor *auditum* tunc *sinit* esse maris. [XI. 485
> *Sponte tamen properant alii subducere remos,* [XI. 486
>   Pars munire latus quisque labore suo. [XI. 487
> *Egerit hic fluctus equorque refundit in equor;* [XI. 488
>   Hic rapit antennas, que sine lege vagant. [XI. 489
> *Bella gerunt venti fretaque indignancia miscent,* [XI. 491
>   Cassus et vlterius fit labor ille viris.
> Tanta mali moles classem compresserat audax,
>   Vt vecors animum laxat abire vagum.
> *Ipse pauet nec se quis sit status ipse fatetur,* [XI. 492
>   Dum timor ex mentis frigore corda gelat.
> *Quippe sonant clamore viri, stridore rudentes,* [XI. 495
>   Rector et in remis fert nichil ipse magis.
> Omnia pontus erat; deerant quoque litora ponto,
>   Regis et ad solium fert sua monstra fretum.
>   (ll. 1675–94)[25]
>
> Beneath the night the sea with swollen waves
> Grew white; the headlong East wind rushed to arms.
> Our captain cried, 'Now bring the topsails down
> And run to reef the sail and bring it in'.
> He shouts, but adverse winds resist his words;
> The ocean roar won't let his voice be heard.
> But others gladly rush to ship the oars,
> And some employ their strength to fix the sides.
> One bales out floods and pours the sea on sea;
> One grabs the yards which flap without restraint.
> The winds wage war and stir indignant seas;
> The crew's endeavours henceforth are in vain.
> So great and bold misfortune crushed the ship
> That he goes mad and lets his mind run loose.
> He fears and won't admit the state he's in,
> Since fear and cold of mind congeal his heart.
> The men cry out and shout and roar and yell;
> The master of the oars can do no more.
> Then all was sea: the ocean had no shores;
> The flood brought monsters to the royal throne.

This verbal usage is not random: not an instance, say, of Gower more or less accidentally recalling matter he had once read or studied, the less than consciously recalled phrases then finding their way through the writer's fingers

---

[25] Gower's l. 1678 ('Clamat; "et ad velum currite", rector ait') compounds *Met.* XI. 483 ('clamat "et antemnis totum subnectite uelum"'), with 'rector' from *Met.* XI. 482; l. 1680 ('Nec fragor auditum tunc sinit esse maris') uses elements of *Met.* XI. 485 ('nec sinit audiri uocem fragor aequoris ullam'); l. 1682 only ends differently from *Met.* XI. 487 ('pars munire latus, pars uentis uela negare'), and l. 1683 differently from *Met.* XI. 489 ('hic rapit antemnas, quae dum sine lege geruntur'); l. 1689 simply substitutes 'quis' for *Met.* XI. 492's 'qui'.

onto the page: 'school-boy plagiarism', in G. C. Macaulay's phrase.[26] Were this so, such unconscious recollections would find themselves evenly distributed, it would be expected, and they are not, occurring instead in patches of concentration.[27] In general, this is the case with the *Visio Anglie*; in this instance in particular, the Ovidian matter is narrowly concentrated (not in random distribution even within the single section) and select: these are the only two points, closely juxtaposed, in the 2150 lines of the *Visio Anglie*—indeed, in the over 10,000 lines of the whole *Vox clamantis*—where such phrases from *Metamorphoses* XI. 410–748 occur.

Nor is the usage imitation, as if Gower, faced with the task of describing a storm at sea, decided that, Ovid having done the same better already, his best approach would be reproduction of the master's work, more or less closely. Gower made imitations of this sort earlier in his career as a Latin poet, as others too had traditionally done, by way of teaching themselves verse composition by close adaptation of canonical predecessors. Were the section of the poem imitative in this way, it would be simple, and it is not. Gower had progressed beyond such a procedure by the time he came to write the *Visio*. The phrases reused from *Metamorphoses* XI. 410–748 are properly allusions, adapted by Gower for his own complex purposes. For the quotations' concentration serves to bring in the whole Ovidian episode, predicting the trajectory of Gower's poem. Another description of a great storm at sea occurs in Ovid: *Tristia* I. 2, recounting the poet's transit of the Mediterranean and beyond it, to his place of relegation at Tomis. In *Tristia* the troubled waters do not give way to greater well-being, for Ovid was to find the shore as wild as the sea had been (elsewhere he says 'plus habet infesta terra timoris aqua' (*Trist.* I. 11. 26: 'that land is more fearsome than the hostile waves')): 'quod faciles opto uentos (quis credere possit?) | Sarmatis est tellus, quam mea uela petunt' (*Trist.* I. 2. 81–82: 'who could credit it that the land I imprecate fair winds for my sails to use for reaching is the Sarmatian?').[28]

Gower knew the *Tristia*, including this item within the collection, but he does not use his knowledge at this point in the *Visio Anglie*.[29] For, by contrast

---

[26] G. C. Macaulay, *The Complete Works of John Gower*, IV: *The Latin Writings* (Oxford: Clarendon Press, 1902), p. xxxii. The alternative approach to the Gowerian usage delineated here is from R. F. Yeager, 'Did Gower Write Cento?', in *John Gower: Recent Readings*, ed. by Yeager (Kalamazoo: Western Michigan University Medieval Institute Publications, 1989), pp. 113–32; for application, see now esp. Maura Nolan, 'The Poetics of Catastrophe: Ovidian Allusion in Gower's *Vox clamantis*', in *Medieval Latin and Middle English Literature: Essays in Honour of Jill Mann*, ed. by Christopher Cannon and Nolan (Cambridge: Brewer, 2011), pp. 113–33.

[27] The point is taken from Harbert, 'Lessons from the Great Clerk', p. 84.

[28] On this piece, where Ovid is himself probably reworking his own earlier description in the sea-storm section of the *Metamorphoses*' episode of Ceyx and Alcione, see Jennifer Ingleheart, 'Ovid, *Tristia* I 2: High Drama on the High Seas', *Greece & Rome*, 53 (2006), 73–91.

[29] *Visio*, l. 2031 ('Desine luctari: referant tua carbasa venti') may recall *Trist.* I. 2. 91 ('ferte (quid hic facio?) rapidi mea carbasa uenti'), though it is nearer *Remedia amoris*, 531 ('Desine luctari:

with the *Tristia* storm that Gower does not use here, the storm that Ovid had conjured up for the Ceyx and Alcione section of the *Metamorphoses*, on which Gower chose to draw, instead yields calm and well-being. By the metamorphosis in Ovid's epic, the loving couple are transformed both to *halcyones*, sea-birds riding calm seas ('tunc iacet unda maris' (XI. 747: 'the sea turned calm then'), 'perque dies placidos' ('throughout peaceful days'), happily together ever after: 'tunc quoque mansit amor nec coniugiale solutum | foedus in alitibus' (XI. 743–45: 'then too their love persisted, nor was their conjugal bond undone in the birds'). And so too in Gower's *Visio Anglie*: the storm that was London in revolution, described conclusively in this chapter in part by means of the *Metamorphoses* quotations, will give way to well-being in Gower's next section when, in answer to prayer ('Vt michi det placidum per mare Cristus iter' (l. 1614: 'Christ, [...] I pray, | Please grant a quiet passage on this sea'), the revolutionary leader will be murdered, the sea-storm calming: 'ex et eo pacificauit opus' (l. 1862: 'this deed brought peace all round').[30]

Patterned Ovidian allusion-making of the same tenor recurs at the beginning of the next chapter of the *Visio*, where Gower makes similar though briefer use of Perseus's rescue of Andromeda from a sea-beast in Ovid (*Met.* IV. 663–789). Here are Gower's opening lines followed by the lines they quote:

> En super hoc *veniens inmenso belua ponto*
> E*minet*, ex cuius naribus *vnda* tonat.
> (ll. 1717–18)

Then next a savage beast arose up from
The sea; its nostrils blared the blast of waves.

> *unda*
> insonuit, *ueniensque inmenso belua ponto*
> in*minet* et latum sub pectore possidet aequor.
> (*Met.* IV. 688–90)

The deep resounded, and, coming on, a beast from boundless ocean towered up and held the wide seas beneath its breast.

The Ovidian section referred to here concludes with the wedding of Perseus and Andromeda, and so the allusion likewise anticipates Gower's concordant outcome, in the calming of the storm of revolution.[31]

Finally, Gower's use of matter from the Ceyx and Alcione episode of the

---

referant tua carbasa uenti'); Gower quotes at least nineteen other lines from *Tristia* I in the *Visio*, at prol. 36, prol. 43–46, ll. 1397–98, 1521–22, 1584, 1589, 1727–28, 1831–32, 1976, 1978, 1991–92, and 2031.

[30] The prayer is repeated later, with more immediate effect, at ll. 1793–1838, where the source appears more Boethian—based on *De consolatione philosophiae*, 3m9—than Ovidian.

[31] For Gower's *inmenso belua ponto* there are biblical analogues: chiefly Apoc. 13. 1–8 ('Et vidi de mare bestiam ascendentem', etc.), though also perhaps allusion to Isa. 27. 1 and Ezek. 29. 3–5; the quotations are from Ovid nevertheless. Though the wedding ensuing from Perseus's

Metamorphoses is clarified too by the other concentrated set of quotations from Ovid used in the same sea-storm passage in the *Visio*, from the other, possibly still more prominent and more consequential, description of troubled waters in Ovid's epic of change, in the flood section at his poem's beginning (I. 244–312).³² Of this Ovid, Gower uses only five lines complete for the section of his *Visio*, though they are weightier ones and more prominently placed. To begin with, Gower incorporates quotations of *Met.* I. 264–65 and 269–70 complete with *Met.* I. 282:

> *Terribilem picea tectus caligine vultum*   [I. 265
>   Ether ab excelso commouet arma fret⟨i⟩s.
> Quatuor ora fremunt ventorum sic, quod inermem
>   Anchora non poterat vlla iuuare ratem.
> Extra se positus *madidis Nothus euolat alis*,   [I. 264
>   Cuius enim gutte dampna furoris agunt.
> Quas sibi non poterat terre ⟨comprendere⟩ virtus,
>   Pendula celestes libra mouebat aquas.
> Sic *defrenato voluuntur in equora cursu*,   [I. 282
>   Quo maris vnda nimis aucta subegit humum.
> Seuiit in nauem ventis discordibus aura,
>   Et maris in remos vnda coacta ruit.
> *Fit fragor*, et *densi funduntur ab ethere nimbi*,   [I. 269
>   Nauis et est variis exagitata malis.
> *Nuncia Iunonis varios* tumefacta *colores*   [I. 270
>   Induit, et vario more refudit aquas.
>   (ll. 1623–38)

> The heaven's face, in pitchy black enclosed,
> From high stirs arms on waters far below.
> The mouths of four winds blow; our helpless boat
> Can't be secured by any anchor's aid.
> Beside itself, on dripping wings, the South
> Wind flies: its drops rain devastating rage.
> On high the hanging balance stirred the wet
> Of skies that earthly power could not contain.
> It poured upon the seas in unchecked streams
> And swelled the sea, which overwhelmed the land.
> As winds conflict, the blast assaults the boat;
> The waves compact and fall upon our oars.
> The thunder claps; thick rains from sky descend;
> Our ship is driven by these varied ills.

rescue is (admittedly) not a well-omened one, Ovid's account imbricates the wedding celebrations with Perseus's pious thanksgiving for safe delivery, in lines (esp. *Met.* IV. 753–64) incorporating reference to all the most potent symbols of social concord that a (pre-Christian) Roman writer could imagine.

³² Harbert, 'Lessons from the Great Clerk', p. 85, notes Gower's collocation of allusions to these three *Metamorphoses* sea-storms.

> Puffed up in many colours, Juno's sign
> In many ways poured waters back to sea.

Then to finish the section, as quoted above ('Omnia pontus erat; deerant quoque litora ponto', l. 1693), Gower puts *Met*. I. 292: 'iamque mare et tellus nullum discrimen habebant: | *omnia pontus erat, derant quoque litora ponto*' (*Met*. I. 291-92: 'no longer was there any difference between sea and land: all was ocean, and an ocean without shore').[33]

By this first flood to which Gower alludes, at the beginning of the *Metamorphoses*, Ovid's Jupiter is punishing impiety, in Lycaon personally, but also generally in all humankind: 'illa propago | contemptrix superum saeuaeque auidissima caedis | et uiolenta' (*Met*. I. 160-62: 'that race contemptuous of the gods above, most avid for savage slaughter and violent').[34] Hence the allusions to and quotations of the Ovidian passage in this section must remind: of Gower's insistent anti-deviance in religion;[35] also, of the more generally held belief (officially promoted) that the events of 1381 were a manifestation of Lollardy;[36] so that, in the representation of the revolt that Gower builds, it was a combination, as if from the Ovidian passage, of both impiety (*contemptus superum* characterizes the rabble's doings) and violence (*saevae aviditas caedis*). A mortal sea-storm, like the Great Rebellion, is what comes of impiety going forth in violence, as it was among the ostensibly Lollard rebels; at the same time, the same allusions to Ovid that Gower uses to characterize the metaphorical sea-storm engulfing London serve also to predict the sea-storm's calming, when 'probis fit renouata salus' (l. 1920: 'safety returned for persons of probity').

Young Chaucer's Ovid and Gower's Reply

Gower's manipulations of Ovid—by means of his knowing, adaptive allusions, from the minute verbal details to the grand thematic matter, made to serve purposes of Gower's own—manifest thorough comprehension; and this is the quality wanting from the earlier employment of the same Ovidiana in Chaucer. Already before 1370, Chaucer had used the Ceyx and Alcione matter for his own probably earliest substantial (non-lyric) composition, *The Book of the*

---

[33] *Met*. I. 264 has 'emittitque Notum' where Gower, l. 1627, puts 'Extra se positus'; *Met*. I. 282 'et' for l. 1631 'Sic'; *Met*. I. 269 'hinc' for l. 1635 'et'; and *Met*. I. 270 'induta' for l. 1637 'tumefacta'. Gower makes other prominent reference to the Ovidian *diluvium* repeatedly in previous sections of the *Visio Anglie*, at ll. 751-54, 821-22, and 939-40; also, he uses post-diluvian matter from the same section of Ovid prominently later, throughout ll. 1901-40.

[34] See esp. *Met*. I. 151-243; Gower quotes *Met*. I. 160-62 prominently, in *Visio Anglie*, ll. 751-54.

[35] There is comment in George R. Coffman, 'John Gower, Mentor for Royalty: Richard II', *PMLA*, 69 (1954), 953-64 (pp. 955-58).

[36] See Margaret Aston, 'Lollardy and Sedition, 1381-1431' (1960), repr. in *Lollards and Reformers: Images and Literacy in Late Medieval Religion* (London: Hambledon, 1984), pp. 1-47.

Duchess. Chaucer's was a daring literary performance, of a sort that might have impressed the elder Seneca's masters of post-Republican declamation by its reckless comic manipulations of a wide range of near-contemporary and other sources, chiefly French. In the *Book of the Duchess* Chaucer juxtaposes rearranged passages from a variety of such modish compositions—the *Jugement dou roy de Behaingne* and *Remede de fortune* of Guillaume Machaut (d. 1377); also, Machaut's *Dit de la fonteinne amoureuse* and the *Paradys d'amours* of Jean Froissart (c. 1330–c. 1405)—introducing their delights into the comparatively refinement-poor English tradition.[37] The low-comic effects Chaucer achieved by so doing have been appreciated: the antic mimicry about wakening Morpheus, the god '[t]hat slep and dide noon other werk' (l. 169), with the horn 'ryght in here eere' (l. 182) and the singular 'his oon yë | Cast up' (ll. 184–85), as well as the monotheist narrator's obtuse proposal of idolatrous sacrifice (cf. l. 114) to placate deities he had not known: 'Of down of pure dowves white | I wil yive hym a fether-bed' (ll 250–51); and so forth. Reckless and indifferent in a consolation, it may seem (Gower's version of the same matter in *Confessio amantis* (IV. 2986–3033) is less distracted).[38] Nevertheless, clever work, to funny effect, Ovid-like perhaps, from a young poet: the *Book of the Duchess* gives every appearance of having been a success with its early public.

Among the source-matter Chaucer incorporated into the *Book of the Duchess* is something of the Ceyx and Alcione tale that Gower too was later to use and to reuse from the *Metamorphoses*, *aliter*, for both the *Visio Anglie* and the *Confessio amantis*. Chaucer need not and so probably did not have recourse to the *Metamorphoses* proper for making his adaptation of the narrative matter to these peculiar purposes of his own in the *Book of the Duchess*; instead, he drew on the French *Ovide moralisé*, close kin of his other sources. Chaucer retells the story of Ceyx and Alcione, at length ('This was the tale' (ll. 62–217)), as a proleptic analogue for the bereavement that occasioned his writing. In the retelling, Chaucer sums up the consolation he has to offer—to the Man in Black within the poem as well as to John of Gaunt, duke of Lancaster, without it—in the words of a god, announced to Alcione through the remains of Ceyx, a reanimate corpse-dummy: 'To lytel while oure blysse lasteth' (l. 211), as if such a transient illusion were what might best be expected of human

---

[37] Chaucer, *BD* (Benson, pp. 330–46). The source-uses are compendiously listed in B. A. Windeatt, *Chaucer's Dream Poetry: Sources and Analogues* (Cambridge: Brewer, 1982), pp. 167–68; generally, I rely on A. J. Minnis, in *Oxford Guides to Chaucer: The Shorter Poems* (Oxford: Clarendon Press, 1995), pp. 91–112, though also, for the particular absence of direct Ovidian borrowing in the *Book of the Duchess*, on Minnis, 'A Note on Chaucer and the *Ovide moralisé*', *Medium Aevum*, 48 (1979), 254–57.

[38] For analysis see Norman Callan, '"Thyn Owne Book": A Note on Chaucer, Gower and Ovid', *Review of English Studies*, 22 (1946), 269–81 (pp. 275–76); and J. A. W. Bennett, 'Caxton and Gower', *MLR*, 45 (1950), 215–16.

happiness. And there Chaucer left the tale, in death, short of the Ovidian transformation.[39]

For the sake of its indecorous verbal antics, Chaucer's poem violates the integrity of the well-known source-story; for in Ovid the point is not that the loving couple are sundered by the death at sea in storm—though briefly they are—but that, despite misfortune, through metamorphosis the two live eternally together, sea-birds riding soft waves in clear light. The inaptness of the adaptation to the circumstance of bereavement may be short-sighted. More likely, the effect may be intentionally comedic, the ineptitude of Chaucer the author only apparent, serving to characterize the Chaucerian narrator as inept, possibly engendering later comic effects at the poem's ending. In either case, Chaucer does not here manifest the same kind of comprehension of what Ovid had done that Gower achieved. Gower corrects the Chaucerian ineptitude, be it authorial or narratorial, when (pointedly to preface his own, most restrained, later retelling of the Ovidian Ceyx and Alcione matter in the *Confessio amantis*) he gives a repetition of the crucial Chaucerian line 'To lytel while oure blysse lasteth', though in a Christian-moral rephrasing, in effect correcting Chaucer. Gower expresses the same sentiment but from the distanced point of view of the divine, *sub specie aeternitatis*, so to say, evoking the possibilities of other, greater perspective: 'Ther mai no worldes joie laste' (IV. 2806).

In the *Confessio amantis* tale, nearly stormless but metamorphic in this way, the point is this possibility of an other-worldly joy that might perdure. The (Chaucerian) topic announced for the tale—ostensibly, the matter of the veracity of 'swevenes' (IV. 2917-26)—is comic misdirection, for Amans-Gower has already averred that, *in amore*, 'I no Sompnolence have used' (IV. 2770).[40] The tale of 'Ceix the king' and 'Alceone' 'his wif', 'Which as hire oghne hertes lif | Him loveth' (IV. 2928-31), that the Confessor-Genius offers in illustration repeats the point the lover has already made about his own erotic perseverance:

> For lich unto the greene tree,
> If that men toke his rote aweie,
> Riht so myn herte scholde deie,
> If that mi love be withdrawe.
> (IV. 2681-84)

---

[39] On Chaucer's ending see A. J. Minnis, *Chaucer and Pagan Antiquity* (Cambridge: Brewer, 1982), pp. 17-18; on the tale's consolatory usefulness for Chaucer see Phillip C. Boardman, 'Courtly Language and the Strategy of Consolation in the *Book of the Duchess*', *ELH*, 44 (1977), 567-79 (pp. 576-77).

[40] Chaucer's grandest discussion is in the probably very late *NPT*, ll. 2922-3156 (Benson, pp. 252-61 (pp. 254-57)), though there had been already the two earlier extensive discussions, in the c. 1379-80 *HF*, ll. 1-58 (Benson, pp. 348-73 (pp. 348-49)) and the c. 1385 *Tr*, v. 358-85 (Benson, p. 565).

Amans's 'herte' stays always by his beloved, he asserts, though his body may wander:

> And yit min herte lith to wedde
> With hire, wher as I cam fro;
> Thogh I departe, he wol noght so,
> Ther is no lock mai schette him oute.
> (IV. 2876–79)

The disembodied 'herte' remains 'with hire overall', no matter the physical realities, with the consequence

> That be hire lief, or be hire loth
> Into hire bedd myn herte goth,
> And softly takth hire in his arm.
> (IV. 2882–85)

'U li coers est, le corps falt obeïr' ('Where the heart is, the body must follow'), goes the refrain of the *ballade* Gower addressed to 'Ma belle oisel, vers qui mon pensement | S'en vole ades sanz null contretenir' ('My beautiful bird, towards whom my thoughts | Fly themselves always, without any opposition'), in which he refers again to the same Ovidian tale:[41]

> Pour remembrer jadis celle aventure
> De Alceone et Ceïx ensement,
> Com dieus muoit en oisel lour figure,
> Ma volenté serroit tout tielment,
> Qe sanz envie et danger de la gent
> Nous porroions ensemble par loisir
> Voler tout francs en nostre esbatement:
> U li coers est, le corps falt obeïr.[42]

> Always keep in mind the fate,
> Moreover, of Alceone and Ceix,
> How God transformed their bodies into birds:
> My desire would be altogether the same,
> That without envy and interference from people
> We would be able together at leisure
> To fly wholly free for our diversion:
> Where the heart is, the body must follow.

When the like gesture—paradoxically, a physical embrace by the arms of a disembodied heart—recurs in Gower's inset tale in the *Confessio amantis*, it

---

[41] It is a *ballade* of 'Saint Valentin'—who has all birds 'en governement' and selects a mate for each 'tout d'un acord et d'un assent', by the teaching of 'Nature'—establishing Gower's familiarity with Chaucer's *Parliament of Fowls*.

[42] *Cinkante Balades*, XXXIV. 25–26 and 17–24, ed. and trans. by R. F. Yeager, in *John Gower: The French Balades*, TEAMS Middle English Texts Series (Kalamazoo: Western Michigan University Medieval Institute Publications, 2011), pp. 106–09.

induces the climactic metamorphosis mentioned in the *ballade* too, though omitted by Chaucer. In 'This Alceone, the trewe queene' of the *Confessio* (l. 3121), 'Hir will stod as it was tofore' (l. 3114): 'And sche, which tok of deth no kepe, | Anon forth lepte into the depe', 'And wolde have cawht him'—'hire oghne hertes lif'—'in hire arm', except that, by the gesture now, the couple are transformed (ll. 3085-87). This is the 'the trowthe of love, | Which in this worthi ladi stod' (ll. 3090-91), that the metamorphosis in it represents and the tale as a whole illustrates: 'Est in amore vigil Venus' (IV. viii. 3). It is not somnolent; rather, as Gower himself Englishes this line from the Latin verses heading the book-section, in the Confessor-Genius's comment following the tale, praising the perseverance of Gower-Amans, 'For love upon his lust wakende | Is ever' (ll. 3181-82). Like Gower's, Ovid's version too 'et ad finem seruatos laudat amores' (*Met.* XI. 743 and 750: 'praises a love persistent all the way to the end'); in Ovid and Gower (and again, unlike Chaucer's version), 'tum quoque mansit amor' ('then too their love persisted').

It is for this perseverance in love, which the metamorphosis makes properly endless, that Alcione is praised at the end of the *Confessio amantis*, where the tale comes up again. Into Cupid's final parliament of lovers, assembled to judge Amans, come four women 'whos feith was proeved in her lyves' (VIII. 2616), whom the assembly reveres 'As thogh they hadden be goddesses | Of al this world or emperesses' (VIII. 2611-12):

> The ferthe wif which I ther sih,
> I herde of hem that were nyh
> Hou sche was cleped Alcione,
> Which to Seyix hir lord al one
> And to no mo hir body kepte;
> And whan sche sih him dreynt, sche lepte
> Into the wawes where he swam,
> And there a sefoul sche becam,
> And with hire wenges him bespradde
> For love which to him sche hadde.
> (VIII. 2647-56)

Gower's Virgil against Chaucer's Ovid

Other evidence for a Gower-Chaucer *agon* over Ovid may come from the one point at which Gower appears to have preferred Virgil, where an Ovidian alternative was available and well known—another case of Ovid redoing Virgilian matter *aliter*—and where Chaucer, unusually, had asserted a preference of his own for the Ovid in place of the especially well-known passage of Virgil: the description of *Fama*'s malign pervasion of the widow Dido's Carthage (*Aen.* IV. 173-97).

First, it needs to be recognized that, by contrast with his thorough knowledge and use of Ovid, Gower used little of Virgil, to such a degree that Gower's knowledge has appeared to be small or none. For even regarding a willingness or capacity to quote Virgil on Gower's part, the evidence is equivocal.[43] In the *Visio Anglie*, for example, to describe the Gower-narrator's doubt during the invasion of London in the Social Revolt, Gower puts 'Mens agiturque diu pugnat sentencia mecum' (l. 1403: 'My mind's astir; my thoughts within dispute'). The post-caesural phrase is a quotation from Ovid, carrying pointed allusion. It comes from the reaction to a vision in sleep of an imperious deity, Hercules, who appears in order to command Myscelus to go into exile, as the Gower-narrator fears he too must go:

> post ea discedunt pariter somnusque deusque;
> surgit Alemonides* tacitaque recentia mente   *=Myscelus.
> visa refert, *pugnatque diu sententia secum*.
> (*Met.* xv. 25–27)

Afterwards, both sleep and the god left him at once; Alemon's son got up and to himself reviewed what of late he had seen, and for a long time his thoughts warred within him.

The phrase Gower substituted at the beginning of his line—'Mens agiturque'—may recall, by ironic inversion, the Virgilian answer to the problem of the kind of mundane uncertainty that Gower's narrator faces at this point, like Myscelus: 'mens agitat molem'. This forms part of the consoling oracular explanation for his troubles that is offered the Odyssean Aeneas, forced from his Trojan home into exilic wanderings, during his underworld passage:

> Principio caelum ac terras camposque liquentis
> lucentemque globum lunae Titaniaque astra
> spiritus intus alit, totamque infusa per artus
> *mens agitat* molem et magno se corpore miscet.
> (*Aen.* vi. 724–27)

From the beginning, a spirit within nourishes the heavens and earth, the liquid plains, the moon's radiant sphere, and the Titanic stars; through each part pervading, mind animates the whole matter and mingles itself within the great material mass.

The same Virgilian lines may as well be said to contain recollection of the beginning of the Gospel of John, 'In principio erat' (1. 1), or vice versa; both passages concern inceptions and cosmic matters, just as both the others concern *mentes* and agitation. But that Gower's first phrase is Virgilian—in the same way that his other half-line is Ovidian—seems dubious.

---

[43] Harbert, 'Lessons from the Great Clerk', p. 86: 'There is no indication that he had extensive knowledge of any Latin poet except Ovid. Although he knew of Virgil, and included stories about him in the *Confessio amantis* (v. 2031–224; viii. 2714–17), he does not use any lines from Virgil in the *Vox*, even in his description of a city in chaos, where *Aeneid* ii might have come in useful.' Cf. Michael P. Kuczynski, 'Gower's Virgil', in *On John Gower*, ed. by Yeager, pp. 161–87.

Those phrases from Virgil that do turn up in Gower are possibly such as might rather confirm Gower's ignorance. A line near the beginning of the *Cronica tripertita*, in praise of the peace that Gower hopes can be installed out of the violence of the Lancastrian usurpation, 'Est tamen hoc clamor: *Omnia vincit amor*' (*prol.* 7), has words from the early pastoral-pacific Virgil: '*Omnia uincit amor* et nos cedamus amori' (*Ecl.* x. 69: 'Love conquers all, so let us give ourselves to love'). Of course, the quoted phrase had attained such currency—crossing over into *fere*-vernacular usage even—that it must have ceased to seem Virgilian.[44] Likewise, Gower's remark about Richard II's propensity for deceit in the *opus infernum* section of the *Cronica tripertita* does have a phrase again from Virgil's early verse:

> Doctoris verba sunt hec—que miror—acerba:
> Dum melius fecisse putes, *latet anguis in herba*.
> (*Cronica tripertita*, II. 345)

The teacher's bitter words are these, and I'm aquake:
You may think you've done well: in grass there hides a snake!

> Qui legitis flores et humi nascentia fraga,
> frigidus—o pueri, fugite hinc—*latet anguis in herba*.
> (*Ecl.* III. 92–93)

Fly away, ye children gathering blossoms and the earth's new berries: in grass there hides a cold snake.

Here, Gower's characterization of the phrase as 'doctoris verba' signals its proverbiality, as opposed to an association of it with a particular *auctor*.[45]

Such quotations from Virgil as may appear to occur in Gower are probably not Virgilian in any meaningful way; certainly, there is in them nothing of the knowingly allusive, taking in episodic contexts, of the sort that characterizes Gower's quotations from Ovid—with yet this one exception, where Gower uses Virgil, unusually but unmistakably and perhaps provocatively. In the *Visio* Gower's prelude to London's invasion is the spread of fear in the city: 'Sperserat ambiguas huius vaga *Fama per vrbes* | Rumoris sonitum, cordaque firma mouet' (ll. 1231–32: 'Fame wanders through the doubtful towns and spreads | This rumour's sound, dismaying once firm hearts'). The form of Gower's remark recalls the Virgilian passage, especially '*magnas it Fama per urbes*' (*Aen.* IV. 173: 'all about the great cities goes Rumour'), though also

---

[44] Other recollections in Gower are *Vox clamantis*, v. 147 ('Sic amor omne domat') and vi. 999 (in *Latin Writings*, ed. by Macaulay, pp. 3–313 (pp. 205 and 259)). The Virgilian phrase is also in Chaucer: *GP*, l. 162 (Benson, pp. 23–36 (p. 26)).

[45] Cf. nos. 13504 ff. in Hans Walther, *Proverbia sententiaeque Latinitatis medii aevi: Lateinische Sprichwörter und Sentenzen des Mittelalters in alphabetischer Anordnung*, 6 vols (Göttingen: Vandenhoeck & Ruprecht, 1963–69). Again, the phrase also occurs twice in English in Chaucer, where it is likewise counted as quotation from Virgil though it can barely function as such: *SumT*, ll. 1994–95 (Benson, pp. 128–36 (p. 132)); and *SqT*, l. 512 (Benson, pp. 169–77 (p. 175)).

Virgil's own repetitions, '*per* umbram | stridens' (ll. 184-85: 'hissing through shadows') and '*magnas* territat *urbes*' (l. 187: 'she affrights the great cities'), both in line-final positions in Virgil that Gower's phrase emulates; also, 'ad regem cursus detorquet' (l. 196: 'to the king she turns her tracks'), where the verb's subject is still *Fama*, moving about others' civic residence.

The invasive traveller that Gower takes from Virgil—'vaga Fama' (l. 1231)— contrasts with the resident figure of the Ovidian rewriting of the Virgil passage, at *Met.* XII. 39-63, which Gower would of course have known as well, but appears to reject in favour of the Virgilian one for the *Visio Anglie*. In the Ovid, 'Fama tenet summaque domum sibi legit in arce' (l. 43: 'Rumour resides, choosing to make her home in a high tower'); information comes to her by various means:

> innumerosque aditus ac mille foramina tectis
> addidit et nullis inclusit limina portis;
> nocte dieque patet.
>
> (ll. 44-46)

she put in countless entry-ways and a thousand portals in the roof; no doorway did she shut up closed; the place is open night and day.

Yet she remains in place; consequently, rather than spreading, Ovid's resident *Fama* comprehends: 'ipsa quid in caelo rerum pelagoque geratur | et tellure uidet totumque inquirit in orbem' (ll. 62-63: 'throughout the whole world, whatever is afoot, be it by sky or sea or land, she sees it and investigates').[46]

As opposed to the Virgilian vagrant that Gower uses, in the *House of Fame* Chaucer substantively depends on Ovid for the resident *Fama*:[47]

> Hir paleys stant, as I shal seye,
> Ryght even in myddes of the weye
> Betwixen hevene, erthe, and see;
> That what so ever in al these three
> Is spoken, either privy or apert,
> The way therto ys so overt,
> And stant eke in so juste a place
> That every soun mot to hyt pace.
>
> (ll. 713-20)

---

[46] That Gower knew the passage of Ovid may be confirmed, aside from other evidence, by his emphatic line-initial 1232, 'Rumoris sonitum', in the same *Visio* passage—the phrase perhaps suggested by the personifications populating the Ovid passage's conclusion, where there is nothing comparable in Virgil: 'illic Credulitas, illic temerarius Error | uanaque Laetitia est consternatique Timores | Seditioque repens dubioque auctore Susurri' (*Met.* XII. 59-61: 'therein is Credulity, therein fearful Error, and vain Joy too, the overwhelming Fears, sudden Discord, and the Whisperings, of unknown author').

[47] Chaucer, *HF*, ll. 661-724, 843-47, and 1023-45 (Benson, pp. 356-57, 358, and 360). See Callan, pp. 276-78. There are recollections of the Virgil in the Chaucer passages, nevertheless; on them see esp. Minnis, *Shorter Poems*, pp. 184-87; also, Charles P. R. Tisdale, 'The House of Fame: Virgilian Reason and Boethian Wisdom', *Comparative Literature*, 25 (1973), 247-61 (pp. 257-58).

The *House of Fame* (c. 1379-80) is probably slightly earlier than the *Visio Anglie*, and there is other evidence to indicate that Gower knew this early work of Chaucer, as well as the others.[48] Gower is reversing fields, here using Virgil when generally otherwise he is Ovidian, in reply to Chaucer's uncharacteristic usage, preferring Ovid where more often he used Virgil, in such writings of his as antedate the composition of Gower's *Visio Anglie*.

Gower and Chaucer, Ancient and Modern

Chaucer's most intimate literary relations were with other vernacular writers, contemporaries and near contemporaries moreover: early in his work, with Guillaume de Lorris (c. 1200-c. 1240), Jean de Meun (c. 1240-c. 1305), Machaut, and Froissart; later, and still more intimate perhaps, with Giovanni Boccaccio (1313-1375)—the writer of vernacular romance, though, rather than the scholarly Latinist. Chaucer also cultivated a special relationship with the *De consolatione philosophiae* of Anicius Manlius Severinus Boethius (d. 524): he translated it into the earliest Middle English *Kunstprosa*, as well as into some of his best realized pentametric verse, in his most mature style (e.g. *Tr.* III. 1744-71). However, Chaucer's relationship with the Boethian writing was much mediated by the 'medieval' Boethius, particularly the medieval French tradition of translation, paraphrase, and comment; Chaucer's translation is often enough from French, rather than the difficult Latin original. His writings' relation to other Latin *auctores*, ancient and modern, was not so close, in any case other than that of Boethius. Be that as it may, such relations as he had with the other Latin *auctores* were again much mediated by vernacular translation and commentary, and such appears to have been the case with Chaucer's knowledge of Ovid. Kindred spirits, it may be felt, in their propensity for the indecorous and inappropriate; the apparent kinship did not induce in Chaucer any impulsion particularly to cultivate Ovidian knowledge.

Ovid was Gower's Boethius; Ovid was Gower's, as Boethius was Chaucer's. Gower would appear to have studied Ovid, moreover, and in a way that engaged him with the Ovidian original, directly and *in extenso*, though of course Gower knew and used the *Ovide moralisé*. Likewise, Gower's intimacy with modern Latin *auctores* is established, in the cases of the *Speculum stultorum* of Nigel Witeker (c. 1135-1198?) (which Chaucer also appears to have known, though not to the same level of verbal intimacy that Gower commanded) and

---

[48] On the date (and textual condition) of the *House of Fame* see Minnis, *Shorter Poems*, pp. 167-72. Gower's line in the *Visio Anglie*, 'Ecce nichil penitus fuerat' (l. 2015: 'Nothing was there!'), may recall the sudden disappearance of the Temple of Glass, in *HF*, ll. 480-91 (Benson, p. 354).

of Peter Riga's *Aurora* (c. 1170–1200).[49] The fact is, however, that Gower did not cultivate a similarly intimate relation with any ancient *auctor* other than Ovid.

There were so few secular English-language writers at that moment that two working in such social and geographic proximity as Gower and Chaucer could not have ignored one another, as all or all but a very few appear to have ignored the distantly north-western *Gawain* poet. Though Gower was senior, possibly by as much as a generation, Chaucer arrived earlier as an English poet, derisory as his earliest work—French and English erotic and religious lyrics; brief lyric-framing narratives such as the *Book of the Duchess*—must have appeared from the perspective of the grander 'public poetry' that both writers contributed to elaborating during the 1380s.[50] Greater, prior success for Chaucer's English writings—evidently widely copied, by contrast with Gower's earliest efforts—may also have engendered a degree of disapprobation in Gower for the younger, less serious, but better-received English writer. Gower's more thoroughly informed Ovidian usage in the *Visio Anglie* represents the superiority of his learning, by contrast with boy Chaucer. The still more thorough command of Ovidianism, still more subtly expressed, in the final *Confessio amantis* reuse of the Ceyx and Alcione matter—where the Chaucerian ineptitude seems still to have offended Gower ('Ther mai no worldes joie laste' topping 'To lytel while oure blysse lasteth')—represents Gower's greater seriousness and knowledge, by comparison with the own, younger self that had engaged thoroughly with the same Ovid, and in the learned language itself, for the *Visio Anglie* section of 1381.

UNIVERSITY OF OTTAWA   DAVID R. CARLSON

[49] Robert R. Raymo, 'Gower's *Vox clamantis* and the *Speculum stultorum*', *Modern Language Notes*, 70 (1955), 315–20, and Paul E. Beichner, 'Gower's Use of Aurora in *Vox clamantis*', *Speculum*, 30 (1955), 582–95; on Chaucer's use see Jill Mann, 'The *Speculum stultorum* and the Nun's Priest's Tale', *Chaucer Review*, 9 (1975), 262–82.

[50] Anne Middleton, 'The Idea of Public Poetry in the Reign of Richard II', *Speculum*, 53 (1978), 94–114.

ROYAL SELF-ASSERTION AND THE REVISION OF CHIVALRY: *THE ENTERTAINMENT AT KENILWORTH* (1575), JONSON'S *MASQUE OF OWLS* (1624), AND *THE KING'S ENTERTAINMENT AT WELBECK* (1633)

Analyses of early modern culture continue to be preoccupied with questions of royal representation; more specifically, of how the nation state was expressed through the person of the monarch. This is never a simple equation between monarch and state, but is rather a process marked by spontaneity and resistance, as well as being constructed out of pre-existing rhetorical and ideological concepts. A key shift in royal representation was occasioned by the change of monarch from Henry to Elizabeth Tudor; this was not the obvious and untroubled inheritance that Elizabeth later stressed through her use of personal iconography, punctuated as it was by the short reigns of her sibling monarchs, Edward and Mary.[1] Significant differences in the royal styles espoused by Henry and Elizabeth are detectable in the ways in which royal entertainments inscribed them into a festive discourse of monarchy and nationhood, with Henry demonstrating a spontaneous and ebullient participation as the foundation of his personal myth; whereas his daughter displayed a presence that appears to have been partly constructed for her by professional writers and their patrons, but nevertheless also showed a queenly detachment from scripted evocations of her iconic presence in royal entertainments, as well as a determination to puncture the fictions scripted for her from time to time in acts of self-assertion. Henry was also compelled to negotiate with the ideological networks he found himself inhabiting to express his royal identity, but there is a very real sense that a web of factors relating to gender, politics, and religion meant that while Elizabeth was the symbolic cynosure for royal festivities, she was often the royal spectator rather than the royal performer, and her iconic self was evoked in the most abstract manner, in keeping with the contemporary ideology regarding the monarch's two bodies, simultaneously spiritual and temporal.[2] Her ongoing struggle with this process of abstraction is amply demonstrated by her responses to the different acts constituting *The Entertainment at Kenilworth*, as she refused to

---

[1] Louis Montrose, *The Subject of Elizabeth: Authority, Gender, and Representation* (Chicago: University of Chicago Press, 2006), pp. 57–62. Montrose shows how Elizabeth exploited portraiture to reinforce her role as Henry's legitimate successor, and comments in his analysis of her representation: 'Elizabeth Tudor was a privileged agent in the production of the royal image, but she was not its master. Her power to shape her own strategies was itself shaped [. . .] by the repertoire of values, institutions and practices [. . .] available to her' (p. 2).

[2] For a classic analysis of the religious thinking underpinning this concept see Ernst Kantorowicz, *The King's Two Bodies: A Study in Medieval and Political Theology* (Princeton: Princeton University Press, 1957).

co-operate with the script and its authors at key moments. In terms of royal entertainments, Henry was not subject to the self-alienation latent in this abstraction of the royal body to the same degree as his daughter, as he was the author of the entertainments he starred in. His position was guaranteed by both his gender and his status, and he clearly did not experience the ontological splitting caused by being a female monarch who was symbolically central yet physically marginal.[3] This shift from performer to audience status for the monarch was entrenched by James I's position as monarch presiding over court masques in Whitehall, his throne the central point for all lines of perspective to meet, apparently codifying the extent and vision of royal power at large, although recent analysis has suggested that more than one viewpoint of the masque was always available.[4] James has been unfavourably compared with Elizabeth, particularly regarding their responses to the entertainments staged to celebrate their entries into London and accession to the English crown: Elizabeth's enthusiastic and intelligent engagement with the devices compared with James's apparent fear of crowds and impatience. Yet James saw himself very much as Elizabeth's successor, to the extent that he adopted many of her signature rhetorical strategies. Furthermore, he emulated her regal detachment at royal festivities, but almost never chose to punctuate scripted events in a spontaneous expression of self, as she did at Kenilworth.[5]

The favoured mythic discourse of the Tudors was neo-chivalric, and the festivities at Kenilworth and Welbeck displayed neo-chivalric set properties, rhetoric, and plot devices, identifying them as part of the Tudor discourse of royal legitimacy. They were also part of the cultural *Zeitgeist*, whereby the recuperation of British history and the charting of British geography were en-

---

[3] While Elizabeth's status as an author was also recognized, this was viewed as an extraordinary achievement relating to her intelligence, learning, and piety, most usually exhibited in the private sphere of letters and poems, and not in the exhibitionist manner of her father's staged theatricals. Her famous speech to the troops at Tilbury plays on the dichotomy between her 'masculine' role as monarch and her weaker female nature. The entrapment of her personal agency is accomplished by this inflexible binary model. See Elizabeth I, *Collected Works*, ed. by Leah S. Marcus and others (Chicago: University of Chicago Press, 2000), pp. xi–xiii.

[4] Stephen Orgel articulates this seminal view on the political implications of masque perspective in *The Illusion of Power: Political Theater in the English Renaissance* (Berkeley: University of California Press, 1975). See also Martin Butler, *The Stuart Court Masque and Political Culture* (Cambridge: Cambridge University Press, 2008), pp. 14–15.

[5] Jonathan Goldberg, *James I and the Politics of Literature: Jonson, Shakespeare, Donne, and their Contemporaries* (Stanford: Stanford University Press, 1983), p. 30; Montrose, p. 44. Among the metaphors Montrose identifies as Elizabeth's borrowing from her half-sister Mary is that of the mother to her people, a metaphor that James would adopt in turn. An exception to this last point is highlighted by Jane Rickard when she describes King James's delivery of an impromptu poem of thanks to Buckingham (*Authorship and Authority in the Writings of James VI and I* (Manchester: Manchester University Press, 2007), p. 184). There is also the infamous incident when he impatiently interrupted the dancing that took place as part of Jonson's 1617 masque *Pleasure Reconciled to Virtue*, as described by Ian Donaldson in *Ben Jonson: A Life* (Oxford: Oxford University Press, 2011), p. 317.

meshed in the broader project of nation-building. Nevertheless, the rhetoric of chivalry is not merely reproduced to reinforce royal and national claims, but interrogated and adapted to express alternative views, and to demonstrate a new kind of democratic, communal chivalry, emphatically embodied by the figure of Captain Cox in *The Entertainment at Kenilworth* and in *The Masque of Owls*, and by the chivalric sports engaged in by the people both at Kenilworth and at Welbeck.[6]

This article will traverse a festive journey from the royal entertainment at Kenilworth in 1575, laid on by Robert Dudley, Earl of Leicester, to Jonson's *Masque of Owls* (1624), and thence to his *The King's Entertainment at Welbeck* (1633). The purpose of this is partly to chart the continuities as well as the discontinuities of cultural inheritance that evolved throughout a growing tradition of royal entertainment; more particularly, the approach will reveal how these entertainments registered resistance to dominant rhetorical and ideological strategies of the day. Thus *The Entertainment at Kenilworth* enabled the Queen's self-assertion in the face of Leicester's ambitious claims and the text's limiting assumptions about her status as a female monarch, as well as enabling a popular appropriation of the traditionally aristocratic mode of chivalry; and this was achieved in the face of Leicester's deliberate recreation of chivalric forms to legitimate his own claims. The most obvious evidence of continuity between these three entertainments relates to physical location: *The Masque of Owls* was also staged at Kenilworth for Charles I, and *Welbeck* was similarly located in the Midlands of England. The location of these entertainments outside of the metropolitan court at Whitehall facilitated the articulation of oppositional discourse: from his own seat of Kenilworth, Leicester was emboldened to query matters of royal jurisdiction such as Elizabeth's policies on marriage and the Netherlands; and later, in *The Masque of Owls* and *The King's Entertainment at Welbeck*, Jonson would exploit the licence granted by distance from the metropolitan centre to scrutinize Charles's withdrawal from the country at large, making way for Puritan dominance of parish authorities.

The Entertainment at Kenilworth has been the subject of much scholarly discussion over the years, thanks to the fact that we possess the most complete account of its proceedings in the shape of Robert Laneham's letter, a detailed text purporting to be the observations of a rather self-important clerk of the council chamber door, as well as *The Princely Pleasures*, George Gascoigne's textual commemoration of his part in composing a good deal of the enter-

---

[6] Perhaps the most obvious example of the rhetorical manipulations and negotiations present in the chivalric rhetoric at Kenilworth is at the outset, when Queen Elizabeth questions the legitimacy of the Lady of the Lake to welcome her to an estate which is technically already royal property. In terms of nation-building, the seminal work of the period was William Camden, *Britannia*, trans. by Philemon Holland (London: George Bishop, 1607), in which national identity was secured through locating a shared history and geography.

tainment. While this has led to extensive analysis of the events at Kenilworth and discussion of the way they engage in the personal and political negotiations between Elizabeth and Leicester, notably in the issues of marriage and potential English intervention in the Low Countries, any attempt to decode the entertainment is made doubly problematic by the complex nature of the source texts, which are not what they appear to be on the surface.[7] The Victorian editor F. J. Furnivall describes Laneham as 'a most amusing, self-satisfied, rollicking chap' whose text takes the format of a letter to his friend and erstwhile colleague, Humfrey Martin, mercer.[8] More recent critics, however, have taken this cue to pick up on the apparently unintentionally ironic resonances within the work, to speculate that it is in fact a satire written by someone who was present at Kenilworth, but certainly not Robert Laneham, whose bumpkin awe of his great patron, Leicester, and self-congratulatory superiority are a joke designed to be shared with a coterie reading public in the know.[9] Such a view is reinforced firstly by the fact that the actual court servant, Robert Langham (or Laneham), protested against the hijacking of his name, and secondly by the existence of a letter to the Lord Chancellor, Lord Burghley, from the probable author of *Laneham's Letter*, William Patten. Patten was part of the literary team responsible for the Kenilworth entertainments, and in the letter to Burghley he apologizes for his part in the spoof, as he had heard 'hoow the book waz too be supprest for that Langham had complained upon it, and ootherwize for that the honorabl entertainment be not turned into a iest'.[10]

The other key source text for information about the entertainment at Kenilworth, *The Princely Pleasures*, was published under Gascoigne's name and he wrote the majority of its material, using the published text to extend his bid for royal patronage.[11] Nevertheless, the text also credits other authors

---

[7] For analysis of the political and personal background to the Kenilworth entertainment see Elizabeth Goldring, 'Portraiture, Patronage and the Progresses of Elizabeth I: Robert Dudley, Earl of Leicester, and the Kenilworth Festivities of 1575', in *The Progresses, Pageants and Entertainments of Elizabeth I*, ed. by Jayne Elisabeth Archer and others (Oxford: Oxford University Press, 2007), pp. 163–88; Susan Doran, *Monarchy and Matrimony: The Courtships of Elizabeth I* (London and New York: Routledge, 1996), p. 67; R. C. Strong and J. A. Van Dorsten, *Leicester's Triumph* (Leiden: published for the Sir Thomas Browne Institute at the University Press, 1964).

[8] *Robert Laneham's Letter: Describing a Part of the Entertainment unto Queen Elizabeth at the Castle of Kenilworth in 1575*, ed. by F. J. Furnivall (London: Chatto and Windus; New York: Duffield, 1907). Further references are given parenthetically. In an attempt to differentiate between the literary character narrating the text and the historical figure behind him, I have followed Furnivall in referring to the narrator as 'Laneham' and I refer to the man himself as 'Langham', an alternative spelling used by contemporary critics.

[9] Sandra Logan, *Texts/Events in Early Modern England: Poetics of History* (Aldershot: Ashgate, 2007), p. 94; Penny McCarthy, *Pseudonymous Shakespeare: Rioting Language in the Sidney Circle* (Aldershot: Ashgate, 2006), p. 5.

[10] McCarthy, p. 5.

[11] 'The Princely Pleasures at Kenelworth Castle', in *The Complete Works of George Gascoigne*, ed. by John Cunliffe, 2 vols (Cambridge: Cambridge University Press, 1910), II, 91–131.

and devisers of the event, suggesting that it was a conglomerate work put together by the printer Richard Jhones; and indeed Jhones's editorial voice is strongly present in it. Logan goes as far as to argue that 'Jhones appears to be the framing voice of the account as a whole [. . .] the text of *The Princely Pleasures* was not "authored" by Gascoigne, but compiled and presented by Jhones'.[12] While this is a reasonable inclusion of the printer's function in the production of this text, it does underestimate Gascoigne's position as an author so obviously concerned to cultivate a literary reputation and his bid for patronage. The material included in *The Princely Pleasures* testifies that Gascoigne was determined to publicize his own efforts on this occasion, albeit not everything he wrote was actually performed or delivered at Kenilworth. Thus, the inclusion of the unperformed masque he composed is significant, although not unprecedented: it does not fit with Jhones's professed agenda of providing a full account of what actually took place at Kenilworth, but it does demonstrate the author's literary abilities and prominence in the preparations for the Queen's visit.[13] By contrast, Jhones's priority was to respond to the growing demand for news, as he makes clear in a preface to the reader in the 1576 edition of the text: 'all studious and well disposed young Gentlemen and others, were desirous to be partakers of those pleasures by a profitable publication'.[14] Thus, both texts trouble traditional notions of authorship, and exist as intriguing palimpsests recording a variety of authors and audiences; that is why they offer rich pickings to the critic seeking to appreciate fully how, in 1575, Elizabeth inserted herself into the pre-existing myth of monarchy and how she shaped it to suit her own purposes.

Louis Montrose's comments about the Queen's restriction by those 'values, institutions and practices available to her' is extended by Susan Anderson to a consideration of how 'the reporting of those [her] actions is shaped by the priorities of the text'.[15] While most contemporary critics accept this notion of compromised royal agency (compromised actually and textually), it would be wrong to underestimate Elizabeth's skill and wit when it came to making her own voice heard, and both texts record key, if brief, episodes when she does just this. The other political figure looming large in this event is, of course, its sponsor and Elizabeth's long-term favourite, the Earl of Leicester. Leicester used the entertainment to proclaim his role as a regional magnate, whose influence within the country at large provided the London-based monarchy

[12] Logan, pp. 107–08.
[13] Masque texts often record sections that were not actually performed, as is the case with part of the epithalamium in Jonson's *Hymeniae* (1606).
[14] Richard Jhones, 1576 Preface to *Princely Pleasures*, in *The Complete Works of George Gascoigne*, ed. by Cunliffe, II, 570.
[15] Susan Anderson, '"A true copie": Gascoigne's *Princely Pleasures* and the Textual Representation of Courtly Performance', *Early Modern Literary Studies*, 14.1 (special issue, 18 May 2008) <http://purl.oclc.org/emls/14-1/article5.htm> [accessed 18 September 2013].

with a platform outside the metropolis. Moreover, much analysis of the Kenilworth entertainment has shown how Leicester exploited the requirements of courtly hospitality and allegorical entertainment to express his own agenda regarding a range of issues, notably that of royal marriage and English intervention in the Netherlands.[16] Thus, the Kenilworth source texts embody the competing requirements and perspectives of authors, literary personae, patron, and monarch, with each voice modulating and adjusting the others in a noisy expression of the aesthetic and political negotiations involved in representing the monarchical state. This aspect of royal entertainments is not limited to those staged away from the court, as Martin Butler has emphasized: 'The court was never hermetically sealed, nor did it speak with a single voice.'[17] Furthermore, the discursive competition inherent in the texts recording the events re-enacts the multilayered and multivocal aspects of the events themselves, which were not only made to speak for different masters, but also made to speak on allegorical, literary, and political levels; as Anderson comments, these entertainments possessed 'a discourse flexible enough to articulate the concerns of the real world within an idealised fantasy, while simultaneously fulfilling the obligations of hospitality'.[18]

The figure of Captain Cox allows us to trace a festive lineage from Henry VIII to Kenilworth in 1575, then again to Kenilworth in 1624, and to Welbeck in 1633; Cox is used as a kind of synecdoche for the history of early modern court entertainments, as he harks back to the scholarly and aristocratic revival of chivalry that was so fundamental to Henry's VIII's attempt to dominate national and international politics, and that was continued in Elizabethan entertainments as a sign of the Tudor crown's legitimacy and continuity with the past. Yet the revival of chivalry was accompanied by satire aimed at its more excessive expressions, as well as at the way in which an aristocratic cultural mode had percolated down to the lower social orders.[19] The rhetoric of chivalry was now employed to provide popular ballad and story plots, and had long been employed to legitimate the pursuit of country

---

[16] James Knowles, '"In the purest times of peerless Queen Elizabeth": Jonson and the Politics of Caroline Nostalgia', in *The Progresses, Pageants and Entertainments of Queen Elizabeth I*, ed. by Archer and others, pp. 247–67.

[17] Butler, p. 21.

[18] Anderson, p. 20.

[19] In his poem 'On the Famous Voyage' (c. 1610) Jonson swiped at the notion of the Arthurian quest by comparing it with an ill-advised expedition to navigate a London sewer, and in his later poem 'An Execration upon Vulcan' (1623) he scoffed at tales of 'The Tristrams, Lancelots, Turpins and the Peers'. See *The Cambridge Edition of the Works of Ben Jonson*, ed. by David Bevington and others, 7 vols (Cambridge: Cambridge University Press, 2012), V, 133; VII, 169. As early as 1589, Thomas Nashe derided chivalric romances as 'worne out impressions of feyned no where acts', in *The Anatomie of Absurditie* (London: I. Charlewood & T. Hacket, 1589), sig. Aii^r. Nevertheless, Prince Henry was actively engaged in promoting chivalric architecture and culture in his masques *Prince Henry's Barriers* (1610) and *Oberon, the Fairy Prince* (1611).

sports, which by 1624 were highly contentious pastimes. By the time Jonson co-opted the ghost of Captain Cox for his *Masque of Owls*, he had become the object of sentimental nostalgia, and Cox rousingly opens the masque with the medieval mummers' proclamation of 'Room, room', providing a vital link between the vigorous neo-medieval chivalry espoused by Henry VIII and the Stuart heir apparent, Prince Charles, for whom it was performed. Jonson takes pains to establish this chivalric lineage by telling us that 'This Captain Cox, by Saint Mary, | Was at Bullen [Boulogne] with King Harry', and then goes on to detail his remarkable library and role in the Kenilworth entertainment of 1575.[20] The 'owls' featured in the masque are a collection of bankrupts, undone by the deceit and sharp practices of others, as well as by political and religious changes. Thus, the masque conspicuously juxtaposes the old-style valour and virtue of Cox with his modern contemporaries, revealing a moral as well as a financial bankruptcy. Most pointed of all, perhaps, is the tale of a maker of embroidery thread, whose business has collapsed with the Puritan abolition of local sports and festivities, for his thread was used by revellers to decorate their clothes. In her analysis of *Pleasure Reconciled to Virtue* (1617) and *The King's Entertainment at Welbeck* (1633), Leah Marcus has shown how closely engaged Jonson was in defending royally sanctioned regional sports and festivities from erosion by local, Puritan parish councils.[21] The succinct *Masque of Owls* shows the same political and cultural preoccupations, castigating the corruptions of the present by contrasting them with the more wholesome ways of the past, epitomized by the neo-chivalric, albeit nostalgic, figure of Captain Cox.

Furnivall was intrigued by Captain Cox, and indeed it was curiosity about him that triggered the 1890 edition of *Laneham's Letter*. Cox was a real person who became a mythical figure in Jonson's reworkings of the Kenilworth entertainment, the mythologizing of him being facilitated by the fact that 'very little is known of Cox beyond the description provided by Laneham'.[22] He was a Coventry mason of standing in the community, functioning as marshall for local musters, as well as alecunner (that is, an officer to ensure the quality and price of ale). Cox participated in the Hock play performed with other

---

[20] Ben Jonson, *The Masque of Owls at Kenilworth (1624)*, ed. by James Knowles, in *The Cambridge Edition of the Works of Ben Jonson*, ed. by Bevington and others, v, 673–84 (p. 677, l. 23; p. 678, l. 23).

[21] Leah Marcus, 'Pleasure and Virtue Reconciled: Jonson's Celebration of the Book of Sports, 1618 and 1633', in *The Politics of Mirth: Jonson, Herrick, Milton, and Marvell and the Defense of Old Holiday Pastimes* (Chicago: University of Chicago Press, 1986), pp. 106–39. Martin Butler's recent analysis of *Pleasure Reconciled to Virtue* largely agrees with Marcus, but he also points out that 'the critique of Comus [in *Pleasure Reconciled to Virtue*] would have cut particularly close to the Whitehall bone' (p. 232).

[22] A. H. Bullen, 'Cox, Captain, of Coventry (fl. 1575)', rev. by Elizabeth Goldring, in *The Oxford Dictionary of National Biography* (Oxford: Oxford University Press, 2004) <http://www.oxforddnb.com/view/article/6517> [accessed 12 April 2013].

citizens for the enjoyment of Queen Elizabeth at Kenilworth, and possessed a remarkable library of ballads, plays, and stories, as well works on philosophy and medicine. Cox's local status is figured by the fact that he is the first to appear in the play of Danes versus Anglo-Saxons: 'Captain Cox cam marching on valiantly before, cleen trust, & gartered aboue the knee, all fresh in a velvet cap (master golding had lent it him) flourishing his tonswoord, and anothers fensmaster with him: thus in the foreward making room for the rest' (p. 14). Laneham's attitude to Cox is patronizing, focusing on his borrowed glories, and jibing at his prominent position among the local craftsmen. Yet we know that Laneham's voice, let alone judgement, is not to be trusted, as Patten's ventriloquism satirizes Laneham's own bumptious pretensions, and rescues Cox from his persona's snide superiority by including an extensive list of the works in Cox's library (pp. 29–31). Cox, then, is not to be dismissed lightly, although his books indicate a taste for popular reading as well as highbrow texts. The majority of the stories he possesses are chivalric romances, with rambling, fantastical plots and titles such as *Syr Eglamour* and *Sir Tryamour*. The inclusion of more folkloric tales, such as *Robinhood*, shows how the cult of chivalry was appropriated by the lower orders: Robin and his men possess a chivalry of spirit although they may not be knights of the Round Table; and Robin's fluid social status—he appears to have risen from commoner to aristocrat—must have particularly appealed to Cox, given his own 'yeoman' status and chivalric interests.

The figure of Robin Hood became even more politically charged in the seventeenth century, as in addition to the egalitarian spirit he embodied, he was closely associated with the defence of country sports under James I and then Charles I.[23] In *The King's Entertainment at Welbeck* Jonson continually emphasizes that the entertainment is culturally and geographically rooted in Sherwood Forest, part of the estates belonging to Jonson's patron, the Earl of Newcastle, and a natural home for following country sports. The Robin Hood games that had been part of rural festivities since medieval times, together with the material from his library, meant that Cox may have viewed Robin Hood as a folkloric defender of the people. Adherence to the community-based values behind the Robin Hood myth must have informed Cox's actions in leading his fellow citizens to petition Queen Elizabeth to reinstate the annual Hock play that had recently been abolished by the Puritan town councillors of Coventry. It may be argued, therefore, that Cox and his library stand for the democratization of chivalry. This defiance of cultural and class boundaries is clearly a source of amusement for Laneham, both in the figure of Cox himself and in the mock chivalric sports engaged in by the

---

[23] Lisa Hopkins, 'Play Houses: Drama at Bolsover and Welbeck', *Early Theatre*, 2.1 (1999), 25–44 (p. 28).

yeoman citizens, but his sneering attitude and language function to disable this scorn by revealing him as a social-climbing upstart. Laneham's apparently throwaway comment on Cox's hat ('master golding had lent it him' (p. 31)) reveals his sense of smug superiority and amusement at Cox's borrowed glories; but the following account of Cox's martial prowess disables Laneham's apparent superiority, as the text starkly juxtaposes the man of action with the smirking civil servant. Jonson underwrites the *Letter*'s legitimation of Cox by presenting him in *The Masque of Owls* as a representative of bygone chivalric codes, whose morality and rhetoric have shaped the development of country sports. For Jonson, although Cox is no aristocrat himself, his close connection to 'King Harry' guarantees his association with military prowess, and its chivalric expression in times of peace.

The presence of Captain Cox links *The Entertainment at Kenilworth* with King Harry's military campaigns in France, including that of the 'Field of Cloth of Gold'. This famous Anglo-French summit and *The Entertainment at Kenilworth* both deployed splendid yet temporary constructions, tented palaces providing venues for important feasts and meetings.[24] Leicester also understood the visual and experiential impact made by these often fanciful constructions, functioning as magnificence made tangible and even inhabitable. Leicester's aspirations to princely status are evinced by his deliberate evocation of Henry's tented splendours in France, when he welcomed Elizabeth, during her journey towards Kenilworth, with a banqueting tent erected at Itchington, seven miles from the castle. Laneham echoes the rhetoric of wonder found in Hall's and Holinshed's accounts of the Field of Cloth of Gold in 1520,[25] when he describes

A tabernacle indeed, for number and shift of large and goodlye roomz, for fair & easy offices, both inward and ooutward, and al so likesum in order & eyesight, that iustly for dignitee may be comparabl with a beautifull Pallais, & for greatnes & quantitee with a proper tooun, or rather, a Citadell [. . .]. This tent had seaven cart lode of pynz pertaining too it: now for the greatness, gess az ye can. (p. 36)

We can only guess how big this 'tabernacle' was, but given that it required seven cartloads of tent pegs it was clearly more than a mere tent housing a banquet. The main banqueting area was separated from a series of smaller 'rooms', doubtless intended to provide privacy for the Queen when required, as well as housing cooks, their equipment, servants, stores, and even the musicians necessary for such a feast. The scale of the tent is indicated by Laneham's

[24] For a full description of the Field of Cloth of Gold (1520) see Jocelyne Russell, *The Field of Cloth of Gold: Men and Manners in 1520* (London: Routledge & Kegan Paul, 1969).
[25] Edward Hall, *The Union of the Two Noble and Illustre Families of Lancastre & Yorke* [. . .] (London: Rychard Graften, 1550), fol. lxxiiii^r; Raphael Holinshed, *The Chronicles of England, from William the Conqueror* [. . .] (London: printed in Aldersgate Street at the Signe of the Starre, 1585), p. 857.

escalating list of comparisons: it was a palace, a citadel, a town. There may be some exaggeration here, intended for comic effect, and accounted for by Laneham's sycophantic attitude towards his master; but, at the very least, it was certainly a large construction divided into several areas for diverse offices, also well ordered and beautiful. It may be that it was dismantled and moved and was the same 'fair pavilion' that was erected at Wedgenall ten days later, to provide accommodation where 'her Majesty [was] too have supped', 'but by meanz of weather not so cleerly disposed, the matter was countermaunded again' (p. 56). Gascoigne's masque of nymphs composed to follow this banquet was also scrapped, which the author attributed to poor weather, but may have had as much to do with the Queen's dislike of the masque's content, as it championed wedded bliss at the expense of chastity.[26] If this is indeed the case, the cancellation of the masque is further evidence of Elizabeth's determination to escape the constricting web of ideology scripted for and about her by others, and instead to reserve her right of non-compliance and self-determination.[27]

The prolonged poor weather at Kenilworth rather belies the mythic fiction underpinning the whole event, co-invented and authored by Leicester, Gascoigne, Laneham, and others, that the gods showered gifts and blessings on the Queen, her host, and the landscape as tokens of their devotion and approval. Towards the end of his account, Laneham becomes carried away by poetic hyperbole and lists the gifts bestowed by various gods, including Aeolus, who made his presence felt by '[h]olding up hiz windez while her highness at any tyme took pleasure on the water, and staying of tempests during [her] abode heer' (p. 46). The ideological pressure in this event is such that Laneham, at the very best, resorts to telling partial truths in an effort to cast the best light on events; given that those who attended the Kenilworth entertainment would have personally experienced the inclement weather, this is a further example of the text undercutting its nominal author, revealing his ability to sacrifice the prickly truth in favour of more palatable fictions or partial truths that help to inflate his patron's prestige. Gascoigne tells us clearly that bad weather prompted the cancellation of his masque, and that the visit was plagued throughout by summer storms, alternately oppressively hot so that the Queen would not venture out, and then wet and windy. By about 19 July, at the time of the cancellation of the Wedgenall banquet, the proceedings were going so badly that 'thear was such earnest talk & appointment of remoouing' (p. 36).

In the event, the Queen stayed for another week, and on her eventual de-

---

[26] On the cancellation of his masque Gascoigne writes: 'The cause whereof I cannot attribute to any other thing, than to lack of opportunitie and seasonable weather' (p. 120).

[27] This point alludes to Montrose's concept of the Elizabethan 'imaginary': those rhetorical and ideological practices that determined the Queen's representation at large. See Montrose, p. 2.

parture Gascoigne composed and performed in a hastily constructed show to accompany her as she left the castle grounds. In the guise of Sylvanus he declared: 'Surely if your highnesse did understand (as it is not to me unknowen) what pleasures for you have been prepared [. . .] [you would] never [. . .] wander any further.'[28] The comment in parenthesis must surely be an ironic jibe at the fact that Gascoigne's major work for the entertainment had been shelved, even after the performers had been ready and in costume for two or three days; this final entertainment represents Leicester's last attempt to address his Queen, and Gascoigne's last chance to lobby for patronage. The soldier-poet draws on all his wit to create a plot where, as Sylvanus, he visited the gods to find 'nothing but weeping and wayling, crying and howling, dole, desperation, mourning and moane' prompted by the news that the Queen intended to depart from Kenilworth shortly. Somewhat neatly, this divine despair was communicated when 'the skies scowled, the windes raged, the waves rored and tossed, but also the Fishes in the waters turned up their bellies, the Dere in the woods went drowping, the grass was weary of growing, the Trees shook off their leaves, and all the Beastes of the Forrest stoode amazed'.[29] Thus intemperate summer weather has been extrapolated into a hellish vision of loss and entropy; and more significantly, it is the Queen who is directly responsible. This artful displacement of responsibility exonerates both Leicester and Gascoigne as the progenitors of the Queen's displeasure, through their roles as patron and composer of the offensive masque that was eventually vetoed, and firmly points to the Queen's determination to leave Kenilworth as the reason for the bad weather and for souring the heavenly bliss first evoked by her arrival. Gascoigne/Sylvanus delivered all this information on foot, following Elizabeth as she rode away, and although the Queen offered to stop he urged her to continue. Thus, we have an image of Gascoigne jogging after the Queen, delivering his lines breathlessly, as she continued to depart; the construction of this leaving entertainment insists on the Queen's departure, which is so essential to its rather disingenuous rationalizing of the less successful aspects of the entertainment which had lasted more than two weeks.

The fate of Gascoigne's masque of *Zabeta*, as well as his hasty composition and personal delivery of the farewell entertainment, underscore that no matter how carefully planned and richly resourced the Kenilworth entertainment was, many of its elements were improvised or scrapped at the last minute as the royal schedule or taste dictated. Some commentators on the representation of Elizabeth have emphasized how she was constrained by the overlapping ideologies of the day regarding monarchy and the gendered sub-

---

[28] Gascoigne, p. 121.
[29] Ibid., pp. 122, 123.

jectivity of women—what Montrose terms the Elizabethan 'imaginary'. This model of the Queen's rhetorical and visual representation is clearly based in a New Historicist understanding of ideology always involving the entrapment of the individual.[30] However, after reading Gascoigne and Laneham carefully it becomes apparent that the schedule of events and planned performances was disrupted not least because the Queen resisted the role she was assigned to play in the Kenilworth script by the co-authors, Leicester and Gascoigne. Thus, the constraints exerted by the Elizabethan 'imaginary' were apprehended in actuality by the Queen, who chose from time to time to assert her royal independence and autocracy by refusing to comply with the scripts already written for her by others. Perhaps the most obvious example of such non-compliance took place in a scenario devised to greet the Queen as she penetrated into the base court of the castle, taking in the lower pool, on the evening of her arrival. *Laneham's Letter* describes how the Arthurian Lady of the Lake appeared on a floating island, ablaze with torchlight, and she delivered lines composed by George Ferrers as she floated to land. These lines briefly sketched the history of the castle to the present time, and the Lady of the Lake then offered up her power and 'the Lake, the Lodge, the Lord' to the Queen's command, pledging to follow her to court. We cannot know how the inventors of this scene expected the Queen to respond, but probably they anticipated some gracious acknowledgement of this expression of loyalty. Such an acknowledgement did not even require speech, but could have been indicated with a physical gesture, which may be why the Queen decided to offer her own pithy rejoinder to these verses, reminding the Lady, and Leicester, that Kenilworth belonged to the monarch as a part of her realm: 'we had thought indeed the Lake had been oours, and doo you call it yourz now? Wel, we will herein common more with yoo heerafter' (p. 7).

In this improvised performance of her own, Elizabeth rejected Leicester's claims dressed in the language and myth of Arthurian chivalry, and instead

---

[30] Montrose, p. 3. Much of what has been written about Elizabeth's representation is a question of emphasis, so that whereas Archer and Knight describe in detail Elizabeth's crucial yet also peripheral presence at pageants staged in her honour, where her role was prescribed for her by others, they also note 'the Queen's strategic use of equivocation and silence' (Jayne Elisabeth Archer and Sarah Knight, 'Elizabetha Triumphans', in *The Progresses, Pageants and Entertainments of Elizabeth I*, ed. by Archer and others, pp. 1–23 (p. 12)). Other scholars tending to this view include John N. King, Carole Levin, and Helen Hackett, whereas Janel Mueller and Anna Riehl focus on episodes where Queen Elizabeth successfully resists the entrapment model of the Elizabethan 'imaginary' to supersede ideologies relating to gender and status, and to assert herself in new ways. See John N. King, 'Queen Elizabeth I: Representations of the Virgin Queen', *Renaissance Quarterly*, 43 (Spring 1990), 30–74; Carole Levin, *The Heart and Stomach of a King: Elizabeth I and the Politics of Sex and Power* (Philadelphia: University of Pennsylvania Press, 1994); Helen Hackett, *Virgin Mother, Maiden Queen* (Basingstoke: Macmillan, 1996); Janel Mueller, *Virtue and Virtuality: Gender in the Self-Representation of Queen Elizabeth I* (Chicago: University of Chicago Press, 2001); Anna Riehl, *The Face of Queenship: Early Modern Representations of Elizabeth I* (Basingstoke: Palgrave Macmillan, 2010).

asserted the power and scope of monarchy, emphasizing her status in its abstract, ideal state, rather than her personal position as a woman, speaking as 'we' rather than 'I'. The Elizabethan manifestation of the 'King's two bodies' theory gave the Queen a masculine status as monarch, a role often in tension with her biological gender. Indeed, Elizabeth seized on opportunities to stress continuities between her personality and reign and her father's, although Henry was much more extensively the author of his own personal spectacle, from the formal exchanges with other monarchs to the display of physical prowess in horsemanship. Henry was the lead actor in his masks and tournaments, the people were the spectators of his personal theatre. Elizabeth was restrained by current notions of acceptable female behaviour, but also liberated by the unarguable fact that she was monarch. So although she became the royal audience of spectacles performed before her by her subjects, rather than a performer in her own right, she exercised the right to step out of the role written for her, to express her own view spontaneously. Thus, she chose to interpolate herself into the prepared scripts written for and about her in unexpected ways, traversing the tensions occasioned by her status as a female monarch.

The neoclassical and pastoral rhetorical structure of the Kenilworth entertainment is not only undone by the poor weather and Elizabeth's non-compliance, but also by its material circumstances; and indeed, the potential satirical content of pastoral, its unravelling from within as its ideal is shown to fall far short of the real, is inbuilt from its earliest manifestations.[31] Thus the predetermined ideological collapse of pastoral as an aesthetic in the Kenilworth entertainment is a further point of contact with Jonson, that most neoclassical of poets, whose seminal country-house poems, 'To Penshurst' and 'To Robert Wroth', register the evocation of a classically based pastoral ideal under threat from modern vice, both from outside the charmed realm of feudal paradise and from within it.[32] Jonson's absorption of Laneham's letter into *The Masque of Owls* and *The King's Entertainment at Welbeck* was established by C. H. Herford and Percy and Evelyn Simpson, and his problematizing of pastoral has been outlined by Raymond Williams.[33] The fractured nature of Jonsonian pastoral has a classical provenance, and while he used the *Letter* as source material for his own festive works, his country-house poems exhibit a consciousness of the internal ironies of the genre that Laneham

---

[31] Jonson's translation of Horace's second epode, 'The Praises of a Country Life', reveals the vision of bucolic innocence to be a fantasy bought through the proceeds of usury and underpinned by it. See *The Cambridge Edition of the Works of Ben Jonson*, ed. by Bevington and others, VII, 279–85.

[32] 'To Penshurst' and 'To Sir Robert Wroth', ibid., V, 209–14, 215–20.

[33] *Ben Jonson*, ed. by C. H. Herford and Percy and Evelyn Simpson, 11 vols (Oxford: Clarendon Press, 1925–52), X (1950), 700; Raymond Williams, *The Country and the City in the Modern Novel* (Oxford: Oxford University Press, 1975), pp. 26–34.

does not—doubtless a further aspect of the satirical intentions of the letter's real author, parodying the aspirational court servant's aping of high culture when he is unable to appreciate its nuanced subtleties. Further resonances between Laneham's narrative of the Kenilworth entertainment and Jonson's pastoral panegyric become apparent when we remember how important patronage from the extended Sidney family was for both, an economic reality always lurking behind the most effusive praise or poised poetry, despite Jonson's poetics emphatically placing the patron in the poet's debt. In pragmatic terms, there is much similarity between Jonson's praise of his patron's conservative values in 'To Penshurst', and Laneham's effusions about the brassy splendours of Kenilworth and Leicester's largesse.[34]

In keeping with the accepted visual scope and direction of movement within pastoral, Laneham first praises the wonders of Kenilworth Castle itself before he moves on to describe the gardens and park generally. He evokes a castle brilliant with glass and light:

euery room so spacious, so wel belighted, and so hy roofed within: So seemely too sight by du proportion without: a day time on euery side so glittering by glasse, a nights by continuall brightnesse of candel, fyre and torchlight, transparent through lightsome wyndz, az it wear the egiptian Pharos. (p. 48)

This brilliance is a result of Leicester's 'advancements', and contrasts significantly with Jonson's Penshurst, which is not 'built to envious show' but is rather 'an ancient pile' which 'joyst in better marks, of soil, of air | Of wood, of water'.[35] Laneham is full of wonder at Kenilworth's garden, to which he was not normally admitted but was given entrance by a friend, possibly a gardener, when the Queen was absent hunting. Furnivall prefaces Laneham's panegyric on the garden with a long note recording that 'the magnificent gardens and spacious parks at Kenilworth were not completed without some oppression on the part of their possessor' (p. 48), who appears to have driven up rents and seized common lands to extend his ground, although Furnivall does question the veracity of some of the more extreme accusations levelled at Leicester. He astutely comments that '[t]he garden mentioned in the text will doubtless remind some readers of those splendid pleasure-grounds which belonged to Lord Burleigh at Theobalds in Hertfordshire and Sir Walter Raleigh's at Shirburne Castle in Dorsetshire' (p. 49); that is to say, Kenilworth was one of the flashy prodigy houses and gardens eschewed by Jonsonian

[34] However, Jonson was not personally enamoured of Robert Sidney, remarking in his conversations with William Drummond that '[m]y Lord Lisle's daughter, my Lady Wroth, is unworthily married on a jealous husband' (*The Cambridge Edition of the Works of Ben Jonson*, ed. by Bevington and others. v, 275). On Jonson's poetics, insisting on the debt owed by patron to poet, see Stanley Fish, 'Authors–Readers: Jonson's Community of the Same', in *Representing the English Renaissance*, ed. by Stephen Greenblatt (Berkeley: University of California Press, 1988), pp. 231–64.

[35] 'To Penshurst', pp. 209–10.

pastoral and its apparent manifestations at Penshurst and at Wroth's estate in Essex. Laneham's evocation of the continual 'Paradys' that is Kenilworth takes in both sculptural and floral wonders, but also the important concept of abundance or *cornucopia*, as the grounds provide a range of seasonal fruit and flowers available at once, from late apples and pears to the early cherry (p. 50). Penshurst too has its abundance of fruit:

> The early cherry, with the later plum
> Fig, grape and quince, each in his time doth come;
> The blushing apricot and woolly peach
> Hang on thy walls, that every child may reach.[36]

Such echoes between the two texts are further evidence that Jonson had read Laneham's letter and that it informed not only The *Masque of Owls* and *The King's Entertainment at Welbeck*, but also his poetry at large. At Kenilworth this magical abundance was linked with Leicester's personal largesse, as well as the plenty provided by his gardens, and was powerfully represented in the welcome staged for the Queen, when she passed a series of iconic pedestals bearing corn, wine, fruit, and birds. In emphasizing the scope of his giving, Leicester underscores his power to give in princely fashion, an attitude that seems to have irritated the Queen from time to time.[37]

Leicester's emulation of princely grandeur was carefully fashioned in terms of late medieval chivalry, and was a bold and risky strategy given his recent family history involving his father's attempt to seize the Crown for Lady Jane Grey and Leicester's brother, Guildford Dudley. If he could not be brother-in-law to a reigning Queen, he could aspire even higher and aim to marry one. This overweening ambition may explain why so much of the Kenilworth festivities were based on a Henrician model, with masques, fireworks, hunting, tilting, banqueting, and so on, all packaged with a neo-chivalric setting and props. There was even bear-baiting, and the presence of the Lady of the Lake made Kenilworth's Arthurian pretensions clear. In presenting himself and his seat in these terms, Leicester declared his status as Henry's natural heir, and thus a meet companion for Elizabeth his daughter, both as a spiritual brother and as an obvious husband. I have already discussed the intriguing figure of Captain Cox, and if Jonson was later right about Cox's history of fighting with King Henry in France, it becomes clear that his pre-eminence at the Kenilworth festivities is at least partly due to the royal associations he brought with him: Kenilworth was presented as the natural stage for Henry's heirs and peers. Nevertheless, Cox's presence and achievements open up a very different

---

[36] Ibid., p. 212.
[37] The Queen's reminder to the Lady of the Lake that Kenilworth belonged to her as part of her realm may be seen as a check to Leicester's insistent display of his generous largesse.

version of chivalry from that espoused by Leicester: that of community and self-discipline, rather than neo-medieval, princely largesse.

While the presence of bear-baiting at Kenilworth underwrites the castle's medieval provenance, other neo-chivalric entertainments are rather more compromised, serving both to connect with an earlier age and to provide a class-based comedy derived from the fact that local countrymen mix rustic festivity with traditionally aristocratic pursuits. In fact, while the Tudor revival of chivalry was part of the serious ideological justification of monarchy, its most overblown productions were always prey to satire, from Nashe's comic take on the neo-chivalric tournament, to Jonson's satirical pastiche of the knightly quest in 'On The Famous Voyage', narrating the navigation of a London sewer.[38] The Kenilworth bride-ale with its neo-medieval tilt may be said to represent a third version of neo-chivalry, neither princely nor communal, but satirical. On Sunday, 17 July a bride-ale was staged for the entertainment of spectators. There are clues in the Laneham text indicating that this was indeed not a real bride-ale but a comic performance of rustic traditions, for the amusement of those who, like Laneham, considered themselves socially and culturally superior to the country folk involved. Yet Furnivall's meticulous scholarship reminds us that while the bride-ale was, like the morris dance, a medieval and rural pastime, it was also enjoyed and performed by the highest rank, and that at the marriage of James I's daughter, Elizabeth, to the Elector Palatine in 1614, the wedding was celebrated with 'draughts of Ippocras out of a great golden bowle' (p. 21). The royal bride-ale was presented in emphatically neo-medieval terms when it was accompanied by the serving of sweet wafers, a great favourite treat of the medieval court. This gesture, however, was more than likely politically motivated, demonstrating the King's support for traditional rural pastimes against erosion from puritanically minded local councils. The King's views and policies in such matters were codified in *The Book of Sports*, published in 1617, three years after the royal wedding, and it explicitly legitimated and promoted the role of traditional pastimes, even on the Sabbath day. So while Furnivall is correct to note this aristocratic bride-ale, it was not typical of aristocratic wedding practices, either in the medieval or the early modern period, but a ritual of the rural parish adopted by King James in 1614 to make an ideological point, and performed at Kenilworth to give further weight to Leicester's personal myth of feudal lordship over the labourers from his estates.[39]

---

[38] Thomas Nashe, *The Unfortunate Traveller*, ed. by J. B. Steane (Harmondsworth: Penguin, 1972), pp. 316–23; Ben Jonson, 'On the Famous Voyage', in *The Cambridge Edition of the Works of Ben Jonson*, ed. by Bevington and others. v, 133.

[39] Ronald Hutton, *The Stations of the Sun: A History of the Ritual Year in Britain* (Oxford: Oxford University Press, 1996), p. 137. Hutton shows how the origin of the bride-ale is related to the festivities of Saint Brigid, and evolved into a rural celebration of spring and ultimately marriage.

Returning to 1575, the bride-ale at Kenilworth was clearly a comedy of country bumpkins, closer to pantomime than to the solemnities of marriage. The humble and improvised attire of the groom and his supporters is emphasized in the Laneham text, the groom's costume rendering him ridiculous, with 'a pen & inkhorn at his bak, for he woold be knowen to be bookish' (p. 22). The comedy in this whole scenario rests on the gap between the aspirations and reality of the performers, an effect which is compounded when the bride-ale gives way to a tournament or tilting at the quintain. The fact that this is a staged performance and not a real bride-ale or tournament is given away when the text says that his actions were as formal 'az had he been a bride groom indeed' (p. 22). Thus the bride-ale was a staged comic performance of rural community life, and the 'featz of arms' ratcheted up the high comedy by presenting yokels aping aristocratic customs. Though it was composed by the inventors of *The Entertainment at Kenilworth* and largely performed by local people, it is nonetheless possible that some professional or semi-professional actors were involved; after all, Gascoigne refers to 'actors' who were to perform his abandoned masque, and 'Actoourz' provided a play that evening (p. 120). Laneham's praise of their performance skills, which made the time seem short 'though it lasted too good oourz and more' (p. 32), indicates that these were professional actors, yet it is impossible that the numbers required by the bride-ale and subsequent tournament could be supplied by a professional troupe of actors alone.

Community participation in *The Entertainment at Kenilworth* certainly took place in the Hock play following the bride-ale, for Captain Cox and other local worthies were the performers of this traditional play presenting a historic battle between the Danes and Saxons. In staging the bride-ale the local community colluded in its own ridicule for the amusement of aristocratic observers. Comedy is forced from the aesthetic discrepancy between rural and aristocratic rituals, and this episode deliberately juxtaposes neo-chivalric with rural pastimes, showing how ridiculous country folk make themselves when they ape aristocratic manners and pursuits, with the young men on horseback falling off and ploughing into the audience in a knockabout pastiche of the chivalric tournament. In this farce, not only are the uncouth yokels the subject of apparent satire, but the cult of neo-chivalry itself is placed under comic scrutiny as it is shown to have percolated through to popular culture to such an extent that it is no longer a viable cultural practice, defining and separating the aristocracy from everyone else. From the point of view of cultural theory, it may be argued that the devaluation of chivalric forms and practices is inevitable: as high culture is desired and appropriated by the lower orders as a sign of status, it no longer operates as high culture or separates the social classes. In our own times, we might call this the Burberry effect. *The*

Entertainment at Kenilworth, then, represents a radical revision of the notion of chivalry—debasing its traditional value, but simultaneously offering a new model of community-based chivalry, evidenced by the true nobility of spirit and action witnessed in the Hock play, where the bravery of English men and women repulsed an invasion of the Danes. While Laneham is quick to laugh at Captain Cox and his peers, they represent a common valour that ensures the safety of the nation. It is significant that, in *The Masque of Owls*, Jonson later seizes on Cox's connection with King Henry and the 1544 campaign in France. Cox and Henry are united by a chivalry of spirit and action that has nothing to do with the usual aristocratic associations.

The audience of this comic bride-ale witnessed the collapse of class-oriented practices into each other as the groom's party processed past the quintain prior to engaging in 'featz of arms' (p. 21), the very aristocratic activity that motivated and was the basis for the meeting of nations at the Field of Cloth of Gold in 1520. The procession was followed by a morris dance 'in the aunciene manner' (p. 22), and then three 'puzels' or maidens, 'bright as a brest of bacon' (p. 23), carried spice cakes before the bride. There is clearly a gendered prejudice at work here, as the 'puzels' and the bride are thirty years old, hardly the young girls who might be expected—and, indeed, the homely bacon simile suggests rather florid and less than youthful complexions. Yet while the women are ugly and old, the men are callow and inept: the young man in charge of the bride cup is described as a 'loovely lubber worts, freklfaced' (p. 23) whose chivalric fortitude of spirit is demonstrated as he swats the flies buzzing around the old sucket barrel which served the office of a bride cup. The bride, as might be expected, is a very unappealing creature: 'a stale stallion [. . .] il smelling, waz she: a thirtie yeer old' (p. 24). If we assume 'stallion' here has the meaning of 'male horse used for breeding', as it is still used, we might think that this description indicates that the 'bride' may have been a male actor cross-dressed for the part. However, Furnivall states that 'stallion' was a term of 'reproval' applied to women, and his citations suggest the sense of an older woman who ensnares foolish victims (p. 24). Semantics aside, it is also very possible that the 'bride' was a woman belonging to the local community, as the Hock festivities traditionally involved the participation of feisty Coventry women who paraded captive 'Danes', and only released their prisoners on payment of a fee. The Laneham text does mention that, at the Kenilworth version of the battle, 'many [were] led captive for triumph by our English wemmen' (p. 32). Again, the implied numbers suggest that more parts were required in this spectacle than could be supplied by a band of professional actors; furthermore, female participation in the Hock play may have been one reason why the local council wished to shut it down. The Coventry men assumed that the spectacle of women parading captive Danes would particularly appeal to their female monarch, specifically as the women were motivated by 'love of their cuntree' and they thought this presentation of female bravery and patriotism 'mooought move sum myrth to her Maiestie' (p. 27). Thus, it appears that women were involved in *The Entertainment at Kenilworth* to a much wider extent than has been acknowledged or was even usual in pageants of this kind, potentially including the Lady of the Lake, the comic bride, and her bridesmaids, and definitely involving the plucky women of Coventry.

More comedy is squeezed out of this pantomime as the bride is determined to dance before the Queen, when clearly she was not skilled in the art. The male equivalent to the apparently feminine courtly accomplishment of dance was 'featz of arms' or tilting at the quintain, and jousting on horseback, which turns out to be a slapstick affair with riders falling off and horses ploughing into the spectators. Laneham assures us that the whole spectacle was funny enough to 'have mooued sum man too a right meery mood, though had it be toold him hiz wife lay a dying' (p. 26). The remarkably poor taste of this metaphor clearly reflects badly on Laneham, but also its extremity is designed to express the extreme humour of the occasion, so the more serious Coventry play may have provided the audience some relief after this increasingly intense, knockabout comedy.

Jonson's imaginative debt to *The Entertainment at Kenilworth* in *The Masque of Owls* (1624), also staged at Kenilworth, has already been described. But this debt is even greater in *The King's Entertainment at Welbeck* (1633), where thematic and linguistic similarities almost suggest a 'sampling' of the earlier festivities, to use an anachronistic term. In Renaissance literary theory, 'sampling' is better understood as *imitatio*, and it is one of Jonson's key poetic strategies. At the core of this literary practice is borrowing from the ancients in order to say something telling about the present, and many critics have written about this aspect of Jonson's work.[40] The obvious question to ask is: what is Jonson trying to tell his audience at Welbeck via *The Entertainment at Kenilworth*? Most obviously, it must be that Welbeck and its owner are the legitimate successors to Kenilworth and Leicester, as pointed out by Hopkins and Knowles. Leicester's role as adviser and confidant to the monarch was aspired to by the Earl of Newcastle, and, while he supported his monarch, he was dissatisfied with Charles's style of personal rule. In *The King's Entertainment at Welbeck* Jonson deliberately appropriated aspects of *The Entertainment at Kenilworth*, and adapted them to state even more clearly that outside the metropolis it is the regional magnate's authority that is of relevance rather than the monarch's, who is a remote and rather abstract entity. This is evidenced

---

[40] See especially Richard Peterson, *Imitation and Praise in the Poems of Ben Jonson*, 2nd edn (Aldershot: Ashgate, 2011).

by the way in which the entertainment draws on the language of masque to eulogize the monarch in abstract philosophical and spiritual terms. The two main characters, Fitz-Ale and Accidence, fail to recognize the King, and furthermore, they prioritize Newcastle.[41] On the one hand, this could be a joke at their expense: revealing the ignorance of rural types was a common strategic opener for the Jonsonian antimasque. Yet both men are learned, and Fitz-Ale quite clearly declares: 'we have nothing to say to the King, till we have spoken with my Lord Lieutenant' (p. 668, l. 57).[42] Fitz-Ale '[h]ath a daughter stale' who is to be wed to one Stub, and what follows is described as a 'bridalty' (p. 673, l. 146) with jousting at the quintain. In *The Entertainment at Kenilworth* bride-ale, the bride was similarly a 'stale stallion', and the great age of both brides is remarked on. The bride-ale has become a bridal tea, but bears the same hallmarks of bowl-bearer and cake-bearer, who appear as twinned clowns. The old-fashioned dress of the bride, 'after the cleanliest country guise' (p. 676, l. 226), is particularly distinguished by a 'great wrought Handkerchiefe' (p. 676, l. 224) presumably decorated in a manner disapproved of by the local parish council. Jonson had already underlined the economic impact of such religiously motivated restrictions on traditional costume in *The Masque of Owls*, where a thread-maker is one of the bankrupts featured.

In *The King's Entertainment at Welbeck* six 'hoods' (p. 673, l. 154), the legitimate successors to Robin Hood, participate in the neo-chivalric exercise of tilting at the quintain—again a deliberate echo of *The Entertainment at Kenilworth*—and Jonson is unable to resist having a jibe at his typical satirical targets: Motley-hood and Russet-hood represent the law and parish authority respectively, and both fall from their horses, while Green-hood (representing the forest) and Blew-hood (representing the yeomen of old England) achieve successful runs. Hopkins asserts that *The King's Entertainment at Welbeck* is not a masque and that it rather fits into the genre of country-house entertainment. Indeed, it is different from the customary Whitehall masque in some key respects: not least, its location in Nottinghamshire emphasizes the authority of Newcastle before that of the King, despite the fact that the King was a spectator and a prime cause of the entertainment. It is not a masque because it lacks the participation of aristocratic dancers (who normally per-

---

[41] Jonson, *The King's Entertainment at Welbeck*, in *The Cambridge Edition of the Works of Ben Jonson*, ed. by Bevington and others. vi, 665–80. Subsequent references are given parenthetically.

[42] Accidence's opening question, 'Which is the King?' (p. 668), allows for an open interpretation: it may be read as a comic swipe at parochial ignorance, when even the local schoolmaster is unable to recognize the monarch; but it may also insinuate that the King's lack of royal charisma or outstanding personal qualities means that he does not stand out from the crowd. As an opening strategy for royal entertainment, this is reminiscent of Jonson's *The Irish Masque at Court* (1614), in which, at the outset, the Irish footmen are unable to pick out the King despite his central position in the audience. Their failure to recognize King James in this instance speaks of the cultural, geographical, and national distance between the English Crown and Ireland.

formed silently), probably being executed instead by a mix of professional actors and amateurs associated with Newcastle's household.[43] Nevertheless, *Welbeck* does feature some of the elements that had increasingly distinguished the developing antimasque up until the accession of Charles I, when there was a shift in royal taste regarding masque as a whole. Prior to 1625, the evolving antimasque featured elements such as dramatic interaction, broad and often bawdy comedy, and comic song, with an emphasis on the material appetites. The fact that Jonson wrote *The King's Entertainment at Welbeck* as a kind of antimasque also speaks tellingly of the limits of royal taste, and asserts the authority and taste of poet and patron. While this is not a Whitehall masque, the gentleman who admonishes the entertainment's characters for their 'rudeness' and declares the King's status as 'Parent' and 'Pastor' reproduces the rhetoric of court masque, stressing the monarch's divine sanction, his exceptional personal characteristics as the basis for strong government, and his vital place in ensuring the succession of the Crown, ending the entertainment with a rousing, pseudo-religious association of Charles and Great Britain:

> Let us pray
> That Fortune never know to exercise
> More power upon him, then as *Charles* his servant,
> And his *Great Britain's* slave: ever to waite
> Bond-woman to the GENIUS of this state!
> (p. 680, ll. 313-17)

Bearing in mind that it was three years since Jonson had last been asked to reprise his long-held role of court poet and compose a Whitehall masque, *Welbeck*'s assertion of political, geographical, and artistic independence fused with an expression of fierce loyalty to the King and Crown seems especially significant for both Jonson and Newcastle, who exploit the precedent of Kenilworth to declare themselves as royalists whose exceptional status should mean that they are at the heart of government, rather than relegated to the edges of power.[44]

Jonson's source text also champions court outsiders and questions the

[43] A. P. Martinich suggests that the philosopher Thomas Hobbes played the character of Fitz-Ale in *The King's Entertainment at Welbeck*. Hobbes had a long association with the Cavendish family, and there are parallels between Fitz-Ale's function as herald and keeper of records relating to Nottinghamshire and Derbyshire, and Hobbes's Latin poem on the wonders of the Peak District, 'De mirabilibus Pecci', published in 1636 but assumed by Martinich to have been in circulation before this date. See A. P. Martinich, 'Thomas Hobbes in Ben Jonson's *The King's Entertainment at Welbeck*', *Notes and Queries*, 45 (1998), 370-72 (p. 370).

[44] In his well-known commonplace book, *Discoveries* (published 1641), Jonson recorded in many places his belief, derived from Horace, that poet-philosophers are obliged to advise monarchs on how to rule justly: for example, 'Learning needs rest: sovereignty gives it. Sovereignty needs council: learning affords it' (*The Cambridge Edition of the Works of Ben Jonson*, ed. by Bevington and others, VII, 499-59 (p. 152, ll. 47-48)). Also in *Discoveries*, he cites a Latin tag taken from Petronius, stressing the poet's unique status and philosophical relationship with the

validity and relevance of traditional courtly modes of behaviour—particularly neo-chivalric affectation—while holding on to the core values at the heart of the chivalric code. We have already witnessed Laneham's attempt to satirize and discredit Captain Cox and his accomplishments on the grounds of class status, and we have seen how an authorial stratum running through the work in turn shows Laneham to be ignorant and unqualified to pass such judgement. As the account of the Hock play proceeds, another rhetorical layer in the complex stratification of voices that is *The Entertainment at Kenilworth* emerges. This is the rhetoric of common chivalry, and the men of Coventry display all the unalloyed valour and clarity of purpose that knights of old were assumed to possess. Furthermore, the ancient provenance of their actions is stressed, indicating the historical and traditional continuity of their actions, just as the ways of feudal chivalry were justified by tradition and precedent. The Hock play, then, is legitimated by its longevity, but its association with Kenilworth and the Queen shows it to be part of the intellectual *Zeitgeist* of the day, embodied by William Camden's *Britannia*, begun in 1577, when historical and geographical analysis of the British Isles was a key aspect of nation-building. For the common men of Coventry, unrequited love for a noble lady was an irrelevant and fanciful conceit, and chivalric behaviour was defined on the battlefield. We are told that the play was performed by 'certain good harted men of Coventree' (p. 26), and while Laneham pokes humour at their actions and appearance, there is every indication that the Coventry men and women take the recreated battle most seriously, unlike the performers of the bride-ale, who deliberately played up the comedy of their performance. Laneham describes the play as an 'old storial show' and rehearses the historical background, stressing that the play has been performed annually since the eleventh century: 'it had an auncient beginning, and a long continuauns' (p. 27). As previously mentioned, the women of Coventry are said to have acted valiantly 'for looue of their cuntree', a further local adaptation of a traditionally masculine code of patriotic chivalry. In the recent past, the Hock play had been put down by local 'Preacherz', yet the text tells us that it was not marred by 'papistry' and 'did so occupy the hedz of a number, that likely innoough woold haue had woorz meditationz' (p. 27). So the Hock play had an improving, didactic effect on its performers, akin to the chivalric code's emphasis on self-improvement and personal discipline. This discipline extends to physical behaviour in the conduct of the battle, with both the Danes and English appearing in formation on horseback, bearing alder poles, 'marcially' (p. 31). The battle was pursued with energy and valour on both sides,

---

monarch: 'Solus rex aut poeta non quotannis nascitur' (p. 208: 'it is kings and poets alone that are not born every year'). It also needs remembering that Jonson was unwell during these last years of his life, a factor compounding his marginalization at court, as described in Donaldson, *Ben Jonson: A Life*, p. 399.

resulting in a 'blazing battail' (p. 31), but despite the fury of the encounter, the participants still showed that physical and inner discipline that allowed them to form into squadrons, and to trace out geometrical shapes (pp. 31–32).

Even Cox is given an Arthurian status concomitant with his artisan profession: 'by profession a Mason, and that right skillfull, very cunning in fens, and hardy as Gawin' (pp. 28–9). There is a significant equation here of his established skill in craft and his chivalric qualities of swordsmanship and physical toughness, showing how the culture of chivalry has moved from its traditional class-bound location, to be adapted and appropriated by others. Cox, in fact, is shown to be the guardian of the chivalric tradition with his extensive library listed, including many Arthurian legends as well as scholarly works on philosophy, poetry, and astronomy, again chiming with the chivalric code's emphasis on self-didacticism and its roots in literature. There is an insistent association in the text of his military prowess and his role as a prominent burgess and craftsman, as we learn that he was 'in the field a good Marshall at musters' and that he was highly regarded and repeatedly chosen to be 'alecunner' (p. 31). The way in which the text worries away at the overlapping of Cox's chivalric status with his middle-class social identity shows this shift in socio-cultural status to be a novelty meriting attention. While Laneham attempts to ridicule Cox in the same way that he jeered at the bride-ale rustics, this attempt at superior class-based satire collapses on two counts: firstly, the Kenilworth villagers satirize themselves, and knowingly play up their performance; secondly, Cox's association with King Henry, his military skill, his pre-eminence in the local community, his skill at masonry, and his learning all combine to elevate him above Laneham's jibes and present him as the guardian of a new, common chivalry that was so essential for national security, rather than the personal distinction pursued by knights of old.

After the Kenilworth bride-ale and Hock play, there was a further play performed by a professional troupe of actors, and then an 'Ambrosiall Banket: whereof, whither I might more muze at the deintynesse, shapez and the cost: or els at the variete & number of the disshez (that wear a three hundred), for my part I coold little tell them' (pp. 32–33). Laneham marvels at the banquet's governing aesthetic of rich plenty and exotic strangeness, associations that identify it as part of masque culture, and indeed it was to have been followed by a masque, cancelled at the last minute due to the lateness of the hour. Yet the wonder of the feast was undercut by its material circumstances: while the Queen 'eat smally or no-thing', 'the coorsez wear not so orderly serued, & sizely set dooun, but wear by and by az disorderly wasted & coorsly consumed; more courtly, me thought, then curteously' (p. 33). The semiotic slippage of 'coorsez', 'coorsly', 'courtly', and 'courteously' shows the court's aristocratic behaviour to be quite other than Laneham anticipated, and shows the semantic fluidity at play here when the court behaves like unpolished yokels and common villagers acquit themselves as chivalrous knights. However, if Laneham was really an inside expert on court culture he would know that the spoiling or ransacking of the banquet or associated masque was a long-established foible of the court, and profoundly linked to the late medieval/Renaissance concept of the monarch's largesse, who is so rich and powerful that he can afford to throw away, or give away without hesitation, priceless and beautiful objects. The Queen seems to be at the edge of this occasion, eating her 'small' meal and refusing to partake of Leicester's largesse—a refusal which may be read as a further act of self-assertion and non-cooperation with the entertainment's prepared script.

At the end of this long day the Queen was still determined to resist the exertions of the 'Elizabethan imaginary': a resolution which she had displayed from her initial encounter with the Lady of the Lake, to her departure followed by the jogging Gascoigne reciting his verse to her. Taken as a whole, *The Entertainment at Kenilworth* displays assumptions about the Queen's behaviour and attitudes, utilizing the rhetoric and stage properties of chivalry to proclaim Leicester's dominance. Nevertheless, just as the Queen refused to be coerced by Leicester throughout, so too did his chosen mode of chivalric action and language slip away from him, as it was shown to be both ripe for comic satire and the property of artisanal classes rather than the aristocracy of old. While this new popular form of chivalry had plenty of comic potential, it was also dignified by the personal achievements of its supporters, particularly the valiant and learned Captain Cox. Ben Jonson recognized the contrary nature of the Kenilworth entertainment, and drew on it for his *Masque of Owls* and *The King's Entertainment at Welbeck*, deploying the notion of community-based chivalry both to support royal policy on country sports and to assert the rights of poet and patron. Taken together, these entertainments show how the comic debunking and serious appropriation of chivalric values and sports by the middle classes are intimately linked with individual self-assertion against dominant ideology—an assertion of self that is also powerfully present in Queen Elizabeth's rejection of Leicester's attempt to exploit chivalric forms and language to serve his own ambitions.

GLASGOW   LESLEY MICKEL

'IL N'Y A PRESQUE PAS DE CES GÉNIES GRANDIOSES QUI ÉTONNENT LE MONDE': UNVEILING GENIUS IN DAVID D'ANGERS'S *PAGANINI*

Pierre-Jean David (1789–1856), usually called David d'Angers after his birthplace, to distinguish him from the painter Jacques-Louis David, was a major innovator in French sculpture of the 1830s. His works, while remaining in dialogue with the classical tradition he had absorbed at the École des Beaux-Arts in Paris, and the neoclassical ideals formulated by Johann Winckelmann in the late eighteenth century, also demonstrate a movement away from the received ideas of his academic education. This is suggested through the adoption of a dramatic and realist approach for which David became well known, executed mostly in his bronze works, with their heavily textured surfaces. As a result, David's œuvre has been considered difficult to pigeonhole. Its merging of 'occasional vague reminiscences of a moderated late neoclassicism, in certain marble monuments and busts' with 'Realism' and a 'Romantic hyperbole' has meant that 'a precise diagnosis and definition of David's historical position has eluded modern scholars'.[1] In his time, however, he was regarded as the sculptor who had brought about a definitive break with international neoclassicism; and the statue which was posited as heralding the French High Romanticism of the 1830s was his marble colossus of Louis XIV's general, the *Grand Condé*, commissioned in 1816. Other works of major importance include the equestrian statue on the tomb of General Gobert in the Père-Lachaise cemetery (1827); the bust of Goethe (1829); the sculptures on the pediment of the Panthéon, showing the main personages in France since the Revolution, grouped around a figure of 'La Patrie' (1830–37); and the *Philopoemen* in the Louvre (1837). Goethe was also celebrated in one of David's five hundred portrait medallions (1815–54), representing almost every major figure, including writers, painters, and musicians of the time. It was during his years of study at Rome that David vowed to devote his art to human grandeur and the glorification of great men, noble causes, and high accomplishments in thought, politics, the sciences, and the arts. In this he was motivated by the neoclassical idea that the immortalizing of exemplary genius could engender spiritual and moral edification. As Suzanne Nash put it, '"Commémorer et instruire": that was David's credo.'[2] Hence, many of the most famous men and women of David's time sat for his busts or medallions. A nearly complete collection of originals or copies is in the Musée des Beaux-Arts, Angers, and it

---

[1] James Holderbaum, 'Portrait Sculpture', in *The Romantics to Rodin*, ed. by Peter Fusco and H. W. Janson (Los Angeles: Los Angeles County Museum of Art in association with George Braziller, 1980), pp. 36–51 (p. 42).

[2] Suzanne Nash, 'Casting Hugo into History', *Nineteenth-Century French Studies*, 35 (2006), 189–205 (p. 191).

offers an interesting display of David's preferences in literature, the visual arts, and music. There are the literary luminaries of the day: Chateaubriand, Byron, Zola, Balzac, Georges Sand, Hugo, and Nodier (the last two names assume an importance in the present study). In painting, David pays homage to all of the great masters of the older generation, such as Jacques-Louis David, Ingres, and Géricault; but also to many contemporary Romantics, including Delacroix. In music, David immortalizes Cherubini, Spontini, and Rossini, but he chose not to celebrate either Chopin or Berlioz, whose work David believed to be marred by an egocentricity which detracted from the lofty moral intentions of art.

One portrait bust—that of the Italian virtuoso violinist and composer, Niccolò Paganini (1782–1840)—is inevitably afforded special, if cursory, mention in art dictionaries and essays devoted to David.[3] 'Arguably the greatest bust of Romanticism' (Holderbaum, 'Portrait Sculpture', p. 40), it has been described as constituting a 'revolution in modelled sculpture',[4] and hailed as 'la plus remarquable des œuvres du même type produites par le XIXe siècle'.[5] Completed between 1830 and 1833, this extraordinary work of art, cast in bronze, measures 60×30 cm, and is also housed by the Musée des Beaux-Arts in Angers (see Figure 1).[6] With this work, David's rapidly developing style, with its bold surface texturing, reached a new peak as he began to realize the more radical possibilities of modelled sculpture. It is said that in 1831 Gustave Planche announced the imminent appearance of the bust in marble, the material into which the clay-modelled Chateaubriand and Goethe had been translated, but the intricacy of surface detail in the Paganini defied the conventional copying techniques in marble or even in sand-cast bronze, and as a result the marble copy never materialized (Holderbaum, 'Portrait Sculpture', p. 41). Instead, in 1832, David was fortunate to discover with Honoré Gonon, a renowned bronze founder, the potential for vigorous expression offered by casting in the lost-wax process. This process allowed for the lightest and deftest of touches in the original clay model to be preserved in the metal. It is for this reason that the bust was not completed until 1833, and first exhibited in the Paris Salon of 1834.

---

[3] As is the case in Jacques de Caso, *David d'Angers: Sculptural Communication in the Age of Romanticism* (Princeton: Princeton University Press, 1992), pp. 172–73, and *The Romantics to Rodin*, pp. 40–42, 211. On David d'Angers see also Marie-Rose and Marguerite-Cécile Albrecht, *David d'Angers: regards autour d'un sculpteur* (Maulévrier: Hérault, 1987); Luc Benoist, *La Sculpture romantique* (Paris: Gallimard, 1994); *David d'Angers: sa vie, son œuvre, ses écrits et ses contemporains*, ed. by Henry Jouin, 2 vols (Paris: Plon, 1878); Joseph G. Reinis, *The Portrait Medallions of David d'Angers* (New York: Polymath, 2000); Paul Schazmann, *David d'Angers: profils de l'Europe* (Geneva: Bonvert, 1973); Alan Windsor, *David d'Angers* (London: Ashgate, 2004).

[4] James Holderbaum, 'Pierre-Jean David d'Angers', in *The Romantics to Rodin*, pp. 211–25 (p. 211).

[5] Edward Neill, *Nicolò Paganini* (Genoa: Fayard, 1990), p. 395.

[6] The illustration may be seen in greater detail, and in colour, in the online version of this article, available at www.jstor.org.

FIG. 1. Pierre-Jean David d'Angers, *Buste en bronze de Paganini*, 1830. Musées d'Angers. © Musées d'Angers, cliché Pierre David

What is particularly interesting about David's sculpture of Paganini, and further justifies it receiving the comprehensive examination that is missing to date, is the manner in which it can be considered in the light of David's own observations about the violinist, recorded in his notebooks, *Les Carnets de*

David d'Angers, published posthumously in Paris in 1858.[7] The present study constitutes the first examination of David's section on Paganini in *Les Carnets*, treating and promoting this writing as a serious and important piece of literature which illuminates an analysis of the sculpture. Almost all of David's account of the violinist (except for the last three paragraphs) is included in Neill's biography of Paganini, in an appendix entitled 'Témoignages des contemporains' (pp. 396–97). Neill introduces David's piece from *Les Carnets* with a few factual remarks (p. 395), but, apart from these, nothing to date has been written on David's description of Paganini. On the sculptured image, the most substantial criticisms are by de Caso and by Holderbaum in *The Romantics to Rodin*. Their views are referred to here, but these critics are not concerned with exploring the relationship between David's sculptured image of Paganini and his verbal account of him in *Les Carnets*, which is the primary focus of this article.

Les Carnets is a collection of personal notes on a variety of subjects, such as architecture, sculpture, contemporary artists, musicians, literary personages, celebrities, philosophical issues such as life and death, but also ordinary, everyday occurrences and childhood memories. However, these writings constitute more than a documentary journal: they have a self-conscious, self-reflexive nature which attempts to provide intimate revelations on the creative state itself. In his introduction to the 1958 edition André Bruel attempts to sum up their content by positing three major areas of reference contained within them: 'biographique, historique, artistique'; but he stresses that there is no attempt to structure or order the notes into any such categories.[8] The section on Paganini occurs in Volume I, 198–202, where in approximately two-and-a-half pages David provides an account of the violinist in performance, as well as stories surrounding some of his meetings with him, during which Paganini sat for preliminary sketches. The pages occur in Carnet 17, which is dated 1831–32, and the Carnet itself contains two dates: one at the beginning, '16 février 1831', and another towards the end, '17 décembre 1832'. In view of the dates, and the positioning of the pages on Paganini, roughly in the middle of Carnet 17, it is logical to assume that David met Paganini and wrote this section after witnessing Paganini perform at the Paris Opéra during the first of the violinist's concert engagements in the city from 9 March to 24 April 1831.[9]

---

[7] *Les Carnets de David d'Angers*, ed. by André Bruel, 2 vols (Paris: Plon, 1958). All further references are to this edition, abbreviated as *Les Carnets*. The latter is the only source of David which refers to Paganini. His correspondence contains only one reference to the violinist, where, writing to Victor Pavie on 20 January 1833, he praises a book of poetry by 'Mme Valmore' (formerly Marceline Desbordes) entitled *Les Pleurs*, which contained verses in honour of Paganini: *David d'Angers et ses relations littéraires: correspondance du maître*, ed. by Henry Jouin (Paris: Plon, 1890), p. 70.

[8] André Bruel, 'Histoire des Carnets', in *Les Carnets de David d'Angers*, pp. i–xix (p. xvii).

[9] Paganini played again from 25 March to 1 June 1832 (all concerts were at the Opéra, apart

These first series of concerts were attended by many of the leading figures in the Romantic avant-garde, including Heine, Liszt, Gautier, Hugo, Nodier, de Musset, de Vigny, Sand, and Delacroix (who also produced his oil painting of Paganini in 1831 after the latter's first Parisian concert engagement).[10] The pages devoted to Paganini in Carnet 17 do not run consecutively, but are broken up, after about one page, by seventeen brief paragraphs of what seem like fragmentary notes on diverse subjects. They include reflections and observations on the following: the relationship between nature, nobility, and sensuality; Saint-Simonism; young girls selling palms on Palm Sunday; the difference in signatures in youth and old age; money-stamping and contemporary materialism; the construction of monuments in towns; and the differences between vegetable and human growth. Although none of these paragraphs mentions Paganini by name, many of the ideas contained within them could be said to relate, by association, to those sections where the violinist is dealt with more directly, as will be shown. Even in those passages where Paganini is undoubtedly the focus of the discussion, David's thoughts on the violinist are often communicated obliquely and by inference in a language that is poetic. Bruel speaks of the 'belle tenue littéraire' of *Les Carnets*, and says of David that 'il avait acquis, à l'époque des *Carnets*, une qualité d'écriture que les écrivains professionels peuvent envier' (Bruel, p. xvii). Nash argues that David saw 'no fundamental difference between writing and sculpture', and underscores the parallels drawn by David between the two mediums in *Les Carnets* themselves (Nash, p. 191).[11] Consequently, part of my analyses of *Les Carnets* aims to highlight how the language employed by David in his consideration of Paganini goes beyond the merely literal and referential to carve out and generate associations and shades of meaning. This is achieved through the use of devices such as the repetition of motifs, the highlighting of key terminology through the use of juxtaposition and the creation of antitheses, and the art of suggestion.

The focal point of David's writing is Paganini's genius. Around this centre pivot a number of topics and concepts viewed in relationship to genius, which will be examined here: contemporary theories of phrenology; sickliness and gaucherie; Romantic notions of the primitive and the natural; the tyranny of

---

from the first, at the Théâtre Italien), and returned again in 1833 to give his final concert at the Paris Opéra on 14 April.

[10] Delacroix's portrait was either commissioned for, or given as a present to, Achille Ricourt, who was then the editor of the Parisian journal *L'Artiste*. The painting now forms part of the Phillips Collection in Washington. For a detailed examination of it, and a comparison of it with an earlier pencil portrait by Ingres (1819, Musée du Louvre, Paris), see my article '"It isn't he!": Ingres's Paganini and Delacroix's Parody', *Journal of Romance Studies*, 11.2 (2011), 35–59.

[11] Nash observes, for example, how David in *Les Carnets* constantly refers to bas-reliefs in linguistic terms, as 'le langage de la sculpture en méplat'; as 'les archives d'une époque', or 'notes explicatives' to be placed at eye level so that they can be easily 'read' (Nash, p. 191).

genius and Paganini's sado-masochistic rapport with his violin; the merging of the figures of Christ and Satan in Paganini's persona; and his associations with German literary depictions of eccentric and genial personages, most notably those by E. T. A. Hoffmann and the *Sturm und Drang* dramatists.

Paganini is first introduced in *Les Carnets* in an unexpected fashion after a short paragraph on the subject of the sculptor in general: 'Le statuaire. Sa tête bouillonne comme un volcan ou comme la fournaise du fondeur; et des bustes, des statues en sortent brillants de vie et de *génie*' (*Les Carnets*, I, 198).[12] The comparison of the sculptor's head to a furnace could well have been inspired by David's friend Victor Hugo. In his ode 'A M. David, statuaire', which Hugo himself recited to David in 1828[13] (and whose title is echoed in David's declamatory 'Le statuaire'), the French poet represents David's own head as the mould from which the image of other men's greatness bursts forth:

> Un métal dans tes veines coule;
> Ta tête ardente est un grand moule
> D'où l'idée en bronze jaillit.[14]

The intertextual allusion reinforces the poetic nature of David's writing, while also managing to establish a type of brotherhood between two geniuses of artistic expression: David and Paganini (an idea to be developed later). For the echo of Hugo clearly makes the 'statuary' of David's prose, who produces works of genius, David himself; and his own genius then serves to 'remind' him, in his free, associative style, of that of Paganini. This is indicated by the repetition of the word 'génie' at the end of the sentence which follows, and which is the beginning of the section devoted to the violinist. The juxtaposed sentences reflect each other in their structure ('Le statuaire. [. . .] génie'; 'Quand Paganini [. . .] génie'):

Quand Paganini a exécuté un passage sublime sur son violon et qu'il a arraché de la poitrine du spectateur de ces exclamations, de ces cris qu'il est impossible de définir, il *découvre* son front avec la main, comme pour *découvrir* le foyer de son sublime *génie*. (*Les Carnets*, I, 198)

From the outset, therefore, David makes it clear that his admiration for Paganini lies in his associations with genius.[15] Genius, for David, is located in the forehead. This is suggested by the allusion to Paganini wiping his brow in

---

[12] The italics here and elsewhere are mine.

[13] David met the French poet in 1827, executed his bust of him in 1837, and formed a solid friendship with Hugo which continued in the form of a correspondence through their respective years of exile as ardent Republicans, until David's death in 1856. In a letter to Victor Pavie, dated 13 August 1828, David speaks of Hugo's recitation of the 'Ode': 'Enfin Hugo m'a lu l'ode faite pour moi; il y a une idée à chaque mot, et cette idée est grande comme Phidias' (*David d'Angers et ses relations littéraires*, ed. by Jouin, p. 33).

[14] Victor Hugo, *Œuvres complètes*, 15 vols (Paris: Laffont, 1985–90), IV: *Poésie* (1985), I, 585.

[15] Although some readers may want to explore a reading of David's admiration for Paganini

performance—presumably pushing his hair back as he does so—and thereby 'unveiling' his forehead, as if to reveal the seat of his genius. Indeed, the first of the aforementioned seventeen short paragraphs dividing the two sections on Paganini reinforces this location of genius. Here David remarks:

La nature semble chercher à annoblir toutes ses productions. C'est ainsi qu'elle a voilé toute la partie supérieure du visage, par la barbe, cette partie qui dénote si bien les goûts sensuels de l'homme; qu'elle a *découvert* la partie supérieure du crâne et du front, où est le siège des facultés nobles. (*Les Carnets*, I, 199)

This passage serves to underscore that Paganini's wiping of his forehead is not merely indicative of the violinist sweating on stage from the heat of the auditorium and the effort of playing. David is also poetically underlining the notion of the forehead, cerebral and lacking in sensuality, as the seat of noble faculties and genius. The point is reinforced linguistically through the repetition of the motif of unveiling (*découvrir*): the term 'découvert' on page 199 intentionally echoes the use of 'découvre' and 'découvrir' on page 198.

More than anything else, it is this concept of Paganini's genius which David is at pains to reveal in his sculptured effigy of the violinist. The most striking impression made by the bust is, in fact, its bulging cranium, which is almost unnaturally prominent, and, importantly, bald. It is true that Paganini's large and high brow was a feature for which he was noted, as, for example, in the 'Notice physiologique sur Niccolò Paganini' published in 1831 by Francesco Bennati.[16] Bennati (mentioned in David's section on Paganini, p. 201) was a Mantuan doctor and a highly recognized member of the Parisian Academy of Science who treated Paganini while he was in Paris. In his 'Notice' he speaks of the virtuoso's 'tête volumineuse' and his 'front haut, large et carré'. However, it is also true to say that David's revolutionary style lay predominantly in what Brooks Beaulieu aptly describes as 'David's hyperbolization of the particular traits of an individual physiognomy',[17] and one suspects that David has exaggerated Paganini's cranial dome to create a dramatic impact. Dorothy Johnson is of the same view. She asserts that David 'explored radical exaggerations in

---

from the point of view of homoeroticism, following the lines dictated by Andrew Elfenbein in his exploration of English literary genius in *Romantic Genius: The Prehistory of a Homosexual Role* (New York: Columbia University Press, 1999), this article prefers not to create such a theoretical framework, which is at variance with David's own reputedly conservative and strait-laced morals (see Holderbaum's remarks in 'Pierre-Jean David d'Angers', p. 216).

[16] Francesco Bennati, 'Notice physiologique sur Niccolò Paganini', *Revue musicale de Paris*, 14 May 1831. Extracts from the article are reprinted in Neill, pp. 367–73.

[17] Brooks Beaulieu, review of 'Portraits publics, portraits privés: 1770–1830', in *Nineteenth-Century Art Worldwide: A Journal of Nineteenth-Century Visual Culture*, 6.2 (Autumn 2007) <http://www.19thc-artworldwide-org/index.php/autumn07/123-portraits-publics-portraits-prives> [accessed 2 January 2011].

the proportions of heads, torsos, and limbs for expressive effect'.[18] As David puts it in *Les Carnets*, 'Le sculpteur [. . .] doit accentuer l'individualité' (I, 5). Nowhere, however, do these exaggerations assume the appearance of caricature, contrary to what Luc Benoist seems to suggest: 'Sous le prétexte que les hommes de génie ont le front très développé [. . .] il leur donne un front hors de toute proportion avec le reste de la tête' (Benoist, p. 185). Paganini's head, in David's rendering, bears, for example, no resemblance to that modelled by Jean-Pierre Dantan in his statuette-caricature of Paganini (1832),[19] where the latter's head is clearly exaggerated to the point of deformity.

By giving the virtuoso a notably large head, David was confirming Paganini's genius, and here the sculptor was much influenced by the contemporary phrenological theories advanced by Johann Gaspar Spurzheim (1776–1832) and Franz Joseph Gall (1758–1828). David's name appears among the founding members of the Parisian phrenological society listed in the first volume of the *Journal de la Société phrénologique de Paris*, published in 1832, and his bronze medallion of Spurzheim is evidence in itself of the much-noted but, to date, insufficiently researched importance he attributed to the science of phrenology.[20] David's interest in phrenology is also well documented throughout *Les Carnets*. For example, he writes:

La nature a mis des bosses sur le crâne de certains hommes et a semblé les signer en leur disant: 'Toi, tu feras telle chose; toi telle autre chose.' Il y en a, sur le front desquels on ne voit que peu de bosses, alors ceux-là sont les enfants gâtés de la nature. (*Les Carnets*, I, 72)[21]

In an introductory outline of the doctrinal principles that comprise the intellectual basis of phrenology, Gall and Spurzheim stated in 1819 that the form of the head or cranium represented the form of the brain, and thus reflected the relative development of the 'brain organs' and the intelligence of the subject.[22] On their numbered phrenological head chart, which would have been well known to David, the thirty-seven brain organs were all given a precise location, and areas with enlarged bumps meant that the patient used that particular organ extensively. The seventeenth brain organ was termed 'Tune', and it denoted 'the organ of musical perception'. It lay roughly mid-

[18] Dorothy Johnson, 'David d'Angers and the Primacy of Drawing', *Master Drawings*, 41 (2003), 140–50 (p. 143).
[19] Dantan's statuette is now in the Musée de la Ville de Paris.
[20] See Charles Blanc, *Les Artistes de mon temps* (Paris: Firmin-Didot, 1876), p. 139; *David d'Angers*, ed. by Jouin, I, 342; Gustave Planche, *Portraits d'artistes: peintres et sculpteurs*, 2 vols (Paris: Lévy, 1853), II, 117–18. Also, more recently, Marc Renneville, *Le Langage des crânes: histoire de la phrénologie*, Les Empêcheurs de penser en rond (Paris: Sanofi-Synthélabo, 2000), p. 89.
[21] See also I, 213–14, 409.
[22] F. J. Gall and J. C. Spurzheim, *Anatomie et physiologie du système nerveux en général et du cerveau en particulier; avec des observations sur la possibilité de reconnaître plusiers dispositions intellectuelles et morales de l'homme et des animaux par la configuration de leurs têtes*, 4 vols (Paris: F. Schoell, 1810–19).

way between and above the ear and the eye, in the region of the temples. In David's bust of Paganini the two temples are particularly pronounced for their swollen appearance and their salient, vertically running veins. The whole of David's reproduction of Paganini's cranium is, moreover, particularly bulbous, and testifies to David's attempt to emphasize the extent to which all of the 'positive' brain organs in Paganini had been developed. In short, the sculpture of Paganini demonstrates how David was able to use the science of phrenology to new expressive and realist effect.

But, as David's prose goes on to suggest, the towering intelligence of this musical genius came at a price. Genius, according to Mario Praz's famous study on Romanticism,[23] is 'sickly', and there follows in David's prose a motif, repeated three times, juxtaposing the weak body and the tyrannical soul. The soul empowers one's genius, and leads to a neglect of the body:

Il vient sur la scène comme un homme qui est poussé par quelque chose qui le maîtrise. Il semble que *l'âme* a une puissance tyrannique sur *ce corps* trop débile. [. . .] Quand *le corps* l'emporte sur *l'âme*, alors il est soigné. Quand c'est *l'âme*, *le corps* est négligé. (*Les Carnets*, I, 198)

This association between Paganini's genius and a resultant sickliness was one commonly employed at the time, and it occurs frequently in reviews of the violinist's Parisian performances of the 1830s, as well as in short stories inspired by those very performances. Aloysius Block's 'Les deux notes', a 'fantastical tale' based on the Faust legend, and published in *L'Artiste* in 1831, announces the arrival of Paganini in the auditorium in the following terms: 'Le voilà, avec son bourreau à ses côtés, son génie, son violon, instrument maigre, jaune et débilité comme lui.'[24] An anonymous entry in *L'Artiste* in 1832 alludes to the ravaging effects of genius on Paganini's face: 'L'empreinte du génie et de la méditation a trop profondément sillonné ce visage.'[25] The contrast between Paganini's vigorous soul driving forward his genius and his frail, debilitated body was therefore one much propagated by the press. Indeed Paganini's first biographer, Eugène Imbert de La Phalecque, wrote in 1830 that the violinist's genius allowed him to energize his body and transcend his physical weakness.[26] Many journal articles and reviews even went so far as to create associations between Paganini's debilitated physique and the great cholera epidemic of 1832, which coincided with Paganini's second concert engagement in the city and claimed the lives of 18,000 of the city's inhabitants. An anonymous review of 23 April in the *Journal des débats* reads: 'Paganini

[23] Mario Praz, *The Romantic Agony*, trans. by Angus Davidson (London: Oxford University Press, 1951).
[24] Aloysius Block, 'Les deux notes', *L'Artiste*, 1 (1831), 116–19 (p. 118).
[25] Anonymous, 'Paganini', *L'Artiste*, 3 (1832), 108–09 (p. 108).
[26] Eugène Imbert de La Phalecque, *Notice sur le célèbre violiniste Nicolò Paganini* (Paris: Guyot, 1830), p. 53.

reparaît dans ces jours de peste, cet homme noir [. . .] au corps brisé.'[27] Nina Athanassoglou-Kallmyer argues that Paganini's appearance became, in the popular imagination, the live embodiment of cholera.[28] Although David's writings on Paganini were composed in 1831, his sculpture, as previously explained, was not finished until 1833. It is therefore highly likely that he was familiar with such representations of Paganini in the Parisian press, and striving above all, as Johnson reminds us, 'to create sculpture that would communicate emotion to a contemporary audience' (Johnson, p. 143), he sought to underscore the by then well-established associations between Paganini's genius and sickliness, which he in no way disputed. As he expresses it in *Les Carnets*, 'Dans les êtres qui ont une imagination ardente [. . .] l'âme dévore le corps' (I, 410). This dichotomy between genius and physical frailty is powerfully conveyed in the contrast between the upper and the lower halves of Paganini's head: the bulky and powerfully modelled cranium overhangs an emaciated lower face, with protruding cheekbones and prominent neck veins. The heavily projected thyroid cartilage of the larynx, intensifying the V shape of the frontal neck bones, adds to the effect of emaciation. Paganini's hollow cheeks (a characteristic feature of other contemporary representations of the violinist)[29] are also suggestive of the painful dental surgery that he underwent in 1828 and again in 1832, resulting in the extraction of the majority of his teeth, and which is referred to later in David's prose, as will be shown.

A further effect of genius which David immediately proceeds to announce is that of awkwardness: 'On sait que les hommes de génie sont maladroits, très gauches; les membres sont des instruments dont ils ne savent pas se servir' (*Les Carnets*, I, 198). This awkwardness is demonstrated in the manner in which Paganini walks on and off stage: 'Quand Paganini est arrivé sur la scène, lentement, pas en ligne droite, toutes les fois qu'il est entré ou sorti de la scène, c'est toujours en lignes diagonales' (ibid.). While having, of course, no literal association with the sculptured image, the crooked lines which Paganini draws on stage, and which for David are clearly symbolic of his genius 'preventing' the proper use of his limbs, cannot fail to steal into the viewer's mind when faced with Paganini's bust. For one of the most striking things the spectator is taken by when confronted with this image is its pronounced lack of symmetry. For Holderbaum this is by far the most daring and exciting aspect of the sculpture. He writes:

[27] Anonymous, *Journal des débats*, 23 April 1832, p. 6.
[28] Nina Athanassoglou-Kallymer, 'Blemished Physiologies: Delacroix, Paganini, and the Cholera Epidemic of 1832', *Art Bulletin*, 83 (2001), 686–710.
[29] See, for example, the lithographs by Franz Barth (Vienna, 1828) and Friedrich Hahn (Paris, 1830), and the marble bust by Paolo Oliveri (Milan, 1835). All three are reproduced in John Sugden, *Niccolò Paganini: Supreme Violinist or Devil's Fiddler?* (Tunbridge Wells: Midas, 1980), pp. 69, 90, and 125, respectively.

The yielding clay is impetuously squeezed and stretched; [...] distortions and asymmetries are inflicted on the strange shape emerging. Brow and crown are pulled upward, much higher on his right than on his left; the nose is ripplingly deflected to his right, but the chin to his left; cheekbones and hollows are completely dissimilar on the two sides. (Holderbaum, 'Portrait Sculpture', p. 41)

As with the exaggerated forehead and brain cavity, David has taken liberties with visible reality in an attempt to capture aspects of Paganini which go beyond the merely physical. Elsewhere in *Les Carnets* he makes it clear that sculpture is not about reproducing reality: 'Quand on regarde un ouvrage de sculpture, il y a une conversation de l'âme: [...] on se trouve en rapport avec la substance impalpable qu'on appelle l'âme, l'âme de l'artiste' (*Les Carnets*, I, 52). The distortions and asymmetries of Paganini's face positively assert the fiery soul of the man who displays them.

Another striking feature of Paganini's face is, of course, his hair. The musician's long black hair was almost as famous as his extraordinary violin-playing. This was because it was blatantly out of step with contemporary fashion. For although most men of Paganini's day would have worn some form of beard and sideburns, it was the custom for them to keep their hair relatively short and pomaded with oil, and Paganini's cascading ringlet curls, so heavily pronounced in David's rendering of him, were fashionable for the *ladies* of his day. For its unusual and dated appearance, references to the violinist's hairstyle abound not only in physiological descriptions of him, but also in reviews of his concert performances: Bennati talks of Paganini as having 'des cheveux noirs et longs retombant en désordre sur ses épaules' (Neill, p. 368); de Ghetaldi writes that 'his hair is black and long, and never dressed';[30] and Leigh Hunt remarks how occasionally during a performance Paganini puts it back.[31] Hair is discussed on many occasions in *Les Carnets* (see, in particular, I, 51-52, 91), and David was especially interested in all of his own subjects' hair, seeing in it a form of 'signature'.[32] Just as he posited what de Caso calls 'an analogue of physiognomy and therefore of character in the [actual] signature of an individual' (de Caso, p. 173), consequently adding in facsimile the signature of the sitter on many of his medallions and busts—the Paganini bust included—so too, according to David, the subject's coiffure revealed much of his or her personality. Two paragraphs prior to the section on Paganini,

---

[30] De Ghetaldi is quoted without a source in Sugden, p. 79.

[31] *Leigh Hunt's Dramatic Criticism 1808–1831*, ed. by Lawrence Huston Houtchens and Carolyn Washburn Houtchens (Oxford: Oxford University Press, 1950), pp. 271-72. See my '"The pale magician of the bow": Leigh Hunt's "Paganini"', *Journal of Anglo-Italian Studies*, 11 (2011), 15-38.

[32] David always paid great attention to the sitter's hairstyle, often exaggerating it wildly to create a dramatic effect. This sometimes resulted in styles which, even by modern standards, might be considered rather daringly avant-garde. See, for example, the coiffures of *Lady Morgan* (marble bust) in Bethnal Green Museum, London; *Mademoiselle Jubin* (plaster bust) in Angers Museum; and *Cuvier* (marble statue) in the Musée d'histoire naturelle in Paris.

David announces 'Les longs cheveux par derrière donnent l'air *sauvage*' (*Les Carnets*, I, 198); and this allusion to the savage is echoed later in the image of Paganini's hair as the 'crinière' of a 'vieux lion' (*Les Carnets*, I, 198–99). In the light of these references, the long and undressed hair of Paganini's sculpture, and the strip of thick, curly, and unkempt beard 'crowning', as it were, his chin and lower jaw, reinforce a sense of the savage and hint at the concept of naturalness, which was an important element that went hand in hand with the concept of original, innate genius, unfettered by laws and 'the Rules of the Learned', as depicted by Edward Young in his critical prose work *Conjectures on Original Composition* (1759): 'Learning inveighs against *natural*, unstudied graces [. . .] and sets rigid boundaries to that liberty. [. . .] Genius is knowledge *innate*.'[33] David's correspondence with Victor Pavie shows him to be an admirer of Young's works—both his *Night Thoughts* (1742) and his *Conjectures*.[34] The latter text was translated into German only a year after its publication, and was extremely popular on the Continent, where it became an important work in the pioneering of Romanticism, influencing Goethe and the view of genius developed by the German eighteenth-century *Sturm und Drang* dramatists, referred to later. Equally, however, in his depiction of Paganini's long hair and untidy beard, David could be making an allusion to a group of students who originally belonged to the atelier of Jacques-Louis David, but who in the late 1790s rejected the values of Davidian classicism in favour of the primitive style of ancient Greece. To the new age of science, industry, and trade they opposed and upheld the ancient world of Homer, Ossian, and the Bible. To demonstrate their faith, and in order to 'separate "themselves" from the world',[35] they dressed like ancient Greeks and grew their hair and beards long. Consequently they were dubbed by Charles Nodier, on his arrival in Paris in 1832, as the *Barbus* or *Primitifs*, and referred to as 'cette société barbue d'hommes de génie' (Delécluze, p. 440). If David intends an allusion to Young or to the *Barbus*, or even to both, such allusions exist to reinforce Paganini's associations with the savage, the primitive, with a sense of otherworldliness, and, of course, with genius.

In addition to the symbolic 'signature' of Paganini's hairstyle, there is, of course, the facsimile of the violinist's real signature, placed near the base of the bust underneath Paganini's neck, and its function is to underscore further

---

[33] Edward Young, *Conjectures on Original Composition: In a Letter to the Author of Sir Charles Grandison* (London: Millar and Dodsley, 1759), ll. 332–33.

[34] *David d'Angers et ses relations littéraires*, ed. by Jouin, p. 24.

[35] Charles Nodier explains how when the leader of the group, Maurice Quay, was asked by Napoleon: 'Pourquoi avez-vous adopté une forme d'habillement qui vous sépare du monde?', Quay replied: 'Pour me séparer du monde' (Nodier, 'Appendice', in E. J. Delécluze, *Louis David, son école et son temps* (Paris: Macula, 1983), pp. 419–47 (p. 441)). For more information on the *Barbus* see George Levitine, *The Dawn of Bohemianism: The Barbu Rebellion and Primitivism in Neoclassical France* (University Park: Pennsylvania State University Press, 1978).

an impression of naturalness and simplicity. In the passage which divides the two sections on Paganini David makes the following remark on signatures in general:

Quand on commence la vie, on signe son nom avec soin. [. . .]. Quand on avance dans la vie, on signe avec effronterie, il n'y a que lorsqu'on écrit à une personne que l'on estime, la signature alors reprend la naïve décence de la jeunesse. (*Les Carnets*, I, 199)

Paganini's signature on the bust does not conform to the theory which David proposes here: there is nothing bold or insolent about it; instead the letters are clearly legible and painstakingly well arranged, suggesting, as David himself puts it, the naivety and simplicity of youth. Both 'signatures', the real one and that of the hairstyle, seem to reinforce David's view of Paganini as a natural genius, of the type extolled by Young, uncorrupted by civilization.

One final observation concerning Paganini's hair leads one to a consideration of David's predilection for the curved as opposed to the straight line. Paganini's coiled locks, whipped by the modelling stick into extravagant waves, allow David to exercise his love of the curved line, expressive, for him, of life and movement: 'La ligne droite est antivivante. Ce sont les lignes courbes qui expriment la vie (le mouvement)' (*Les Carnets*, I, 196). Noteworthy in this respect too is the fact that Paganini's head is not held upright in a straight line, but tilted. Towards the end of the first section on Paganini David tells us of the violinist's reaction to his suggestion that he model him with his head slightly forward and to the side, as if he were playing the violin:

Quand je lui ai dit que je voulais lui faire pencher la tête en avant et de côté, comme un homme qui joue du violon (dans son buste) il me dit: 'Oui, car je tire de mon intérieur pour impressionner l'extérieur.' Il approuva beaucoup le parti que j'ai pris de faire un buste de Rossini, la tête dans la pose d'un homme qui écoute. (*Les Carnets*, I, 199)

David, by depicting Paganini's head in a playing position, heightens the impression of naturalism and movement, and frees the spectator from the idea of witnessing the representation of a subject who has posed for the artist. The forward tilting of Paganini's head is also interesting from an additional point of view. The invisible violin over which Paganini's head inclines makes of it a limb-like extension of the limbless bust. David intends an irony here, for this real instrument has become an ever-present limb which the violinist knows only too well how to handle; while, since he is a man of genius, his flesh-and-blood limbs are 'instruments he does not know how to use', to adapt the phrase quoted above from *Les Carnets*, I, 198. David is suggesting that Paganini's violin has become an organic part of his frail body, and, like his soul, exerts a tyrannical power over him. This idea emerges quite forcefully in David's prose, where the relationship between Paganini and his violin is presented as a violent and tempestuous one. To underscore this, there is the repetition of the verb *frapper*. David recounts how on one of the mornings he visited Paganini, no sooner had the latter set his fingers on one of the strings of the violin than it broke violently and whipped him across the face, drawing blood: '[la corde] se rompit avec violence et fut le *frapper* au visage, de manière à faire couler le sang' (*Les Carnets*, I, 201). The verb *frapper* is also used to describe Paganini's playing in performance, in particular, the manner in which he concludes a piece—he 'strikes' the bow on the strings, and the bow seems to 'strike' the air, stamping it with sound: '[Les cordes] ont été *frappées* par l'archet qui semble *frapper* l'air et lui imprimer les sons' (*Les Carnets*, I, 198). Paganini, we are told, directs the orchestra with a similar sense of forceful imperiousness, but conversely, off stage he is a different man, with movements which are slow and tired. The contradiction is underlined in David's prose by the juxtaposing of two highly different images: the first of the on-stage violinist with energetic and authoritative gestures; and the second of the Paganini he saw that particular day, seated in his armchair, weighed down by a heavy fatigue: 'Il a un geste, pour commander à l'orchestre, qui est extrêmement impérieux. J'ai été le voir aujourd'hui. Il était assis dans son fauteuil, comme un homme accablé par une longue fatigue' (*Les Carnets*, I, 198). Three sentences later, the contrast is exposed once more: 'Cet homme a une démarche excessivement lente et il a une âme de feu' (*Les Carnets*, I, 199). The on-stage energy and the off-stage lethargy are inextricably yoked together: the tyranny exerted by the violin whips the artist into vigorous performances which leave the man shattered and spent.

The inclined head of the bust, therefore, encapsulates the sado-masochistic rapport between Paganini and his instrument. It also recalls that of Christ on the cross, an image charged with a sense of persecuted martyrdom. Nina Athanassoglou-Kallmyer wrote of Paganini's thinness:

his extraordinary gaunt face and emaciated body were ambivalent, double-edged signifiers of the supernatural: on the one hand, they evoked hallowed Christian martyrs, even Christ himself miraculously risen from the dead; on the other, they called forth unholy devils and vampires gone astray from their graves. Boldly, therefore, if not blasphemously, Christ and Dracula merged as the inextricable two facets of Paganini's mystifying character. (Athanassoglou-Kallymer, pp. 703–04)

This merging of the holy and the satanic, of good and evil, was characteristic of the contemporary Romantic movement in art and literature, and was underlined in Victor Hugo's *Préface de Cromwell*, which Hugo read aloud to David in November 1827:[36]

La muse moderne [. . .] sentira que tout dans la création n'est pas humainement beau,

---

[36] David writes to Victor Pavie from Paris on 10 November, 1827: 'Hugo [. . .] vient de nous lire sa préface de *Cromwell*. Quelle profondeur de pensées! A elle seule, cette préface est un code de littérature!' (*David d'Angers et ses relations littéraires*, ed. by Jouin, p. 25).

que le laid y existe à côté du beau, le difforme près du gracieux, le grotesque au revers du sublime, le mal avec le bien, l'ombre avec la lumière. [. . .] [C]'est de la féconde union du type grotesque au type sublime que naît le génie moderne.[37]

It could well be that David was influenced by Hugo's view,[38] for, in spite of the sacred connotations of Paganini's tilted head, there are suggestions of witchery and the satanic in that 'rippingly deflected' hooked nose, and Paganini's jutting, pointed chin. In *Les Carnets* allusions to the diabolic aspects of Paganini are very pronounced. David recalls how he will never forget the expression of the violinist the day he had his teeth pulled out (a 'painful remedy' for the problem of his rotting gums, which reinforced what John O'Shea calls Paganini's 'masochistic personality disorder').[39] Dr Bennati visited him, and when he exclaimed that Paganini must be mad to have had his teeth extracted, the frenzied Paganini shouted in answer: 'Je te dis que je veux devenir beau garçon, que je veux me faire mettre des dents neuves, enfin je le veux!' (*Les Carnets*, I, 201). He then erupted into a long, continuous laugh, the likes of which, David says, had never before been produced by a human being, while blood trickled out of the corners of his mouth:

Alors, il se mit à rire, de ce rire long et continu, qui ne ressemble nullement à celui des autres hommes [. . .]. En même temps le sang lui sortait des coins de la bouche, ce qui donnait une terrible expression à son masque. (*Les Carnets*, I, 201)

Paganini never, of course, had false teeth fitted, and he proceeded to perform with a toothless mouth, which added to the satanic appearance which for a short time he coveted. The vampiric imagery which David obviously intends here displays his acquaintance with the tales of devilry which surrounded Paganini, originating in Vienna on Paganini's arrival there in March 1828, where, as Geraldine de Courcy explains,[40] young Romantics were drawing inspiration from ancient folklore, embroidering it with elements of diablerie. Largely through the writings of Hoffmann in Germany, Michelet in France, and Sir Walter Scott in England, the Romantic period saw a revival of interest in witches and witchcraft, and the figure of Paganini merged with that of

[37] Victor Hugo, *Préface de 'Cromwell'* (Paris: Larousse, 1949), p. 5.
[38] He could equally have been inspired by Delacroix's *Portrait of Paganini*, produced in 1831, two years prior to David's sculpture, a portrait suffused precisely with this Romantic merging of the sublime and the grotesque. See n. 10 above.
[39] John O'Shea, in his chapter on Paganini in *Music and Medicine* (London: Dent, 1993), pp. 66–89, posits Paganini's consumption of mercury (then the mainstay of treatment for syphilis) as the cause of his rotting gums and teeth. In 1828 the latter were discovered by the Italian dentist, Vergani, to be literally 'hanging by a thread' (Paganini had threaded them together in order to be able to chew). O'Shea links practically all of Paganini's other ailments (including a 'productive' cough, 'tunnel vision', erethism, gastro-intestinal problems, and laryngeal pain and voice change) to the mercury poisoning, and claims that Paganini 'had a veritable obsession with painful remedies' of which he became the victim (p. 85).
[40] Geraldine de Courcy, *Paganini: The Genoese*, 2 vols (New York: Da Capo, 1977), I, 257.

Faust, who had sold his soul to the Devil in return for supernatural abilities.[41] Paganini initially reinforced his associations with witchcraft, which boosted box office receipts, composing pieces with satanic allusions, including the celebrated 'Caprice No. 13', subtitled 'La risata del diavolo' (1818). It is precisely this composition which David alludes to above in his description of Paganini's 'inhuman' laughter. The violinist, however, began to discourage his Mephistophelian links when they merged with tales of murder. David hints at one such tale when he recounts how once, arriving at Paganini's house, he seemed to hear noises which resembled the stifled cries of a young girl being assassinated, only to discover that the sounds were being produced by Paganini's violin (*Les Carnets*, I, 201). The allusion is to the rumour that Paganini had passed eight years in prison for murdering his mistress (when in fact he had spent eight days incarcerated owing to an unfortunate liaison with a young girl)[42]—a tale perpetuated by Louis Boulanger's lithograph *Paganini en prison*,[43] which Paganini saw twice on display: in a print shop on the Boulevard des Italiens in 1831, and again in the pages of *L'Artiste*, causing his outburst of protest in a letter to the editor of the journal, which was published in the second issue of *L'Artiste* in 1831.[44]

Perhaps David was also familiar with the declaration made in *L'Artiste* by the eminent Parisian musicologist François-Joseph Fétis, that Paganini was the living embodiment of the eccentric Krespel, the lawyer, violin-maker, and violinist of Hoffmann's well-known story *Rat Krespel* (1818):

Vous souvenez-vous de ce conseiller Crespel, si bien peint par Hoffmann, et du violon de Crémone, qui, sous ses doigts, rendait des sons merveilleux qu'aucun autre instrument ne pouvait produire? Cette création fantastique, Paganini la réalise.[45]

David's correspondence displays a certain reverence for Hoffmann,[46] and Krespel's unpredictability lurks behind the sculptor's allusions to the temperamental aspects of Paganini's character, oscillating, with his son, between playfulness and a more terrifying attitude:

[41] See Maiko Kawabata, 'Virtuosity, the Violin, the Devil . . .: What Really Made Paganini "Demonic"?', *Current Musicology*, 83 (2007), 85–109.

[42] The girl in question (possibly a prostitute) was the twenty-year-old Angelina Cavanna, whom, in a long-drawn-out case, Paganini was found guilty by the courts of abducting, seducing, and impregnating. In a letter to his lawyer friend Luigi Germi, dated 5 July 1815, Paganini denies paternity of her child, who died at birth: Niccolò Paganini, *Epistolario*, ed. by Roberto Grisley (Milan: Skira, 2006–), I: (*1810–1831*), pp. 76–78.

[43] Boulanger's *Paganini en prison* (1831) is now in the Bibliothèque Nationale de France Richelieu Musique fonds estampes.

[44] 'Au directeur de *L'Artiste*', *L'Artiste*, 2 (1831), 159–60.

[45] François-Joseph Fétis, 'Concert de Paganini', *L'Artiste*, 2 (1831), 109.

[46] Alfred de Musset, in a letter to David (1832), makes an allusion to the latter's familiarity with Hoffmann's works, and David, in a letter to the German artist Neo Rauch (18 May 1847), asks Rauch to find him an original sketch of Hoffmann's hand. See *David d'Angers et ses relations littéraires*, ed. by Jouin, pp. 68, 272.

Son enfant joue avec lui, à peu près comme un petit chien mis dans la loge d'un lion. Il lui tire le nez, les cheveux. Mais un jour qu'il avait égaré quelque chose dont Paganini avait besoin, ne répondant point aux demandes de son père, celui-ci prit son expression terrible et l'enfant eut, toute la journée, la pâleur du papier. (*Les Carnets*, I, 201)

That David is alluding here to something more than the anger of a parent towards his misbehaving child is reinforced by the anecdote which follows, telling of a young German who, on keeping close company with the violinist, became increasingly disturbed by the 'strange things' he witnessed in his presence. Significantly, this is the precise reaction of the young German narrator vis-à-vis Krespel in the Hoffmann story, who becomes seized with horror at the strange behaviour and rapid mood-swings of Krespel, who seems to want to draw him down with him 'into the abyss of madness':[47]

Un jeune Allemand de Bâle, fils d'un marchand de musique, a suivi notre musicien par enthousiasme. Il le sert, mais on a vu, de jour en jour, l'expression de la mélancolie s'imprimer sur ce visage, avant si calme. Il semble qu'il a vu des choses étranges, qui lui font désirer de retourner vers son père. Il doit partir sous peu de jours. (*Les Carnets*, I, 201–02)

In addition to Hoffmann, the reference to Paganini's frightening unpredictability, his vampiric laughter, his 'expression terrible', and Dr Bennati's pronouncement 'tu es fou!' (*Les Carnets*, I, 201) also reminds one of the genius-protagonists of the German eighteenth-century *Sturm und Drang* dramatists.[48] The latter were influential in establishing the Romantic conception of genius as belonging to someone driven by a force beyond his control, and with a (Faustian) ability that exceeds the human mind, making genius almost identical with the notion of divine madness or frenzy. Even though a precise identification of Paganini with a particular *Sturm und Drang* hero is not possible, David's writing clearly demonstrates how he shared the movement's identification of genius with madness or frenzy: 'L'expression du *génie* est une certaine ivresse. C'est pour cela que les hommes froids croient qu'un homme inspiré est *fou*, et qu'à la vue de l'expression de cette *frénésie*, on voit, sur les lèvres des gens nuls, l'expression de la pitié' (*Les Carnets*, I, 67–68). The *Sturm und Drang* writers were, moreover, known to David through his close acquaintance with Goethe, who in his early years was one of their members. David's admiration for the work of Herder and for Goethe's friend

[47] 'Councillor Krespel', in E. T. A. Hoffmann, *Tales of Hoffmann*, selected and trans. by R. J. Hollingdale (London: Penguin, 1982), p. 173.

[48] The most significant writers of the *Sturm und Drang* included Lavater (1741–1801), Herder (1744–1803), the young Goethe (1749–1832), Klinger (1752–1831), Schiller (1788–1805), and Müller (1811–1825). The genius-protagonists (the *Kraftgenies*) of their dramas tend to be 'mad' and 'frenzied': examples include Karl Moor and his band of robbers in Schiller's *Die Räuber*; the pathological 'Guelfo', who commits fratricide in Klinger's *Die Zwillinge*; and 'Wild', the hero consumed with desire for Jenny Caroline in the play *Sturm und Drang*, from which the movement took its name.

Schiller is recorded in his correspondence,[49] and he would also have been acquainted with Lavater's contribution to the movement through the interest he took (explained in Holderbaum, 'Portrait Sculpture', p. 40) in Lavater's *Physiognomische Fragmente* (1775–78), where Lavater speaks of the science of physiognomy in relation to poetic genius.

As shown, therefore, David's prose resonates with allusions to Paganini's associations with dark and sinister literary creations. These allusions are reinforced by the stern and gloomy countenance of David's bust; the tension suggested in the vertical and horizontal lines of his deeply furrowed brow; and by the particular method used to render Paganini's eyes: in contrast to neoclassical sculpture, where the eyes were left blank, David's sculpturing of the iris and pupil allows Paganini's eyes to stare, detached and aloof, 'comme le cercle de la lune à travers un léger nuage' (*Les Carnets*, I, 403). The use of bronze, as opposed to the marble employed for figures such as Lamartine and Béranger (1828), Chateaubriand and Goethe (1829), also underscores this notion of darkness, and indeed David's decision to experiment with the technique of lost-wax bronze casting for the bust of Paganini was clearly a deliberate one. While the complex and highly skilled procedures involved in this technique make it a fiendishly difficult hit-and-miss process, it also attains thereby something of the thaumaturgical and the divinely creative, concepts which seem to inform the ideas of Hugo's ode to David and David's remarks on the sculptor in *Les Carnets*, I, 198, quoted above. Hence, the association of the *cire perdue* method with alchemical forging made it an appropriate form in which to convey the diabolical aspects of Paganini's character, and its innovative departure from the tradition of carving in marble well suited the distinction and novelty of Paganini's personality and playing.

David was very conscious of the importance of the first impression created by a work of art. Two pages prior to the section on Paganini, he writes: 'La première impression est toujours la seule forte. C'est pour cela que l'artiste doit arranger ses lignes de manière qu'elles frappent d'une manière irrésistible' (*Les Carnets*, I, 196). If one were made to identify one particular feature of David's bust which creates a first, overriding impression among its plethora of representational nuances and overtones, it would have to be Paganini's huge brain cavity, that exaggerated cranial dome, underscoring the towering genius of the composer-violinist. The word 'génie' is, in fact, repeated constantly in the two sections on Paganini. In addition to the aforementioned literary reference to the sculptor bringing forth from his head-like furnace busts and statues 'brillants de vie et de *génie*' (p. 198), there are four more allusions to genius in the first paragraph alone:

[. . .] comme pour découvrir le foyer de son sublime *génie*.

[49] *David d'Angers et ses relations littéraires*, ed. by Jouin, pp. 76, 124, 146.

Il ne rit jamais, il a trop de *génie*.
Quand on est électrisé par un grand *génie* [. . .]
On sait que les hommes de *génie* sont maladroits. (*Les Carnets*, I, 198)

Another occurs in the opening of the second section on Paganini in a passage devoted to town monuments:

Les monuments élevés sont comme des phares dans une ville. Ils détruisent la monotonie des lignes, mais, à mesure que la civilisation avance, ils disparaissent. Les monuments deviennent plus commodes, moins vilains, moins malsains, que dans les âges passés; mais l'aspect est moins pittoresque. Il en est de même des hommes. Il n'y a presque pas de ces *génies* grandioses qui étonnent le monde. (*Les Carnets*, I, 200)

This passage creates a parallel between a certain type of town monument regrettably ceasing to exist and men of genius—they too becoming more rare. The monuments David extols are likened to lighthouses: towering, powerful works of art. They aim not to beautify reality, but to represent it in all of its ugly and unwholesome aspects. For their potential to shock, they resemble men of genius. David's sculpture of Paganini not only commemorates and instructs, but also acts as a lighthouse monument (anticipating the imagery of Baudelaire's 'Les Phares'). Its own genius lies in its magnification of the real traits of Paganini's physiognomy; and its representation of Paganini's large and protuberant cranium has the same dramatic impact and shock effect that Paganini's personality and performances had on his audiences. In this way, the sense of genius-brotherhood, alluded to at the very start of David's writing on Paganini through the intertextual echo of Hugo's poem, resonates once more, and the musical and sculptor geniuses do indeed unite.

ROYAL HOLLOWAY, UNIVERSITY OF LONDON   VIVIENNE SUVINI-HAND

MAUPASSANT'S *BEL-AMI* AND THE SECRETS OF *ACTUALITÉ*

When Georges Duroy, hero of Maupassant's 1885 novel *Bel-Ami*, attends his first dinner party, he regales fellow guests with recollections of his years spent in North Africa. Impressed, M. Walter, owner of the novel's fictional newspaper, *La Vie française*, requests a series of newspaper articles from the young man. Algeria, it seems, is newsworthy:

Mais faites-nous tout de suite une petite série fantaisiste sur l'Algérie. Vous raconterez vos souvenirs; et vous mêlerez à ça la question de la colonisation, comme tout à l'heure. C'est d'actualité, tout à fait d'actualité, et je suis sûr que ça plaira beaucoup à nos lecteurs.[1]

The stuff of dinner-party conversation constitutes news in *Bel-Ami*. The true significance of the commission, however, will emerge only later in the narrative: the newspaper's interest in North Africa does not stem from the simple curiosity of its readers (and, indeed, M. Walter notes the question of entertainment value almost as an afterthought). Rather, *La Vie française* aims to manipulate public opinion, to shape foreign policy, and, ultimately, to profit from the French occupation of Morocco. Behind apparently innocent conversation, therefore, lurks a complex network of political and financial interests.

In the exclusivity of the private party the limits of *actualité* are thus established in such a way as to promote personal ambitions. The scope of such plotting raises various questions: if the newspaper is simply a front, a means to a lucrative end, what is the nature of *actualité*? By what criteria is it defined? Who is ultimately responsible for its definition? And how might it gain traction among the public? Indeed, that the novel takes as its subject the production of *actualité* is a fact complicated by the ways in which the text itself references the specificities of its own political moment, from the Naquet divorce law of 1884[2] to the occupation of Tunisia in 1881, the colonial project incorporated into Maupassant's text under the guise of the Moroccan Affair.[3] In its treatment of the news, therefore, *Bel-Ami* emerges as a text emblematic of an important thesis recently advanced by Marie-Ève Thérenty: the novel testifies to the sense of exchange, crossover, and overlap Thérenty deems

---

[1] Guy de Maupassant, *Romans*, ed. by Louis Forestier (Paris: Gallimard, 1987), p. 217. All subsequent references to this edition will appear in the text.

[2] See Nicholas White, *The Family in Crisis in Late Nineteenth-Century French Fiction* (Cambridge: Cambridge University Press, 1999), p. 87.

[3] André Vial, *Guy de Maupassant et l'art du roman* (Paris: Nizet, 1954), pp. 316-29; Gérard Delaisement, 'Les Chroniques coloniales de Maupassant', in *Maupassant et l'écriture: actes du colloque de Fécamp 21-22-23 mai 1993*, ed. by Louis Forestier (Paris: Nathan, 1993), pp. 53-59.

characteristic of relations between fiction and the press in nineteenth-century France.[4]

Nowhere is such exchange more evident than in the slippage between the concerns of Maupassant's North African journalism and the plot of his 1885 novel. And yet *Bel-Ami*, I shall argue, represents a crucial moment in the nineteenth-century novel's fascination with *actualité* not simply because of the text's debt to an array of prevailing contemporary debates: in its depiction of the news *Bel-Ami* challenges, undermines, even provokes the very terms in which current affairs are discussed. Beginning with the idea of *actualité* and how this pertains to colonial politics of the Third Republic, I shall explore Maupassant's journalistic attempts of the early 1880s to write the history of the Tunisian Affair before turning to *Bel-Ami* with the aim of tracing the ways in which the novel probes the processes of corruption and manipulation which underlie the news. Through an exploration of the connections between colonial politics and the press, it is my contention here that *Bel-Ami*, alongside Maupassant's journalism regarding the Tunisian Affair, represents an interrogation of the values which lie at the heart of *actualité*, sketching its rise, its continual reaffirmation, and, ultimately, its manipulation.

Media Manipulation: 'Le Secret de l'affaire tunisienne'

The myriad connections between Maupassant's fiction and the press have proved a subject of critical interest.[5] A point crucial to such scholarship is the sense of slippage between the news and the literary text, the ways in which Maupassant's fiction develops and transfigures themes, debates, and *causes célèbres* prominent in the press. *Bel-Ami*, furthermore, bears many of the characteristics of the *roman d'actualité*, a genre chiefly defined by its 'intertextualité avec le périodique'.[6] Mining his extensive journalism on North Africa and the Tunisian Affair (Maupassant was also sent to Algeria as a correspondent for *Le Gaulois* in 1881),[7] the origins of the novel's conspiracy plot lie in journalism, in the reporting of colonial politics *au jour le jour*.

Taking *actualité* as its explicit subject, *Bel-Ami* probes news—now lost—

[4] Marie-Ève Thérenty, *La Littérature au quotidien: poétiques journalistiques au XIXe siècle* (Paris: Seuil, 2007). See e.g. pp. 11–46.

[5] See e.g. Marie-Claire Bancquart, 'Maupassant journaliste', in *Flaubert et Maupassant: écrivains normands*, ed. by Joseph-Marc Bailbé and Jean Pierrot (Paris: Presses Universitaires de France, 1981), pp. 155–66; Noëlle Benhamou, 'De l'influence du fait divers: les Chroniques et Contes de Maupassant', *Romantisme*, 97 (1997), 47–58; Adrian Ritchie, 'Maupassant en 1881: entre le conte et la chronique', in *Guy de Maupassant*, ed. by Noëlle Benhamou (Amsterdam: Rodopi, 2007), pp. 11–20.

[6] Marie-Ève Thérenty, *Mosaïques: être écrivain entre presse et roman (1829–1836)* (Paris: Champion, 2003), p. 438; Thérenty, *La Littérature au quotidien*, pp. 90–120.

[7] For details of Maupassant's travels see Marlo Johnston, *Guy de Maupassant* (Paris: Fayard, 2012), pp. 372–97.

familiar to the contemporary reader. A form of social knowledge of the contemporary, taken for granted in its sheer ubiquity, *actualité* shapes many of the innumerable discourses prominent under the Third Republic, a point explored in Marc Angenot's *1889: un état du discours social*:

'Tout le monde' doit posséder un savoir élémentaire sur le Général Boulanger, (son cheval noir et sa barbe blonde), sur Jules Ferry, sur Prado (l'assassin de cocottes), sur le 'Drame de Meyerling', sur Buffalo-Bill et sur l'épidémie d'influenza. C'est parce que ces objets de discours relèvent d'une convivialité doxique créée par le champ journalistique même qu'ils peuvent être traités différemment, en clé 'concierge' par *le Petit Journal* et en clé distinguée par *le Figaro*.[8]

The seemingly discreet facts and events which constitute *actualité* are ultimately the product of a set of pre-existing values, closely tied to the doxa (that which, according to Angenot, 'dénoterait [. . .] l'ordre de l'implicite public, du *trivium*, du langage des carrefours').[9] Discussing *1889*, Fredric Jameson underlines the foundational nature of *actualité*, not simply to stress its role in informing the terms of prevailing contemporary debate, but to emphasize its capacity to structure the limits of social discourse itself:

As for *Actualité*, the power to determine and classify what happens as such is a more subtle and intangible, yet perhaps even more significant new force, that reaches even more deeply into private life and has its say in the way people tell themselves their own biographical stories.[10]

Journalism, of course, proves of critical importance to Angenot's account of the production of such discourse, defining the preoccupations of the present, *l'air du temps*.

It follows from Angenot's explanation of *actualité*, furthermore, that 'everyone' must have had some basic knowledge of the Tunisian Affair. *Kroumir* provocation on the Algerian frontier in March 1881 served as a 'pretext' for the invasion of Tunisia, seemingly concluded by the famous *traité du Bardo* of 12 May, the terms of which established Tunisia as a French protectorate.[11] Subsequent unrest in the south of the country provoked continued hostilities brought to a close only by the end of 1881. A prominent feature of the news, the invasion spawned a variety of theories of complicity, collusion, even conspiracy on the part of government, high finance, and the press: the intervention, it was claimed, formed part of a wider scandal of exploitation and

[8] Marc Angenot, *1889: un état du discours social* (Longueuil: Le Préambule, 1989), p. 595.
[9] Ibid., pp. 29–30.
[10] Fredric Jameson, 'Marc Angenot, Literary History, and the Study of Culture in the Nineteenth Century', *Yale Journal of Criticism*, 17 (2004), 233–53 (p. 248).
[11] See Louis Forestier's discussion of *Bel-Ami* in his edition of Maupassant's *Romans*, p. 1328; Vial, *Guy de Maupassant et l'art du roman*, p. 318. For further analysis of the historical context see Jean-Marie Mayeur, *Les Débuts de la Troisième République 1871–1898* (Paris: Seuil, 1973), pp. 124–33; Charles-André Julien, *L'Affaire tunisienne 1878–1881* (Tunis: Dar el-Amal, 1981).

financial enrichment. At the centre of this media storm lay radical journalist Henri Rochefort, who, under the headline 'Le Secret de l'affaire tunisienne' in *L'Intransigeant* of 27 September 1881, famously outlined the extent of government collusion with finance over the Tunisian intervention: 'MM. Gambetta et Roustan avaient formé une association dont le but était de faire d'abord tomber au prix du papier les obligations de la Dette tunisienne, et de les racheter ensuite pour quelques liards.'[12] Central to Rochefort's claim, therefore, was the allegation of financial chicanery on the part of Roustan, French consul in Tunisia, whom the journalist accused of conspiring to manipulate the value of Tunisian debt so that it might be subsequently bought and sold for immense profit.

Key to this plot was the newspaper *La République française*,[13] which was deemed to have played a critical role in generating a climate of opinion favourable to the scheme:

Ce journal qui, au grand étonnement de ses lecteurs, ne souffle plus mot aujourd'hui des affaires tunisiennes, consacrait alors une place relativement considérable aux affaires de ce petit État. Les articles du journal de M. Gambetta — voir la collection de la *République française* de 1875 et 1876 — avaient tous la même tendance: déprécier la valeur des titres tunisiens, afin d'en rendre le drainage plus facile et moins onéreux, et ramener au pouvoir le ministre Sidi-Mustapha-Khasnadar, qui favoriserait plus tard les projets de ses protecteurs, MM. Roustan et Gambetta.[14]

Such claims followed a similarly inflammatory article by Maurice Talmeyr (24 September 1881), uncompromising in its condemnation of Gambetta, and formed part of a series of articles aimed precisely at denouncing the occupation. The apparent difficulty in locating the *Kroumirs* (the pretext for the invasion itself) became a running gag for this strand of opposition, with the refrain 'Où est le Kroumir?' becoming ubiquitous.[15] At heart, these allegations probed questions concerning the complicity of the press, the value of its information. Rochefort's newspaper did not go unchecked: Roustan took the radical journalist to court, and the subsequent trial, recorded in Albert Bataille's *Causes criminelles et mondaines de 1881*, further highlights the perceived extent of media involvement in the apparently shadowy world of colonial politics. As has been noted, the trial—one in which Rochefort was accused of defamation—became in effect an interrogation of Roustan's

---

[12] The importance of the newspaper has notably been stressed by Vial, *Guy de Maupassant et l'art du roman*, p. 321, and Delaisement, in Guy de Maupassant, *Chroniques*, ed. by Gérard Delaisement, 2 vols (Paris: Rive droite, 2004), II, 1483. For further commentary on the period see Delaisement's discussion of Maupassant's 1881 *chronique*, *Zut* (II, 1410–15).

[13] Forestier notes the evident parallels with Maupassant's fictional *La Vie française* in Maupassant, *Romans*, ed. by Forestier, p. 1332.

[14] *L'Intransigeant*, 27 September 1881, p. 1.

[15] Vial, *Guy de Maupassant et l'art du roman*, p. 327; see also Julien, *L'Affaire tunisienne 1878–1881*, p. 47.

competencies and conduct as consul.¹⁶ Witness M. Gay de Tunis was particularly virulent on the subject of the consul's innumerable failings, echoing Rochefort's allegations: 'J'ai ici [. . .] une lettre de l'ancien premier ministre Khérédine, qui se plaint des articles de la *République française*, articles publiés en vue de déprécier les valeurs tunisiennes.' His conclusion was similarly unambiguous: 'M. Roustan, conclut-il, s'est mis entre les mains d'hommes de finance qui lui ont dit: "Marche, marche, et tu avanceras vite! autrement, nous te briserons!" (Sensation.).'¹⁷

Borderline hysterical, the courtroom denunciation epitomizes precisely the line of attack adopted by *L'Intransigeant*, referencing hands ('mis entre les mains'), moreover, as the privileged metonym for underlining the extent of press corruption. Readers of *Bel-Ami* will immediately recognize not only the details of the plot but its surrounding discourse. The idea of conspiracy is evident in the collusion of political and journalistic realms in the novel: 'Les inspirateurs et véritables rédacteurs de *La Vie française* étaient une demi-douzaine de députés intéressés dans toutes les spéculations que lançait ou que soutenait le directeur' (p. 290). In the narrative's explanation of the newspaper's structure, this elite band of conspirators forms the beating heart of *La Vie française*'s media operation, the additional array of journalists, *chroniqueurs*, and the like serving chiefly as foil to its crucial mission of self-enrichment. The notion of 'véritables rédacteurs' naturally betokens the existence of false editors, and yet it is precisely those uninitiated journalists—those outside 'la bande à Walter' (p. 290)—who furnish the operation with an air of normality, contributing ultimately to its success: 'Et *La Vie française* "naviguait sur les fonds et bas-fonds", manœuvrée par toutes ces mains différentes' (p. 290). Hands repeatedly figure in the formulation of the newspaper's rise, an ascension tied symbiotically to the social triumph of Maupassant's protagonist: 'Du Roy devenait célèbre dans les groupes politiques. Il sentait grandir son influence à la pression des poignées de main' (p. 366).

While central to *Bel-Ami*, media manipulation, the very etymology of which evokes *la main*, equally plays a significant role in Maupassant's North African journalism; it forms, moreover, a crucial element of wider Third Republic discourses on the press. In his study of the media imaginary in nineteenth-century France, Guillaume Pinson explores the debate about press manipulation, noting the sense in which the newspaper was deemed to play a starring role in the corrupt and corrupting political and business culture of the Third Republic. Evoking Angenot's influential notion of 'Publicistique', a diverse sector of discursive production principally concerned with mapping, and ultimately shaping, the twin social forces of *actualité* and public opinion, Pinson

---

¹⁶ See Maupassant, *Chroniques*, ed. by Delaisement, II, 1483.
¹⁷ Albert Bataille, *Causes criminelles et mondaines de 1881* (Paris: Dentu, 1882), pp. 339, 341.

considers an array of critiques of journalism, such as Eugène Soleilhac's *Le Grand levier; ou, De la presse et de son influence politique et sociale à notre époque*: 'La presse est un "grand levier", pour reprendre l'expression d'un analyste [Soleilhac] qui tente, au début du xxe siècle, de convertir en réflexion sociale approfondie ce que Maupassant avait illustré dans *Bel-Ami*.'[18] Closely tied to Pinson's notion of the *roman du scandale*, a later evolutionary stage in the development of the nineteenth-century novel of journalism, epitomized not simply by *Bel-Ami* but by novels such as Zola's *L'Argent*, this strand of public discourse paints a picture of underhand deals, backscratching, the selfish pursuit of financial remuneration at any cost. In a lengthy sequence of media scandals and affairs, furthermore, the debate about Tunisia figures as an early example of this wider culture of newspaper suspicion, a staging post to the more significant crises of the Panama Canal and the *emprunts russes*.[19]

Maupassant's journalistic pronouncements on Tunisia suggest a certain ambivalence in the novelist's attitude toward this much-discussed debate. To a certain extent he defended Roustan in the article 'Choses du jour', and his reflections on the affair evolve over the course of the 1880s.[20] From his earliest depictions of the subject, however, a concern for the role of the media in shaping, and ultimately manipulating, public opinion is evident. Writing in *Le Gaulois* on 10 April 1881 in a *chronique* entitled 'La Guerre' (some months before the eruption of the Rochefort–Roustan scandal), the journalist depicts France beset by rumours of impending military conflict in Tunisia:

> Un frisson court d'un bout à l'autre de ce pays de gobe-mouches. On murmure.
> —La guerre! la guerre! Tunis, Roustan, Maccio, Roustan!
> Et tous les bourgeois exaltés brandissent leur journal au coin du feu en criant à leur femme et à leurs mioches, devant leur servante stupéfaite:
> —A Tunis, à Tunis!
> Aussitôt, les hommes du pouvoir se disent:
> —Il faut tenir compte de l'opinion publique.
> Et on arme, on déplace les régiments, on réquisitionne les transatlantiques, on fait du bruit du diable, avec cette pensée secrète:
> —Il sera toujours temps de voir ce qui peut arriver.[21]

---

[18] Guillaume Pinson, *L'Imaginaire médiatique: histoire et fiction du journal au XIXe siècle* (Paris: Classiques Garnier, 2012) p. 145. See also Marc Martin, 'Retour sur "l'abominable vénalité de la presse"', *Le Temps des médias*, 6 (2006), 22–33.

[19] See Pinson, *L'Imaginaire médiatique*, pp. 93–97. The connection with Zola's *L'Argent* gestures towards that other crucial historical phenomenon evoked in *Bel-Ami: le krach de l'Union Générale*. See, in particular, Delaisement's study of questions of money, the press, and *le krach* in *Les Chroniques politiques de Guy de Maupassant*, ed. by Delaisement (Paris: Rive droite, 2006), pp. 236–69; see also Dorian Bell's discussion of *L'Argent*, 'Beyond the Bourse: Zola, Empire, and the Jews', *Romanic Review*, 102 (2011), 485–501.

[20] See Guy de Maupassant, *Lettres d'Afrique (Algérie-Tunisie)*, ed. by Michèle Salinas (Paris: La Boîte à documents, 1997), p. 278. See, in particular, Salinas's 'Présentation', pp. 7–45.

[21] Maupassant, *Chroniques*, ed. by Delaisement, I, 189.

This sketch deftly connects government policy with the proverbial reader, whipped into an apparently delirious frenzy of colonialist zeal by his newspaper, vehicle of colonial knowledge. Brandishing his 'journal', the bourgeois is positively enthused by the prospect of military intervention. But, as Maupassant's article suggests, the sources behind this story prove elusive: who, after all, has inspired such lust for military conflict? That talk of war in Tunisia is everywhere evident and yet nowhere specific emerges in the journalist's manipulation of the pronoun 'on', sign of the homogenized times. The ambiguity associated with this 'on' will prove crucial to *Bel-Ami*: inscribed into its seeming innocuousness are the actions of unseen and yet ever-present authorities, organizing a specific version of *actualité* convenient to their own political ambitions. Emblem of the doxa, the 'on' masks an apparently invisible process of government manipulation.[22] Indeed, just as M. Walter's remarks at the dinner party (with which we began) suggested a hierarchical relationship between those responsible for *les actualités* and those destined simply to consume them, 'La Guerre' equally evokes a distinction between 'les hommes du pouvoir' and the sense of ignorance characteristic of 'les bourgeois exaltés', their dependence on the media as food for political thought.

Crucial to Maupassant's early reaction to the occupation, therefore, is the sketching of a triangular relation between authority, ignorance, and manipulation, a relation, moreover, which stresses the pyramidal structure governing the dissemination of information under the Third Republic: *actualité*, it seems, is no democracy. Maupassant's 'Balançoires', an article published 12 May 1881, paints a bleak picture of the media, slavishly trumpeting the (fatally compromised) glory of French military victory. In the image of the *balançoire*, the journalist stresses the vacuity at the heart of press reports on the Tunisian Affair. A seemingly uncontrollable lurching of political momentum from one side to another proves characteristic of the media's fascination with this foreign-policy episode, which—once launched—takes on a life of its own. Maupassant is swift to undermine the supposed heroism of his fellow reporters:

Les journaux, depuis six semaines, sont pleins de dépêches héroïques; les reporters eux-mêmes étaient mis en campagne, la plume d'une main, le revolver de l'autre. On savait le nombre des bataillons pris à tous les coins de la France.[23]

Once again, the vagueness of the pronoun 'on' gestures towards the sense in which newspaper discourse comes to dominate public opinion, shaping the

---

[22] On this pronoun see also Dominique Kalifa, 'Les Tâcherons de l'information: petits reporters et faits divers à la "belle époque"', *Revue d'histoire moderne et contemporaine*, 40 (1993), 578–603 (p. 594): 'Le "je", *a fortiori* la signature y étaient absents, hormis quelques textes d'envoyés spéciaux ou certains récits d'exécutions capitales, genres plus "nobles". A l'inverse progressa l'emploi du "on", qui établissait un amalgame suspect entre le journaliste, le lecteur et l'opinion.'

[23] Maupassant, *Chroniques*, ed. by Delaisement, I, 201.

ubiquitous and yet unquestioned *actualité*. However, Maupassant's depiction of the fictionalization of this conflict, its manipulation ('la plume d'une main, le revolver de l'autre'), poses a challenge to the epistemological pretensions of the press, questioning not simply the extent of French military triumph but the discourse given to the perpetuation of such triumphs:

Enfin, on se décide à tenter l'assaut. [. . .] Un général marche en tête, bravement, cherchant la gloire et le danger. On monte, on monte encore, on monte toujours: pas *plus de Kroumirs que sur la main*. Voici le faîte. Le général y parvient le premier, en hardi soldat, et il trouve en face de lui... un vieil abruti de Kroumir qui devait chantonner dans sa barbe blanche:

Allah! Tralala!
Les voilà,
Ces bons Français-là!

Et la campagne est terminée!!! Enfin, ce qui n'empêcha point les journaux du soir d'annoncer pompeusement en tête de leurs colonnes: *l'Assaut et la prise du fameux marabout de Djebel-ben-Abdallah*.[24]

Military columns thus prove as flawed as their journalistic counterparts, the two bound together in a symbiotic relation of mutual dependence (and, ultimately, mutual fabrication).

What emerges from 'La Guerre' and 'Balançoires', therefore, is a profound pessimism concerning the sincerity of the various official languages which dominate French society;[25] the satire of misinformation calls into question the political logic underpinning colonial expansion. Indeed, misinformation is an ever-present theme in Maupassant's writings on Africa and constitutes, moreover, a crucial aspect of much of his prose in general. The often-evoked 'La Parure',[26] structured around misunderstanding and ignorance, encapsulates the critical role played by fakes and falsehoods in Maupassant's fiction. That social discourses propagate a variety of misleading fictions is an observation pertinent to many of Maupassant's discussions of the press. In an article at pains to stress media hypocrisy, entitled 'Vive Mustapha', the limits of the newspaper's colonial knowledge and the inconsistency of (what we might term) its colonial conscience are exposed: 'Il est bien difficile, vraiment, de se fier aux renseignements que nous fournit la presse française.'[27] Such a denunciation of the press's epistemological confidence is a frequent feature of much of Maupassant's journalism: invariably, the newspapers have simply

---

[24] Ibid., pp. 201–02.

[25] The question of poverty of language proves crucial to Maupassant's journalism, and is evoked by Trevor A. Le V. Harris, *Maupassant in the Hall of Mirrors: Ironies of Repetition in the Work of Guy de Maupassant* (Basingstoke: Macmillan, 1990), p. 32.

[26] See Maupassant, *Contes et nouvelles*, ed. by Louis Forestier, 2 vols (Paris: Gallimard, 1974–79) I, 1198–1206.

[27] Maupassant, *Chroniques*, ed. by Delaisement, I, 230.

got it wrong. From the press (and it should also be noted that *Bel-Ami* was serialized in *Gil-Blas*), the novelist thus fights journalism with journalism.

Crucial to Maupassant's particular vision of newspaper inadequacy, furthermore, is an overriding concern with outlining the personal dynamics underpinning political developments.[28] The sense of slippage which links the private dramas of men and women to the public world of diplomacy represents an underlying thematic concern common both to Maupassant's journalism and to his work as a novelist. In 'Choses du jour', for example, foreign policy—in a fashion typical of Maupassant—proves to be intimately linked with personal liaisons: 'Tous les secrets de cabinet devenaient des secrets d'alcôve, et réciproquement.'[29] The secrets of the Tunisian Affair, it therefore follows, become inseparable from those of Roustan's personal affairs.[30] This notion of overlap, the innumerable connections between the bedroom and the wider political world, lies at the heart of *Bel-Ami*'s treatment of media corruption, a point critical to Robert Lethbridge's reading of the text: 'the manipulation of words becomes synonymous with the manipulation of others, whether for speculative or seductive ends'.[31] The disruptive presence of manipulation at virtually every social level accounts for the novel's more complex reflection on the nature of *actualité* and, as we shall see, on the success—and perpetuation—of certain corrupted values.

The Value of News: 'On manœuvre'

Angenot identifies literature as that discourse which comments upon all others; following wider discursive trends, it interrogates the nature of social discourse itself: 'Literature is to be considered as a *supplement* to the

---

[28] The question of Maupassant's status as a political writer (and, indeed, *Bel-Ami* as a political novel) has been the subject of some debate. See Christopher Lloyd, *Maupassant: 'Bel-Ami'* (London: Grant and Cutler, 1988), p. 84. For a different reading see Adrian C. Ritchie, 'Maupassant et la démocratie parlementaire', *Studi francesi*, 78 (1982), 426–34; Harris, *Maupassant in the Hall of Mirrors*, pp. 25–36. On the question of the relation of public to private, note Bancquart's introduction to her edition of *Bel-Ami* (Paris: Imprimerie nationale, 1979), pp. 9–40 (p. 35): 'Si *Bel-Ami* comporte, plus que tout autre roman de Maupassant, des traits du roman balzacien, l'enchaînement des causes et la relation de la vie privée aux choses publiques sont plus précipités chez Maupassant.'

[29] Maupassant, *Chroniques*, ed. by Delaisement, I, 405.

[30] The question of Roustan's relationship with the prominent Mme Elias was a central feature of the debate about the consul's inadequacies; see 'Choses du jour', in Maupassant, *Chroniques*, ed. by Delaisement, I, 404–07.

[31] See Lethbridge's 'Introduction' to Maupassant's *Bel-Ami*, trans. by Margaret Mauldon (Oxford: Oxford University Press, 2001), p. xxxii. Lethbridge's study not only details the novel's historical context but explores 'the triangulation of money, sex, and power' (p. xix). His above comments on manipulation, moreover, highlight a further theme crucial to *Bel-Ami* explored later in my discussion: 'the *language* of duplicity' (p. xxxii). On such questions of manipulation, note also Pinson's discussion of the nature of the *roman du scandale* in *L'Imaginaire médiatique*, p. 94: 'La manipulation de l'information est à la source du scénario des romans du scandale médiatique.'

social discourse; its moment is afterward, which contributes to its trouble-making character.'[32] The apparently *supplementary* quality of literary fiction, according to such arguments, transforms the tedium of the everyday into the super-relevant, postponing literature's powers of intervention in favour of a sense of wider historical perspective: 'Il s'agit de connecter l'actualité transitoire et la vérité éternelle.' This comment of Angenot's, cited in Jameson's analysis of *1889*, prompts the following critique:

> This is then contextualization with a vengeance, in which the contextualized object ends up being completely volatized by the ever more completely researched context and by our own fuller knowledge.[33]

In tracing the debate about Tunisia—and Maupassant's own journalistic pronouncements on the subject—I have endeavoured to adhere to such critical principles. And yet, the nature of Maupassant's commentary on the news and its foundations will lead not only to an appreciation of some (highly specific) contextual *cause célèbre*: at stake in *Bel-Ami* is an exploration of the limits of *actualité*, an analysis of how a given social discourse comes to dominate others. The novel, therefore, does not simply map what—in Angenot's terminology—we might refer to as some specific 'socio-discursive moment', but offers its own explanation as to how certain discourses succeed in arresting public attention.[34] Furthermore, the proximity of newspaper and literary text (a proximity epitomized by the innumerable connections between Maupassant's journalism, his shorter fiction, and his work as a novelist) serves to highlight the complexity of literature's *supplementary* character: while the novel questions the validity of *actualité* as defined by the likes of M. Walter, the text nevertheless adopts various discourses associated with the newspapers, its plot shaped by the intricacies of recent scandal. While the Tunisian Affair furnishes the novel with a plot of political corruption, therefore, the thematic concerns of financial chicanery and political manipulation equally occasion a more subtle reflection on the nature of *actualité* itself.

Bel-Ami details how *actualité* circulates incognito throughout the social world, seemingly naturalized as fact. And yet, the narrative equally demonstrates how such *actualité* invariably proves subject to manipulation, to the corruptive logic characteristic of the Moroccan plot. After all, Duroy's rapid ascension comes to depend upon the success of M. Walter's politico-financial intrigue, their fates intertwined with the convoluted circulation of capital. Indeed, as has been noted, questions of cost, scenes of financial transaction,

---

[32] Marc Angenot, 'What Can Literature Do? From Literary Sociocriticism to a Critique of Social Discourse', trans. by Robert F. Barsky, *Yale Journal of Criticism*, 17 (2004), 217–31 (p. 219).

[33] Angenot, *1889: un état du discours social*, p. 836. Cited in Jameson, 'Marc Angenot, Literary History, and the Study of Culture in the Nineteenth Century', p. 247.

[34] Angenot, 'What Can Literature Do?', p. 220.

however small, are ubiquitous in *Bel-Ami*.[35] The narrative documents the evolution of a certain set of values: the Moroccan debt, the authenticity of newspaper copy, and the personal wealth of the various characters (not least Duroy himself) become symbiotically linked in what is ostensibly a disconnect between financial and moral values. This issue of the connection between economic enrichment, the literary text, and a debased and transgressed moral code lies at the heart of Maupassant's novel, which, in a fashion distinct from Balzac, probes the question of how a given text's (literary or journalistic) referential qualities might be warped or undermined by corrupt and corrupting discourses. Christopher Prendergast's influential reading of Balzac in *The Order of Mimesis* explores the circulation of forgeries and fakes in such texts as *Illusions perdues* and *Splendeurs et misères des courtisanes*, noting their disruptive propensity to call into question any definitive notion of value, even subverting the authority of the narrator's discourse itself. Lucien de Rubempré, in Prendergast's account, epitomizes such insecurity: 'He is a space of "values" that vary according to the laws of circulation.'[36] The same point, of course, might be made of Duroy: like Balzac's ill-fated poet, Maupassant's protagonist elects to change his name in a bid for social elevation. Such an alteration epitomizes his lack of fixed value, his ability to shift in accordance with social expectation.[37]

The difference between such questions of value for the respective protagonists of *Illusions perdues* and *Bel-Ami* lies in their degree of success, however: put simply, duplicity works for Duroy. Maupassant's narrative does not therefore simply evoke a social world in which forgeries, fakes, and copies threaten to deform what is authentic, original; rather—and perhaps more radically—his is a universe comprised almost in its entirety of such forgeries, fakes, and copies. All values appear relative in *Bel-Ami*, a narrative in which the boundaries separating the fictions of personal ambition and the realities of the social world prove (like the territorial limits of France itself) flexible. Manipulation, therefore, figures as social principle. Knowledge, furthermore, essentially corresponds to the appearance of knowledge, a point Forestier makes to Duroy early in the text:

> Il se tut, réfléchit quelques secondes, puis demanda:
> 'Es-tu bachelier?'
> —Non. J'ai échoué deux fois.

---

[35] Lethbridge, 'Introduction', pp. xix–xxi.

[36] Christopher Prendergast, *The Order of Mimesis: Balzac, Stendhal, Nerval, Flaubert* (Cambridge: Cambridge University Press, 1986), p. 99. Prendergast's chapter on Balzac (pp. 83–118) is of particular relevance here.

[37] On such questions of name changes (and, indeed, broader issues of originality and repetition) see Harris, *Maupassant in the Hall of Mirrors*, Ch. 6, pp. 83–104, especially p. 100.

—Ça ne fait rien, du moment que tu as poussé tes études jusqu'au bout. Si on parle de Cicéron ou de Tibère, tu sais à peu près ce que c'est?
—Oui, à peu près.
—Bon, personne n'en sait davantage, à l'exception d'une vingtaine d'imbéciles qui ne sont pas fichus de se tirer d'affaire. Ça n'est pas difficile de passer pour fort, va; le tout est de ne pas se faire pincer en flagrant délit d'ignorance. On manœuvre, on esquive la difficulté, on tourne l'obstacle, et on colle les autres au moyen d'un dictionnaire. (p. 202)

Conversation, according to Forestier, thus constitutes a series of acts of manipulation ('On manœuvre'). This lesson in social comportment, however, might double for an education in the art of writing newspaper copy. Indeed, the elusive pronoun 'on' resurfaces in the journalist's response to Duroy's admission of his want of writing experience: 'Bah! on essaye, on commence' (p. 204). Elsewhere in *Bel-Ami*, a slippage between speech and text, between *parole* and *mot*, will prove typical of the narrative's strategy of outlining the confused origins of *actualité* (a point reinforced through the novel's repeated episodes of dictation).

Central in Forestier's enigmatic call for Duroy to transcend his humble beginnings is the notion of the copy ('on colle les autres au moyen d'un dictionnaire'), a capacity Duroy is swift to master ('répétant comme de lui des choses qu'il venait d'entendre' (p. 220)). From the (aptly named) fellow journalist Saint-Potin's explanation of how to interview various foreign dignitaries (p. 244) to the protagonist's repeated transcribing of his original article, 'Souvenirs d'un chasseur d'Afrique' (p. 402), the ability to copy has long been associated with Maupassant's narrative of *arrivisme*. Primed in the imitative arts, Duroy emerges as an extreme example of a literary character whose psychological motivation might be best described by René Girard's theory of mimetic desire.[38] His early decision to accompany Forestier to the newspaper offices is couched in terms which prefigure the protagonist's winning ability not simply to copy but, ultimately, to assimilate the actions, behaviours, even the lives of others: 'Je te suis' (p. 201). In a narrative in which Duroy will be repeatedly likened to Forestier, the protagonist's profound debt to his would-be mentor is thus early established. Later, the spectre of his wife's former husband becomes something of an obsession: 'Il ne pouvait plus prendre un objet sans qu'il crût voir aussitôt la main de Charles posée dessus' (p. 369). Hands, it should be noted, figure in Maupassant's depiction of the paranoia of copy, an anxiety of influence which, like the disembodied hand of his short story 'La main d'écorché', refuses to leave the protagonist alone.

[38] René Girard, *Mensonge romantique et vérité romanesque* (Paris: Grasset, 1961). See also Gerald Prince, '*Bel-Ami* and Narrative as Antagonist', *French Forum*, 11 (1986), 217–26 (pp. 219–20 and 222). See also Noëlle Benhamou, 'L'Imitation dans *Bel-Ami*', *Bulletin Flaubert-Maupassant*, 12 (2003), 33–48.

That social behaviour follows this imitative logic is further evidence of its complex entanglement with newspaper copy. Indeed, that the press takes responsibility for producing (and reproducing) *actualité* is a point central to Angenot's analysis; conversation follows the newspaper, a faded copy of those widely circulated discourses which construct *actualité*: 'les discours journalistiques [...] sont venus nourrir et informer de plus en plus la conversation bourgeoise "privée", au point de réduire celle-ci à un simple épicycle de l'imprimé d'actualité'.[39] Various episodes in *Bel-Ami* underline the nature of this influence; Duroy's meeting with Mme Walter and friends, for example, reveals the extent to which social knowledge of the contemporary figures as a subject of rote learning: 'Ces dames discutaient ces choses de mémoire, comme si elles eussent récité une comédie mondaine et convenable, répétée bien souvent' (p. 286). Maupassant's narrative, however, equally subverts (and inverts) this causal relation. That everyday conversation constitutes newspaper copy is a point stressed in Duroy's private observation that he might simply transcribe Clotilde de Marelle's remarks into the newspaper: 'Il l'écoutait, pensant: "C'est bon à retenir tout ça. On écrirait des chroniques parisiennes charmantes en la faisant bavarder sur les événements du jour"' (p. 252). The journalist is alive to the possibilities of integrating any aspect of his personal life into the newspaper, seemingly conscious of the intricate mirroring which renders social life the inverted imitation of newspaper copy (and vice versa). Indeed, the narrative's interest in copy ends neither in the derivative behaviour of its protagonist nor in the derivative nature of the texts he produces: *actualité* is itself profoundly derivative. Far from a simple *compte rendu* of salient public events, it depends upon the doxa—that which is taken for granted—and is inscribed into some pre-existing narrative of the supposedly novel, the newsworthy. Notions of replication thus prove critical to *actualité* as it emerges in *Bel-Ami*: a social discourse propagated through continual reaffirmation.[40]

Via an array of metaphors stressing such interrelated notions as similarity, copy, imitation, mirroring, the novel underlines a derivative logic at work in the perpetuation of news. Such emphasis on the derivative is not the only strand of the text's meditation on the operations of *actualité*, however: the interrogation of its value becomes, in fact, a kind of privileged *passetemps* during Duroy's first dinner party. Maupassant's men and women content themselves with unpicking a hidden logic behind the news:

Et on discuta sur ce cas d'adultère compliqué de chantage. On n'en parlait point comme on parle, au sein des familles, des événements racontés dans les feuilles publiques, mais

---

[39] Angenot, *1889: un état du discours social*, p. 652.

[40] Angenot explores the repetitive aspect of *actualité* and, citing Walter Benjamin, defines it as 'l'éternel retour du même', in *1889: un état du discours social*, p. 597.

comme on parle d'une maladie entre médecins ou de légumes entre fruitiers. On ne s'indignait pas, on ne s'étonnait pas des faits; on en cherchait les causes profondes, secrètes, avec une curiosité professionnelle et une indifférence absolue pour le crime lui-même. On tâchait d'expliquer nettement les origines des actions, de déterminer tous les phénomènes cérébraux dont était né le drame, résultat scientifique d'un état d'esprit particulier. Les femmes aussi se passionnaient à cette poursuite, à ce travail. Et d'autres événements récents furent examinés, commentés, tournés sous toutes leurs faces, pesés à leur valeur, avec ce coup d'œil pratique et cette manière de voir spéciale des marchands de nouvelles, des débitants de comédie humaine à la ligne, comme on examine, comme on retourne et comme on pèse, chez les commerçants, les objets qu'on va livrer au public. (pp. 214-15)

These merchants of public information engage in a peculiar reading of *actualité*, concerned less with questions of substance than with its potential value ('pesés à leur valeur') in an economy of perennially circulating news stories. At stake in the conversation of this media-enlightened gathering, then, is the secret history of *actualité*, a history bent on tracing the contours, the ambiguities of social knowledge itself. *Bel-Ami*, it should be noted, takes up a position in such an economy, for the novel is explicitly concerned with multiple cases of adultery. This self-reflexive turn epitomizes the narrative's complex relation to *actualité*: dependent upon the newspaper (even indebted to it) for the details of thematic content, *Bel-Ami* nevertheless contrives to illustrate not simply the commercial logic underpinning *actualité* but the process of manipulation, evident throughout society, which such commercial activities necessarily engender.[41] Crucial to this interrogation (as noted in previous examples), the pronoun 'on' here serves to obscure the question of who is ultimately responsible for this social knowledge, shrouding issues of agency and identity in its lack of specificity.

The enigma of what lies behind the stuff of *actualité* is, therefore, a question confronted by Maupassant's circle of media insiders. While such characters blithely discuss the limits of the news, the narrative's well-documented obsessions with duplicity and language posit a more fundamental interrogation of the manipulative logic at the heart of social interaction. Increasingly apparent is the notion that conversation itself betrays some hidden agenda. In contrast to this inaugural dinner party, the Café Riche provides the setting for a scene characterized by various 'ruses de langage':

Ce fut le moment des sous-entendus adroits, des voiles levés par des mots, comme on lève des jupes, le moment des ruses de langage, des audaces habiles et déguisées, de toutes les hypocrisies impudiques de la phrase qui montre des images dévêtues avec des expressions couvertes, qui fait passer dans l'œil et dans l'esprit la vision rapide de tout ce qu'on ne peut pas dire, et permet aux gens du monde une sorte d'amour subtil

---

[41] See Richard Terdiman's *Discourse/Counter-Discourse: The Theory and Practice of Symbolic Resistance in Nineteenth-Century France* (Ithaca, NY: Cornell University Press, 1985), in particular pp. 117-46.

et mystérieux, une sorte de contact impur des pensées par l'évocation simultanée, troublante et sensuelle comme une étreinte, de toutes les choses secrètes, honteuses et désirées de l'enlacement. (p. 258)

In the gap between the first attempts to fathom some hidden significance of *actualité* and the various unsubtle layers of suggestive language deployed in this second social gathering ('des voiles levés', 'on lève des jupes', 'des images dévêtues avec des expressions couvertes'), the extent of the protagonist's education emerges: Duroy becomes fluent in a language of 'sous-entendus'. Indeed, the language of uncovering is not simply deployed as an obvious means of evoking supposedly hidden desires (which in fact have never really been concealed) but rather serves to stress the novel's fascination with eliding the personal with the political, the private with the public. Playing on the term *découvert*, the narrative's close echoes precisely this interest: waiting for Duroy's marriage ceremony with Suzanne Walter to begin, Jacques Rival, 'chroniqueur d'actualité' (p. 290), remarks to the poet Norbert de Varenne of Madeleine Forestier: 'Elle doit être charmante au découvert' (p. 475). Later, the poet advances his own version of events behind Duroy's marriage to Suzanne: 'il [Duroy] tenait le père [M. Walter] par des cadavres découverts, paraît-il, des cadavres enterrés au Maroc' (p. 476). In the space of a single conversation, therefore, the repetition of *découvert* betokens two seemingly distinct (but in fact interconnected) acts of discovery. The colonial conspiracy (and indeed, the etymology of this term indicates the idea of 'breathing together') is intricately bound up with the novel's various amorous adventures in an evident elision of sexual and military conquest.[42]

The novel thus traces a slippage between covering, uncovering, and covering-up—all terms, of course, relevant both to social discourse (conversation and journalism alike) and to the various secretive liaisons critical to the narrative's arc. Such a slippage, however, is particularly evident in *Bel-Ami*'s characterization of *les échos*, that section of the newspaper chiefly concerned with gossip and social life. *Les échos*, in fact, come to resemble precisely the kind of duplicitous language evident during the scene at the Café Riche:

C'est par eux [les échos] qu'on lance les nouvelles, qu'on fait courir les bruits, qu'on agit sur le public et sur la rente. Entre deux soirées mondaines, il faut savoir glisser, sans avoir l'air de rien, la chose importante, plutôt insinuée que dite. Il faut, par des sous-entendus, laisser deviner ce qu'on veut, démentir de telle sorte que la rumeur s'affirme, ou affirmer de telle manière que personne ne croie au fait annoncé. Il faut que, dans les échos, chacun trouve, chaque jour, une ligne au moins qui l'intéresse, afin que tout le monde les lise. (p. 289)[43]

[42] See White, *The Family in Crisis in Late Nineteenth-Century French Fiction*, p. 88, for a reading sensitive to this elision.
[43] Lethbridge notes the connection between these discourses (and indeed briefly contrasts *les*

The passage is saturated with impersonal constructions ('on', 'il faut'). And yet central to *les échos* is the imperative that such impersonal rhetoric serve some personal interest. As Gerald Prince explains, the narratives produced in *Bel-Ami* may lack interest but prove invariably 'interested'.[44] Indeed, we might add to this observation that journalistic narratives seemingly generate interest (in the financial sense), such is their role in an illicit scheme of personal enrichment. While intent on stressing the derivative nature of much social interaction—and the term *les échos* necessarily highlights this point—the novel thus equally traces a crisis of linguistic clarity: language, it would seem, is given solely to the perpetuation of 'interested' discourses, to various ulterior motives. *Actualité*, therefore, lies somewhere between the unthinking repetition of social knowledge (the doxa) and the more elusive hidden agenda, concealed behind the apparently innocent, the innocuous. Thriving on the *sous-entendu*, news—it would seem—is of value only as long as its private (and 'interested') origins remain obscure, invisible, secret.

Conclusion

In its depiction of *actualité* and its limits, Maupassant's novel of journalism not only stresses what Richard Terdiman sees as a defining element of the modern news industry ('at times the "world" and the "news" might almost seem to have merged for us') but sketches a still more insidious phenomenon: the 'world' emerges simply as a fiction propagated by the 'news'.[45] After all, the novel explores the newspaper's capacity to produce *actualité*, to profoundly shape (indeed, to define) the limits of social knowledge. Nothing could summarize the nature of this confused entanglement of newspaper and social world more effectively than the title of Maupassant's fictional newspaper, *La Vie française*. At stake in *Bel-Ami*, therefore, is an exploration of the fictions at the heart of *actualité*, fictions which rise to such prominence as the result of adroit manipulation on the one hand, and uncritical repetition on the other. While the text evokes the hierarchical structure underpinning *actualité*, it equally interrogates the more ambiguous elements crucial to its propagation: the unthinking reaffirmation of social knowledge by various pawns, the profound duplicity characteristic of all manner of social intercourse. In an episode redolent of Duroy's first encounter with M. Walter, such concerns come to the fore; the director again requests some *actualité* on the subject of Morocco:

échos and conversation of the Café Riche), underlining the fact of linguistic duplicity: 'Above all, in both the private and public domain, language is seen as a substitute for reality rather than a reflection of it' ('Introduction', p. xxxii). See also Prince, '*Bel-Ami* and Narrative as Antagonist', p. 219.
[44] See Prince, '*Bel-Ami* and Narrative as Antagonist', p. 221.
[45] Terdiman, *Discourse/Counter-Discourse*, p. 118.

'Mais il me faudrait quelque chose d'intéressant sur la question du Maroc, une actualité, une chronique à effet, à sensation, je ne sais quoi? Trouvez-moi ça, vous' (p. 401). Duroy has no difficulty in obtaining such news and reproduces a simple transcription of his inaugural 'Souvenirs d'un chasseur d'Afrique'. The protagonist sees fit to transcribe a fictionalized account of his African experience largely written by someone else (and, ultimately, serving the interest of some higher power): 'Et Du Roy s'en alla fouiller dans la collection de *La Vie française* pour retrouver son premier article' (p. 402). It is a strategy utterly emblematic of *actualité* as it operates in *Bel-Ami*: fictional, derivative, manipulative.

GONVILLE AND CAIUS COLLEGE, CAMBRIDGE   EDMUND BIRCH

GIL Y ZÁRATE AND
CARLOS II EL HECHIZADO

Carlos II el hechizado (1837) offers us one of the most paradoxical examples of Spanish Romantic theatre (perhaps only Joaquin Francisco Pacheco's *Alfredo* (1835) is comparable in this respect). In spite of its success on the stage and the considerable political and religious controversy which surrounded it after its first performance, this play by Antonio Gil y Zárate is nowadays considered by scholars of nineteenth-century Spanish theatre to be only a minor work, and it remains half-forgotten beneath the ever-lengthening shadow of other plays now regarded as more representative of Spanish Romanticism in the 1830s, such as Martínez de la Rosa's *La conjuración de Venecia* (1834), Larra's *Macías* (1834), Rivas's *Don Álvaro* (1835), García Gutiérrez's *El trovador* (1836), or even Hartzenbusch's *Los amantes de Teruel*, first performed, like Gil y Zárate's play, in 1837.

Despite the social and political implications that could arise in the 1830s from putting on a historical play set in the time of Carlos II, the same monarch inspired works by various other Romantics.[1] While we now know from modern historical and medical studies that his illness was due to 'la endiosada y demencial política matrimonial que [los Austrias] practicaron una y otra vez sucediéndose sin interrupción los matrimonios consanguíneos',[2] the figure of this king, lonely and misunderstood, manœuvred by power-hungry nobles and politicians, proved irresistible to a number of nineteenth-century authors who, drawn to the character of the last monarch of the House of Austria, saw in him the perfect incarnation of Romantic cosmic injustice.[3]

Nowadays it is generally accepted by critics that behind the writing of a play such as *Carlos II el hechizado* we can discern clear evidence of a political intention on the part of the author with respect to contemporary Spanish

[1] To mention a few: Isidoro Gil y Baus, *Una aventura de Carlos II: comedia en un acto* (Madrid: Imprenta de Yenes, 1846); Tomás Rodríguez y Díaz Rubí, *La corte de Carlos II: comedia histórica en dos partes y seis cuadros* (Madrid: Imprenta de Yenes,1846). Carlos II is also the subject of a novel by Torcuato Tarrago y Mateos, *Carlos II El hechizado* (Madrid: Editorial Pena, 1855).

[2] José Calvo Poyato, *La vida y la época de Carlos II el hechizado* (Barcelona: Planeta, 1996), p. 21.

[3] In his entry speech to the Royal Academy of Medicine in Valencia entitled 'Pericia médica: la otra mirada', Dr Alejandro Font de Mora Turón, on the basis of the portrait of the king by Juan Carreño de Miranda, diagnosed the illness of the last of the Austrian monarchs as obviously having nothing to do with diabolical possession. After describing the physical symptoms revealed by the portrait—'el cráneo con abombamiento frontoparietal, la intensa palidez, el acusado prognatismo habsbúrgico llevado aquí al extremo y la deformidad de las extremidades'—Dr Font de Mora concludes: 'Nuestro diagnóstico aquí sería el de *Raquitismo*, *Anemia* (tal vez de origen palúdico) y un más que posible *déficit intelectual*, siquiera de carácter leve.' See Alejandro Font de Mora Turón, 'Pericia médica: la otra mirada. Discurso de entrada a la Real Academia de Medicina de la Comunidad Valenciana', *Anales Reial Acadèmia de Medicina de la Comunitat Valenciana*, 13 (2012) <http://www.ramcv.com/50-anales2012.html> [accessed 15 May 2014] (p. 8 of 20).

society. Only thus can we explain the survival throughout the nineteenth century of a work which was for forty years emblematic of liberal ideas in Spain. At its first performance on 2 November 1837, as Spain had emerged from the tyranny of Fernando VII and was undergoing a full-scale political revolution, the play was instantly understood to be calling for the separation of the powers of Church and State, and as reflecting 'los abusos de poder de un estamento clerical que impone sus dictados al propio poder civil'.[4] The same would happen in the decade of the 1860s, when the newborn Unión Liberal tried desperately to control the populist impulses which would come together at the time of the 'Glorious' revolution. In each case, the neo-Catholic factions interpreted the play as a frontal attack on their political pretensions and, as Borja Rodríguez Gutiérrez points out, reacted to it 'con la misma furia que antes y con un rencor que desde 1837 no se había extinguido'.[5]

The huge success of the play, and its criticism of the Roman Catholic Church as an institution that was dangerously detrimental to the political progress of the country, would continue in the following year with the premiere of Hartzenbusch's *Doña Mencía o la boda de la Inquisición* (1838). Although Aureliano Fernández Guerra attributes its success mainly to the sensationalism of its plot,[6] it is obvious, as Inés Bergquist suggests, that *Doña Mencía* 'expone la actitud anticlerical del romanticismo liberal más extremo, criticando la beatería y las actitudes ultracatólicas ejemplificadas en la persona de la protagonista',[7] showing also how the Holy Inquisition was a recurrent subject of repression and confinement in the works of liberal writers.[8]

Critics dealing with the work of Gil y Zárate have traditionally agreed to classify it as eclectic.[9] Indeed, over time the term has become a commonplace

---

[4] Víctor Cantero García, '*Carlos II el hechizado* o el teatro ecléctico de Antonio Gil y Zárate', *Estudios Humanísticos: Filología*, 30 (2008), 57–82 (p. 78).

[5] Borja Rodríguez Gutiérrez, 'De retractaciones y falsificaciones: Antonio Gil y Zárate y Carlos II el hechizado', in *Desde la platea: estudios sobre el teatro decomonónico* (Santander: Universidad de Cantabria, 2010), pp. 35–76 (p. 44).

[6] Aureliano Fernández Guerra, *Hartzenbusch: estudio biográfico-crítico* (Madrid: Sáenz de Jubera, [n.d.]), p. 9.

[7] Inés L. Bergquist, 'Convento e Inquisición en *Doña Mencía* de Hartzenbusch', *Bulletin of Spanish Studies*, 79 (2002), 563–73 (p. 564).

[8] See Daniel Muñoz Sempere, *La Inquisición española como tema literario: política, historia y ficción en la crisis del Antiguo Régimen* (Woodbridge: Tamesis, 2008), pp. 155–79.

[9] Besides the classic works of Edgar Allison Peers, *A History of the Romantic Movement in Spain*, 2 vols (Cambridge: Cambridge University Press, 1940; trans. into Spanish by José M. Gimeno as *Historia del movimiento romántico español*, 2 vols (Madrid: Gredos, 1967)), and Ricardo Navas Ruiz, *El romanticismo español* (Madrid: Cátedra, 1983), see, to mention just a few: Derek Flitter, *Spanish Romantic Literary Theory and Criticism* (Cambridge : Cambridge University Press, 1992), pp. 76–78; Félix San Vicente, 'Continuidad del drama histórico', in *Historia de la literatura española: siglo XIX*, ed. by Víctor García de la Concha (Madrid: Espasa Calpe, 1997), pp. 384–99; Felipe González Alcázar, *Procesos de la poética clasicista: los tratados de perceptiva españoles del siglo XIX* (Murcia: Universidad de Murcia, 2005), pp. 66–72; Cecilio Alonso, *Historia de la literatura española*, v: *Hacia una literatura nacional (1800–1900)*, ed. by José Carlos Mainer

of Gil y Zárate criticism, though few have tried to define it or to specify what it denotes. The description seems to have grown out of the dramatist's own theoretical conception of drama. Thus, in his accession speech to the Real Academia de la Lengua, 'Sobre la poesía dramática' (1839), he spoke of the need to create a new mode of national theatre in which 'se refundan todas las literaturas especiales, ostentando por consiguiente las dotes más sobresalientes de cada una de ellas'.[10] Only in this way, taking the best elements from earlier models, could dramatic literature achieve its full perfection. It would then be possible to 'fijarse las reglas de este nuevo género, reglas que serían adoptadas y seguidas con escrupulosidad por los ingenios que se dedicasen al teatro, los cuales tendrían asi las pautas que habían de conducirlos al acierto, ventaja que no podemos tener los que vivimos ahora en estos tiempos de transición y revoluciones'.[11] Accordingly, he would affirm two years later in 'Teatro antiguo y teatro moderno' (1841), while again discussing the need to renew the theatre in Spain:

Tres son pues las fuentes que han de concurrir a la formación de nuestro nuevo teatro nacional. Las comedias antiguas, la literatura clásica y los dramas románticos: en las tres hay defectos de los que huir, pero tambien bellezas que imitar. La brillante poesía de las primeras, la regularidad, el buen gusto de la segunda; el movimiento y pasión de los últimos son prendas que deben hermanarse para producir una composición perfecta.[12]

However, any attempt to apply this theory to a specific work such as *Carlos II el hechizado* raises serious difficulties. Víctor Cantero García faces them in his article when, having defined eclecticism as a mixture of 'lo clásico y lo romántico', he tries to justify this view in relation to Gil y Zárate's play, but can only manage to mention two kinds of love—that of Froilán versus that of Florencio—and the regular alternation of scenes of high dramatic tension with others that are of more marginal interest to the audience, such as the exorcism and its rituals.[13]

The problem that arises when one tries to apply the concept of eclecticism to *Carlos II el hechizado* resides in the fact that Gil y Zárate attempted from the outset to write a play commensurate with the Romantic dramas of the 1830s. In complete theoretical disaccord with both the Romantics and the

(Barcelona: Crítica, 2010), pp. 371–73; and Raimundo Cuesta, 'La huella francesa en la génesis de la historia escolar en España', in *Francia en la educación de la España contemporánea (1808-2008)*, ed. by José María Hernández Díaz (Salamanca: Universidad de Salamanca, 2011), pp. 273–322 (pp. 306–10).
[10] Antonio Gil y Zárate, 'Sobre la poesía dramática', *Revista de Madrid*, 3 (Madrid: Imprenta de Tomás Jordán, 1839), 147–57 (pp. 156–57).
[11] Ibid., p. 157.
[12] Antonio Gil y Zárate, 'Teatro antiguo y teatro moderno', *Revista de Madrid*, 3.1 (Madrid: Imprenta de D. Fernando Suárez, 1841), 112–24 (p. 122).
[13] Cantero García, '*Carlos II el hechizado*, o el teatro ecléctico', p. 76.

traditionalist school of dramatic writing, his previous play, *Blanca de Borbón* (1835), was well received by one side but furiously attacked by critics on the Romantic side, who found it tepid.[14] This alignment of the later play's text with the postulates of the Romantic school did not pass unnoticed by critics at the time. Eugenio de Ochoa, in his introduction to the collected plays of Gil y Zárate (1850), would affirm:

> [. . .] de esta funesta carcoma de las sociedades, el espíritu del pandillaje, que así en lo literario como en lo político es el mayor obstáculo para la razón y el bienestar de la especie humana, sindicaba al Señor Gil de 'clásico puro', ya por esa [*Blanca de Borbon*] como por sus anteriores obras. Su amor propio se sintió herido, y por ello cometió un error, pero error que dio lugar a otro de mayor consecuencia, componiendo el *Carlos II*.[15]

Much the same view was taken by the theatre critic Fermín Gonzálo Morón in a series of articles on the work of Gil y Zárate published in the *Revista de España y del Extranjero* in 1842. After analysing the qualities and the success of the latter's early *Blanca de Borbon* and *Rodrigo*, as well as two very early comedies, *El entrometido* and *Un año despues de la boda*,[16] on turning to *Carlos II el hechizado* he complains of 'la nueva marcha adoptada en su carrera'.[17] Gonzalo Morón harshly criticizes the fact that Gil y Zárate should here have followed 'casi en todo la malhadada escuela, y la perjudicial moral del autor de *Nuestra Señora de París*, hasta parecer a veces una imitación'.[18] At the same time, the alignment with the manner of the Romantic school perceived by critics in *Carlos II el hechizado* involved not merely questions of form but also of content, a fact which did not remain unnoticed by contemporary critics. Gonzalo Morón himself, in the article cited, declares that 'el frenesí de su vergonzosa pasión hacia Inés nos recuerda esa funesta moral de los dramáticos y novelistas franceses, que han dado en pintar las pasiones mas criminales como una cosa necesaria, y que no era posible reprimir al hombre'.[19] Similarly to Ochoa in the introduction mentioned above, 'pareció peligrosísimo que viniese el nuevo drama a favorecer las exageraciones y los extremos de la moda, dándoles autoridad y peso con el brillo de su mérito y con el nombre ya respetable del autor'.[20]

Eleven years later, the publication of Gil's memoires, amid the polemic produced by the appearance in the magazine *La Esperanza* of a supposed

---

[14] Alonso, *Historia de la literature española*, v, 372.
[15] *Obras dramáticas de Don Antonio Gil y Zárate*, ed. by Eugenio de Ochoa (Paris: Baudry Librería Europea, 1850), p. xii.
[16] Fermín Gonzalo Morón, 'Juicio crítico delas tragedias y comedias de D. Antonio Gil y Zárate', *Revista de España y del Extranjero*, 2 (1842), 185–92.
[17] Ibid., p. 185.
[18] Ibid., p. 189.
[19] Ibid.
[20] *Obras dramáticas de Don Antonio Gil y Zárate*, ed. by Ochoa, p. xii.

withdrawal by Gil y Zárate from the ideas expressed in *Carlos II*, simply reinforced his original intention to write the play in the Romantic manner:

Decíase por los partidarios de la nueva escuela que si persistía en la antigua era por falta de ingenio y por incapacidad de escribir un drama romántico; y yo, que siempre he creído mucho más difícil hacer una buena tragedia, me propuse darles un solemne mentís, y probarles que me sobraban facultades para hacer lo que ellos creían estaba sólo reservado a los más sublimes genios.[21]

Bearing in mind the clear intention of the author, the aim of this article will be to analyse *Carlos II el hechizado* as a work belonging precisely to this subversive Romanticism of the 1830s, noting both its fresh contribution to that genre and its connections with other works staged in the same decade.

Gil y Zárate based the construction of his play on two different series of events which interact with each other as the plot progresses and which converge, at least indirectly, in the final scene of the play. On the one hand, we see the court intrigues which emerged during the last days of the reign of Carlos II, with his courtiers divided between the supporters of the House of Austria and those of the French crown. In the end it will be the last who, aided by the Pope, will take over the Spanish throne.[22] In addition, alongside the political aspects of the play, the main plot concerns the overwhelming passion

[21] Rodríguez Gutiérrez, 'De retractaciones y falsificaciones', p. 42.

[22] It is important to recognize that, in spite of the negative opinion expressed by Gonzalo Morón with regard to the treatment of the historical background to the play, it actually reveals an unusual fidelity to history, especially if we think of the general tendency of nineteenth-century Romantic plays to make use of historic elements simply as a means of satisfying the public's taste for spectacle. If we ignore the obvious historical inexactitude of the description of Spain's economic situation by Froilán at the beginning of the play, which is justified dramatically by the need to underline the contrast between it and the anguish of the king amid the factions which are struggling with each other to dominate the kingdom, and the story of the illegitimate daughter of Carlos II, the text contains various well-founded references to historical events which in the end play an important role in the development of the plot. The first of these is the scene of the exorcism of the king in Act II, which, according to Gil y Zárate himself, was taken from the *Proceso criminal fulminado contra el Rmo Fray Froilán Díaz* (1787), from which he drew 'varios personajes, como el vicario de las monjas, y muchas de las frases o expresiones que están en el segundo acto del drama, frases que se me han atribuido a mí siendo textualmente copiadas sin mas diferencia que la necesaria para ponerlas en verso' (quoted by Rodríguez Gutiérrez, p. 59). The second historical reference has to do with 'el grave motín popular que provocó la caída del ministro Conde de Oropesa y que estuvo propiciado por los altos precios alcanzados en la corte por el pan' (Calvo Poyato, p. 102). This is used by Gil y Zárate to justify Inés's attempt to flee and the final flight of Florencio, who now leaves the stage until the play's last scene. This careful attachment to the facts may well reflect Gil y Zárate's own concept of history, which emerges from his *Introducción a la historia moderna* (Madrid: Imprenta de Repullés, 1841), and which is closely linked to his political views. For him, when a people possesses 'una vida política animada y fuerte', 'la historia se hace práctica, esperándose de ella instrucciones análogas a las necesidades que experimenta y la vida que nos anima' (p. 3). The role of the writer as a transmitter of history thus acquires a meaningful dimension since 'es preciso que los hombres y los acontecimientos resalten a los ojos del entendimiento, no solo para interesarle y divertirle, sino para revelarle cómo se adquieren, se ejercen y se defienden sus derechos, la libertad y el poder, cómo se combinan las opiniones, los intereses, las pasiones, las necesidades de las circunstancias, todos los elementos de

which the king's confessor, Froilán Díaz, conceives for Inés, who is betrothed to Florencio. Rejected by Inés, the confessor, having won over a member of the Inquisition with the promise of a political post, succeeds in having her accused of witchcraft and of being responsible for bewitching the king. This is what leads, at the close of the play, to the death of Inés at the stake and the killing of Froilán by Florencio.

In the late 1830s and throughout the 1840s, the debate about the 'nueva escuela' of Romanticism took on heavy moral overtones. The violence of the attack on 'la satánica escuela' (to cite Ochoa) amply confirms that a sector of the Spanish intelligentsia in the nineteenth century was fully aware of the fact that the ideological and existential crisis which underlay the most subversive Romantic dramas undermined the most solid principles of Christian doctrine. This subversive and provocative spirit had reached a peak of self-manifestation in 1835, when Pacheco in his *Alfredo* dramatized the incestuous relationship between the central character and his father's wife. Gil y Zárate follows to a certain extent this transgressive tendency in Romantic drama when he makes the mainspring of his play the sacrilegious passion of the king's confessor for the young Inés, with whom he is infatuated.

The first act, which takes place in the king's private room, introduces the two parallel plots which will be developed through the rest of the play. The references to the king's mysterious illness and to his behaviour lead his page, Florencio, to affirm right at the beginning of the text: 'Parece, Dios me perdone, un endemoniado.'[23] This introduces the theme of demonic possession which near the end will play a crucial role in the plot's evolution. Although Father Froilán brushes aside this possibility as 'dichos del vulgo' (p. 4), faced with the seriousness of the king's illness and the impossibility of discovering its causes, he announces 'que el tribunal de la fe | ha llegado a tomar cartas en el asunto' (p. 4). This brings in the Inquisition, whose role will give rise to the main political criticism contained in the play.[24]

Similarly, from the earliest scenes, the spectator can sense intuitively the

---

la política activa. Esto es lo que viene a ser la historia de los pueblos libres' (p. 4). For Gil y Zárate, what distinguishes modern nations is the rise in them of political activity (p. 6), and it is precisely in this that lies the important role played by history in interpreting the world which surrounds modern man, who thus acquires 'la facultad de examinarlo todo bajo sus aspectos y descubrir cuanto encierra' (p. 7). Hence, Gil y Zárate concludes that 'la historia encierra las leyes del mundo político, en ella es donde deben observarse, y observándolas con cuidado, con meditación, con imparcialidad, se encontrarán sin duda' (p. 17).

[23] Antonio Gil y Zárate, *Carlos II el hechizado* (Madrid: Imprenta de Repullés, 1844), p. 4. Subsequent citations within the text are from this edition.

[24] In the *Juicio crítico de 'Carlos II el hechizado'*, written a year before his death, Gil y Zárate reflected on the political aim of his play, stating that one of his objectives was 'anatemizar a la Inquisición' because of its permissive attitude towards the principles and the political extremism of the Austrian monarchy. He went on to reaffirm that 'el odio justo que se debe tener a la Inquisición resulta de las escenas de los hechizos y del conjuro, como igualmente de la persecución

mysterious past which brings Froilán into contact with Florencio's betrothed Inés. When Florencio announces to the confessor his future marriage and reveals the bride's name, the friar's insistent questions arouse the distrust and suspicion of the page, who asserts: 'Los ojos se os encandilan, padre, mala señal es' (p. 5), later adding after hearing the friar's evasive replies: 'poco me gusta este fraile... mala alma debe tener' (p. 6). We could likewise mention the third scene of the first act, which contains, besides elements that prefigure the tragic ending, Carlos II's confession that he has an illegitimate daughter whom he never recognized, as a result of a youthful escapade: 'Si, padre, yo la adoré | lo confieso con rubor | y en mi criminal ardor | dulces momentos pasé' (p. 12). The description of the girl and the time of her birth allow the spectator to see in Inés this illegitimate daughter that the king has kept out of his life and whom he would now like to get back. It is at once clear that, following the pattern of the most recent Romantic plays which he is striving to imitate, Gil y Zárate constructs these scenes with great care, bringing in characters and speeches which, like that of Preciosilla in Rivas's *Don Álvaro*,[25] or even that of Alfredo in Pacheco's play,[26] are intended to prefigure the fate which will later doom the characters.

Subversive Romantic drama in the 1830s revolved structurally around two fundamental presuppositions. In the first place stood love, seen as an absolute, and as supreme over all the other political, social, and even religious forces believed to govern humanity. The Romantic hero neither understood nor obeyed any other law save that of the heart's dictates, even when—as in *Don Álvaro* or *Macías*—this meant consciously opposing any form of social organization which stood in the way of achieving his heart's desire. The search for the fulfilment of such a love became almost an existential imperative for the hero in question, since it offered the only possibility of mitigating the existential malaise consequent on his entire loss of confidence in divine Providence.

The second of these two central principles involves, clearly, the force of destiny, a codified reference in the more subversive Romantic plays to divine injustice.[27] Romantic heroes and heroines are, and know themselves to be, victims: of family, of circumstances, of a society which oppresses them and does not understand them, but above all of adverse fate, of a *devil world* which conflicts with any harmonious interpretation of the human condition. The Romantic hero, above all after *Don Álvaro*, is one who lives a life of desper-

de personas tan puras e inocentes como Inés y Florencio, hechos todos que están sacados de otros verídicos y de documentos irrefragables' (quoted by Rodríguez Gutiérrez, pp. 59–60).

[25] Duque de Rivas, *Don Álvaro o la fuerza del sino*, ed. by Miguel Ángel Lama (Barcelona: Crítica, 1994), p. 87.

[26] Joaquín Francisco Pacheco, *Alfredo: drama trágico en cinco actos* (Madrid: Imprenta de Tomás Jordán, 1835), pp. 8–9.

[27] Richard Cardwell, 'Don Álvaro or the Force of Cosmic Injustice', *Studies in Romanticism*, 12 (1973), 559–79.

ation owing to his awareness of struggling against an overwhelming force in response to which he can do nothing but suffer and die. The characters who appear in *Carlos II el hechizado* not only fit the pattern of Romantic drama, but draw directly on the earlier plays, confirming the idea that the theatre of the 1830s should be seen as a whole which is easier to analyse when the plays are taken together.[28] Thus the characterization of Inés, which is at least formally the most elaborate and rich in light and shade, fits the pattern which in Romantic drama begins with Laura (in *La Conjuracion de Venecia*) and develops in Elvira (*Macías*), Leonor (*Don Álvaro*), and Isabel (*Los amantes de Teruel*), although she never reveals the split personality typical of other Romantic heroines, which derives from the contradiction between their presentation as literary characters belonging to their own age and the accepted social values of nineteenth-century Spain which they anachronistically confront. We recall that the role of the main feminine characters was to express sweetness, sacrifice, resignation, and dedication to the family—Gil y Zárate's play begins with the announcement of Inés's forthcoming marriage—but above all to offer consolation to her male counterpart after the onset of his spiritual and existential crisis. Inés, as a character, falters at this point not only because she does not show signs of a split in her dramatic personality, but also because Florencio, as we shall see, reveals no traces of an inner existential conflict, nor does he undergo any kind of real tragic evolution towards insight. He thus prevents Inés from performing her fundamental dramatic function.

Nevertheless, this does not prevent her from being presented largely through religious terminology, nor, if we look at the scattered references to the passion she has awakened in Florencio, do these fail to be subordinated to a supposedly consolatory role. Despite the general references to her physical beauty—'bella' (pp. 5, 18, 54), 'linda cara' (p. 18), 'hermosa niña' (p. 18), etc.—all the qualities attributed to her relate to spiritual features: 'modesta' (p. 4), 'aureola pura' (p. 5), 'fuente de vida' (p. 5), 'más pura que el sol' (p. 59), etc. Especially noteworthy is the fact that when, in the first scene of Act I, Florencio, without realizing whom he is addressing, describes his betrothed to the sinister and curious Froilán, he does not hesitate to compare Inés to the Virgin Mary, claiming with the almost irreverent impetuosity of the Romantic figure that 'Así tan pura y tan bella | se muestra mi amada Inés | y cual los ángeles aman | así la adoro también' (p. 5). This spiritualization of the Romantic heroine was clearly not unnoticed by Gil y Zárate. Following the pattern established by Martínez de la Rosa, Larra, and the Duque de Rivas, *ángel* is the noun most frequently employed to characterize his Romantic heroine. Towards the end of the first act, when Florencio presents Inés to the

---

[28] Donald L. Shaw, 'El drama romántico como modelo literario e ideológico', in *Historia de la literatura española: siglo XIX*, ed. by Víctor García de la Concha (Madrid: Espasa Calpe, 1997), pp. 314–52 (p. 319).

sick and suffering king, and she sings to him to bring him comfort, the king responds with a speech which contains undeniable echoes of Martínez de la Rosa:

> REY El ángel eres sin duda
> que el cielo me proporciona
> en medio de tantos males
> para sanarlos... Pues sola
> puedes la salud volverme,
> quédate a mi lado, pronta
> siempre a calmar mis delirios
> con canciones seductoras.
> (p. 65)

This capacity for loving is the main quality which defines the characters. Inés and Florencio seem to subordinate everything that society demands and hopes from them to the law of love, though in point of fact they always seek approval and the fulfilment of their love in accordance with the social and religious expectations of the world around them. We recall, in this respect, Florencio's speech at the beginning of Act III before the fatal appearance of Froilán, who is destined to radically alter his life and that of Inés, a speech full of Romantic irony in the light of what follows:

> FLORENCIO Juramentos, bien lo sé,
> no ha menester mi pasión;
> mas es tan pura esta llama
> que nos abrasa a los dos,
> tan bella que bien merece
> la contemple el Hacedor.
> (p. 60)

In the same third act, as everything is being prepared for the lovers' marriage and just before Inés is handed over to the Inquisition branded as a witch, Florencio expresses a love which transcends human limitations: '¡Amarte! Aún después de muerto | que allí hay también amor' (p. 60). Inés makes a similar speech in Act IV when, as a result of Froilán's vengefulness, she is imprisoned along with Florencio. In it, before the people in rebellion against Oropesa break into their prison, Inés in turn speaks of an absolute love which goes beyond the limits of human existence:

> INÉS Fija los ojos en mí
> que sin dejar de mirarte,
> tú me escucharás allí
> con firme voz el darte el sí
> que en el altar debí darte.
> De los hombres a despecho,

> templo la hoguera será
> o de rosas blando lecho;
> donde al fin en lazo estrecho
> nuestra unión se cumplirá;
> y en vez de que al expirar
> nuestros amores se acaben,
> se verán acrecentar
> de cuanto los celos saben
> más que los hombres amar.
>   (pp. 85–86)

However, though he paints an accurate picture of Romantic love, as the plot develops Gil y Zárate makes a decision which affects the whole dramatic conception of the play: the love of Froilán for Inés remains unrequited. Hence Gil y Zárate perforce reduces the role of Florencio, whose love for Inés is fully requited, to a subordinate figure, as he places Froilán's passion for Inés at the centre of the play. When his love is not returned, the jealousy and hatred of Froilán professed in 'Tu desdén, tus odios | todo sufrirlo resignado puedo | mas verte ajena! No, desventurada | ¿sabes tú que son los celos?' (p. 26), far from presenting him as a hero, turn him into a villain. His longing for vengeance when Inés once more rejects him turns *Carlos II el hechizado* from being a love story into the story of a sordid and hypocritical vengeance on the part of a cowardly and spiteful lover who cannot take no for an answer. From this point on—'Amaos, infames, mas será por poco, | temblad, pronto veréis lo que puedo' (p. 27)—the plot will no longer centre on whether the love story of Florencio and Inés will have a happy ending (adverse fate will prevent it) or whether the king will be able at the last moment to save his daughter from the stake, but on whether Inés, despite her innocence, will be able to escape the vengeance of the king's confessor.

Froilán's conception of love in absolute terms reflects what we expect from a Romantic play. Although, in line with Romantic sensibility, we should normally evaluate it in terms of its spiritual effects on the confessor, it is expressed in physical ones: 'ardiente', 'fuego', 'fiera pasión', 'corazón de fuego' (p. 29). Still, the spiritual effects remain: 'Tú serás mi delicia | mi único bien, mi Consuelo; | así me perdone el cielo mi injusticia' (p. 111). His love becomes the equivalent of life itself, fitting in with the Romantic equation of love with life. Thus when Froilán visits Inés in her prison cell, just before she is to be burnt at the stake, he reminds her that he alone can prevent her death, and once more expresses his love for her: '¡Cuál otro es mi amor! A par que ardiente | firme le probarás: si cuando te amo | es por la vida, por la vida juro | a tus plantas estar rendido, esclavo' (p. 77). This absolute conception of love entails that if its fulfilment means life, its denial inevitably involves the death of the lover: 'Sálvame, por piedad, de este delirio' (p. 79).

Such a conception of love causes the lover to carry it to its utmost extreme, in conflict with prevailing political and social values which, functioning as instruments in the hands of destiny, prevent its fulfilment. In this case we must also add religious values, not with regard to Inés, since she has not been married to Florencio, but with regard to the vows of chastity taken by Froilán. When they first meet in the play, Inés reminds him of his vows, while he responds by asserting the impossibility of struggling with the bonds that bind him:

> FROILÁN Mis votos no olvidé, ni necesito
> que me los recuerdes tú, que al cielo ofendo
> lo sé también, lo sé... Juzga ahora
> cuán grande es mi pasión, pues lo consiento.
> (p. 24)

The struggle of Romantic passion against overwhelming forces is thus transferred from Florencio to Froilán, and with it the awareness of fate. Throughout the play the confessor remains torn between his hopeless passion and the impossibility of consummating it, not only because of Inés's rejection, but also because of his religious vows. In his brief soliloquy in Act I, Scene 7 he speaks of them disdainfully: '¡Mis votos! Bien lo se... | duro, tremendo, | imposible deber fieros me imponen | cambiando en crimen inocente afecto!' (p. 24), but then finally complains: 'Destino injusto, hado ciego' (p. 25). In line with his attempts to restrain his feelings, as the plot advances he begins to give up the effort, becoming ever more conscious of the futility of continuing a struggle which he is condemned to lose:

> FROILÁN ¡Inútil batallar! Sólo combato
> para ser más vencido... Presa horrible
> de algún genio maléfico encargado
> de mi condenación, ya abierto miro
> el infierno a mis pies y en él me lanzo.
> (p. 76)

The transfer to Froilán of the love plot tends to compromise the effect of the other major theme in Romantic drama: adverse fate, seen after *Don Álvaro* and *Macías* as a malignant force which governs events here below and before which human justice—here represented by the king—and even divine Providence are powerless. As the counterforce to love, fate sets in the path of the protagonists every possible obstacle preventing its fulfilment and condemning them to experience pain, suffering, and death. Their personalities are permanently split as a result of unremitting psychological stress.

The first references to fate in our play have to do with the figure of the king. In the brief monologue before his confessional dialogue with Froilán near the beginning of the play, we hear a series of references to the 'funesto mal' (p. 7) to which he attributes all the misfortunes that have pursued him during his lifetime: the lack of a childhood and his premature enthronement—'de niño al solio subí' (p. 7); his weakness in the face of the savage political struggles during his reign—'y entre encontradas facciones | juguete de mis pasiones | solo rey en nombre fui' (p. 8); his constant illness—'Siempre enfermo, el peso grave | no resistí al reinar' (p. 8); his lack of descendants and the political chaos which, as a result, characterizes his reign—'En vano por mi lució | la antorcha nupcial dos veces, | que sordo el cielo a mis preces | mi lecho estéril dejó' (p. 9); and the abuse of the power he left to his favourites, which reduced the country to economic poverty and political instability:

> REY ¿Es esta, cielos, la España
> de Europa un tiempo terror?
> Con mi funesto vivir
> su poder eché por tierra,
> y la discordia y la guerra
> son mi legado al morir.
> (p. 9)

The king lives in a state of anguish, torn in two directions, but in his case they derive not from love but from the political problems and the instability arising from his lack of an heir. This shift away from love and fate is the second major factor that compromises the fully Romantic development of the plot:

> REY Amor y un deber sagrado
> al Austria mis votos dan,
> pero por la Francia están
> prudencia y razón de Estado.
> (p. 10)

The last trick that fate plays on the king is seen in the final scenes of the play when Inés escapes from the procession—which is carrying her to the fire of the Inquisition—and bursts into the king's palace to proclaim her innocence and beg him to grant her his pardon. When he sees on her finger the jewelled ring which he had given her mother, Leonor, he realizes that she is the daughter he had dreamt of finding again. In one of the play's most melodramatic scenes he exclaims: '¿Con que al fin te puedo hallar | objeto de mi deseo? | Te abrazo y apenas creo | de tanta dicha gozar' (p. 110). But the discovery comes too late. When Inés, having realized who she is, sees in this discovery the way to a royal pardon, she asks her father: '¿Y qué importa? ¿No sois el rey? | ¿Quien vuestro poder contrasta?', and he responds crushingly:

> REY ¡Ah! Que mi poder no basta
> ante su inflexible ley.
> ¿Ignoras que no hay perdón

> cuando lanza su anatema?
> ¿Ignoras que aun mi diadema
> la humilla la inquisición?
> ¿Lo sabes, y no te espantas,
> que yo al oír su sentencia,
> mudo quedo en su presencia
> y tiemblo, y caigo a sus plantas?
> (p. 112)

Gil y Zárate was only too well able to discern that the main figure in the kind of Romantic drama he was striving to create was not only fully conscious of belonging to a *devil world*, but also of the fact that even divine Providence could not control, much less thwart, the action of fate. We recall in this connection Don Álvaro's reproaches to God at the end of Rivas's play because of his lack of benevolence towards the two central characters. Similarly, characters in *Carlos II* invoke God numerous times in order to question his failure to intervene in their lives. In Act IV, for example, after a visit from Froilán, who once more offers her freedom if she will accept his love, Inés calls on God:

> INÉS ¡Dios mío! ¡Mírame aquí!
> Humillada en tu presencia,
> ¡ah! yo imploro tu clemencia
> mas no la imploro por mí.
> Si alguna vez te ofendí
> sufra yo sola el castigo.
> Tu cólera yo bendigo
> si a mí solamente alcanza,
> pero es sobrada venganza
> perder a mi bien conmigo.
> (p. 80)

Froilán also reproaches God from near the start of the play. In Act I, when face to face with Inés he confesses to her that he can neither forget her nor lessen his love for her, he goes on:

> FROILÁN Mira este cuerpo flaco, estenuado,
> contempla este semblante macilento,
> son aún más que desayunos y cilicios,
> estragos del amor que arde aquí dentro.
> Pues tanto sacrificio Dios no acepta,
> a mi pasión de hoy más todo me entrego.
> (p. 25)

Later, again facing Inés, he recognizes the immutability of his feelings and the growth of his passion, and again timidly raises his voice against a God who has placed him in such an unbearable situation: 'Pensé que Dios tan penitente vida | al fin premiaría sofocando el fuego | de mi funesto amor... ¡Vana esperanza! | ¡Cuanto más penitencia más deseos!' (p. 26).

Yet it is in the presentation of fate that Gil y Zárate further underlines the difference and distance between this play and genuinely subversive Romantic drama. Despite the feeble reproaches occasionally directed against God in the play, his sovereignty is never fully questioned or cast into doubt. Indeed, as we have just seen, Inés shortly before her death proclaims: 'Tu cólera yo bendigo' (p. 80). Later, when Florencio proposes suicide as a solution to the blows of fate and the impossibility of enjoying their love in liberty, Inés, who earlier had accepted his offer of poison—'Dámelo luego... Morir | mi aciago destino es ya; | pero al dejar de existir | al menos el no sufrir | tu esposa te deberá' (p. 84)—changes her mind, fearing that her actions could offend the sovereignty of God:

>   INÉS En este mundo de horror;
>   mas reunirnos debemos
>   en otro mundo mejor,
>   y amarnos allí podremos
>   con puro y eterno amor.
>   Esta halagüeña esperanza
>   me da en mis males aliento;
>   pero ¡ay! el celeste asiento
>   solo la virtud le alcanza
>   y es criminal nuestro intento.
>   Suframos, mi bien, suframos...
>   ¿qué importa una hora sufrir
>   si siempre puros quedamos
>   y así felices logramos
>   al trono de Dios subir?
>   (p. 85)

It is precisely this scene which allows critics such as Ochoa, who harshly censured other aspects of the play, to regard *Carlos II el hechizado* as a 'moral' drama. Florencio and Inés give up the idea of suicide—a key symbolic feature of the subversive Romantic world-view—'alumbrados por un sentimiento sublime de virtud y religión',[29] against which Froilán's machinations are powerless. In Ochoa's view this scene introduces the play's final development. He asks:

¿Pudiera acaso el más estricto moralista reprobar de una manera tan sólida y filosófica el atentado del suicidio, aún en el caso en que podría hallar disculpa en la justicia de los hombres? Esta y otras escenas del mismo drama le justifican sobradamente ante los ojos de la crítica imparcial, y con esa composición escrita como por despique, bajo los principios de una escuela que no eran los de la suya, contestó victoriosamente a los que

---

[29] *Obras dramáticas de Don Antonio Gil y Zárate*, ed. by Ochoa, p. xiii.

en la ceguedad de su entusiasmo pueril por las novedades, suponían neciamente que el alazán acostumbrado a la rigidez del freno es incapaz de romperle y ostentar en plena libertad el brío y lozana guardia de su peculiar naturaleza.[30]

Finally, let us consider the symbolic elements visible in the play. To a man of the theatre such as Gil y Zárate, the symbolic dimension underlying the motivations and dramatic resources present in Romantic drama must have been quite obvious. In fact, many such elements were employed so arbitrarily, and sometimes absurdly, that it becomes clear that this form of drama cannot be interpreted realistically, so that recourse must be had to a symbolic approach. From Rivas's *Don Álvaro* onwards—this being the play which established the model—the majority of these symbolic elements, most notably the prison or the Church, became important emblematic spaces on the stage, as Joaquin Casalduero has pointed out.[31] In both *Don Álvaro* and *El trovador* the hero enters the sacred place seeking a refuge, a shelter and protection from the ceaseless attacks of passion. But when the attempt fails, the sacred place attains its full symbolic importance: the world is seen as a *devil world*: not one governed by divine Providence, but one in which God turns his back on those who seek his help and protection.

The image of the Church appears in sundry forms in *Carlos II el hechizado*, but most of all it dominates Act II, Scene 7, which takes place in the sacristy of the Convent of Atocha. From the standpoint of the play's political message, the critique of the religious outlook is obvious in the planning of the exorcism, in which no one—not even those who participate—believes. Hence the Church is presented as a political institution which does not hesitate to manipulate events as it pleases, in order to achieve the end its followers consider to be in their best interest: the assumption of the Spanish throne by the Bourbon monarchy.

Gil y Zárate can be seen to be indicating the danger arising from interference by the Church in matters affecting the State. However, from the standpoint of the Romantic world-view, he fails to make proper use of the symbol, since the scene in the charnel house is not really related to the love plot but instead to the question of the succession to the throne. The same is true of the prison symbol when Florencio and Inés are confined in a dungeon. In previous Romantic plays the hero often finds himself literally and figuratively imprisoned: literally, because of having broken some social or political rule in the course of his obsessive search for love as the only source of happiness and reconciliation with life; and symbolically because, as we have seen, the Romantic hero struggles not so much against society or mankind, as against

---

[30] Ibid.
[31] Joaquín Casalduero, 'Don Álvaro o el destino como fuerza', in id., *Estudios sobre el teatro español* (Madrid: Gredos, 1967), pp. 232–69 (pp. 235–40).

a *devil world* which destroys any universal harmony, even for the innocent. Hence, as we see in *Don Álvaro* when he escapes from prison, he meets with a fate which is worse than the one from which he is attempting to flee, a major example of Romantic irony. As in the case of his use of the Church symbol in various ways, Gil y Zárate does not entirely present the prison as a metaphor which figures the Romantic world-view. If Inés had returned Froilán's love and they had been imprisoned for setting their passion above social and religious regulations, the prison would have taken on the symbolism it acquires in plays like *Don Álvaro*. Likewise, if the death of Inés had been the result of the hostility of adverse destiny conquering love as the highest ideal: in that case her death would have been a further example of the formula 'love, crossed by fate, ending in death', which is at the heart of subversive Romanticism. But since in this case it represents only vengeance for Inés's rejection of Froilán, we are closer to melodrama than to the symbolic expression of love as the highest ideal characteristic of the most authentic Romantic theatre.

Finally, we need to glance at the scene of Froilán's death towards the end of the play. It takes a form hitherto unknown in the subversive plays of the 1830s, one that is very unusual in post-Romantic historical drama. With regard to the political message of the play, the death of Froilán represents the victory of the power of the State over the interference of the Church in state affairs, so that the play becomes emblematic of liberal ideas in Spain. As such, it remained relevant to much of Spain's chaotic political history in the nineteenth century, and was still powerfully effective fifty years after its premiere, as theatre criticism of the period amply reveals.[32]

Still, contemplated from the standpoint of the subversive Romanticism which Gil y Zárate was striving to emulate, this death faces us with some theoretical difficulties connected with the management of the plot. The absence of a tragic evolution in Florencio prevents him from seeing death as the only possible outcome of an existential conflict, which he does not feel. In this, he is unlike other subversive Romantic heroes. Moreover, since Froilán is not hero but villain, his death cannot be attributed to the intervention of the *devil world* operating to destroy the passion felt by the lovers. In this case it is more related to poetic justice, and hence is ultimately more suitable for melodrama.

Again, we must note the fact that the death of Froilán comes at the hands of Florencio, who takes justice upon himself. As already noted, this type of event

---

[32] Cantero García includes in his cited article an extract from a Madrid newspaper at the end of the century, which deals with the staging of Gil y Zárate's play in a theatre in Almería. The report states: 'Al concluir el drama el público llamó a grandes voces a los actores. Estos se presentaban en escena, pero aquel tumulto no se calmaba aún después de salir cuatro o cinco veces. El Sr. Méndez, todavía vestido de las hopalandas, preguntó valiéndose de la mímica, qué querían los espectadores, y [uno] de las primeras filas, contestó: "¡Que le maten a usted otra vez!". Volvió a presentar El Sr. Cacht y sepultó de nuevo el puñal en el pecho del fraile. El público se retiró tranquilamente' (*El Imparcial*, 6 January 1883). See Cantero García, p. 81.

is most unusual in nineteenth-century drama. In the subversive Romanticism of the 1830s the hero's death—often by suicide—is always the result of his recognition of the impossibility of thwarting destiny. Death becomes the hero's only way out when he realizes that his love cannot be fulfilled in a world in which the sovereignty of a benevolent God is in question. The fading of Romantic subversion was replaced by a type of historical drama which sought, by returning to the Middle Ages and the Golden Age, to defend a particular vision of society—Catholic, monarchical, and medievalizing—wherein justice would be meted out to the villain by a Golden Age monarch. This left action in the hands of another force to which reactionary Romanticism returned: divine Providence. Nonetheless, the fact that Florencio takes justice into his own hands should not be interpreted as a negation of justice but as a further element of melodrama which takes over in the play because of the absence of the symbolic presentation of human existence characteristic of subversive Romanticism.

Despite his prior experience as a dramatist, it is clear that Gil y Zárate could not entirely manage a plot in which the political theme and its message prevail over the love theme. As a result, what could have been a story of love crossed by fate—the basic theme of the plays he was endeavouring to emulate—turns into mere melodrama in which the suspense is generated not by whether Inés can consummate her love for Florencio, but whether she will be able to escape from the vengeance which the resentful Froilán has in store for her. Although the play exhibits clear formal links with the subversive Romantic plays of the 1830s, Gil y Zárate fails in his attempt to construct a play modelled on their pattern, since his drama does not confer on the love between hero and heroine an absolute value to which all other social norms and political values must be subordinate, nor is the love of Inés and Florencio crossed by adverse fate. The characters, except for Froilán, tend to lack self-insight, and are never presented as playthings of a cruel destiny which God himself cannot control, since, in the play, divine Providence is never questioned or cast into doubt.

All the same, although the play does not fully succeed as an attempt to present the world-view of the most radical Romantics, the importance of *Carlos II el hechizado* derives from the way it reveals the conflict of ideas after the mid-1830s in Spain concerning radical Romanticism and the social and religious implications of its message, which its opponents regarded as pernicious. The political and literary polemics which followed its first staging are more than sufficient to make Gil y Zárate's play worth considering as one of the leading works of the decade, in view of its contribution to the debate about Romanticism and its provocative social message amid the convulsions of the nineteenth century in Spain.

UNIVERSITY OF NORTH TEXAS

HOME AND HOMELESSNESS IN WORKS BY NOVALIS, DOROTHEA SCHLEGEL, AND TIECK

Longing for the unity of an ideal past (often classical in coloration) from the standpoint of a fragmented present is one of the predominant themes in late eighteenth-century thought, from Winckelmann to Schiller. This derives in large measure from the struggle into, or with, modernity; yet in David Constantine's account of Hölderlin's development as a poet there is also a more personal dimension, one that resists total identification with the march of modernization. According to Constantine, 'childhood in an ideal homeland became a central component of his whole mythology. [. . .] Hölderlin's childhood, in real places in Württemberg, must despite its sorrows have had sufficient persuasive power to enter his poetry as the archetype of a once and future ideal condition.'[1] The notion 'once and future' has powerful implications for a theme that I intend to explore in relation to three narratives of self-development[2] from the period—Novalis's *Heinrich von Ofterdingen*, Dorothea Schlegel's *Florentin* ('perhaps the most overlooked work of *Fruehromantik* [sic]'[3]), and Ludwig Tieck's *Der Runenberg*—the question, namely, of ontological security. This term denotes 'a stable mental state derived from a sense of continuity and order',[4] which can also be expressed in the concept of 'home' (understood in a spiritual or emotional, rather than a material, sense). Peter Blickle has explored collective social constructions of *Heimat*, arguing that '[i]n its premodern longings *Heimat* stands in (an often only implied) contrast to familiar modern experiences such as urban alienation, the industrial workplace, the technologized mode of existence, mass politics, and the nation-state'.[5] Although there is considerable overlap between my approach and his, I am concerned here with the experience of *individuals* as portrayed in these works and with the individual's sense of home and stability, which is an implicit preoccupation of all three texts. Anthony Giddens (who is also an important thinker for Blickle) contends that '"basic trust"

---

[1] David Constantine, *Hölderlin* (Oxford: Clarendon Press, 1988), pp. 1–2.

[2] There is no space here to rehearse the critical debate that has for decades surrounded the term 'Bildungsroman', often applied to texts in this vein; and since the term implies a level of fulfilment which, in my view, neither Florentin nor Tieck's Christian attains (and, moreover, *Der Runenberg* is not a novel), I shall avoid it here.

[3] 'Introduction', in Dorothea Mendelssohn Veit Schlegel, *Florentin: A Novel*, translated, annotated, and introduced by Edwina Lawler and Ruth Richardson (Lewiston, NY: Mellen, 1988), pp. i–cxli (p. cii). I follow Liliane Weissberg in referring to the author simply as 'Dorothea Schlegel'. See Dorothea Schlegel, *Florentin: Roman — Fragmente — Varianten*, ed. by Liliane Weisbberg (Berlin: Ullstein, 1987).

[4] Tony Bilton and others, *Introductory Sociology*, 4th edn (Basingstoke: Palgrave Macmillan, 2002), p. 532.

[5] Peter Blickle, *Heimat: A Critical Theory of the German Idea of Homeland* (Rochester, NY: Camden House, 2002), p. 28.

[as developed through the loving attentions of early caretakers] forms the original nexus from which a combined emotive-cognitive orientation towards others, the object-world, and self-identity, emerges'.[6] Attention to the relation of parent (the major implication of Giddens's term 'early caretaker') and child in these narratives by Novalis, Schlegel, and Tieck, then, will help to bring this most intimate, or originary, aspect of 'being at home' into relief. Even this relationship, and its portrayal, will always be shaped in part by the times. *Der Runenberg*, for example, is poised on the boundary between premodern and modern: Andrew Cusack reads the protagonist's disjointed relationship to the patriarchy as an allegory of the position of the intellectuals who made up the Romantic movement, 'driven by a pressure to innovate, to devise their own *modus vivendi*, and to generate new knowledge [and who as a result] found themselves uniquely at odds with their philosophical and religious traditions'.[7] Yet the attempt by the protagonists in all three tales to establish a stable path between origins and destinations ('once and future') also has a timeless relevance, and to an extent transcends the late eighteenth- and early nineteenth-century context from which they emerged.

Heinrich von Ofterdingen, *Florentin*, and *Der Runenberg* lend themselves particularly well to comparison because they all derive from the impetus of 1799, an important year in the development of Early Romanticism.[8] Novalis and Tieck met in July, sowing the seeds for an unusually close friendship; October saw the arrival in Jena of both Dorothea Veit (later Schlegel, born Brendel Mendelssohn) and Tieck as residents, following close upon Friedrich Schlegel's return from Berlin, and expanding the group which had consisted of the Schlegel brothers and August Wilhelm's wife, Caroline; and in November Novalis visited the group in Jena, sharing with them his latest poetry and his important essay 'Die Christenheit oder Europa'. Both *Ofterdingen* and *Florentin* were begun in 1799; in 1801 *Florentin* was published (anonymously, with Friedrich Schlegel's name as editor on the title-page), and Novalis's untimely death in March 1801 broke off the composition of *Ofterdingen*. Although *Der Runenberg* was composed slightly later, in 1802, its conceptual roots lie in 1799. That was the year in which Tieck met the mineralogist Henrik Steffens, another associate of the Jena circle, whose nature philosophy

---

[6] Anthony Giddens, *Modernity and Self-Identity: Self and Society in the Late Modern Age* (Cambridge: Polity, 1991), p. 38.
[7] Andrew Cusack, *The Wanderer in Nineteenth-Century German Literature: Intellectual History and Cultural Criticism* (Rochester, NY: Camden House, 2006), p. 92.
[8] Theodore Ziolkowski has posited 1794–95 as the year of greatest significance in the development of new intellectual currents in Jena, not least because of the explosive arrival there of Johann Gottlieb Fichte: see *Das Wunderjahr in Jena: Geist und Gesellschaft 1794/95* (Stuttgart: Klett-Cotta, 1998). Ziolkowski's argument has many merits, but activity on the Jena scene was so intensive, and changes in or additions to its personnel so frequent, that each year between the arrival of Fichte and the departure of the Schlegel brothers in 1801 had its own distinct bearing on developments.

was a major source of inspiration for *Der Runenberg*. Tieck seriously contemplated writing the conclusion to *Heinrich von Ofterdingen* after Novalis's death, but although he was eventually persuaded otherwise, in 1802, together with Friedrich Schlegel, he brought out an edition of this and other unpublished works and fragments by Novalis. *Ofterdingen* was therefore very much on his mind as he wrote *Der Runenberg*.⁹

The spirit of discussion and collective enterprise that characterized the Jena scene caused ideas to develop quickly for the Early Romantics; but they were also in flux. Novalis and Dorothea Schlegel, writing at the same time, produced strikingly divergent treatments of the theme of self-development. Furthermore, Tieck's creative engagement with Novalis seems, in this instance, to have been a critical one, for *Der Runenberg* pulls in a very different direction from *Ofterdingen*, and even from his own earlier contribution to the theme, *Franz Sternbalds Wanderungen* (1798). Indeed, for Roger Paulin it remains 'one of the ironies of German Romanticism that Tieck's name should be so intimately bound up with that of Novalis [. . .]. Novalis's work is as little Tieckian as Tieck's own differs from that of his friend.'¹⁰ *Heinrich von Ofterdingen* is striking for the optimism with which it depicts family bonds: psychological conflict between the generations is noticeably absent, and Heinrich's self-development is aided in no small part by a continuous (though also developing) parental presence. In *Florentin* and *Der Runenberg*, by contrast, the protagonists' progress is much more limited. Andrew Cusack takes 'Tieck's *Runenberg* as an example of a fiction in which the wanderer motif is employed in a contrary sense to that prevailing among the early Romantics, for whom it was a more or less unproblematic emblem of dynamism',¹¹ and Schlegel's *Florentin* is a further instance of that countervailing trend. Florentin is caught between murky origins and a blurred destination, and struggles both to find and to establish a home. Tieck's Christian, for his part, oscillates between commitment to and rejection of his father's world, until that world almost ceases to exist, not just in his mind, but also in reality.

Heinrich von Ofterdingen charts the protagonist's journey from one home, that of his parents, to another, that of poetry. Heinrich's development—indeed, the development of the novel itself—always involves a return in some form: the all-important move out into new territory generally entails a move into deeper levels of familiarity also, and origins and destinations are intimately linked. This pattern is traced in both the metaphysical *and* the physical

⁹ *Ofterdingen* itself has often been read as a response to, or at least influenced by, Tieck's own novel *Franz Sternbalds Wanderungen*. Robert L. Kahn, for example, writes of 'memory clusters' in *Ofterdingen* that 'demonstrate a unique process of assimilation of Tieck's novel by Novalis'. See 'Tieck's *Franz Sternbalds Wanderungen* and Novalis' *Heinrich von Ofterdingen*', *Studies in Romanticism*, 7 (1967), 40–64 (p. 54).

¹⁰ Roger Paulin, *Ludwig Tieck: A Literary Biography* (Oxford: Clarendon Press, 1986), p. 142.

¹¹ Cusack, *The Wanderer in Nineteenth-Century German Literature*, p. 93.

spheres: Nicholas Saul observes that 'the gradual integration into a temporal unity of past, present and future runs parallel with the gradual integration into a spiritual unity of ideal and real'.[12] Although the mode of *Ofterdingen* could hardly be described as realist, particularities such as geographical location and the details of everyday life (work, leisure, nourishment, environment) have a particular charge in the novel, and are more than a simple backdrop for abstract speculation.[13] This is particularly true of the first part of the novel as we witness Heinrich's journey, in the company of his mother and a group of merchants, from his parents' home to that of his maternal grandfather Schwaning. This 'real' world so present at the beginning gradually recedes from view as Heinrich comes closer to the ideal, and it is not restored in Part One after Klingsohr's *Märchen*. It is not completely obscured, however, even in Part Two, which is subtitled 'Die Erfüllung': on the contrary, the mirroring of elements (especially constellations of characters) between what is commonly, if somewhat misleadingly, known as the 'frame' narrative and the allegorical tales that complement it keeps the novel's broader poetic vision rooted in what Stuart Curran has called 'the sheer energy of life or its resolute thingness'.[14]

The pattern of development and return is established in the famous dream sequence with which the novel opens. The dream itself is triggered by tales that a stranger has told Heinrich and which, by their very strangeness, have released in him a deeper sense of understanding: 'Ich glaubte, ich wäre wahnsinnig, wenn ich nicht so klar und hell sähe und dächte, mir ist seitdem alles viel bekannter.'[15] From his bed at home, he experiences in his dream 'neue und niegesehene Bilder' (*Werke*, p. 242), which mark the first stage of his journey to self-fulfilment. The combination of novelty and deep familiarity that occupies Heinrich's mind in the opening scene is mirrored in his physical journey. The significance of place in the trajectory of the individual is particularly clear in the example of Augsburg, his mother's home town. This is his destination in Part One, although it is clear by Part Two, which opens (after verses spoken by Astralis) with his second arrival at Augsburg, that he has journeyed far beyond it in the interim. Early in Part One the text registers the

[12] Nicholas Saul, *History and Poetry in Novalis and in the Tradition of the German Enlightenment* (London: University of London Institute of Germanic Studies, 1984), p. 166.

[13] *Pace* Georg Lukács, for whom '[d]ie Wirklichkeit [bei Novalis] ist allzu belastet und beladen von der Erdenschwere ihrer Ideenverlassenheit, und die transzendentale Welt ist zu luftig und inhaltlos wegen ihrer allzu direkten Abstammung aus der philosophisch-postulativen Sphäre des abstrakten Überhaupt' (*Die Theorie des Romans: Ein geschichtsphilosophischer Versuch über die Formen der grossen Epik* (Berlin: Cassirer, 1920), pp. 151–52).

[14] Stuart Curran, 'Romantic Poetry: The I Altered', in *Romanticism and Feminism*, ed. by Anne K. Mellor (Bloomington: Indiana University Press, 1988), pp. 185–207 (p. 190).

[15] Novalis, *Werke in einem Band*, ed. by Hans-Joachim Mähl and Richard Samuel (Munich: Hanser, 1984), p. 240. Further references from this volume (hereafter simply *Werke*) will be given after quotations in the main body of the text.

pain caused to the young Heinrich by his separation from his own birthplace. Soon afterwards, however, Heinrich notices a 'strange sensation', 'als werde er nach langen Wanderungen von der Weltgegend her, nach welcher sie jetzt reisten, in sein Vaterland zurückkommen, und als reise er daher diesem eigentlich zu' (*Werke*, p. 251). And this is a return, for Heinrich as well as for his mother, for it is strongly implied in these words of his father's that Augsburg was the place of Heinrich's conception: 'In seinen Reden kocht der feurige wälsche Wein, den ich damals von Rom mitgebracht hatte, und der unsern Hochzeitabend verherrlichte [. . .]. [L]ange war in *Augsburg* keine lustigere Hochzeit gefeyert worden' (*Werke*, pp. 244–45). It is, therefore, the return to the purest point of origin—a return which itself will be repeated—that enables Heinrich to progress towards his goal.

Novalis was intimately involved in the development of early Idealist thought, and this pattern resonates with the work of other thinkers—above all with Hegel's *Phänomenologie des Geistes*.[16] It has been observed that '[h]istory, for Hegel, is a march of the human spirit homeward';[17] and David Ciavatta has explained the importance of familial relations in Hegel's philosophy, especially in relation to the issue of ontological security:

the individual who is appropriately recognized by familial others is afforded the possibility of developing a basic and enduring sense of belonging, of having a recognized, stable, and meaningful place in the world [. . .]. [T]his basic, existential experience of being at home, as uniquely generated by distinctively familial practices of recognition, functions for Hegel as an original modality of our experience of the world generally.[18]

For Hegel, the sister-to-brother relation is 'the ethical dimension by which to measure the character of all distinctively familial relationships',[19] but Novalis devotes his attention to a different axis. The relation of parent and child is a crucial dimension of the dual movement towards origins and destinations in *Ofterdingen*. The novel opens with the words 'die Eltern', and parents feature in all the narratives. Heinrich's relationship to his father, in particular, follows that spiral pattern of progress that characterizes his development as a whole. This is reflected in the novel's structure: early in Part One there is a move away from the father and his world, while Part Two sees a return to that part of his life through the character Sylvester, who knew Heinrich's father. Midway through the novel, Heinrich's grandfather Schwaning observes:

---

[16] See my essay '*Im flüßgen Element hin und wieder schweifen*: Development and Return in Goethe's Poetry and Hegel's Philosophy', *Goethe Yearbook*, 20 (2013), 166–77, for an analysis of a different literary variation on this theme.

[17] John Neubauer, 'Bakhtin versus Lukács: Inscriptions of Homelessness in Theories of the Novel', *Poetics Today*, 17 (1996), 531–46 (p. 533).

[18] David V. Ciavatta, *Spirit, the Family and the Unconscious in Hegel's Philosophy* (Albany: State University of New York Press, 2009), p. 5.

[19] Ibid., p. 73.

Er sieht seinem Vater ähnlich; nur scheint er weniger heftig und eigensinnig. Jener war in seiner Jugend voll glücklicher Anlagen. [...] Es hätte mehr aus ihm werden können, als ein fleißiger und fertiger Künstler. (*Werke*, pp. 318–19)

In his grandfather's perception, Heinrich is neither the simple image nor the simple opposite of his father. Instead, he shares some of the same traits, and at the same time has the potential to develop beyond his father. This is anticipated in the opening pages: we discover that, in his youth, Heinrich's father also had a dream about a flower, which prompted him to return to Germany and to marry; but whereas Heinrich cannot stop dwelling on the significance of his version of the dream—which marks the dawn of his notion of that ideal sphere towards which he will journey—his father firmly refuses to be distracted by dreams. In other words, Heinrich both repeats and advances his father's experience.

The depiction of motherhood in the novel is more problematic. At the very least, gender roles are constructed along profoundly normative lines. Moreover, mothers and female lovers—and, as has frequently been observed,[20] the boundary between the two is fluid in *Ofterdingen*—are both fetishized, and they die with disproportionate frequency. Certainly, the sacrificial killing of the mother in Klingsohr's *Märchen* is a prime example of the 'formal, symbolic violence'[21] that tends to be visited on women, and of the absence that (except in the case of Heinrich's own mother) seems not always to be properly motivated in this text. In addition, Martha Helfer has observed that *Ofterdingen* poses a challenge to the perception—widespread in scholarship—that inspiration always springs from the female muse in Romantic writing:

in *Heinrich von Ofterdingen* the process of *autopoiesis* is coded as male. Man—not woman—is the true source of poetic inspiration in the novel, and the subject Heinrich is constructed at the nexus of multiple male discourses, indeed *as* the nexus of multiple male discourses.[22]

In Helfer's interpretation, women in Ofterdingen play a marginal role in the process of poetic inspiration, and a similar argument could be made in relation to mother figures in the development of the protagonist. For all that Heinrich's mother travels with him, her character is only vaguely delineated, and the task of helping Heinrich to intellectual self-fulfilment is very much left to the male characters. This runs counter to the premiss of Friedrich Kittler's study *Dichter — Mutter — Kind*, namely that the transition to the nuclear family model in the eighteenth century brought about a recoding

---

[20] See e.g. James R. Hodkinson, *Women and Writing in the Works of Novalis: Transformation beyond Measure?* (Rochester, NY: Camden House, 2007), p. 41.

[21] Michael Minden, *The German Bildungsroman: Incest and Inheritance* (Cambridge: Cambridge University Press, 1997), p. 201.

[22] Martha B. Helfer, 'The Male Muses of Romanticism: The Poetics of Gender in Novalis, E. T. A. Hoffmann, and Eichendorff', *German Quarterly*, 78 (2005), 299–319 (p. 305).

of relations, in which 'das altüberlieferte Familienoberhaupt namens Vater durch eine Familienmitte namens Mutter [abgelöst wurde]'.²³ Although Kittler's analysis is insightful, it understates the role of father figures in Romantic writing. Moreover, the notion that intimacy and care in family relations is a relatively recent development, resulting from an unprecedented centralizing of the mother from the eighteenth century onwards, has been the subject of intense historiographical debate, and has been partly discredited.²⁴ Nonetheless, the gesture in Klingsohr's *Märchen* of drinking the mother's ashes is one sign, however problematic, that she remains essential to the symbolic economy of the text: 'Sie war jedem gegenwärtig, und ihre geheimnisvolle Anwesenheit schien alle zu verklären' (*Werke*, p. 361). Her presence 'transfigures', and is thus fundamental to the integration of the ideal and the real. Indeed, although this is technically the mother of Eros, she is referred to throughout simply as 'die Mutter', which confers on her the status of an archetype. Here I agree with Kittler's contention that '[d]as Individuum scheint vollständig, weil die Liebe zu und aus der Mutterliebe es familiarisiert'.²⁵ The treatment of female figures in *Ofterdingen* is likely to be quite unpalatable to a twenty-first-century readership, but mothers do retain an important role in the development of the protagonist.

Parents are thus a crucial instantiation of the origins that run like a red thread through Heinrich's progress; but the most significant figures he meets along the way, and who guide him towards his goal, also share deep connections with his parents. Michael Minden posits a link between Mathilde and Heinrich's mother on the one hand, and between Klingsohr and Heinrich's father on the other. Heinrich is woken from his dream of the blue flower, allied with Mathilde in the image system of the novel, by his mother's voice, so that 'both Mathilde and his mother are associated with the same deepest yearning'; and Klingsohr is a superior artist, 'an intensified version' of Heinrich's father.²⁶ Avatars of parents proliferate, therefore, throughout the text.

²³ Friedrich A. Kittler, *Dichter — Mutter — Kind* (Munich: Fink, 1991), p. 15.

²⁴ It is true that the concept of the relationship between parent and child underwent profound changes from the late eighteenth century, not least in the wake of 'Rousseau's "Copernican turn" to the child'; see e.g. Loftur Guttormsson, 'Parent–Child Relations', in *The History of the European Family*, ed. by David I. Kerzter and Marzio Barbagli, 3 vols (New Haven: Yale University Press, 2001–03), II: *Family Life in the Long Nineteenth Century, 1789-1913* (2002), pp. 251–81 (p. 253). Yet Steven Ozment, among others, contests the thesis, which finds its focal point in the work of Philippe Arières, that 'the premodern family was only a "moral and social unit," not yet a sentimental one'; see *Ancestors: The Loving Family in Old Europe* (Cambridge, MA: Harvard University Press, 2001), p. 11. One of Ozment's counter-arguments is that, far from being a development associated with the rise of the 'modern' family, the recognition of children as having 'special needs and vulnerabilities [. . .] has been documented all the way back to antiquity' (p. 56). Linda A. Pollock's chapter on 'Parent–Child Relations' in *The History of the European Family*, I: *Family Life in Early Modern Times, 1500-1789* (2001), pp. 191–220, represents a similar view.

²⁵ Kittler, *Dichter — Mutter — Kind*, p. 195.

²⁶ Minden, *The German Bildungsroman*, p. 183.

The constellation that develops around Klingsohr is also an instance of *textual* heightening. Earlier on, in the story of a young man and his beloved princess told by the merchants, both fathers and fathers-in-law played a crucial role: the two fathers (the old man, and the king) have invested everything in their children, and their children's devotion to them is matched only by their tenderness towards their new fathers. Now, the roles of both the old man (provider of wisdom, and educator of the young man) and the king (father of the young woman, and father-in-law to the man) are merged in Klingsohr, who towers above the earlier characters in significance. In this intensification of a pre-established pattern, the text performs what it describes. Finally, Heinrich has a premonition that he is moving towards his parents, biological and adopted, as well as beyond them. At the end of Chapter 6 he dreams both of Mathilde's death and of their reunion beyond mortality; and when Heinrich, on rediscovering his beloved, asks 'Wo sind wir, liebe Mathilde?', she replies 'Bey unsern Eltern' (*Werke*, p. 326). Thus parental figures, in addition to biological parents, are involved in the transforming process of development and return. They facilitate the transition between the real and the ideal, providing the protagonist with orientation throughout; and they can be expected to be present, in some permutation, at the end of the journey as well as the beginning. This is precisely the pattern that is missing, and overtly missed, in *Florentin*.

Florentin is most commonly compared with Friedrich Schlegel's *Lucinde*. Both novels offer innovative theoretical perspectives on marriage, and the love affair between their respective authors might seem to reinforce their status as partner texts. Elena Pnevmonidou argues, however, that 'es war wohl auch nie Dorothea Schlegels Absicht, ein Pendant zu *Lucinde* zu entwerfen', and highlights the many differences in the conceptualization of marriage and the construction of gender in the two texts.[27] Moreover, the persistent coupling of *Florentin* and *Lucinde* has obscured the potential for reading Dorothea Schlegel's novel as a foil to *Ofterdingen*. Although *Florentin* and *Ofterdingen* were written in the same year, and with many of the same models in mind (*Wilhelm Meisters Lehrjahre* and *Franz Sternbald* foremost among them), the differences between them are conspicuous. Schlegel populates her novel with impressive female figures, above all Clementina, who, with her combination of physical frailty and profound spirituality, anticipates the figure of Makarie in Goethe's *Wilhelm Meisters Wanderjahre*. As Edwina Lawler and Ruth Richardson observe, 'by making Clementina priestess and musician, [Dorothea] speaks out against the centuries-long ban against women interfering in either the sphere of theology or that of music'.[28] Moreover, as we shall see, Schlegel devotes

[27] Elena Pnevmonidou, 'Die Absage an das romantische Ich: Dorothea Schlegels *Florentin* als Umschrift von Friedrich Schlegels *Lucinde*', *German Life and Letters*, 58 (2005), 271–92 (p. 272).
[28] 'Introduction', in Schlegel, *Florentin*, trans. by Lawler and Richardson, p. lxv.

more attention both to the components of a successful family model and to the everyday workings of family life than either Novalis or Tieck. The link between *Florentin* and *Ofterdingen* is the theme of self-development, which is in the foreground of both novels, but it is in fact here that they diverge most significantly of all. There is a good deal to be said for the claim that *Florentin* is 'a developmental novel', portraying 'the apprenticeship of the romantic hero from love to life and the numerous stages of development through which he must go to reach self-actualization'.[29] But what is not made explicit here is that this apprenticeship is full of impediments and traumas, and that there is much less in the novel to convince the reader that Florentin will achieve 'self-actualization' than we find in *Ofterdingen*. As far as we can judge (for Novalis died before the completion of Part Two), there are 'no obstacles in [Heinrich's] path to self-fulfilment':[30] Heinrich moves seamlessly from one sphere to another. Florentin's journey, by contrast, is jagged, his progress by no means assured; and, significantly, he lacks the stable parent figures and a secure sense of home by which to orient himself.

The major point of contrast between *Florentin* and *Ofterdingen* is arguably the question of origins. While origins are crucial in Heinrich's progress, Florentin is in ignorance of his: 'So weit mich mein Gedächtnis zurückträgt, war ich eine Waise und ein Fremdling auf Erden.'[31] In a lengthy retrospective account towards the middle of the novel, Florentin describes two childhood dwellings in Italy, neither of which offers a stable point of origin. His first home is on a small, unnamed island; but despite the loving care of a 'gute, freundliche Frau, die Sorge für mich trug und mich keinen Augenblick verließ' (*Florentin*, p. 42), his life there is a disrupted one. The other occupant of the house, an older, Charon figure,[32] periodically brings a glamorous, aristocratic lady in his boat, of whom Florentin says 'ich mußte sie Mutter nennen' (*Florentin*, p. 42). Although he describes a level of attachment between them, the use of the verb 'mußte' betrays the element of force in the relationship. Florentin also speaks of considerable reciprocal hostility between himself and the woman's male companions: an equally glamorous man, and a priest. Such is his alienation from the men that he professes astonishment at hearing that his father has died: 'ich konnte es nicht fassen, ich wußte nicht, wer mein Vater gewesen sei, ich hatte diese Benennung gar nicht zu brauchen gelernt' (*Florentin*, p. 44). It has to be explained to him that it is the handsome com-

[29] Ibid., p. xxxiii. Lawler and Richardson's argument is especially important in the context of the traditional, dismissive reception of *Florentin* as merely another *Trivialroman*.
[30] Saul, *History and Poetry*, p. 160.
[31] Dorothea Schlegel, *Florentin: Roman — Fragmente — Varianten*, ed. by Weissberg, p. 16. Further references to this volume (hereafter *Florentin*) will be given after quotations in the main body of the text.
[32] See Heike Brandstädter and Katharina Jeorgakopulos, *Dorothea Schlegel, 'Florentin': Lektüre eines vergessenen Textes* (Hamburg: Argument, 2001), p. 61.

panion of his 'mother' who has died. Following the death of his 'father', he is torn away from his life on the island and taken to live with his 'mother', whose house is run in a manner profoundly inimical to his own nature. He describes it as a claustrophobic place, devoid of colour and light; indeed, his description of the schoolroom is reminiscent of the study in which Goethe's Faust feels so confined at the beginning of Part One of the tragedy: 'Das Zimmer war groß und hoch, gotisch gewölbt, die Fenster ganz oben, und zum Überfluß noch vergittert, die nackten grauen Wände nur von finstern Heiligenbildern verziert' (*Florentin*, p. 45). The dark icons are emblematic of the religious fanaticism that infiltrates the family in the absence of a father figure, and which oppresses and stifles Florentin. The eventual revelation, some years later, that the woman whom he has had to call mother is not, in fact, his biological mother is wholly in keeping with this history of alienation and spiritual homelessness.

Florentin, then, has neither the established sense of home nor the confidence in his parentage that Heinrich possesses, and his destination is almost as obscure as his origin. As he nears the end of the narration of his life story, he professes to be driven in a manner that is in many respects 'typically Romantic':[33] 'Mich treibt etwas Unnennbares vorwärts, was ich mein Schicksal nennen muß. [. . .] [I]ch muß meinen Endzweck, ich muß das Glück, das ich ahnde, wirklich finden' (*Florentin*, p. 82). The insufficiency of language to which Florentin refers ('etwas Unnennbares') was certainly a major preoccupation for Early Romantic writers and thinkers, but there is also a sense here of the formlessness of his future, which contrasts markedly with Heinrich's assured progress. Florentin cannot find a more appropriate name for his direction than 'fate' because his own sense of it is indistinct. At the opening of the novel he is bound for America, a land characterized at that time by its formlessness. The American Declaration of Independence had been made well within living memory when *Florentin* was written, but vast areas of that continent still lay unexplored. Florentin hopes that this destination will also solve the problem of origins: '"So weit mich mein Gedächtnis zurückträgt, war ich eine Waise und ein Fremdling auf Erden, und so denke ich das Land mein Vaterland zu benennen, wo ich zuerst mich werde Vater nennen hören." — Er schwieg, und sein Blick senkte sich trübe und ernst' (*Florentin*, p. 16). Becoming a parent himself ought to assuage the pain caused by the absence of a trusted parent figure in his own life. Yet his melancholy as he says this derives from the impossibly fractured experience from which he has recently emerged. None of the stations in the period between leaving the military academy (which, with his friend Manfred, was his escape from his unhappy circumstances) and encountering the Schwarzenberg family has met

---

[33] 'Introduction', in Schlegel, *Florentin*, trans. by Lawler and Richardson, p. xxiv.

with much success. His stays in Venice and Paris are taken up with gambling, the latter sojourn in particular serving only to reinforce his sense 'daß ich nirgends hinpasse' (*Florentin*, p. 74). In Rome, his artistic labours seem only to run to dilettantism, and his brief but obsessive partnership with one of his models ends abruptly when she terminates her pregnancy in his absence. His stay in England dissolves into virtual destitution. Only his visit to a Swiss friend seems to provide some stability, and even here, the terminal illness of that friend's wife is a reminder of the transience of all things.

Even the two stations on Florentin's journey that occupy the main part of the novel are problematic. The first, the Schwarzenberg estate, is ostensibly a social utopia, infused with progressive ideas. The respect for the autonomy of children and for the views and rights of subordinates, together with the leading role taken by the Countess in these innovations, all reflect Dorothea Schlegel's 'revolutionary' desire to 'restructur[e] the ordering of relations in her society'.[34] Schwarzenberg certainly forms a positive contrast to Florentin's own unhappy background. Yet it soon becomes clear that this cannot represent the 'Endzweck' (*Florentin*, p. 82) to which Florentin feels inexorably drawn: for Juliane, the eldest daughter, whom he desires, is intended for Eduard, which reduces, even eradicates, the opportunity for Florentin to integrate into the family. Moreover, Schwarzenberg is not drawn uncritically,[35] and its limitations are most evident in the figure of Juliane. Juliane is beautiful, but two-dimensional by comparison with her impressive mother. Her aunt, Clementina, intervenes several times to warn that her marriage to Eduard, for which the Count in particular is pushing, is premature. Moreover, her foray, in male clothing, into the forest and into a thunderstorm reveals a lack of resilience and independence; as Martha Helfer observes, 'her one "manly" venture into the real world reduces her to a pathetic creature who realizes how dependent she is on an aestheticized existence characterized by limits and creature comforts'.[36] Whether we see this as an absence of resourcefulness on Juliane's own part, or as a sign that this family model, seemingly so flexible, has the capacity to hinder and restrain, it is clear that, in her case, the Schwarzenberg method has yet to prove itself.

Florentin's final station in the novel is Clementina's house. He leaves the

[34] Ibid., p. lv.

[35] John Hibberd concludes an examination of this 'precarious idyll' as follows: 'the author remains ambivalent in her attitude to the precarious idyll she portrays: she seems to agree with her hero's demands for greater freedom and naturalness than society appears able to give, but also, with him, to admire and envy the refined superiority of Clementine and the civilised calm of Eleonore. The problem of defining and creating a golden age [is] to discover an Elysium that is not a hell of monotony, and that takes equal account of individual yearnings and social reality' ('Dorothea Schlegel's *Florentin* and the Precarious Idyll', *German Life and Letters*, 30 (1977), 198–207 (pp. 206–07)).

[36] Martha B. Helfer, 'Dorothea Schlegel's *Florentin*: Constructing a Feminist Romantic Aesthetic', *German Quarterly*, 69 (1996), 144–60 (p. 155).

Schwarzenberg estate quite suddenly, unsure as to his own motivations—though, with a touch of whimsy, he suspects himself of having taken fright at lacking the appropriate clothing to wear for Juliane's wedding. A good deal of suspense has been generated around the character of Clementina, to the extent that the reader and Florentin alike have come to expect that it will bring the revelation of both his origins and his 'Endzweck'. Florentin has felt an instinctive connection to her ever since he saw her portrait on his first morning at Schwarzenberg, and we have been led to suspect that she might be Florentin's mother. Yet the mystery is increased by her reaction to Florentin when they finally come face to face in the temple at her house:

Einige Augenblicke blieb sie, weit hervor sich beugend, in derselben Stellung, ihre Augen fest mit sichtbarem Erstaunen auf ihn geheftet; eine schnelle Röte überflog den Marmor ihres Gesichts, dann erblaßte sie wieder, ihre Augen schlossen sich, und sie sank ohnmächtig zurück. (*Florentin*, p. 148)

Clementina's inability to move her gaze from Florentin, her blushing, and her loss of physical control suggest a moment of profound recognition, which matches the pull that Florentin has felt to her:

Warum, dachte er, warum ist diese Clementina und alles was sie umgibt, grade mir wie eine Erscheinung, da sie doch unter den übrigen Menschen wie eine längst bekannte Mitbürgerin wandelt? Warum wird jede ferne Erinnerung wieder wach in mir? Was tut sich die Vergangenheit, dies längst verdeckte Grab, gegen mich auf? (*Florentin*, p. 148)

Florentin comes close here to experiencing the deep familiarity which is essential to Heinrich's progress. For Heinrich, it announces itself in the form of a visionary dream, which takes him far beyond the limits of his everyday experience; and for Florentin, likewise, it is closely allied to foreignness. Clementina seems strange, even ghostly, to him precisely because she triggers the release of sensations which are familiar, but have long since been buried.[37] The notion of the past as a grave opening itself up, however, bodes ill; and the moment of anagnorisis is incomplete, the nature of the connection between them remains unconfirmed. Instead, Clementina's doctor informs Florentin that she is not well enough to see him again that day, and the novel jolts to a finish with his disappearance.

Florentin remained incomplete: a move to Cologne compounded Dorothea Schlegel's indecision about what Gerald Mackenthun calls '[das] Schicksal ihres ungebundenen Helden', and condemned the novel to remain a

[37] Florentin's experience corresponds in many ways to Freud's exploration of the uncanny. For Freud, following Schelling, 'das Unheimliche' is not a negation of that which is 'heimlich'; rather, the 'uncanny' effect derives from the rootedness of that which has been uncovered in the familiar. See Sigmund Freud, *Gesammelte Werke*, ed. by Anna Freud and others, 18 vols (London: Imago, 1946–[68]), XII: *Werke aus den Jahren 1917–1920* (1947), pp. 227–68.

fragment.³⁸ Yet, by contrast with *Ofterdingen*, which was cut short by Novalis's death, *Florentin* remained unfinished for reasons that arguably go beyond sheer force of circumstance. Just as the form of *Ofterdingen* reflected its central idea, so incompleteness inheres in the very fabric of *Florentin*, and is its principal theme. Even the planned continuation of the work (it was to have ended with the establishment by the main characters of a new colony in America) was also to deny Florentin a meeting with his mother. One version of the manuscript (which, appropriately enough, has been lost) allegedly depicted Florentin (now called Florestan) receiving confirmation that Clementina (now called Camilla) is indeed his mother and returning to Europe from America, only to find her dead.³⁹ That productive return, which figures so strongly in Heinrich's trajectory, is repeatedly denied to Florentin. This persistent incompleteness is not, I think, a reflection of cynicism about family relations *per se*. A stable home is held up throughout as an ideal, and Florentin is not a wanderer because he has rejected family ties.⁴⁰ On the contrary, he genuinely desires that sense of belonging, as his reflections on the word 'Vaterland' or his fury and despair at his wife's abortion make plain. Rather, the novel, despite the humour and whimsy in its pages, expresses a deep yearning for ontological security in this life and, arguably, deep pessimism about the possibility of achieving it. This could be attributed in part to the perspective of unending marginality from which Dorothea Schlegel was writing, as a female intellectual and a Jewish apostate at the end of the eighteenth century. Yet her protagonist is neither female nor Jewish, though he is an apostate; and the pessimism of *Florentin*, if it finds no echo in *Heinrich von Ofterdingen*, certainly resonates with *Der Runenberg*.

In *Der Runenberg* Tieck makes a partial return to the quasi-mystical, quasi-magical world of *Ofterdingen*. At first sight, reflections of *Ofterdingen* abound in *Der Runenberg*, despite the difference in the length of the two narratives. Just as the homeless mother Zulima gives Heinrich her golden hair ribbon 'mit den unbekannten Buchstaben' (*Werke*, p. 285), so the tablet given to Christian by the mysterious beauty in the Runenberg 'schien eine wunderlich unverständliche Figur mit ihren unterschiedlichen Farben und Linien zu bilden'⁴¹—although, of course, Zulima explains the meaning of the inscription,

---

³⁸ Gerald Mackenthun, 'Dorothea Schlegel und die Poesie des Lebens', in *Bedeutende Frauen des 18. Jahrhunderts: Elf biographische Essays*, ed. by Elke Pilz (Würzburg: Königshausen & Neumann, 2007), pp. 63–82 (p. 75).

³⁹ See Liliane Weissberg, 'Nachwort', in Schlegel, *Florentin*, pp. 205–38 (pp. 226–27). The fluidity of names here could be seen as symbolic of the instability of personal identity with which Florentin has been struggling throughout the first part of the novel.

⁴⁰ For this reason, Weissberg's claim that '[e]r muß die Familie bewußt aufgeben, um seine wahre Herkunft zu entdecken' ('Nachwort', p. 232) seems slightly wide of the mark. 'Family' *per se* is not the obstacle, nor does the renunciation of family lead to the discovery of his true origins. He desires both, but both remain elusive.

⁴¹ Ludwig Tieck, *Schriften in zwölf Bänden*, ed. by Hans Peter Balmes and others (Frankfurt

whereas Christian is left to conjecture. The description of Arctur's palace at the opening of Klingsohr's *Märchen* resonates with that of the interior of the Runenberg in Christian's vision. The palace garden is full of 'Metallbäumen und Krystallpflanzen [. . .] bunten Edelsteinblüthen und Früchten', and 'die Lebhaftigkeit der Lichter und Farben gewährte das herrlichste Schauspiel' (*Werke*, p. 339); and similarly, Christian finds himself looking upon a chamber 'der wunderlich verziert von mancherlei Gesteinen und Kristallen in vielfältigen Schimmern funkelte, die sich geheimnisvoll von dem wandelnden Lichte durcheinander bewegten' (*Schriften*, VI, 191). Furthermore, the theme of the subterranean explored in Chapter 5 of *Ofterdingen* pervades *Der Runenberg*: Christian more than shares the Bohemian miner's 'heftige Neugierde [. . .] zu wissen, was in den Bergen verborgen seyn müsse' (*Werke*, p. 286), and indeed disappears down a mine shaft when he leaves home for the final time.

It is in this context, however, that the crucial differences between the two texts become apparent. For Christian, the subterranean world becomes an obsession, to which he sacrifices all else. Theodore Ziolkowski, for example, interprets Christian's final disappearance as 'a symbolic act that clearly represents a sexual coupling with the seductive, maddening spirit of the mountains'.[42] In *Ofterdingen*, by contrast, neither the miner nor the hermit, whom the miner's party encounters deep inside the mountain cavity, forgets the importance of human ties. The miner remarks that, in his profession, the worker 'gedenkt in seiner Einsamkeit mit inniger Herzlichkeit seiner Genossen und seiner Familie, und fühlt immer erneuert die gegenseitige Unentbehrlichkeit und Blutverwandtschaft der Menschen' (*Werke*, p. 292). The hermit, for his part, goes out every day, maintains a few contacts in the area, and explains that, in his view, solitude can be successful only if it is predicated on significant experience of the world; indeed, despite his isolation, the impression he makes is this: 'Er war sehr freundlich und offen, und verrieth eine große Bekanntschaft mit der Welt' (*Werke*, p. 304). It is precisely this combination of meditative self-discovery and sociability which characterizes Heinrich's path, too, but which Christian is unable to maintain: and Tieck depicts this conflict against the background not of 'society' in general but of the family in particular.

Unlike Florentin, Christian is in no doubt about his origins: when we first meet him, he has recently left his parents' home, determined to forge a different path from that of his father (and here, once again, it is the father,

---

a.M.: Deutscher Klassiker Verlag, 1985–), VI: *Phantasus*, ed. by Manfred Frank (1985), p. 192. Further references to this volume (hereafter *Schriften*, VI) will be given after quotations in the main body of the text.

[42] Theodore Ziolkowski, *German Romanticism and its Institutions* (Princeton: Princeton University Press, 1990), p. 53. Ziolkowski devotes an entire chapter to the various symbolic associations of the mine in Romantic writing.

rather than the mother, who looms large). Unlike Heinrich, however, he takes a meandering, dislocated course; he vacillates between participation and extreme isolation, and between the wholehearted imitation and the wholehearted rejection of his father's career as a gardener. Return in this text tends to be regressive rather than productive: it is nostalgia that pulls him from his pursuit of the life of the hunter (a more solitary, and more aggressive, occupation) back into his father's world, and into the world of the family. He longs for the home he has left as he wanders alone in the mountains at the opening of the story; and when, after his vision of the mysterious beauty in the Runenberg, he happens upon a village, he is seized with 'unbeschreiblich süßer Wehmut' (*Schriften*, VI, 193). The description of this village, '[d]ie engen Gärten, die kleinen Hütten [...], die gerade abgeteilten Kornfelder' (*Schriften*, VI, 193–94), recalls Christian's evocation of his father's world: 'der kleine beschränkte Garten meines Vaters mit den geordenten Blumenbeeten, die enge Wohnung' (*Schriften*, VI, 188). Consonant with the recurrent adjective 'eng', it is a life of self-limitation which, initially, he cultivates as he settles, becoming a gardener after all, marrying Elisabeth, and starting his own family. When his father comes to live with them, the course seems set for Christian's life to be a simple continuation of his father's: seemingly secure, but with none of the progress that characterizes Heinrich's relationship with his father. Differentiation can only be achieved, it seems, in extreme forms. His perception of things diverges once again from that of his father when a stranger deposits a sum of money in his house, and above all when he finds the bejewelled tablet that he had lost:

'Seht', rief er ihm zu, 'das, wovon ich Euch so oft erzählt habe, was ich nur im Traum zu sehn glaubte, ist jetzt gewiß und wahrhaftig mein.' Der Alte betrachtete die Tafel lange und sagte: 'mein Sohn, mir schaudert recht im Herzen, wenn ich die Lineamente dieser Steine betrachte und ahnend den Sinn dieser Wortfügung errate.' (*Schriften*, VI, 204)

Christian believes that he has found his own true 'Endzweck' (to use Florentin's term), that his calling is the discovery of treasures which outstrip ordinary human understanding. He believes that he has grasped the 'truth' about the natural world: 'in den Pflanzen, Kräutern, Blumen und Bäumen regt und bewegt sich schmerzhaft nur eine große Wunde, sie sind der Leichnam vormaliger herrlicher Steinwelten' (*Schriften*, VI, 202).[43] He is con-

---

[43] Ziolkowski observes that this represents 'a curious inversion of the usual theory' (*German Romanticism and its Institutions*, p. 52), namely the belief, which lasted from classical antiquity to the eighteenth century, 'that stones and metals grew beneath the earth like organic matter' (p. 29), and which, despite the familiarity of many Romantic thinkers (Novalis among them) with modern geology, frequently appealed to their sensibility. It is possible, then, that Christian's words represent a satirical critique of that belief on Tieck's part.

vinced that he has been 'called' by the 'Waldweib', who merges in his mind with the mysterious beauty of his vision.

There is, then, in *Der Runenberg* a juxtaposition of spheres that could for a moment be designated 'real' (that of the family and the village) and 'ideal' (that of visions and precious stones), which, superficially, brings the text parallel with *Ofterdingen*. Yet Christian's behaviour before his disappearance speaks of paranoia, and his father reads only danger into the tablet, rendering Christian's discoveries dubious: the comparison with Novalis stalls because of the friction between the two spheres in Tieck. There is no sense of the progressive integration of the two that is so characteristic of *Ofterdingen*; on the contrary, Christian is driven uncomfortably from one to the other, and there is little progress in the story. There is one equivalent to the parental avatars stationed so conveniently along Heinrich's journey, namely the old man (the first 'stranger' in the text) whom Christian meets at the beginning of the story. He has a paternal air, comforts him in his loneliness by listening to his tales of home, and 'dünkt [. . .] dem Jünglinge bald ein alter Bekannter zu sein' (*Schriften*, VI, 187); but the destination to which he guides him is the ominous Runenberg. Pursuing or indulging the supposed ideal entails the destruction of the real, and not just for Christian. Shortly after starting his own family, he discovers that in his absence (which includes his first exposure to the world of the Runenberg) his parents' home has withered away, and his mother has died. Although his father joins him and Elisabeth, and more children are born, the death of his birthplace is a portent of things to come. Once Christian has devoted himself wholly to his ideal, his father dies, as do Elisabeth's parents, and the stable environment that they have built up falls away: their livestock perish and their servants begin to cheat Elisabeth. It is true that death and loss, above all of family members, also figure strongly in *Ofterdingen*, and Heinrich's position at the beginning of Part Two is bleak. Yet, in *Ofterdingen*, loss itself is part of the gradual process of integration, and the characters are able to move beyond it. In the first allegorical story told by the merchants, after a painful period of separation the king's daughter is restored to him, complete with son-in-law and grandson. By the time Heinrich loses Mathilde, he has progressed too far beyond that simple story for there to be such an easy solution; but he is quickened by a vision of his beloved, who comforts him and restores his confidence in his journey. Negation is itself negated. In *Der Runenberg*, by contrast, there is nothing, no progressive or integrative movement, to contain devastation.

Der Runenberg has been interpreted variously as making 'eros, nature organism, and underground mystery into one agency, whose sole aim is to delude, ensnare and destroy',[44] and as an allegory of 'the emerging bourgeois

---

[44] Paulin, *Ludwig Tieck*, p. 143.

accumulation of material wealth that becomes the driving force of social change during the early industrial period'.⁴⁵ To these a further dimension can be added, the novel's reflection on the fragility of 'home' and on the vulnerability of those ties from which we derive a sense of security. Twice in *Der Runenberg* a seemingly stable home is dispelled as if it were a mirage: first Christian's birthplace and then the life he has established with Elisabeth. This has its echo in Tieck's *Kunstmärchen* of 1811, *Die Elfen*. There, too, an apparently sturdy and bounteous home life turns out to be wholly dependent on the activity of a kingdom of elves; at the disclosure of their presence, that life withers away and the surviving family members are forced to seek a meagre existence elsewhere. There might seem to be a causal link in *Der Runenberg* between Christian's actions and the fate of his family—that is, that his desertion of them and indulgence in a dangerous fantasy bring about their destruction—but Tieck offers more than a simple moralistic lesson: after all, he devotes his most impressive and mesmeric writing to the passages concerned with the Runenberg. Without absolving him of responsibility, it is also possible to see Christian's fate and that of his family as different expressions of the same fundamental problem, namely the precariousness of human existence and the constant challenges posed to our ontological resilience. Despite the limitations of the Schwarzenberg model, it remains just possible to explain Florentin's experience away as the fate of an unfortunate outsider; this is not the case with *Der Runenberg*, however, for not only Christian but even those who comply and conform are shown to be tragically vulnerable. With this text Tieck was, I suggest, refusing to offer a vision of poetic progress and fulfilment in the vein of *Heinrich von Ofterdingen*, choosing instead to depict hope, and home, blossoming and withering away by turns.

Writing in 1920, Georg Lukács coined the notion of 'transcendental homelessness'. 'Die Form des Romans', he argued, is 'ein Ausdruck der transzendentalen Obdachlosigkeit. [. . .] In einer unentwirrbaren Verschlungenheit kreuzen sich [in der nachgriechischen Zeit] die Gattungen als Zeichen des echten und des unechten Suchens nach dem nicht mehr klar und eindeutig gegebenen Ziele.'⁴⁶ For Lukács, the novel is the form that best expresses the loss of that organic unity embodied, at least for the German philosophical tradition, in ancient Greece. In Lukács's interpretation, Novalis tried, and ultimately failed, to achieve a complete synthesis between reality and transcendence in his recasting of the *Wilhelm Meister* scenario.⁴⁷ John Neubauer comments that 'Lukács adopts from Hegel the notion that the novel is the

---

⁴⁵ Ulrich Scheck, 'Tales of Wonder and Terror: Short Prose of the German Romantics', in *The Literature of German Romanticism*, ed. by Dennis F. Mahoney (Rochester, NY: Camden House, 2004), pp. 101–23 (p. 105).
⁴⁶ Lukács, *Die Theorie des Romans*, pp. 23–24.
⁴⁷ Ibid., pp. 151–52.

epic of a prosaic and bourgeois world [...], without sharing Hegel's ultimately optimistic vision.'[48] Implicit in this observation is the key, I suggest, both to Lukács's objection to Novalis and to the radical difference between *Heinrich von Ofterdingen* on the one hand, and *Florentin* and *Der Runenberg* on the other. The 'optimism' that can be detected in both Hegel and Novalis derives from their lasting commitment to a 'Platonic–Christian ontology',[49] however unorthodox its expression in their works. This orients itself towards 'a final cause, *telos*, of saving grace, and an intrinsic soteriology (salvation)':[50] qualities which are noticeably absent from *Florentin* and *Der Runenberg*. Indeed, there is in both texts a strong undercurrent of religious doubt, conveyed in Florentin's apostasy and Tieck's ironic choice of the name 'Christian' for his protagonist. By the eve of the nineteenth century, the process of secularization had cast a shadow over religious certainty; this is a latent concern in all three texts, and may account for the differences between them. If *Heinrich von Ofterdingen* is an unreserved affirmation of the Platonic–Christian ontology, *Florentin* and *Der Runenberg* reflect no such faith. The struggle to establish and maintain ontological security is a perennial theme in cultural production. But the ambivalence of secularization is more specific (though it is by no means unique) to this particular context; and it can be seen to infiltrate other dimensions of security, such as family life, in these narratives.

MURRAY EDWARDS COLLEGE, CAMBRIDGE   CHARLOTTE LEE

[48] Neubauer, 'Bakhtin versus Lukács', p. 533.
[49] Pio Colonnello, 'Homelessness as *Heimatlosigkeit*?', in *The Ethics of Homelessness: Philosophical Perspectives*, ed. by G. John M. Abbarno (Amsterdam: Rodopi, 1999), pp. 41–53 (p. 42).
[50] Ibid.

REVIEWS

How to Read Literature. By TERRY EAGLETON. New Haven and London: Yale University Press. 2013. x+216 pp. £18.99. ISBN 978-0-300-19096-03.

After *How to Read a Poem* (Oxford: Blackwell, 2007) and the twenty-fifth anniversary edition of his *Literary Theory: An Introduction* (Minneapolis: University of Minnesota Press, 2008), here is another introductory work from Terry Eagleton, one which, according to the jacket blurb, 'is the book of choice for students new to the study of literature'. A reading of the book itself, however, suggests significant grounds for doubting this assertion. There are certainly some fine analyses, some very neat formulations of central critical problems, and Eagleton is particularly good at articulating the shifts in strategy, focus, and approach between the grand realist projects of the nineteenth century and the modernist novels of the early twentieth century. Problematically, however, for a book to which a beginner might look for a model of critical writing, Eagleton's tone throughout is matey, his prose littered with throwaway comments ('Lady Macbeth', he writes, 'has an indeterminate number of children, which may prove convenient when applying for child benefit' (p. 46)) and marked by a seemingly compulsive recourse to distracting 'illustrative' imagery. Buying into the illusion of a literary work, he argues, is to collude with the author, 'rather as we collude in the illusion that a toddler is the President of the International Monetary Fund if this yields him some momentary pleasure' (p. 80). On another occasion (one of many such moments), an important critical point about the riches of everyday language is diluted by Eagleton's inability to resist tagging on another of his flippant asides: '[Language] is the most magnificent artefact humanity has ever come up with. It even surpasses the movies of Mel Gibson in this respect' (p. 179).

The book has a simple structure: the first chapter, 'Openings', considers the incipit of a wide range of texts, from *Wuthering Heights*, *A Passage to India*, and *Macbeth* to the Bible and *Pride and Prejudice*, demonstrating how openings prime readers for what is to come, often in ways not immediately evident to the first-time reader. From the focus on the 'micro' business of word-choice, punctuation, and rhythm, Eagleton moves in his subsequent chapters to broader, 'macro' issues: first 'Character', then 'Narrative' and 'Interpretation'. A shorter, concluding chapter addresses the notion of 'Value'.

Eagleton notes in his first chapter that 'learning to be a literary critic is, among other things, a matter of learning how to deploy certain techniques' (p. 7). One wonders whether Eagleton's techniques would be welcome in the essays of the students at whom the book is aimed. Richardson's Clarissa Harlowe, we read in the 'Character' chapter, 'is not the kind of woman one would gladly accompany on a pubcrawl' (p. 53); later, in the 'Value' chapter, Eagleton observes that 'Shakespeare's Cordelia, Milton's Satan and Dickens's Fagin are fascinating precisely because we are unlikely to encounter them at Walmart's' (p. 181). The 'Interpretation' chapter includes a lengthy exposition of *Great Expectations*, which provides many insights and examples of excellent critical practice, but one might question the merits of extending to ten pages in the same chapter a reading of 'Baa Baa Black Sheep' which, no sooner finished, is discredited as an example of criticism that overlooks the question of genre. Additionally, across different chapters we find the author making very similar points that overlap even in their phrasing, which highlights a lack of care taken in the structuring and editing of the work. Eagleton is one of our most important critics and he appears to have enjoyed writing this book. It is unlikely, however, to be particularly useful as an introduction for those genuinely in need of critical guidance.

University of Exeter   Adam Watt

Jenseitsästhetik: Literarische Räume letzter Dinge. By Verena O. Lobsien. Berlin: Berlin University Press. 2012. 438 pp. €34.90. ISBN 978-3-86280-044-5.

Verena Lobsien explicitly addresses her book not only to specialists (p. 8) but also to that broader audience interested more generally in questions concerning the connection between literature, philosophy, theology, and the reality of experience (p. 391). She regards these questions as implicit in literary works dealing with the hereafter (in the religious sense) or with utopias generally, both of which are suggested by the German word *jenseits*. Leaving her theoretical reflections for her brief conclusion, she proceeds inductively—in an admirably clear and jargon-free prose—from text to representative text, beginning appropriately with Thomas More's *Utopia*.

Given her primary focus on aesthetic form rather than substantive content, Lobsien is very much concerned with spatial terms ('Topopoetik', p. 7) in the works: depictions of the other-world and the relationship of the figures to that world. In the case of More's 'utopia' various ideological systems come into play—Communism, Stoicism, Epicureanism, Platonism (p. 50)—but in the highly ambiguous text with its 'pluralistic play' (p. 33) none is thought through to its conclusion. Rather, the discussants' standpoints vary from moment to moment, reflecting More's 'performative gift' (p. 25), which was furthered by his rhetorical training at school and enhanced by his legal practice. The imaginary space, the 'no-where' that More creates and presents with constant humour, enables the reader to examine and question the nature of his 'utopia' as well as the values of the 'real' world of the present from which it is viewed.

In a disproportionately lengthy chapter on Spenser's *Faerie Queene*, Lobsien discusses the topopoetic aspects of allegory and the nature of pastoral, which is not so much 'naive' as, rather, a play with the seeming simplicity of the pastoral life (p. 96). And then, proceeding by association rather than by logic, the author jumps forward three and a half centuries to an author who was also a scholar of sixteenth-century English literature, C. S. Lewis. His *Chronicles of Narnia*, Lobsien demonstrates, display pronounced analogies to Spenser's allegory. The figures, though youthful, behave in a knightly manner and speak much as do Spenser's heroes and heroines, both series consist of seven books, and both address a lofty moral goal—in Lewis's case, the Christian story of salvation. Lobsien analyses Lewis's concept of allegory, which as a medievalist he treasures but which, as a modern writer, he distrusts because of its tendency to didacticism. As in Spenser's work, the allegory ends ultimately in an apocalypse, when the children close the door on the flooded Narnia for ever. But they are left with the knowledge that 'the real Narnia' lies in another realm altogether and that the Narnia they have known was simply an allegory for their own world (p. 215). What connects the two worlds on either side of the cabinet door is the quest motif, and this also provides the transition to the next chapter on Bunyan's *The Pilgrim's Progress*. But whereas Lewis's figures experience adventures mainly in the other-world of Narnia, for Bunyan's Christian the journey and the conditions and circumstances under which the pilgrim finally arrives are central (p. 240). Lobsien makes the point that this notable novel of progress, which provided an influential source for later novels of development, is not yet a *Bildungsroman* because Christian himself undergoes no transformation: he must remain constant because he is a representative type (p. 247).

Lobsien turns unexpectedly from canonical names to Sibylle Lewitscharoff, a contemporary writer who, though a recent winner of the Büchner Prize (2013), is still largely unknown and untranslated in other countries. Again the transition is wholly by association, here from Lewis's Aslan (the central Christological image in Narnia) to the imaginary lion that accompanies the philosopher 'Blumenberg' in the novel of that title (which displays the lion on its cover) from his study to the lecture hall, seen by almost no one but himself. The actual philosopher Hans Blumenberg (1920–1996) was indeed known for his interest in lions, and this short novel features not only Blumenberg himself but also four of his students, all of whom come to untimely ends. The concluding chapter, where they are reunited, along with the lion, in a cave (with its reminiscences both of Plato and of St. Jerome with his lion), provides the novel with an other-worldly dimension that is more Platonic than Christian: the real Blumenberg also published a philosophical-anthropological rumination entitled *Höhlenausgänge* (1989).

A chapter on Arcadias begins, as it must, with Sidney's allegory (in its original unedited form as *Old Arcadia*) and Longus's pastoral romance of *Daphnis and Chloe*, to establish the genre. But it moves quickly to two writers who illustrate the impossibility of Arcadia in the modern world. The Swiss novelist C. F. Ramuz (most familiar as the librettist for Stravinsky's *L'Histoire du soldat*) used the mountain world of the Valais as the setting for most of his works, which translated 'the modus of the other-world-pastoral' into the style of classical modernism (p. 367). In his later novels, however—notably *Grande peur dans la montagne* and *Présence de la mort*—he exposed the dark side of Arcadia, where mountains can suddenly burst into avalanches that destroy entire villages. Accordingly, 'Ramuz's mountain world is and is not Arcadia' (p. 347). The chapter ends with the work of another Büchner Prize winner, Felicitas Hoppe (in 2012), who unites the motifs of her predecessors, excursion fiction, apocalyptic narratives, images of Utopia and Arcadia, and the idea of a gate to the beyond that opens in everyday experience. In *Der beste Platz der Welt* that gateway is represented by the long tunnel through which the train bears the narrator from the world below up to the symbolically loftier monastic retreat in the Alps where she remains forever an outsider, unable to share the true spirit of the place, which remains 'a point of departure, but not a transition to Arcadia' (p. 379).

Lobsien's study ends with a consideration of railway stations as points of departure—like the cabinet door to Narnia or the railway tunnel to the Alpine Arcadia—and as modernizations of the knightly quest or the pilgrim's journey. In the principal example, W. G. Sebald's *Austerlitz*, the narrator, who originally came to England as a refugee from Nazi Germany in the 'Kindertransport', has an epiphany when he happens upon the waiting room in Liverpool Street station and realizes that it was the gateway through which he arrived from Germany to the sanctuary of England. But Sebald's aesthetics of the beyond is inverted (p. 392) because his doorway leads not from present-day reality to a higher Arcadia but, instead, back into the horrors of the German and European past, exposing possibilities that remain unfulfilled or irretrievably lost; and the author's filmic technique of dissolving scenes produces 'a modern travesty of the allegory' (p. 402).

The brief conclusion recapitulates the principal findings. The aesthetics of the beyond is characterized, first, by an interpenetration of here and there (p. 405). The means through which that goal is achieved involve a journey (whether knightly quest, pilgrimage, pastoral wandering, train ride, or some other). The journey, in turn, necessitates a topology of the places through which the traveller passes, either in real time or, chronotopologically, in past or future. In the process of its depiction 'the linearity of the path-narrative acquires spatial quality' (p. 409). The contemporary narratives, unlike ancient or Renaissance pastoral, sometimes run the risk of letting the other-world be dismissed as purely subjective or even psychopathological (p. 410). This other-world literature is ultimately motivated by an 'eschatological fascination with unity' of both realms (p. 412). Yet the texts examined turn out repeatedly to be preliminary prior stages in this world to a further or higher beyond (pp. 414–15). Why, in a secular world, should we care about works dealing with such 'consciousness of the beyond' (p. 415)? Apart from the fact that they appear to be an anthropological constant, they offer us the possibility of contemplating the things of this world from a radically different perspective. One of the most ancient and effective means of achieving this goal is allegory, which enables us to experience unity and alterity simultaneously (p. 417). 'Jenseitsästhetik', Lobsien concludes, enables us 'to experience the non-apparent in the world of appearances' (p. 418).

Lobsien has written a provocative study. Her profound erudition is modestly tucked away into the endnotes of each chapter, her theoretical speculations are reserved for the conclusion of her inductive work, and her literary culture is evident in the many graceful asides that enrich the text. The book, which begins so powerfully with four famous examples, might have chosen more familiar examples for the second half than the two German prizewinners. Swift's *Gulliver's Travels* and Heinse's *Ardinghello* could have provided transitions from the Renaissance to the present. Huxley's *Brave New World* or Orwell's *Nineteen Eighty-Four* are obvious examples of modern dystopias. But we should be grateful to the author for providing us with useful tools for the analysis of other examples of other-world literature and with the larger literary context into which they may be placed.

PRINCETON UNIVERSITY   THEODORE ZIOLKOWSKI

Philologie et théâtre: traduire, commenter, interpréter le théâtre antique en Europe (XVᵉ–XVIIIᵉ siècle). Ed. by VÉRONIQUE LOCHERT and ZOÉ SCHWEITZER. Amsterdam and New York: Rodopi. 2012. 276 pp. £51. ISBN 978-90-420-3587-4.

The fifteen essays contained in this volume explore various aspects of the reception of ancient theatrical texts by the European Renaissance and Classical periods. The overarching emphasis is on the rediscovery of the texts' dramatic potential, and the particular focus is on the role of translator in both interpreting them and recreating them as performance blueprints for the early modern stage. In this context, the term 'translator' is very widely interpreted, including as it should textual commentators, editors, adaptors, and performers; by investigating the work of all of these, the essays aim to 'esquisser une typologie des opérations de sens qui sont à l'œuvre autour du texte' (p. 14), moving from pure explanation via correction towards interpretation. The works studied cover comedy as well as tragedy, and relatively minor as well as canonical plays. The first of four groups of essays, 'Les Métamorphoses du commentaire', covers paratextual elements in Italian publications of Seneca, in German translations of Terence, and in González de Salas's 1633 Spanish translation of Seneca's *Troades*, and has as its centrepiece a rich analysis by Véronique Lochert of the illustrative material contained in publications from 1493 to 1730, bringing out particularly well the different functions that such illustrations may serve: 'd'annonce, de synthèse, d'explication ou de visualisation' (p. 57). The second group, 'Interpréter la comédie', contains essays on Marolles's translations of Terence and of Plautus, on Mme Dacier's 1683 translation of Plautus, and on eighteenth-century French translations of Aristophanes. The multiplicity of Marolles's role as both popularizer and erudite theorist is underlined by Florence de Caigny, while his important interactions with more practical critics such as La Mesnardière and d'Aubignac are brought out by Ariane Ferry. Pierre Letessier's analysis of Mme Dacier gives most interesting insight into how her imposition of classical act and scene divisions onto Plautus's structures was underpinned by a coherent theoretical position: 'Mme Dacier fait plus qu'opérer des coupures dans le texte: elle en oriente la lecture et façonne un théâtre de Plaute qui est conforme à l'idéal classique' (p. 131). 'Interpréter la tragédie' contains three essays, two dealing with French translations of Sophocles' *Elektra*, and one ranging more widely over French, English, and Italian translations of Seneca's *Thyestes*. The whole section, unsurprisingly, is dominated by the issue of *bienséance*, as violent and unpalatable works are both adapted for the stage and incorporated within evolving theoretical positions about the utility and morality of tragedy. The final section, 'Lectures de l'œuvre antique et théories du théâtre moderne', uses several early modern adaptations of Sophocles' *Oedipus rex* to explore links between interpretation and hermeneutics: plays whose very subject is interpretation lend themselves suggestively to such metatheatrical investigation. This section also brings machine-plays and early operas helpfully into the frame. Some interesting running themes emerge: the perceived need to clean up the 'vilaines mœurs' of ancient theatre to comply with *bienséance* blurred the distinction between translation and adaptation; printers and illustrators contributed more than we might expect to a genuinely theatrical interpretation of the works being transmitted, even where performance was not envisaged; the international range of the papers reminds us (as does Larry Norman in his *Avant-propos*) that in practice the 'république des théâtres' had boundaries as porous as those of the 'république des lettres'. All the essays are in French. Material in other languages is given in the original and in French translation. The volume is neat, clean, and easy to read, but its usefulness as a research tool would be enhanced by an index, and its cumulative bibliography appears rather sketchy considering the range of material covered: just over forty items, barely a third of them post-2000, and eight pre-dating the Second World War.

UNIVERSITY OF BRISTOL   EDWARD FORMAN

Taken for Wonder: Nineteenth-Century Travel Accounts from Iran to Europe. By NAGHMEH SOHRABI. New York: Oxford University Press. 2012. x+179 pp. £45. ISBN 978-0-19-982970-5.

In this book Naghmeh Sohrabi challenges the dominant historiographies surrounding nineteenth-century Persian travelogues or *safarnamah* to Europe, which, she argues, overemphasize Europe as travel destination. This Eurocentric bias, she argues, has led both to the misremembering of nineteenth-century Iranian culture through the telescope of the Constitutional Revolution of 1907, and to the critical neglect of those travelogues with an anti-European outlook as being unenlightened or 'limited' (p. 22). Instead, Sohrabi puts forward the need for the historicization of the travelogue as 'a rhetorical text in the service of its origin's concerns and developments' (p. 5). She traces the emergence of the *safarnamah* within Persian court culture as a propagandistic tool intent on representing the grandeur of the Qajar dynasty, rather than Europe.

Each chapter takes as its focus an individual travel writer from the four Qajar monarchies in order to adjust this Eurocentric focus. Sohrabi revises previous criticisms of the 'frivolity' of *Hayratnamah* or *Book of Wonder* (1809) by Mirza Abul Hasan Khan Ilchi, Ambassador Extraordinaire for Fath ᶜAli Shah to King George III. She rereads Ilchi's self-indulgence as indicative of Iran's confidence in its status as a 'buffer state' in British foreign affairs at this time (p. 42). She analyses Mirza Fattah Khan Garmrudi's *Chaharfasl* (1838), not as an account of his failed diplomatic mission on behalf of Muhammed Shah to Queen Victoria (1838), but in terms of Garmrudi's discourse of 'new geography' (p. 48), which sought to situate Iran in a prominent position in relation to the rest of the world. Similarly, she stipulates that Nasir al-Din Shah's changing policy from territorial expansion to political stability underpins this monarch's late turn to travel writing in 1867, twenty years into his reign. The final chapter of the book strengthens Sohrabi's hypothesis considerably by contrasting the late-century popularization of the travelogue with these earlier courtly texts. Through Hajji Pirzadah's (1886) and Ibrahim Sahhafbashi's (1896–97) travelogues, Sohrabi details how later texts both engaged with and deliberately flouted earlier travel-literary conventions in order to establish an oppositional, anti-monarchical discourse.

Taken for Wonder is not merely of importance from a historical viewpoint. Informed by both Iranian and Anglo-American literary studies, Sohrabi provides a nuanced analysis of the historicization of the *safarnamah* as a literary form and of its textual production throughout the nineteenth century. She uses original archival research to challenge the textual authority of modern editions of travelogues such as the *Chaharfasl*, which reduce the heterogeneity of discourses embedded within this form. This combination of literary with historical analysis offers some exciting new insights: Sohrabi's use of the rhetorical trope of 'hypnotyposis' to politicize her reading of Shah's travelogues, for instance, is particularly impressive (pp. 95–96).

Sohrabi is her own worst critic, describing her book as 'attempting to dislodge a boulder with a toothpick' by using a small selection of texts to shift the focus of an established critical heritage (p. 125). However, she succeeds in creating a clear picture of the extensive influence of these travelogues in the absence of any systematic study of Iranian manuscript or book circulation for this period by highlighting the intertextuality of the travelogues themselves. Her in-depth, literary-historical treatment of each text is enhanced by a seamless comparison of thematic and stylistic intersections between writers from chapter to chapter, thus providing a convincing account of the changing political motivations determining the evolution of the *safarnamah*. This book should not only be a vital reference point for historians interested in the Qajar dynasty, but should also be considered an invaluable resource for Iranian literary studies in tracing the evolution of the *safarnamah* as a literary mode.

BANGOR UNIVERSITY   REBECCA BUTLER

Gothic Topographies: Language, Nation Building and 'Race'. Ed. by P. M. MEHTO-NEN and MATTI SAVOLAINEN. Farnham and Burlington: Ashgate. 2013. xiv+243 pp. £60. ISBN 978-1-4094-5166-2.

Distancing themselves from understandings of the Gothic that are narrowly defined in relation to a predominantly Euro-American tradition encompassing a 'canon' of texts published between the late eighteenth and early nineteenth centuries, editors P. M. Mehtonen and Matti Savolainen turn their collective gaze towards minor literatures that 'co-exist with and question' (p. 1) said canon. Rather than the more traditional designations of Gothic as a genre or a mode, 'Gothic sensibility' is employed as a more fitting umbrella term to comprehend the range of historically, geographically, and aesthetically diverse novels, short stories, and films covered within the collection. The novelty and critical value of *Gothic Topographies* lies in its wide coverage of Gothic literatures to which little attention has previously been paid.

Following an introduction that outlines the theoretical frameworks of minor literature and 'Gothic sensibility', the collection is split into three sections. The first, 'European Gothicisms in, between and through Languages', contains essays as loosely linked as the heading might suggest. This is followed by a section devoted to '"Race", Society and Power in a Global Perspective', which deals with the use of Gothic as a means of discussing historical traumas in slave-holding America, a South Africa still haunted by the 'Spectres of Apartheid', colonial Australia, and a post-Soviet Russia that has failed to overcome the romanticized vision of its Soviet past. Critically rigorous and genre-defining, this section stands out as the one that most convincingly moves beyond a tedious reiteration of Gothic tropes in order to indicate what the Gothic can (or indeed cannot) *do*. The section is united by the idea that the Gothic can have an ethical function; as Jack W. Shear suggests, 'by inspiring pathos through fear' (p. 98) readers are implicated, which can engender social critique or social action. Teresa A. Goddu, in a nuanced chapter on 'Antislavery Discourse and the Gothic Imagination', nevertheless highlights the potential limitations of the Gothic to effect social change, owing to its tendency to 'validat[e] the viewer's voyeurism as benevolence' and (in the case of her selected texts) effectively reproduce the horrors of slavery 'as a commodity for mass consumption' (p. 84). In another exemplary essay from this section, Dina Khapaeva explains the international vampire boom in terms of a 'deep disdain for humans' (p. 125) and a renegotiation of beliefs in human exceptionality. Khapaeva's essay identifies an emerging 'post-Soviet Gothic' in which vampires often occupy positions of political power while humanity is often incidental to the plot, a move that she suggests mirrors a 'new medievalism' in Russia (p. 134). This essay is distinguished by its convincing political critique and its novel and insightful take on a subgenre of vampire literature that is too often dismissed as frivolous and devoid of critical value.

Finally, a section on 'The Challenge of the North' concludes the collection, though essays collected under this subheading are somewhat blighted by a tendency to justify texts *as* Gothic through a laborious identification of common themes, motifs, and intertexts, without foregrounding an argumentative agenda. However, *Gothic Topographies* boldly goes where relatively few have gone before in mapping out new territories in Gothic literature and film. Perhaps this early cartographic work will pave the way for future critics to provide more analytical accounts, safe in the knowledge that the groundwork of defining these 'minor' Gothic literatures has been done.

As a whole the collection suffers from its baggy framework: the justification for bringing this particular set of essays together is not adequately articulated, as is apparent from the subtitle 'Language, Nation Building and "Race"', which at once covers everything and nothing. Nevertheless, Mehtonen and Savolainen's collection comprises a number of genre-defining and perceptive essays and as such marks important new interventions into particular Gothic literatures. *Gothic Topographies* will be particularly attractive to postgraduate scholars and researchers of the specific texts and national literatures outlined in this study.

LANCASTER UNIVERSITY   SARAH ILOTT

Capital Crimes: Crime Fiction in the City. Ed. by LUCY ANDREW and CATHERINE PHELPS. Cardiff: University of Wales Press. 2013. xii+149 pp. £90. ISBN 978-0-7083-2586-5.

This edited volume, the latest in the University of Wales Press 'European Crime Fictions' series, explores the diverse ways in which capital cities have been figured in crime fiction from the nineteenth century to the present day. Drawing on the 2009 'Capital Crimes' colloquium at Cardiff University, the book brings together contributions from academics and practitioners (authors Cormac Ó Cuilleanáin and Ian Rankin) on crime fiction set in Cardiff, Dublin, Edinburgh, London, Paris, the Vatican/Rome, and Stockholm. Its focus is thus on the capitals of the UK, the Republic of Ireland, and Europe, and its explorations and analyses—of works ranging from police procedurals to thrillers to urban noir—are wide-ranging, varied, and stimulating.

In their introduction editors Lucy Andrew and Catherine Phelps argue convincingly for 'capital crime fiction' to be viewed as a unique genre whose features distinguish it from the broader category of 'urban crime' (p. 5). The capital is set apart by its status as the centre of the body politic and as a space where extremes are especially visible: wealth and poverty; respectable society and its criminal underbelly; local, national, and global identities. In contrast to rural crime fiction, which typically delivers a reassuring closure, capital crime also provides a 'more complex engagement with criminality', ultimately asserting that 'crime itself cannot be contained' (p. 138). All of these threads are fruitfully developed in the volume's main chapters.

The first two contributions form a neat, complementary pair: Ian Rankin explores the Edinburgh of the Rebus series from a practitioner's and city dweller's perspective, while Gill Plain traces the evolution of the capital's portrayal in the seventeen Rebus novels, moving from the literary inflections of early instalments to the more precisely mapped city of later works, which look beyond the national to the global. These are followed by Catherine Phelps's welcome exploration of overlooked crime fiction set in Cardiff's Tiger Bay, which is used to 'corral' the perceived dangers of vice, foreignness, and miscegenation, and Cormac Ó Cuilleanáin's thoughtful examination of Dublin's portrayal in a variety of crime novels, with an emphasis on the use of 'symbolic geography' to explore the urban/rural divide.

Kerstin Bergman's chapter on Stockholm crime fiction examines how the capital has been used to highlight and critique power structures in modern Swedish society. Her fine comparative analysis of novels from the 1970s (Sjöwall and Wahlöö), 1990s (Marklund), and the new millennium (Lapidus) once again illuminates the shift from national to global following the expansion of the EU. The Blainville novels of Jean-François Vilar are the focus of Margaret Atack's essay, which deftly places the series in the larger context of French writing on Paris, and highlights Vilar's commemoration of the city's disappeared, particularly Jewish citizens deported during the Nazi Occupation. The final two contributions look back to the city mysteries of the nineteenth century: Maurizio Ascari's examination of Dan Brown's best-selling religious thrillers helpfully places the texts in the context of anti-clerical urban mysteries by Del Vecchio and Mistrali, while Stephen Knight provides a rich insight into the depictions of Paris and London in the highly popular 'Mysteries of the Cities' by Sue and Reynolds.

In sum, this volume provides a valuable contribution to the fields of European and urban crime fiction studies, yielding an extensive and thought-provoking set of analyses. One final observation: at the time of publication, both editors were doctoral students at Cardiff University. Their achievement in putting together such a polished volume is to be applauded, as is the support they received during the editing process from the university's Crime Narratives in Context Network and the University of Wales Press. It is to be hoped that this excellent model, which provides early career researchers with invaluable experience, is one that can be replicated elsewhere.

SWANSEA UNIVERSITY   KATHARINA HALL

The Time before Death: Twentieth-Century Memoirs. By CONSTANTIN V. PONO-
    MAREFF. Amsterdam and New York: Rodopi. 2013. 165 pp. €35. ISBN 978-
    90-420-3612-3.

Constantin V. Ponomareff's book is a collection of fifteen essays that consider a cross-cultural selection of literary memoirs of the twentieth century. In the two-page introduction and equally sized conclusion the author argues that the last century was a particularly 'tragic' period in history, and autobiography was a profound personal means of dealing with trauma or psychological problems. Accordingly, each author countered a sense of tragic reality through life writing in which refuge may be sought by returning to childhood or through metaphoric displacement. The wider suggestion is that out of the trauma, which may involve mental illness, a sense of human worth emerges. For example, the essay entitled 'Katherine Mansfield's *Notebooks*: The Chameleon Self' begins by stating that five months before her death, Mansfield left a letter and legal will deposited in a bank security box intended for her husband, John Middleton Murry. 'In it she asked him to look after her literary remains.' For Ponomareff, 'this trust is perhaps indicative of how much she still loved him', despite later critical claims that he 'manipulated her literary inheritance' (p. 124). One would presume, given the title, that the central aim, and the connecting theme, of this book is to focus solely on a poignant revelation in the life of the literary author prior to their death. However, the book's title is a misnomer, because this theme is not apparent throughout. To add further confusion, the title of the Mansfield essay is borrowed from Antony Alpers's *The Life of Katherine Mansfield* (London: Penguin, 1982), in which he argues that Mansfield was obsessed with the question: 'Who am I?' (Alpers, p. 129). This prompts Ponomareff to give a potted biography of Mansfield's illness and her 'romantic attachment' to a fellow sufferer from tuberculosis, Anton Chekhov. The matter of Mansfield's *Notebooks* is dealt with only in a cursory manner, from which Ponomareff concludes that as her life was nearing its end, she reverted to 'a belief in yet another escape, a transformation so much in keeping with her restless chameleon self' (p. 136). It is thus rather difficult to deduce the connection between entrusting Murry with her literary remains and the question of Mansfield's 'restless chameleon self'.

The failings of the book recur—lack of coherent theme, and absence of original analysis. Ponomareff offers pithy biographical accounts that are reliant on other 'definitive' sources, from which the anticipated autobiographical revelation during 'the time before death' is never sufficiently explained. In his introduction he acknowledges the 'pitfalls' of life writing, while stating that he will 'let them speak for themselves' (p. 7). This is an odd admission, given that Ponomareff often presents quasi-psychological readings. 'Virginia Woolf's *Moments of Being*: The Silence Within' puts forward a familiar argument that writing was a therapeutic and healing process, and Woolf's 'reminiscences were less autobiographical than biographical' because she rarely talks about herself (p. 121). This time, the underwriting biography is Hermione Lee's *Virginia Woolf* (London: Vintage, 1997). However, Lee, in her excellent introduction to *Moments of Being: Autobiographical Writings* (London: Pimlico, 2002), offers a far more convincing account of the rich complexity of Woolf's final memoir, 'Sketch of the Past', accepting that it is about 'inhibition, evasion and silence', for a great deal isn't spoken of (Lee, p. xiv). According to Ponomareff, Woolf escapes to the past, the first quarter-century of her life, in her autobiographical writings, 'when her mental illness had not yet so severely disfigured the world around her' (p. 123). And yet according to Lee, Virginia's first mental illness occurred during this time, which was mentioned in an earlier, rejected version (Lee, p. 176). Ponomareff's general point is partly valid, but it is only that—a partly valid, general point.

As self-contained biographical exercises, each one of the fifteen essays will not satisfy the knowing, academic specialist. Where this book could have succeeded is in creating an overarching critical narrative, but Ponomareff's theoretical or philosophical acumen falls short too: 'And yet, human beings have survived all the evil spawned by the twentieth century' (p. 7). This overall view contradicts the biographical view that for Primo Levi, a Holocaust survivor, 'the camp experience proved too powerful to be overcome' (p. 69). Ultimately, this book may appeal to non-academic readers, serving as an accessible collection of pithy biographical accounts on seminal twentieth-century authors.

UNIVERSITY OF LEICESTER   SCOTT FREER

The Poetics of the Margins: Mapping Europe from the Interstices. Ed. by ROSSELLA M. RICCOBONO. Bern: Peter Lang. 2011. viii+211 pp. €53.50; £40. ISBN 978-3-0343-0158-9.

This volume of nine essays explores identity in the European context across a range of modern and contemporary literatures and cinema, including contributions concerning Italian, Portuguese, French, German, Spanish, and English cultural production. Many of the texts examined are bilingual or multilingual, or include regional dialects, and unravel the intricacies of mobility and migrancy in the European context.

In her theoretically informed introduction Rossella Riccobono describes Europe as a territory of wounds, within which the interstices (or Deleuzian folds) 'add depth to our revised map of Europe' (p. 2). The collection aims to 'establish the equality and dignity of all those mosaic stones that compose our multicultural, postcolonial Europe' (p. 3). A key concept is therefore identity's relationship to place (lived, left behind, revisited), as the contributors seek to investigate a 'third space', neither central nor marginal, but somewhere in between; several of the essays achieve precisely this aim.

In the opening chapter Ubaldo Riccobono employs the expression 'isle-solitude' to unpack Sciascia's construction of Sicily as an island, both marginal and central, and its relationship to the globe. Several Sciascian texts are employed to exemplify how Reason is the author's primary means for connecting 'isle-solitude' to the global context; unfortunately, the essay neglects to engage with the copious existing scholarship on Sciascia, thus seeming to accept his words at face value.

In the second essay Marina Spunta clearly defines provincialism and marginalism in the contemporary Italian context, moving then to the specific case of Piersanti's fiction as a product of a regional literary environment. Spunta cogently explores how Piersanti's œuvre depicts middle-aged men often living in silence, isolation, and displacement in a regional setting, thus incarnating non-belonging. For Spunta, Piersanti descends from a line of authors (Tozzi, Bilenchi, etc.) whose prose is set in a provincial milieu, yet his works reveal a postmodern rearticulation of the province's typical themes, while nevertheless stressing the mediocrity of those who attempt to return 'home' to the province.

In Chapter 3 Rossella Riccobono analyses Tondelli's *Camere separate* (1989) via the relationship between protagonists Leo and Thomas. Leo travels through European capitals in the aftermath of Thomas's death from cancer, and moves through three phases of mourning: from pain to destruction to reconstruction. Tondelli's work, while revealing a desire for major European cities (especially London), also uncovers a strong drive to return to the author's 'provincial' home town, Correggio. In *Camere separate*, Riccobono maintains, post-war Europe is juxtaposed with

Thomas's diseased body and is conceptualized as decayed and scarred (evoking the Deleuzian 'fold'), yet Leo's journey results in a promise of 'healing.'

Margherita Sprio examines how Matarazzo's film *Vortice* (1953) has served the Italian community in Britain in the creation of collective memory and cultural identity. Sprio's thoughtful piece is based on interviews conducted with Italian migrants in London and Italy; it would have been interesting, however, to read examples of the film's retelling in the interviewees' own words. Cross-cultural migrancy is considered also by Eleni Papargyriou in her analysis of contemporary Greek-born author Panos Karnezis. Papargyriou delineates how Karnezis draws on Greek literary and filmic traditions (*ethographia*) in his narratives, which are loosely based in actual or historical Greece but also influenced by magic realism and mythology. Karnezis—who hails from a 'marginal' country in today's Europe—chooses an adopted language (English), thus facilitating his engagement with a global literary context.

Using Deleuze's and Guattari's theories of nomadology, assemblage, and space, Kate Roy's thought-provoking, original essay constitutes a highlight. Roy contends that the writings of Turkish German Emine Sevgi Özdamar and French Algerian Leïla Sebbar, through their very materiality, present a history that is not anchored in a limited national (i.e. German, French) space but rather always already includes the Other in its making. Both writers intermingle 'documents and fiction' (p. 111), with the result that Sebbar's texts utilize haptic space to 'disturb official French histories by activating their Algerian elements' (p. 117). For Roy, both writers' textual 'collective assemblages' problematize standardized notions of (national) history, bringing it into the 'European present' (p. 117).

Christina Johnson investigates the significance of Marseille in films by Ducastel/Martineau and Guediguian. Johnson illustrates how these films portray Marseille as neither a landlocked city nor a transitional port, but rather as a truly trans-national urban centre which opens up to the rest of Europe, and thus facilitates hybridized identities.

Claudia Nocentini discusses contemporary writer Laura Pariani, whose transnational prose concerns the socio-cultural interplay between Italy and Argentina, in its exploration of migrants' lives between countries and languages (Italian, Spanish, and Lombard dialect). Nocentini's piece provides a descriptive overview of women's intergenerational experience in Pariani's *Di corno o d'oro*, *Il pettine*, and *Quando Dio ballava il tango*.

Raquel Ribeiro traces the Portuguese writer Llansol's use of the literary figures of Pessoa, Musil, and Kafka in her œuvre, above all in *Lisbonleipzig 1* and *Lisbonleipzig 2*. Using Deleuze's and Guattari's theories on minor literature and 'becoming', along with Braidotti's 'nomad', Ribeiro illustrates how Llansol engages with these three key European authors, in particular via the tropes of *fulgor* and 'figure'.

While all the essays in this volume concern questions of identity in the modern and contemporary trans-European context, some engage more fully with the notions of marginality and centrality than others; overall, the collection provides a useful and multifaceted exploration of the textual representation of European mobilities and migrants.

UNIVERSITY COLLEGE CORK   SILVIA ROSS

The Friction of the Frame: Derrida's 'Parergon' in Literature. By SIMONE HELLER-ANDRIST. (Swiss Studies in English) Tübingen: Franke. 2012. 277 pp. £51.90. ISBN 978-3-7720-8426-3.

This book was originally a doctoral dissertation and as such is extremely impressive: it has considerable intellectual range, is written in impeccable English, and is notable for its clarity (not something one can usually say about books on Derrida). It also seems to be the first study that attempts fully to apply Derrida's concept of the *parergon* to literature, in this case the novel. Derrida himself applies it to painting, sculpture, and architecture in his book *The Truth in Painting*, first published in French in 1978. Simone Heller-Andrist quotes the following passage from it:

The *parergon* inscribes something that comes as an extra, *exterior* to the proper field [. . .] but whose transcendent exteriority comes to play, abut onto, brush against, rub, press against the limit itself and intervene in the inside only to the extent that the inside is lacking. It is lacking *in* something and it is lacking *from itself*. (Derrida, trans. by Geoff Bennington and Ian McLeod (Chicago and London: University of Chicago Press, 1987), quoted on page 69)

The *parerga* Derrida focuses on are the frame around a painting, clothing on sculpture, and pillars around a building. Heller-Andrist then adopts Derrida's concept, which 'when transposed from the visual arts to literature, provides a tool with which to investigate, understand, and interpret the working of literary frames that hold the power to influence our readings' (p. 11). The term 'friction' is what Heller-Andrist uses for the procedure Derrida describes, and she elaborates: '[There is] interaction [that] works dialogically in both directions, from frame to work and back, or vice-versa. Thus, it takes the form of an oscillation' (p. 16).

Heller-Andrist also supplements Derrida (perhaps an ironic procedure): 'This study attempts to combine a close analysis of Derrida's parergon in literature with one of the main tenets of Reader-Response criticism, namely that the reader plays a central role in the decoding of texts' (p. 56); use is also made of Barthes's *The Pleasure of the Text*. The question raised by this is whether Derrida's concept of the *parergon* still retains its power and integrity in the process of this transposition to literature. In relation to the novels Heller-Andrist discusses, it seems rather to have more of an analogical relation to the Derridean concept and therefore can be applied with a good deal of metaphorical freedom, for mainly deconstructive purposes.

Middlemarch is a key text. It provides a very pertinent epigraph to the whole study: 'Every limit is a beginning as well as an ending' (p. vi). It is one of the few novels (I do not know of another one) where the word *'parerga'* is actually used, and

Heller-Andrist discusses that quite effectively in relation to frames within frames. However, her main focus is on the issue of gender in the novel, a much-discussed topic in Eliot criticism, and one could argue that her discussion does not add much that is new to it. One had hoped rather that the *parergon* might have moved discussion of the novel onto less familiar ground. Heller-Andrist's main claim is that the concept of the *parergon* can help deconstruct Eliot's adoption of a pseudonym which she reads as male: in assuming 'a feigned male perspective through her pseudonym [. . .] she [. . .] avoids being judged in the manner in which she herself judges the average writer of her own sex' (p. 87), a reference to Eliot's essay on 'Silly Novels by Lady Novelists'. However, in that essay Eliot was attacking not women novelists as such, but a type of novel that had become associated with women, to the detriment of fiction written by women, in Eliot's view. She admired many women novelists (Austen, Gaskell, Charlotte Brontë, among others). Heller-Andrist also ignores some fairly obvious empirical reasons why Eliot adopted a pseudonym. She had no alternative but to hide her identity at first since as a 'fallen woman' no respectable publisher would have taken her on; but by the time of *Middlemarch* the pseudonym provided no disguise since virtually every reader would have known she was a woman, and exchanging it for her real name would almost certainly have drawn attention to her 'fallen' status. Heller-Andrist assumes that her choice of the name 'George' affirms the 'submission to the rule of writing as a male sphere (represented in the male name)' (p. 88), overlooking the fact that the most famous female novelist in Europe was also called George (Sand). The claim that the narrator of *Middlemarch* is unequivocally male is also disputable as there is no gendered reference to the narrator after her first two works of fiction.

This is not to say that *parergon* as a concept is equally problematic in critical terms in relation to all of the novels discussed. The fact, however, that Derrida himself did not apply it to literature might indicate an awareness on his part that such an application might lead to an overly metaphorical use of it, resulting in some loss of critical precision. Despite that being a potential problem with this study, it is still of value for its full and clear discussion of *parergon* as a concept not just by Derrida but by other critics and especially in relation to its Kantian and Aristotelian contexts.

UNIVERSITY OF DUNDEE K. M. NEWTON

Communicational Criticism: Studies in Literature as Dialogue. By ROGER D. SELL. (Dialogue Studies, 11) Amsterdam: Benjamins. 2011. xi+392 pp. €99; $149. ISBN 978-90-272-1028-9.

Any teacher, critic, or lover of literature who has felt either uncertain or defensive about literature's social and pedagogical roles in the twenty-first century will be cheered by Roger Sell's new book. Its author does not shy away from large claims about literature's efficacy in helping to produce solutions for the problems of the new millennium. 'The writing, reading, and discussion of literary texts can make their own kinds of contribution' to 'attempts to bring justice to every corner of the earth' (p. 3), Sell boldly asserts. He seems confident that the increasingly global aspect of literary studies helps to make it an effective tool in addressing global problems, and his optimism is bracing: 'To work through the medium of literary criticism for improved communicational practices which could result in a thawing-out of rigid attitudes, and in a more widespread solicitude for the rights and sensitivities of every individual and grouping, is not unrealistic here' (p. 49). The book has much of the same energy and optimism of the first Obama campaign, and indeed, at the very end of Sell's theoretical introduction President Barack Obama makes a brief appearance as a 'post-postmodern writer who has championed hope' (p. 50). For readers who are constitutionally opposed to optimism, do not despair: Sell's version frequently enters into a dialogue with a despondent scepticism. 'In all areas of human life, distorted communication apparently triumphs time after time' (p. 48)

An urgently dialogical mode of discourse, literature, for Sell, provides effective models for other forms of communication: 'By studying communicational genuineness in so-called literary texts, where it has always prospered, [critics] will be working to promote the same quality in other forms of communication as well' (p. 46). Notable for its 'communicational exemplariness', literature often takes as its subject failures in communication, 'communicational dysfunction' (p. 369). It forges communities through its power to communicate, sometimes by foregrounding failures of communication between and among characters themselves. Sell is careful, however, not to privilege the literary over other modes of discourse: 'so-called literary texts are not more hospitable to inner contradiction than communication of other kinds' (p. 37). Nevertheless, individual chapters treat mostly canonical authors and texts: Shakespeare, Pope, Wordsworth, Dickens, Eliot, Orwell, and Pinter, with Churchill's autobiographical *My Early Life* and a novel for young adults, Lynne Reid Banks's *Melusine: A Mystery*, stretching the canon ever so slightly. It may be Sell's contention, '[a]s post-postmodernity gathers apace, all of us are hybrid now, as one might put it' (pp. 38–39), that partially explains and justifies the conservative choices of texts to investigate.

Keats's celebration of Shakespeare's 'negative capability'—the dramatist's remarkable ability to dwell 'in uncertainties, mysteries, doubts, without any irritable reaching after fact and reason'—undergirds all the analyses in *Communicational Criticism*. For Sell, 'Negative capability is the main psychological and ethical precondition for any genuine communication—for any uncoercive community-making—at all' (p. 37). Consequently, Shakespeare, and in particular a Keatsian Shakespeare, plays an important role in the articulation of principles in a long introductory chapter, which draws examples from *King Lear* and *Macbeth*, and leads into a consideration of strong and weak language in *Henry V* in the first full chapter of applied criticism. For Sell, Shakespeare is an exemplary dialogical thinker and writer who 'was unrepressive of his own complexities' (p. 37). He was also a master of what Sell calls 'genuine communication', a phrase that receives an unexpected turn in Sell's work. The term 'communication' has been largely misunderstood 'as a unidirectional transfer of something' (p. 52). But, for Sell, genuine communication is precisely that which 'floods us with' uncertainties, mysteries, and doubts. After all, 'the uncertainties and disagreements are in no small part what *constitutes* a literary community' (p. 37). In *Henry V*, for example, the communicationally self-conscious Shakespeare 'draws the audience into the characters' philological efforts, highlighting, above all, the scope for both error and disagreement' (p. 79). By contrast, what Sell labels 'distorted communication' is often the clearest, resulting from ideological hegemony and the motive to coerce, and accomplishing a 'distorting passivization of the human other' (p. 48). For Sell, dialogical writers such as Keats and Shakespeare offer a necessary and altogether more humanizing alternative to 'the semiotic and linguistic model of communication as a basically transitive and persuasive process, whereby a message is unidirectionally sent from a more active party to a more passive' (p. 37)

Although he is not the first critic to do so, Sell insists on talking about postmodernism in the past tense. According to Sell, we no longer live in a postmodern world, but rather in post-postmodern times. The former era produced a politics of recognition that could be repressive: 'members of a particular community could be urged to conform with a group identity script which was seriously limiting' (p. 2); the latter regards 'world literature as an affiliation of the different' (p. 4). Postmodernism keeps coming up for critical scrutiny in this study: for example,

Postmodern notions of sociohistorical positionality were sometimes too essentialist and simplistic, seeing a particular position as, in the first place, fixed, unchanging, and completely walled off from every other position, and, in the second place, as definable in terms of features which are mutually compatible in a very strong sense. (pp. 35–36)

Postmodern literary critics need an infusion of Keatsian negative capability, for they are (or were) frequently 'less negatively capable than postmodern theologians and philosophers such as Tillich, Bultmann, Derrida, and Vattimo' (p. 46). Sell recognizes that postmodernism did have 'emancipatory achievements', but these need to be consolidated by a 'post-postmodern follow-through' (p. 49) that allows for forms of community based on internal difference, and forms of communication and globalization that resist hegemony. Sell's characterization of postmodernity may strike some readers as too rigid, a means to more confidently and conveniently demarcate a new post-post period. His version of post-postmodernism may strike many as corresponding to what they have for many years considered 'postmodern'. Nevertheless, this important contribution to dialogue studies strikes me as a valuable and vigorous—and surprisingly non-defensive—defence of literature for our time. It manages to shun the hierarchies associated with the sacralization of literature by earlier ages, and redefines communication for whatever age we happen to call ours, finding tonic examples of the most 'genuine' forms of communication in texts that have become canonical not because they are universal in meaning but because they are insistently dialogical in spirit, both open to and helping to foster heterogeneity.

UNIVERSITY OF ROCHESTER   JONATHAN BALDO

Sartorial Strategies: Outfitting Aristocrats and Fashioning Conduct in Late Medieval Literature. By Nicole D. Smith. Notre Dame: University of Notre Dame Press. 2012. xiii+281 pp. $35; £29.95. ISBN 978-0-268-04137-3.

In *Sartorial Strategies* Nicole D. Smith considers how four medieval texts—Marie de France's *Guigemar*, Heldris de Cornuälle's *Roman de Silence*, *Sir Gawain and the Green Knight*, and Geoffrey Chaucer's Parson's Tale—use courtly attire as a didactic tool to highlight the transformative potential of vestments and 'interrupt the strong current of negative moral commentary on medieval dress promulgated by clerics' (p. 6).

The study begins with an introduction that outlines the aim of the book and establishes romance as 'fertile ground for an investigation of clothing and conduct' (p. 7). Though the Parson's Tale is not a romance, Smith makes a case for including it alongside the other texts.

The first chapter considers *Guigemar* in the light of the remarkable transformation in twelfth-century fashion that resulted in aristocratic attire becoming 'tightly fitted across the body with belts, knots, and laces' (p. 23). Smith sees a 'pedagogical strategy' in Marie's representation of the lovers and their courtly dress which inverts clerical diatribes against fitted attire and recasts tight, knotted garments as a 'sign of positive corporeal restriction' (p. 55). Thought-provoking and original, this is one of the strongest chapters in the book.

Smith's ensuing discussion of the thirteenth-century *Roman de Silence* in Chapter 2 uses similar methodologies to reconceptualize transvestism as a 'moral barometer' that allows Heldris de Cornuälle to examine 'the sins that plague aristocratic courts' (p. 20). Setting the text's moral work against the influence of the sartorial regulations introduced in the canons of the Fourth Lateran Council (1215), the argument is at once refreshing and restricting. Smith successfully circumvents the gender issues at the heart of most *Silence* criticism to offer an exciting new evaluation of the text, yet the chapter is less satisfying in its exploration of the connections between Heldris's 'sartorial strategy' and other prominent themes explicitly aligned with the heroine's cross-dressing, such as language, feudalism, and economic power.

Chapter 3 argues that the *Gawain* poet 'manipulates the common clerical understanding of a richly embroidered garment that indicates pride [i.e. Lady Bertilak's girdle] into a penitential garment that at once signifies absolution and performs satisfaction of sin' (p. 135). Reading *Sir Gawain and the Green Knight* against the backdrop of another fundamental change in fashion history—the introduction of tailored, form-fitting garments in the fourteenth-century—Smith charts the ways in which Gawain's adoption of the girdle reinvests 'courtly life and its symbols' with 'new, spiritually sound meaning' (pp. 99–100). Though more predictable than the conclusions drawn elsewhere, this opinion is undoubtedly sound and accentuates the benefit of re-evaluating well-known texts within their socio-historical frameworks.

The final chapter, on Chaucer's Parson's Tale, is by far the strongest. Despite some repetition (see, for example, the subject of tailored garments first explained on pp. 2–3, and repeated at pp. 15–16, 97, 137–38, and 141), Smith carefully explains how the text moves from casting 'pleasure-in-dress as sinful to pleasure-in-dress as salvific' (p. 174). She confidently draws on medieval theories of visual cognition and spectatorship to offer a dazzlingly original and important account of the tale and its relationship with other accoutrements in *The Canterbury Tales*: most notably in the General Prologue.

Overall, the ambitious coverage of this monograph, with its unremitting concentration on how writers across three centuries use a 'sartorial hermeneutic' (p. 35) to promote virtue through fine dress, is both a strength and a weakness. At times it is difficult to escape the feeling that Smith spreads herself too thinly and draws her conclusions together too quickly, particularly when one is left wanting to know more about the implications of each 'sartorial strategy' for our understanding of other aspects of the texts studied, such as Gawain's arming scene or the description of Morgan le Fay. On the other hand, the tight focus on vestments and the breadth of the book prove that Smith's methodologies can be applied with equal success to a range of vernacular literature. Smith's meticulous coverage of the social and ideological changes informing medieval fashion allows her to place medieval garments under a metaphorical microscope and offer new insights into the redemptive power of noble attire. *Sartorial Strategies* makes a valuable contribution to the field of medieval studies.

UNIVERSITY OF LIVERPOOL   SARAH L. PEVERLEY

Banished: Common Law and the Rhetoric of Social Exclusion in Early New England.
    By NAN GOODMAN. Philadelphia: University of Pennsylvania Press. 2012.
    206 pp. $59.95; £39. ISBN 978-0-8122-4427-4.

The vast historiography of New England features a plethora of studies on banishment from—and by—seventeenth-century Puritan communities. While these have deepened our understanding of the topic, the central thesis of this engaging book by Nan Goodman is that too much stress has been placed on the religious motivation behind exclusion orders. That is, New England banishment and the sense of community membership it forged have hitherto been observed solely through the prism of heresy. This, Goodman argues, has obscured our view of other important factors at play in Puritan community-building, pre-eminently the legal basis and rhetorical potential of social exclusion.

To rectify this imbalance, and drawing on an array of pamphlets, trial testimonies, histories, and affidavits, the author chooses five salient case studies, re-examining the banishments of Anne Hutchinson, Thomas Morton, Roger Williams, the Quakers, and the Indians. Before this, an introductory chapter locates the book's thesis within a theoretical framework indebted to the writings of Carl Schmitt, Girgio Agamben, and Jacques Derrida, among others. Thus, the alignment of community with 'maddeningly vague' notions of nationalism (p. 8), which has characterized much previous scholarship in this field, is subordinated by the author to transnational perspectives asserting the porousness of geographic boundaries. In this analysis, present-day concepts of space and borders not only help us better comprehend New England banishment but may also inform current debates on migration, sovereignty, and jurisdiction.

The opening chapter, on Hutchinson and Morton, is particularly persuasive, partly owing to the early modern transatlantic context in which it is situated. The long-established role of hospitality—the imperative to 'entertain strangers' which was mandated by the common as well as canon law—in Catholic England was, Goodman reminds us, vitiated in the Protestant Reformation by an increased focus on institutionalized charity, a development transported with alacrity to New England. Church-based charity, unlike hospitality, 'helped the needy without making them part of the community' (p. 32). Set against this backdrop, John Winthrop's influential 'Model of Christian Charity' was designed, perhaps primarily, to strengthen pre-existing notions of civic identity among the Massachusetts brethren (see p. 33). Hence, though religious dispute played no small part in their banishment, it was when Morton and Hutchinson overstepped the bounds of hospitality, Goodman argues, that their fates were sealed. In the colony he established at Mare Mount, Morton, trader and religious rebel, incurred the wrath of the Plymouth Pilgrims chiefly through championing an all-inclusive brand of hospitality. This included the erection of a maypole—an incendiary blend of the pagan and visual—which evidently appealed to Indians as well as European settlers. For their destabilizing effects on community, Puritan authorities were loath to accept 'people who came in as guests [. . .] but turned into hosts in short order' (p. 58); consequently Morton was banished three times between 1628 and 1630.

Hutchinson held religious meetings in her Bay Colony home which were—notoriously—open to all. Her antinomian challenge to church doctrine was controversial enough, but the platform her hospitality provided for inhabitants and strangers to mix, along with her violation of normative gender and public–private realms, was equally instrumental in her eventual exclusion following a trial in 1637. Thus, she is 'figured as a religious leader usurping religious authority when in fact she was offering a rival to the secular realm as well' (p. 65). Implicit here is a subtheme of contemporary resonance explored more explicitly in the rest of the book: the advantages, as perceived by the banished, of heterogeneous communities. Though Goodman perhaps too ambitiously—if never stridently—invites parallels with our own contested notions of social diversity, she has succeeded here in identifying a significant new dimension to seventeenth-century New England expulsion.

BIRKBECK, UNIVERSITY OF LONDON   PHILIP MAJOR

Performing Authorship in Eighteenth-Century English Periodicals. By MANUSHAG N. POWELL. (Transits: Literature, Thought & Culture, 1650–1850) Lewisburg, PA: Bucknell University Press. 2012. xii+291 pp. £51.95. ISBN 978-1-61148-416-8.

Manushag N. Powell's *Performing Authorship in Eighteenth-Century English Periodicals* is yet another timely entry in Greg Clingham's series for Bucknell University Press. In this monograph Powell examines in detail the ways in which the essay periodical both shaped and expressed early conceptions of professionalized authorship in the early and mid-eighteenth century. To be sure, scholars of the period have long acknowledged the formative influence of Addison, Johnson, and other leading periodical writers on the literary marketplace. By placing the eidolon (or fictional persona) firmly at the centre of her readings, though, Powell substantially expands our understanding of specific types of authorial attitudes amidst the ebb and flow of a commodity culture. To this end, her methodology neatly brings together performance studies, the history of the book, authorship theory, and formalism, among other approaches.

Performing Authorship also ventures an admirable—and increasingly necessary—attempt to make connections between eighteenth-century manuscript culture and the twenty-first-century blogosphere. Indeed, the author makes a convincing case for the claim that, technological differences notwithstanding, we do share with the early modern period a perversely pervasive treatment of professional writing as at once a viable form of self-commodification and a vituperative rejection of it. There has been a lot of important work produced on the theoretical underpinnings of anonymous, allonymous, and pseudonymous writing in recent years. By outlining the various material issues associated with the marketplace, such as developments in copyright law and the habits of booksellers and readers, Powell instead outlines the figuration, circulation, and recycling of various well-known and perhaps long forgotten personae, many of which outlived their users. This study, in other words, offers a healthy tranche of examples to support what I take to be a key thesis: 'Despite the eidolons' earnestness and conservatism about what an author ought to be—masculine, genteel, disinterested—there was a great deal of tension between the real identities of periodical authors and their eidolons' (p. 4). Such a claim for the intrinsic crisis of the writer's authority convincingly builds on well-established claims in the field, such as Dror Wahrman's influential account of the emergence of the modern self in the early modern period (*The Making of the Modern Self* (New Haven: Yale University Press, 2004)), or perhaps Judith Pascoe's notion of heterodox and fluid notions of self as tied to the theatrical playing of a part (*Romantic Theatricality* (Ithaca, NY, and London: Cornell University Press, 1997)). To put it another way, Powell's multifaceted approach allows for yet another way to respond to Ian Watt's ground-breaking if ultimately reductive treatment of the rise of the novel across all textual media (*The Rise of the Novel* (Berkeley: University of California Press, 1957)). She also firms up Walter Graham's indispensable if now dated work on the periodical (*English Literary Periodicals* (New York: Nelson, 1930)), with its perspective on 'the nursery of literary genius' (quoted on page 17). And Powell's book vividly demonstrates the ways in which periodicals invented a space for their authors to think out loud, in often stark terms, about what it meant to earn a living by the pen.

Above all else, this new monograph contributes greatly to recent scholarship on the professionalization of authorship in the eighteenth century, not merely in terms of the logistics of the modern marketplace but, more importantly I think, in terms of the authors' own attitudes to their profession. The liveliest sections of *Performing Authorship* explore various skirmishes that largely arose in the periodical press, such as the 1709 spat between two competing versions of the same periodical, the *Female Tatler* (a title once derided by Richard Steele as a literary parasite on his canonical body—quoted in Powell, page 51), along with the *Female Tatler*'s nearly simultaneous war with another competitor, the *British Apollo*. Further 'paper wars' examined here include the well-known but always entertaining tiff between Henry Fielding and John Hill, along with a whole host of wits and dunces waiting in the wings. Indeed, this book is alive with scuffles, death threats, textual pirating, and, in short, the insatiable itch for writing that drove many into the perilous world of print.

UNIVERSITY OF DUNDEE   DANIEL COOK

Charles Dickens's Networks: Public Transport and the Novel. By JONATHAN H. GROSSMAN. Oxford: Oxford University Press. 2012. xi+256 pp. £25. ISBN 978-0-19-964419-3.

The first instance of direct speech in Charles Dickens's first novel, *The Pickwick Papers*, is a cry: 'Cab!'. It comes early on in the book, as Mr Pickwick looks out upon the world beneath his London window. More than simply a rallying call to begin the circulatory adventures that await him, however, this appeal for a 'cab'—a term newly coined in the 1820s as an abbreviation for the two-wheeled cabriolets that were increasingly criss-crossing metropolitan Britain—registers Pickwick's place 'in the midst of an up-to-date accelerating transport network' (p. 86). So suggests Jonathan H. Grossman, maintaining that Pickwick's cry illustrates that right from the outset Dickens's serialized fiction was shaped and energized by the author's recognition that a progressively powerful passenger transportation system was not only complicating the ways in which communities and individuals were connected, but was also transforming 'the art of the novel, which provide[d] a means for its comprehension' (p. 5). Thus advancing an argument that binds aesthetic form to material infrastructure, Grossman's stimulating and engaging study proposes that first and foremost among Victorian writers Dickens shines a light on the nineteenth-century 'history of public transport's systematic networking of people and the difference it makes—how it revolutionized perceptions of time and space, how it involved re-imagining community, and how the art form of the novel played a special role in synthesizing and understanding it' (p. 3).

Grossman examines three novels in order to elaborate this central thesis: *The Pickwick Papers* (1836–37), *The Old Curiosity Shop* (1840–41), and *Little Dorrit* (1855–57). Chapter 1 refuses *Pickwick* as 'a last hurrah for Olde England and the simple country days of rambling coaches and cozy coaching inns' (p. 12), and thus refuses the juxtaposition that holds horse-drawn transport as a pre-modern counter to the steam-driven, modernizing power of the railways. Instead it examines how in his first novel Dickens was drawn to the notion that stagecoaching standardized space and time, helping form a new kind of networked yet variously oriented and individuated community. Where this chapter foregrounds a link between an emerging public transportation network and the capacity of the serial novel to represent social cohesion, Chapter 2 suggests Little Nell's fatal intercity journey in *The Personal Adventures of Master Humphrey: The Old Curiosity Shop* gives the lie to the harmonious vision of unity in diversity with which *Pickwick* is associated. Although Grossman frames his work as a study of the transport system as a system, and not 'as an economic entity' (p. 227), his contention that the novel 'shows that the same forces holding together a community ironically rip it apart' (p. 92) is a reading that, to my mind at least, lends significant weight to the idea of Dickens as a writer concerned with the fact that uneven development, exploitation, and ruin are a systemic consequence, not an anomaly, of the way industrial capitalism works. Moving beyond the manner in which the passenger transport revolution impacted upon the novelistic conceptualization of the nation state, Chapter 3 shows how in *Little Dorrit* Dickens imagined an internationally networked community. Here Grossman argues that by the 1850s the steam-powered compression of global space and time was reflected by the way in which Dickens plotted international terrains criss-crossed by dizzyingly extensive interrelations and meetings, playing with the limitations of narrative perspective in order to reveal the heightened connectivity and complexity that marked the modern world.

What stands out about *Charles Dickens's Networks* is the clever and convincing manner in which historical and theoretical insights concerning the Victorian transport system are used to illuminate particular episodes, generic features, and textual strategies from Dickens's fiction. It is true, as Grossman acknowledges, that his critical methodology does not work through Dickens's networked aesthetic with relation to the politics and economics of the period. But in developing such a compelling and nuanced account of the way in which the public transport revolution both impacted upon and was mediated by Dickens's fiction, this study opens up spatio-temporal dimensions of Victorian society and culture in a manner that deserves and will reward further work.

UNIVERSITY OF EXETER   PAUL YOUNG

Dickinson Unbound: Paper, Process, Poetics. By ALEXANDRA SOCARIDES. Oxford: Oxford University Press. 2012. xi+211 pp. £32.50. ISBN 978-0-19-985808-8.

Alexandra Socarides's first book offers an insightful, lucid, and fascinating intervention into recent work in Dickinson manuscript studies by demonstrating that critical attention to the manuscripts makes visible Dickinson's writing practice, creative process, and poetics. Historically locating the materiality of these scenes of composition and pointing out the often multiple manuscript contexts of individual Dickinson poems, Socarides considers the intricate relationship between the poems Dickinson wrote and the paper on which she wrote them. In the process, Socarides hypothesizes that Dickinson's compositional methods and materials reveal her development of a theory of poetry in which poems are complex and multifaceted physical objects that defy their subsequent translation into print. This impressive book challenges those who view Dickinson's printed poems as 'well-wrought urns' existing independently of the material, historical, and social factors that shaped them (Cleanth Brooks, *The Well Wrought Urn: Studies in the Structure of Poetry* (New York: Harcourt Brace, 1947)). Instead, examining the multiple manuscript incarnations of Dickinson's poems and her penchant for revising poems to suit new material contexts and different occasions, it offers convincing evidence of Dickinson's resistance to the idea that a poem has a fixed, final, and definite identity.

Focusing on such material sites of composition and advancing recent scholarship that questions the notion that Dickinson wrote isolated lyrics, Socarides shows that in their manuscript state Dickinson's poems are always drawn into interpretative relations with other texts and artefacts. The meaning of a given poem, then, derives from its formation out of one or more of its material contexts and her compositional practices. Each of the book's five chapters focuses on the materiality and historicity of one of these compositional practices that also represents a different stage in her writing career. The first and fourth chapters argue that individual folded sheets of stationery were the primary material sites of Dickinson's compositions; taken together, these chapters show that while initially poems on folded sheets significantly and explicitly related to each other, after 1865 poems on individual pieces of paper resisted such relations. The second chapter considers how a poem on a folded sheet takes on a different meaning when it is embedded within the prose of or functions as a letter. The third chapter considers the significance of Dickinson's practice, from 1858 to 1865, of sewing together individual folded stationery sheets into homemade books, often called fascicles, and shows that the poems within a given fascicle disrupt the possibility of the interpretative closure and determinacy of individual poems within these sewn-together sheets. Feeling confined and restricted by her own practice of book-making and use of formal stationery, Dickinson, according to the fifth chapter, began from 1876 onwards to write poems on used envelopes, the backs of shopping lists, advertisements, bills, and recipes, and the materiality of these scraps of paper significantly informed the poems she wrote.

This book also convincingly shows that attention to the paper on which Dickinson wrote and circulated her poems demonstrates her engagement with and response to nineteenth-century literary genres such as the elegy, and her conforming to and deviating from the compositional conventions and material features of women's letter-writing, copying of verses in albums and commonplace books, and book-making practices. If this excellent book has a flaw, it is in its recurring tendency to move, at times, beyond the evidence it offers to make definitive statements about

Dickinson's intentions and the meaning of her writing practices and poetics. The real strength of the book, in contrast, is the way it opens up interpretative possibilities, pointing to new directions for future scholarship, as well as the persuasive case it makes for the importance of giving due critical attention to Dickinson's manuscripts that unsettle prevailing critical and editorial procedures and biases.

UNIVERSITY OF PORTSMOUTH   PÁRAIC FINNERTY

The Politics and Poetics of Displacement: Modernism off the Beaten Track. Ed. by MASSIMO BACIGALUPO and LUISA VILLA. Pasian di Prato: Campanotto. 2011. x+174 pp. €25. ISBN 978-88-456-1256-5.

Modernism, it seems, is an ever-expanding concept, and its deterritorialization (to adapt a Deleuzian term which seems particularly apt here) continues apace in this highly eclectic but richly fascinating collection of essays on the 'nomadic geographies' of modernism (p. 11). While there are some familiar canonical co-ordinates in the volume—with essays on Forster, Lawrence, and Durrell—the emphasis is firmly on the non-canonical and unfamiliar. The collection seeks to explore some of the uncharted textual and geographical byways of modernism, particularly in relation to questions of cultural, psychological, or political displacement; and, to this end, most of the essays certainly go well off the beaten track of standard discussions of modernism. Even where the subjects appear initially familiar, as with the authors just mentioned, the focus tends to be on less-known works: Forster's travel writings on Egypt ('The Greek-Alexandrian *Genius Loci* and E. M. Forster's Literary Epiphany', by Angelica Palumbo); Lawrence's proto-postcolonial engagement with the ancient cultures of New and Old Mexico ('Forever in Transit: D. H. Lawrence's Displacement', by Stefania Michelucci); Durrell's poetry in the Cairo-based literary magazine *Personal Landscape* ('The Dissolution of the Self: Location and Identity in *Personal Landscape* and *The Alexandria Quartet*', by Silvia Panizza). Indeed, with essays on figures such as the late Victorian *Daily Mail* war correspondent G. W. Steevens, the polar explorer Apsley Cherry-Garrard, and the obscure inter-war German-language writer Essad Bey/Lev Nussimbaum, it is a moot point whether the volume in places veers so far off the beaten track as to lose all recognizable modernist bearings—but there is an admirable spirit of adventure here and all the essays yield relevant insights and are well informed, finely detailed, and compellingly written. Apart from the regrettable lack of an index, the book itself has been handsomely produced and skilfully edited, with just a few minor typographical errors—e.g. 'negected' (p. 12), 'Boshevist' (p. 128), 'fist-hand view' (p. 130)—and a breakdown in the referencing system in the eighth essay.

As already indicated, the collection takes in a broad sweep of writers and contexts—and, in addition to the six subjects touched on above, there are also essays devoted to Kazuo Ishiguro's novels, Vita Sackville-West's travel writing (especially *Passenger to Tehran* (1926)), Rose Macaulay's Turkish travel novel *The Towers of Trebizond* (1956), and Robert Byron's classic travelogue *The Road to Oxiana* (1937).

This latter essay, 'A Modernist Transcultural Quest', by Laura Colombino, is one of the strongest in the collection and perhaps best exemplifies the benefits to be gained from straying 'off the beaten track'. Byron's work may be well known and highly valued among other travel writers, but, in terms of literary criticism, his 'masterpiece' remains 'still largely unexamined' (p. 74). Colombino's fine analysis of Byron's complex multivocal style seems timely, therefore, and establishes him convincingly as a major modernist while also bringing into sharp focus just how widely spread and deeply rooted modernist writing practices had become by the 1930s.

Although Apsley Cherry-Garrard's name does not often trip off any critic's tongue as an acknowledged modernist, Nicoletta Brazzelli's essay, 'A Symbolic Geography of Ice: Apsley Cherry-Garrard and Modernity', neatly situates him within the *Zeitgeist* of his period and makes a very persuasive case for viewing his memoir of Antarctic exploration, *The Worst Journey* (1922), as a symptomatic modernist text. Brazelli pays careful attention to questions of language, style, and form in her discussion, and this is a welcome feature of several other essays in the collection too—of particular note in this respect is Luisa Villa's precisely observed study of 'Modernist Style and Imperialist Politics' in G. W. Steevens's war correspondence.

Massimo Bacigalupo's 'Essad Bey: Fictional Islam and International Modernism' is unlikely to send the reader racing to buy any of Bey's books (even if we could be sure of what he wrote), but the fun is in the chase, as they say, and Bacigalupo's intriguing search for his shadowy author is something of a modernist creation in its own right and certainly conjures up the spirit of nomadic modernism. The final essay by Wayne Pounds, 'The Sorrows of Exoticism: Kazuo Ishiguro's Sinking World', provides a sophisticated conclusion to the collection in its subtle ideological analysis of Ishiguro as a postmodernist 'polycultural' author. The argument becomes a little over-elaborate in places, but Pounds interestingly inverts the underlying premiss of the other essays by considering Ishiguro as an essentially 'rooted' writer whose 'displacement' has been experienced not geographically or psychologically so much as stylistically, in response to the exigencies of a globalized publishing world where transnational markets require authors to write with a view to translation and where 'the ideal translatable text is one in which the strong colors of culture and language are diluted ("grayed-out," as the software makers say) in order to ease the labor of translation' (p. 153). Such a bleak Orwellian development seems something of a parody of the modernists' own more profound 'crisis of representation'—which, in this contrastive light, is given especially forceful expression in a statement cited earlier in the volume from the Antarctic memoir of the aforementioned Cherry-Garrard: 'This journey beggared our language: no words could express its horror' (p. 52).

MILLSTATT, AUSTRIA   PAUL POPLAWSKI

Americanizing Britain: The Rise of Modernism in the Age of the Entertainment Empire. By GENEVIEVE ABRAVANEL. (Modernist Literature and Culture Series) Oxford: Oxford University Press. 2012. xii+206 pp. £40. ISBN 978-0-19-975445-8.

Very rarely, a new volume of cultural or literary criticism appears which is so obvious in its aims that it seems startling that it has not already been written. This superbly crafted book is precisely this and represents a landmark in modernist and transatlantic studies. Abravenal positions British modernism as a reaction to America's cultural colonization of Great Britain during the early decades of cinema and jazz. *Americanizing Britain* has impressive breadth and imaginative narrative architecture: it moves through H. G. Wells, Rudyard Kipling, Virginia Woolf, and Aldous Huxley in 'Ameritopias'; the influence of jazz in 'Jazzing Britain'; the dominance of Hollywood in 'The Entertainment Empire'; and in its final two chapters discusses two key players in the reshaping of Britishness against the influence of America—F. R. Leavis in 'English by Example' and T. S. Eliot in 'Make it Old'. This book offers a fascinating story of the rise of one empire against the fall of another and is academically rigorous while revelling in some wonderful historical anecdotes. We learn, for example, that Hitchcock's *Blackmail* (1929), Britain's first 'talkie', was advertised as featuring 'English as it should be spoken' (p. 88). These moments never detract from the core project of illuminating a British culture facing 'a new style of world power; one predicated more obviously on global commercialism and standardization than on occupation and colonial rule' (p. 7).

The first chapter coins the term 'Ameritopias': 'the use of America as the raw material [of the literary imagination] with which to dream the future, even if that future is sometimes a nightmare' (p. 25). It moves through variations of this, beginning with the opposing views of Kipling, who repeatedly characterized America's empire as impotent or in a state of arrested development, and Wells, who saw England's greatest threat as its obsession with 'tradition'. This opposition moves into the later, more sophisticated 'Ameritopian' ideas of Woolf and Huxley. The term remains fluid, though, pertaining generally to the British and English 'imaginative production through and against the idea of the United States' (p. 26).

The second and third chapters retain a strand of literary criticism but focus on the emergent influence in Great Britain of jazz and Hollywood. The discussion of jazz examines its arrival in the 1920s, charting a movement from a subversive alien form to a distinctly British jazz, mutated through a transatlantic field of exchange by the 1950s. The third chapter is particularly interesting read alongside David Seed's recent account of the relationship between literary modernism and the rise of cinema, which discusses the influence of cinema on American literary modernism (*Cinematic Fictions: The Impact of the Cinema on the American Novel up to World War II* (Liverpool: Liverpool University Press, 2011)). It charts Britain's suspicion of a Hollywood imperialism from before the Film Acts of 1927 and 1934 up to and beyond the establishment of the British Arts Council in 1944—upon which John Maynard Keynes declared 'Death to Hollywood' (p. 85). This hyperbole was ubiquitous: Abravenal cites an assertion from the *Daily Express* in 1927 which read: 'We have several million people, mostly women, who, to all intent and purpose, are temporary American citizens' (p. 87).

The final two chapters focus on Leavis and Eliot, whom Abravanel identifies as playing integral roles in establishing a reactionary British modernism hugely invested in 'tradition' and propelled by a wilful distrust of popular American culture. The chapters go into great depth, respectively, on the manners in which Leavis invented modern literary criticism and Eliot perpetuated Leavis's emphasis on tradition in his poetry. Incredibly, Abravanel finds room in her 'Afterword' to discuss the Harry Potter phenomenon as an example of a British culture which still 'rests upon narratives of heritage, history, and little England much like those that began most clearly to be told in the early twentieth century' (p. 161). This is an outstanding contribution to the scholarship of British and American cultures of modernism, to transatlantic studies, and to modernist literary studies; rigorous and immensely enjoyable.

NEWCASTLE UNIVERSITY/BISHOP GROSSETESTE UNIVERSITY   ARIN KEEBLE

Be a Good Soldier: Children's Grief in English Modernist Novels. By JENNIFER MARGARET FRASER. Toronto: University of Toronto Press. 2011. x+270 pp. $55; £38.99. ISBN 978-1-4426-4313-0.

Jennifer Margaret Fraser sees the effort to express childhood grief as central to a number of modernist texts: Joseph Conrad's *Under Western Eyes*, Jean Rhys's novellas, Rebecca West's *Return of the Soldier*, Ford Madox Ford's *Parade's End*, Virginia Woolf's *The Waves*, and James Joyce's *Finnegans Wake*. Each author occupies a chapter, and the chapters can be paired: Fraser progresses from two authors writing on childhood memory, to two with silent children, and finally to two with child narrators. In each of these texts, the relationship is exposed between the repression of childhood grief and the ability of adults to perform cruel acts. Modernist authors of grief frequently allude to *Hamlet*, and, following from Ovid's story of Niobe, often deploy the trope of turning to stone in the suppression of tears. Fraser's key theoretical text is Derrida's 'Circumfession', through which she radically rereads his work, and reveals the importance of the grieving child not only to modernism, but to writing more broadly. Indeed, Fraser brings new material to the case for a special relationship between writing and trauma.

In Conrad's novel Razumov is portrayed as wanting paternal affection and unable to grieve childhood miseries; because of this, he is able to act cruelly and without remorse. After betraying Haldin, Razumov reconnects with his childhood grief—a task depicted as breaking apart stoniness—through writing. He records his grief in incoherent Russian, which the narrator chooses not to translate into English. Rhys presents characters seeking children to abuse, and wanting to treat women as if they were children. In such a world, children become stony and cynical. Like Razumov, Rhys's Rochester is unwittingly ruled by his repression of childhood grief. Here, again, expression of such grief is impossible in English: Antoinette finds comfort only in Christophine's Creole. In West's novella, Chris is not only a stony member of the infantry, but has to grieve for the loss of his son. His cousin, Jenny, desires his safety, but ultimately decides that Chris cannot remain a child: he must be cured and return to war, to the delight of his wife. The hero of *Parade's End* suffers shell shock and emotional suppression from childhood onwards. Ford's Christopher fights against society and faces his grief in order to reach his son; the child is silent, but a central motivating figure. In *The Waves*, interior monologue enables children to appear to speak, but their words do not reach the outside world. This silencing of emotion is directly linked to the oppressing of natives, and the processes of empire-building. Woolf challenges this oppression: in letting children narrate, her text creates a space for the soldier, and the grieving child, to return to. To speak of a child's grief, Joyce creates an experimental language of his own, Wakese: he tells in reverse the story of parents comforting a child crying in bed. For Woolf and Joyce, access to grief is equally access to joy, codified in Joyce's neologism 'laughtears' (p. 9).

Fraser powerfully proves the continuing importance of her account of suppressing childhood grief. She begins by telling of her own family's traumas, and ends by asserting that we still value the repression of grief today. The grief of children and soldiers is expressed but boys are still taught to 'man up', and for a man to cry is 'girly'. As Fraser crucially notes, when society values this stony censure of childhood grief, those who most successfully crush their grief, and can perform acts of cruelty, are rewarded with positions of power and authority. Fraser's work builds on the inexplicably sparse discussion of modernism and childhood with insight and urgency, in her discerning readings of childhood grief as lying at the heart of key modernist texts.

QUEEN MARY UNIVERSITY OF LONDON   ANEESH BARAI

The Letters of Samuel Beckett 1941–1956. Ed. by GEORGE CRAIG, MARTHA DOW FEHSENFELD, DAN GUNN, and LOIS MORE OVERBECK. Cambridge: Cambridge University Press. 2011. xciii+791 pp. £35. ISBN 978-0-521-86793-1.

The first volume of Samuel Beckett's selected correspondence covered the years 1929 to 1940 and gave us a sense of an erudite, ambitious, and ultimately unsettled young man. Increasingly alienated from an Ireland that was becoming a nation, Beckett moved restlessly between Dublin and London, travelling also to Germany and France, always deeply conscious of his desire to become a writer. When approached to translate De Sade's *Les 120 Journées de Sodome*, in February 1938, Beckett explains to George Reavey that while 'it fills [him] with a kind of metaphysical ecstasy' (p. 607), he is concerned about his reputation as a writer: 'I don't mind the obloquy, on the contrary it will get more of me into a certain room. But I don't want to be spiked as a writer, I mean as a publicist in the airiest sense' (p. 604). By 1940 Beckett had other concerns. Germany had invaded Western Europe and Paris, where Beckett now lived, was occupied. Beckett joined the French Resistance in 1941, working in the réseau Gloira SMH. Less than a year later, the cell was broken by the Gestapo and Beckett and his companion, Suzanne Deschevaux-Dumesnil, fled to the Unoccupied Zone. *The Letters of Samuel Beckett 1941–1956* opens with an acknowledgement of the silence of the war years: 'I am sorry to hear that my family is without news of me. I write them regular cards', Beckett explains to the Irish Legation in January 1945 (p. 9). It also offers a vision of ruins: 'St. Lô is just a heap of rubble, la Capitale des Ruines as they call it in France' (p. 18), which became the haunting quatrain 'Vire will wind in other shadows | unborn through the bright ways tremble | and the old mind ghost-forsaken | sink into its havoc' ('Saint-Lô', in *Samuel Beckett: Selected Poems 1930–1989*, ed. by David Wheatley (London: Faber and Faber, 2009), p. 49); and about which Beckett wrote a broadcast for Radio Telefís Éireann—'The Capital of the Ruins'— describing his work for the Red Cross there.

The effect of the Second World War on Beckett's writing cannot be overestimated. Beckett's novel *Watt*, written while he was in hiding in Roussillon— disparaged by the author as 'an unsatisfactory book, written in dribs and drabs, first on the run, then of an evening after the clodhopping, during the occupation' (p. 55)—is, nonetheless, a pivotal work in which confidence in systems and reason is increasingly undermined even as the protagonists of the novel are trapped within increasingly bizarre and destabilizing conceptual schemes. The Beckett that emerges after the war is stripped and bare, like Giacometti's tree in Jean-Louis Barrault's 1961 production of *Waiting For Godot* (Beckett describes Giacometti as 'subtle in a granite-like way, all stunning perceptions' (p. 294)). Fired with a sense of urgency, he wrote with intensity and drive. Between 1945 and 1956 Beckett completed the novels *Mercier et Camier*, *Molloy*, *Malone meurt*, *L'Innomable*, short prose pieces 'L'Expulsé', 'Le Calmant', *Textes pour rien*, and began writing for the stage with *Eleutheria* and the play that would make his name, *En attendant Godot*. Feeling increasingly alienated from his mother tongue, Beckett wrote more frequently in French, admitting to Reavey in December 1946: 'I do not think I will write very much in English in the future' (p. 48). Later, in a letter to Georges Duthuit in June 1949, he describes English as a 'horrible language, which I still know too well' (p. 170).

When thinking of Samuel Beckett's attitude to his writing, and to the artistic act, scholars often turn to the 'Three Dialogues with Georges Duthuit'. That complex and recalcitrant piece becomes, in the correspondence on which it is based, a vibrant and honest dialogue that lays bare Beckett's sense of the possibilities of art. Beckett is at turns brilliant and astute—of his friend Bram Van Velde (whom he describes as 'my great familiar' (p. 305)) he writes:

I think continually of his last paintings, miracles of frenzied impotence, streaming with beauties and splendours like a shipwreck of phosphorescences, decidedly one is literary all one's life, with great wide ways along which everything rushes away and comes back again, and the crushed calm of the deep. (p. 295)

Yet, he is also exhausted: 'On paper all I'm good for now is going on into silliness, ignorance, impotence and silence' (p. 279). The letters reveal that Beckett was deeply immersed in the writing of his contemporaries in Paris, reading Maurice Blanchot, Pierre Klosowski, and Maurice Heine: yet of all of them 'Blanchot is by far the most intelligent' (p. 225). He is delighted that Jean-Paul Sartre and Simone de Beauvoir think *Molloy* is good (p. 261), and responds warmly to Bataille's comments that his novel is 'remarkable', as we learn in a particularly apposite note by the editors (p. 259, n. 1). He is deeply immersed in the publication and production of his work, as his letters to Jérôme Lindon, Mania Peron (on whom he relied for advice on linguistic matters), Pamela Mitchell, Roger Blin, and Barney Rosset reveal. He is sanguine about failure—on the Miami fiasco of *Waiting for Godot*, he writes: 'Success and failure on the public level never mattered much to me, in fact I feel much more at home with the latter, having breathed deep of its vivifying air all my writing life' (p. 594). Indeed, he considers failure to be integral to his aesthetics: 'Aesthetically the adventure is that of the failed form', he writes to one of the first critical analysts of his dramatic work, Alec Reid (p. 596). At times, a vulnerable Beckett emerges. Two years after the death of his mother in 1950, he writes to Duthuit: 'My heart falls backwards down precipices every night, as it did when I was twenty, followed by nightmares, back in the family, floods of tears, fists swinging into the faces of the dear departed' (p. 310).

The Letters of Samuel Beckett 1941–1956 provides a vital support for the development of critical strands that underline how embedded the writer was in the literary and philosophical milieu in Paris in the post-war years, while maintaining strong connections with Ireland (his enthusiasm for Jack Yeats's Paris exhibition in 1954 is palpable (p. 444)). Annotated with detail and precision by Fehsenfeld, Overbeck, and Gunn, the many letters written originally in French are expertly translated by George Craig, who explains his process eloquently in his introduction, and his slim volume *Writing Beckett's Letters* (London: Sylph Editions, 2011). The edition is a triumph of scholarship. It makes available to a global readership the kinds of insights and details previously accessible only to those able to travel to one of the excellent Beckett archives. It reveals a writer who, though intensely private, found in his writing the means to articulate an ethics in which the connection between margin and centre is vital and necessary.

GOLDSMITHS, UNIVERSITY OF LONDON   DERVAL TUBRIDY

The Political in Margaret Atwood's Fiction: The Writing on the Wall of the Tent. By THEODORE F. SHECKELS. Farnham: Ashgate. 2012. vii+188 pp. £55. ISBN 978-1-4094-3379-8.

Theodore F. Sheckels is no stranger to critical analysis in relation to Margret Atwood's writing. The front cover of his monograph features a charming picture of Atwood reading from one of her most recent novels, *Oryx and Crake* (2003), at Randolph-Macon College, the academic institution where Sheckels works as a professor. His authorial credentials on the back cover of the book state that he is the founding editor of the academic journal *Margaret Atwood Studies*, and the current President of the Margaret Atwood Society. With *The Political in Margaret Atwood's Fiction*, Sheckels provides a detailed and thorough explication of this facet of his subject's twelve novels (excluding *The Penelopiad* (2006)). He is aware that by studying her novels only rather than her poetry, short fiction, or essays he joins 'a fairly long list of critics who have given primacy to Atwood's novel-length fiction in discussions of her work' (p. ix). Therefore, the originality of his research lies in his choice of theoretical approach. Sheckels offers a lucid and meticulous close analysis of what he means by 'political' in the preface and introduction of his book. 'Political', as Sheckels explains, does not refer to specific parties or to people voting in elections, but to the constant and solid presence of power in every human relationship. Atwood 'wants us, her readers, to see who is power-down because these are the victims in a political world that is depicted by Atwood' (p. viii). Sheckels observes that because quite often the people who are oppressed and injured by various power structures are women, Atwood's humanism comes very close to her feminism, which is used by Sheckels along with formal realism and postmodernism; all the political issues Atwood addresses are real and she rarely offers a tidy, reassuring ending to her readers.

Sheckels explains how he is going to use the concept of power to excavate and evaluate the considerable depths of Atwood's novels. Power is explored within the framework of two theorists, one economic and one literary: Kenneth Boulding and Michel Foucault. Boulding helpfully categorizes power: based 'on how the power operates interactively, there is threat power, exchange power and love power. Based on the power's results, there is destructive power, productive power and integrative power' (p. 3). These varied faces of power operate in three realms: the political, the economic, and the social. Foucault on the other hand writes on the disciplinary function of power, but more importantly on the interior nature of power in human relations, especially in sexual relations. By using Boulding's theory on the exteriority and Foucault's theory on the interiority of power Sheckels's aim is to offer an insightful reading of Atwood's novels that will bring out her complex and fascinating relationship with the political. His critical examination moves through a precise chronological order of Atwood's novels, although he also clusters them under the headings of Exteriority (I), Politics Foregrounded, Interiority, and Exteriority (II).

At its best the book offers an elegant, detailed, and reflective analysis of Atwood's presentation of power and resistance in all human relationships and contexts. The overall estimation of love, power, and perhaps hope seems to be somehow bleaker than the analyses of the novels deem appropriate. However, *The Political in Margaret Atwood's Fiction* is a useful critical companion for any level of study of Atwood's novels. The political is and will always be bleeding into any literary creation by Atwood. Sheckels's book encourages the reader to cast or recast an attentive critical eye on the manifestations, actions, and consequences of the political in all of Atwood's novels analysed here.

NORTHUMBRIA UNIVERSITY   KIRIAKI MASSOURA

Historical Dictionary of French Literature. By JOHN FLOWER. Lanham, MD: Scarecrow Press. 2013. xxxviii+587 pp. £80. ISBN 978-0-8108-6778-9.

In a general dictionary of French literature, the author/editor inevitably has to make choices about breadth of coverage and those authors, works, and movements to include or omit. It would seem, therefore, that John Flower has made the brave decision to ignore a number of what are commonly agreed to be major writers, such as Montaigne and Pascal, and to focus instead on an array of less-known authors: Drieu la Rochelle, for example, is accorded 155 lines of text, almost three times longer than the entry devoted to Proust, and five times longer than the lines on Corneille, Molière, and Racine combined. And the information on the latter three is not only sketchy but at times inaccurate or misleading: Racine, we are told, was educated by the Jesuits, and Molière's plays 'while technically not tragedies, are dark and disturbing' (p. 354). It is only in the bibliography that the reader is informed that 'the historical dictionary focuses on imaginative prose works and poetry only' (p. 543), which might explain why no single play by the aforementioned dramatists is named and why Beaumarchais receives no entry at all. Yet, even here little consistency is shown, as all of Genet's and Sartre's plays are listed, but, in the case of Ionesco's theatre, only *La Cantatrice chauve* receives a mention. Marivaux (who, rather worryingly, appears as a nineteenth-century writer in the bibliography) is discussed in a suitably lengthy article, but nothing is written on his substantial dramatic output. Although it was refreshing to find a piece on Marie de Sévigné, for instance, it was less explicable that such a prolific novelist as Madeleine de Scudéry from the same century should be omitted. French thought seems to receive only cursory treatment, with Derrida, Descartes, and Foucault notable absentees. Various historical events, such as the Revolution, the Commune, the Franco-Prussian War, the two World Wars, the Algerian War, and May 1968, are given full and interesting entries of their own, yet other conflicts, such as the Wars of Religion and the Fronde, which themselves spawned significant literary offerings, do not feature.

If one decides to approach this book less as a reference tool than as a selection of mini-essays, then there are many useful and delightful insights to be gained. Flower's sympathies are markedly in favour of post-1800 literature, and the articles on writers such as Duras, Echenoz, Mauriac, Modiano, Vigny, and Yourcenar display the author's expertise and interests to best advantage. And even if a writer such as Drieu la Rochelle is given undue prominence, it is refreshing to see fuller analysis of authors who have been given short shrift in other recent literary histories.

Readers requiring a general survey of all periods of French literature may wish to look elsewhere, but those wishing to gain knowledge of previously neglected (and predominantly twentieth-century) writers will find much of value in this volume.

UNIVERSITY OF CAMBRIDGE NICHOLAS HAMMOND

Shaping Courtliness in Medieval France: Essays in Honor of Matilda Tomaryn Bruckner. Ed. by DANIEL E. O'SULLIVAN and LAURIE SHEPARD. (Gallica, 28) Cambridge: Brewer. 2013. xii+295 pp. £60. ISBN 978-1-84384-335-1.

Matilda Tomaryn Bruckner's lively and important contributions to the study of medieval French and Occitan literature are well reflected in this affectionate collection of seventeen essays, which are framed by an introduction by the editors, a list of Bruckner's publications from 1975 to 2011, and a poetic 'envoi' by Sarah White. The selection of papers ranges from the core twelfth-century courtly texts (Chrétien de Troyes, Thomas d'Angleterre, Marie de France) to fifteenth-century *remaniements* and illustrated compilations. Most of the chapters are literary studies, and most make an explicit statement in their introduction about how they develop an insight or approach formulated by Bruckner. A handful take a more historical, or socio-cultural, approach. The volume is divided into four parts, in order to reflect their dedicatee's exceptionally wide-ranging body of published work. Part I, 'Shaping Real and Fictive Courts', opens with Peter Haidu's proposal to 'desublimate' the courtly in terms of theory, literary texts, and case studies. Donald Maddox examines 'courts' differently in a fifteenth-century collection of acts of the Parlement de Paris. Michel-André Bossy offers a close reading of the contents and illustrative programme of a compilation that was completed after the accession of Henry VII to the throne of England (British Library, MS Royal 16 F ii). The six studies in Part II explore narrative romances, all from the High Middle Ages, except for Joan Tasker Grimbert's study of a fifteenth-century Burgundian rewriting of Chrétien's *Cligès*. Kristin Burr emphasizes the importance of the lady Lidoine to *Meraugis de Portlesguez*; David Hult offers further thoughts on Thomas's *Tristan*, and Virginie Greene makes anew the case for the importance of the *Conte du Papegau*, while Logan Whalen suggests that Marie de France's *Lai* of *Guigemar* discusses themes of fecundity and sterility. Evelyn Burge Vitz's suggestion that the *Roman de la Rose* could have been performed (based on workshops with her students) is strikingly original. Part III offers four chapters, reflecting Bruckner's contributions to the study of women's writing. Elizabeth Wilson Poe makes an intriguing link between a poetic exchange about the Albigensian crusade and the famous Na Lombarda debate. Nadia Margolis explores Christine de Pisan's translation into her political context of the tropes of courtly romance. Daniel E. O'Sullivan makes a fresh case for the validity of studying Marian themes in troubadour lyric poetry. There is also an intriguing exploration by William Schenk of the contrasting written witnesses of the life of the twelfth-century countess of Brittany and reluctant nun, Ermengarde of Anjou (d. 1146). Part IV, 'Shaping the Courtly Other', offers four approaches to ongoing interest in questions of intercultural contact. Laine Doggett applies Bruckner's insights into the theme of hospitality at court to the reception of 'outsiders' in the *Tristan*–*Cligès* tradition and the *Lai* of *Lanval*. E. Jane Burns explores the paradoxical depiction in the *Ordene de chevalerie* and a French treatise composed for Saladin of Eastern, Muslim silk as a sign of chivalry. Nancy Freeman Regalado analyses the courtly reinterpretations of bestiary lore in Richard de Fournival's

Bestiaire d'amours, chiefly in terms of the illustrative programme of the famous compilation from Metz, Oxford, Bodleian Library, MS Douce 38/London, British Library, MS Harley 4972. Laurie Shepard proposes that Charles I of Anjou's court may have promoted new debates concerning French courtly concepts of nobility and love in the secular literary circles of the Italian communes.

UNIVERSITY OF READING   CATHERINE LEGLU

Manuscrits et pratiques autographes chez les écrivains français de la fin du moyen âge: l'exemple de Christine de Pizan. By OLIVIER DELSAUX. (Publications romanes et françaises, 258) Geneva: Droz. 2013. 615 pp. €70.14. ISBN 978-2-600-01702-2.

This monograph is the latest in a series of publications inspired by Charity Willard's suggestion (*Studi francesi*, 27 (1965) 452–57) that BnF, MS fr. 580 might contain an autograph copy of Christine de Pizan's *Epistre a la reine*. Her article opened up a fruitful line of enquiry, notably in studies by Gilbert Ouy and Christine Reno that culminated in their *Album Christine de Pizan* (Turnhout: Brepols, 2012), completed in collaboration with art historian Inès Villela-Petit and a number of other scholars, including Olivier Delsaux. Out of some 200 manuscripts, Ouy and Reno identified fifty-four as being contemporaneous with the date of composition, twenty-five of which, they argued, were copied wholly or partly by scribe X, and the remainder by P and R, all three scribes and some twelve illuminators working together in a Paris scriptorium in the late fourteenth and early fifteenth centuries. At the centre of their analysis is the persuasive but still contested thesis that X is Christine. These considerations will contextualize Delsaux's monograph, based on a doctoral dissertation (Université de Louvain, 2011), which he must have been completing before and during his collaboration on the *Album*. Delsaux accepts the Ouy/Reno arguments as a working hypothesis, though he has re-examined all the relevant manuscripts. Inevitably, therefore, there is considerable (and understandable) overlap in the material covered by the two works.

They are, however, very different. Where the *Album* is a monumental inventory, Delsaux's study focuses on the status of the autograph manuscript in the late medieval period, and the questions this poses. What value (if any) was attached to autograph production at the time? How does this compare with the status of an autograph manuscript in the modern world? What were the issues at stake when a medieval author chose to copy works in his/her own hand? What do we know of medieval representations of the author/scribe? After proposing a quite intricate terminology, Delsaux guides us authoritatively through these issues over three main chapters, each reflecting one stage in manuscript production: composition, edition, publication. To ensure perspective and depth, he casts his net far and wide over non-Christinian works, while subjecting a representative sample of Christine's manuscripts to meticulous analysis. The wealth of technical material covered, though rewarding, is challenging, and some changes would have made the volume a little more reader-friendly: for example, a layout based on three sections further subdivided into self-contained chapters might have been preferable, while cross-references of the type 'cf. Chapter III' would have been more useful as page references, given the length of the chapters involved. Whether interested or not in codicological studies, Christine specialists will find much to intrigue them. For example, it is touching to note the impact of personal memories when Christine acts as author and scribe (p. 440). In the *Advision-Cristine*, recalling her husband's death, she refers to 'sa fin comme bon catholique en la fin de Beauvais' (a revealing slip for 'la ville de Beauvais'). General readers will be interested to register the distance that separates medieval and modern conceptions of autography. Our medieval ancestors did not accord it the same value as we do, who live in the world of the printed book where autograph manuscripts may be rare. When Christine copied or corrected manuscripts in her own hand, it was more often than not for reasons of finance and efficiency: the author could dispense with intermediaries, make additions, or alter names of dedicatees at the last minute. In other words, autography had everything to do with the needs of the producer, not the expectations of the reader. A handful of slips provides a reminder that we are all still subject to scribal error (e.g. p. 45, lines 17–18; p. 191, line 1; p. 421, line 10 . . .).

UNIVERSITY OF GLASGOW   ANGUS J. KENNEDY

Female Intimacies in Seventeenth-Century French Literature. By MARIANNE LEGAULT. Farnham: Ashgate. 2012. ix+250 pp. £55. ISBN 978-0-7546-6945-6.

This monograph is a revised and translated version of an earlier work published in French, *Narrations déviantes: l'intimité entre femmes dans l'imaginaire français du dix-septième siècle* (Quebec: Presses de l'Université Laval, 2008). As Marianne Legault points out, French literary critics are generally reticent to explore the possibility of homoeroticism in the lives and texts of the women of the *Grand Siècle*. One can therefore appreciate the author's decision to make this investigation more accessible to a wider English-speaking readership, especially since Anglo-American scholarship has increasingly attempted to give voice to obscured and marginalized accounts by and of women, and in lesbian and queer studies, to reveal the same-sex erotic entanglements evidenced in a variety of texts. To this end, the book offers a useful contribution and serves as a good introduction to certain material which has hitherto received little attention. Throughout, the readings are informative and well researched, even if the historical overview of the first chapter (a new section added to the original French version) lacks lustre. In attempting to 'rediscover a genealogy of female friendships and of intimate bonds between women in Early Modern France' (p. 7), Legault often has recourse to rather overly extensive citations of feminist theorists which at times hinder the flow of her own prose. Psychoanalytic readings are kept to a minimum and Legault's analysis focuses more on the historical backdrop and the textual strategies of the specific works she examines.

Legault's definition of female intimacy includes both friendship and lesbian love, and often the blurring of the two. Mainly concerned with the analysis of literary works, the volume examines several genres and sources, including dictionary treatise, moral reflection, maxim, novel, comedy, fairy tale, harangue, and excerpts from Madeleine de Scudéry's private correspondence. In a division of readings between male and female literary discourses, the 'male imagination' is presented through Honoré d'Urfé's novel *L'Astrée* and Isaac de Benserade's comedy *Iphis et Iante*. Legault seeks to underscore these writers' sexual fascination in evoking female encounters, combined with a distinct apprehension over such closeness and a determined effort to reject and ridicule female intimacy. In contrast, the chapter on 'women's imagination', illustrated through Scudéry's novel *Mathilde (D'Aguilar)* and Charlotte-Rose de Caumont de la Force's fairy tale *Plus belle que Fée*, emphasizes how these writers stand out by daring to privilege the erotic ties between women and by resisting heteronormative expectations, either openly or obliquely. Although structurally very neat, the divisions between the male and the female perspectives seem rather too binary. Legault views Benserade's comedy as a tool to mock the same-sex desire of the characters and argues that through the miraculous metamorphosis at the end which transforms Iphis into a man, the play ultimately restores the patriarchal order and erases any of the subversive elements the same-sex desire of the characters had originally provoked. However, this ignores substantial evidence in the text to suggest that Benserade presents a more nuanced and positive vision of lesbian love where truth-telling and lying, male and female, passive and active forms of desire, the real and theatrical world cannot be easily differentiated.

More convincing is the third chapter, in which Legault examines the 'précieux' movement as bold and feminocentric and which, she argues, helps contextualize Scudéry's specific depiction of female friendships. This section offers insightful and detailed readings of Scudéry's *Mathilde*, explored beyond its façade of a traditional love story. Likewise, Legault's analysis of La Force's much-neglected text highlights well the audacious nature of the tale. Legault teases out how La Force manipulates the magical world of the fairy tale to present a world of intense female intimacy and erotic playfulness.

CLARE HALL, UNIVERSITY OF CAMBRIDGE   EMILIA WILTON-GODBERFFORDE

Stendhal's Less-Loved Heroines: Fiction, Freedom, and the Female. By MARIA C. SCOTT. London: Legenda. 2013. x+131 pp. £40. ISBN 978-1-907975-71-4.

This monograph offers a refreshing reconsideration of four of Stendhal's less socially compliant heroines: Mina de Vanghel, Vanina Vanini, Mathilde de la Mole, and Lamiel. Thoughtfully reading against the grain of a range of critical appraisals of these female characters—including feminist ones—Maria C. Scott argues that these women are cast as freer and more self-serving than previously believed. She builds on and departs from a fascinating range of sources, including excerpts from the author's correspondence with his sister, Pauline Beyle, and Simone de Beauvoir's analysis of Stendhal's heroines. Scott demonstrates that the condemnation of these characters as pointlessly rebellious and selfish—inherent in 'normative, androcentric criticism' (p. 1)—is skewed, reductive, and marginalizes their narrative significance. Basing her analysis on the existential conception of freedom, Scott convincingly shows that Stendhal's most independent heroines emerge instead as champions of their own liberty, positively subversive of the restrictive, traditional female role. This results in characters who are not set up to fail, but who are instead 'well-loved, by readers at least' (p. 6). Scott specifically takes issue with the view that Realist fiction is inherently antagonistic to female freedom, in two ways. The first is by arguing against the claim that Stendhal's male heroes simplistically 'express the author's own thoughts and preferences' (p. 4). This is achieved in part through an analysis of the author's attitude to female freedom revealed in his correspondence. The second is to challenge the view, *pace* Naomi Schor, that Stendhal's female characters are restricted by the Realist narrative. Scott traces the author's championing of freedom as 'the ability to determine the direction of one's own life' (p. 12) back to his admiration for Destutt de Tracy's *Éléments d'idéologie* (1801–15), explained in detail in the first chapter. She then convincingly argues that Stendhal's view is akin to Sartre's conception of freedom as inherently dependent on the possibility of constraint (p. 16). Scott counters interpretations based on the view that the fates of these heroines offer 'evidence of the author's ultimate censure of the self-determining female figure and preference for the self-abnegating heroine' (p. 28). She argues instead that the lenient treatment given to Stendhal's heroes by commentators is evidence of a sexual double standard in criticism rather than revelatory of the author's own attitude to women. This case is particularly well drawn in the second chapter on Mathilde de la Mole, where Scott argues that Mathilde's theatricality does not show her as a flawed or inauthentic heroine, but rather 'frees her to be herself in the presence of other people' (p. 49). In this, she parallels these qualities with the role-playing abilities for which Mathilde's mirror character, Julien Sorel, is traditionally praised. The third chapter, on *Lamiel*, does not attempt to iron out the difficulties posed by the different versions of the text and its unfinished state, but views the disordered structure of the emergent novel—and the central presence of the character Lamiel—as positively liberating. Scott presents a reading of *Lamiel* as a 'writerly' text in the Barthesian sense—a text to be troubled over, and one which does not play down the importance of its eponymous protagonist. This is a concise, elegant, and original reassessment of some of Stendhal's most important and, as it turns out, misunderstood heroines that will be of equal interest to both specialist scholars and students keen to challenge the dominant critical view of these female characters as limited and frustrated by their narrative possibilities.

UNIVERSITY OF WARWICK   SUSANNAH WILSON

Le Tremblement de Terre de la Martinique: drame en cinq actes, suivi de documents inédits. By CHARLES LAFONT and CHARLES DESNOYER. Ed. by BARBARA T. COOPER. Paris: L'Harmattan. 2012. xlv+184 pp. €23. ISBN 978-2-296-96600-0.

On 11 January 1839 an earthquake struck the French Caribbean island of Martinique. It destroyed the city of Fort-Royal and may have killed as many as 700 people. In her comprehensive introduction to *Le Tremblement de Terre de la Martinique* by Charles Lafont and Charles Desnoyer, Barbara Cooper argues that the earthquake prompted more than the coalition of relief efforts to aid the devastated colony; it inspired three dramatic representations, of which *Le Tremblement de Terre* by Lafont and Desnoyer rehearsed an ongoing debate between France and her colonies on the issues of slavery and a racialized social hierarchy in the ever-expanding French Empire of the 1830s.

The play, which opened on 14 January 1840, is less concerned with the impact of the natural disaster than with imagining the social and political consequences of slavery in a colony linked to a nation with republican ideals. Its romantic plot juxtaposes characters from each class and racial group on the island. Dominique, the play's villain, is a French-educated freeman of colour, who literally embodies the conflict between Enlightenment principles and the exigencies of a slave-labour force in a capitalist economy. Having twice saved the Count of Beaumont's daughter's life, he is appointed overseer by the Count, but Dominique wants to marry Julie. When he asks the Count for her hand in marriage the old man refuses. Interestingly, he adds that were they in France, he would be willing to entertain the proposal, suggesting that the chief obstacle is the racially polarized society of the colony and not Dominique's African ancestry. The Count, however, does not know just how mistaken his enlightened view is; Dominique has murdered not only Julie's first suitor, but also the Count's only son and heir to the Beaumont plantations. Dominique then organizes the slave revolt that threatens the island seconds before the earth begins to quake. The audience must decide whether it is a sign of divine intervention or retribution. In addition to Barbara Cooper's richly detailed introduction, this volume includes illustrations, excerpts from the original manuscript, and contemporary reviews of the 1840 production at the Theatre of Porte-Saint-Martin in Paris. For both scholars and students, this volume is an important contribution to the rich archive of the colonial period of the Caribbean.

COLLEGE OF WILLIAM AND MARY   M. LYNN WEISS

French Divorce Fiction from the Revolution to the First World War. By NICHOLAS WHITE. London: Legenda. 2013. x+195 pp. £45. ISBN 978-1-907975-47-9.

In times and places where marriage was indissoluble, the permanence of marriage formed the central problem of many novels. How would unhappy spouses cope? It was not self-evident which problems, if any, would remain for novelists to address once legal divorce took hold. Through his analysis of late nineteenth- and early twentieth-century novels, Nicholas White shows that the option of divorce—legal in France from 1792 to 1816, and then from 1884—did not obliterate family drama, but rather brought with it new problems for writers to explore.

White's focus is not how one might use fiction about divorce to better understand the place of divorce in French history, but rather 'the ways in which divorce informed the development of French fiction' (p. 1). The introduction provides White's critical framework, presenting the work of sociologists Anthony Giddens (favourable to new, more flexible family arrangements) and Zygmunt Bauman (critical of a system in which the family becomes disposable). This background allows for precision in White's subsequent discussions of modernity.

Chapter 1 traces the history of divorce in France. While divorce became legal during the Revolution, its first run was brief. It was only decades later, with the efforts of Alfred Naquet—presented impeccably by White—that divorce returned. White presents the incidence of divorce when legal, but also the debates surrounding its reintroduction, including differences of opinion among feminists.

The remainder of the book focuses on the novels themselves. In Chapter 2 White begins with works written during the years when divorce was first permitted. After 1816, French authors wishing to depict something like a French divorce could relocate a narrative to Switzerland, where divorce was legal. White's analysis of the female author André Léo's 1866 *Un divorce* reveals mid-century anxieties about the possibility of legally ending a marriage. White then brings us to the post-Loi Naquet years. Once divorce is reintroduced, White shows through his reading of Claire Vautier's 1889 *Adultère et divorce* that conflicts within a marriage become public, impacting women's reputation in unprecedented ways.

Chapter 3 looks at 'retrospective jealousy' (p. 106) in post-Loi Naquet novels. Had society reached a point at which men would accept women with other living (ex-) lovers? Chapter 4 treats novels in which fathers and daughters confront divorce as a family, including Alphonse Daudet's *Rose et Ninette* (1892). In Chapter 5 White expands upon his initial observation that the 'shift from linear to serial lives had profound implications for narrative', including the use of serial fiction to depict a protagonist having multiple relationships (p. 166).

White's prose, while elegant, can be challenging. Certain sentences (e.g. 'In the Baumanesque language of fluid dynamics, these three patriarchs of the French novel—France, Daudet, and Rod—are all keen to register the "drag force" of heavy modernity which resists liquid motion' (p. 163)) contribute to the sophistication of White's analysis, but can impede comprehension. In addition, the title is somewhat misleading, as most of the fiction discussed was published after 1884.

These minor criticisms aside, *French Divorce Fiction* is an important contribution to the study of nineteenth-century French literature and the family. The authors covered are an exciting selection of, as White puts it, 'unknown women and forgotten men' (p. 106). He displays tremendous knowledge of the corpus and authors, but also of the eras and literary movements discussed. His inspired choice to conclude with American novelist Diane Johnson's 1997 *Le Divorce* brings his story to the present, but also contributes to his broader argument about the literary value of texts beyond the canon.

PRINCETON   PHOEBE MALTZ BOVY

The Livres-Souvenirs of Colette: Genre and the Telling of Time. By ANNA FREADMAN. (Research Monographs in French Studies, 33) London: Legenda. 2012. xii+178 pp. £40. ISBN 978-1-906540-93-7.

Anna Freadman's *The Livres-Souvenirs of Colette* provides a new and convincing account of genre and autobiography in a selection of Colette's more autobiographical writings. Freadman argues that Colette's 'semi-autobiographical' works employ a variety of genres and modes to recount stories from Colette's life while simultaneously calling into question the relationship between a life and a work of writing. Freadman draws on a wide range of Colette scholarship as well as on recent and classic scholarship on autobiography, including the works of James Goodwin, Philippe Lejeune, and Michael Sheringham. This book will be indispensable for scholars of Colette and those interested in the genre of autobiography.

The book can be divided into three parts: the first treats Colette's most autobiographical works, which Freadman describes as 'anything but an exercise in self-revelation' (p. 22). Freadman focuses here on *Mes apprentissages* and 'Le Miroir', a short story from the 1908 collection *Les Vrilles de la vigne*. Freadman argues that these two pieces reveal not Colette's authentic self, but rather her fundamental distrust of autobiography as a genre. Freadman reads *Mes apprentissages* in terms of the genre of memoir, focusing in particular on Colette's deployment of portraits of her contemporaries. Freadman argues that Colette undermines the grand scale of the memoir by restraining herself to a modest scale and focusing on the colourful ephemera of her life rather than providing a sweeping narrative.

The second part treats Colette's collections of autobiographical writings, *La Maison de Claudine*, *Sido*, *Le Fanal bleu*, and *L'Étoile vesper*. Freadman describes Colette's writing in these works using a variety of concrete metaphors: the memory-book, the bundle or bouquet, tapestry, cobbling, and still life. All of these metaphors suggest that Colette gathers together memories without a coherent narrative, in a fragmentary and disconnected form. For Freadman, this form also indicates a particular phenomenology of time, according to which Colette uses the present to collect the past. Freadman also explores Colette's use of a number of different genres to recount the past, including the portrait, formal genres of mourning, and the anecdote.

The third part proposes a new reading on this basis of *La Naissance du jour*, a work whose relationship to autobiography is murkier. Freadman convincingly argues that the fictional plot is an allegory of reading in which Colette draws attention to the problem of autobiography, and is intended to teach readers how to approach Colette's fictional œuvre. The text is a cautionary tale about autobiographical reading, a story about love stories, rather than a love story itself.

In her reading of Colette's autobiographical writing as generically distinct from her fictional writings, Freadman makes an important intervention into Colette scholarship. This is because, as Freadman points out, there has been a tendency to approach Colette's fiction (and perhaps the fiction of women writers in general) as documentary of their lives. By treating Colette's autobiographical writings in a generic context, rather than a biographical one, Freadman calls attention to the fact that not all of Colette's writing was autobiographical and that none of her writing was straightforwardly revelatory of the facts of her life. Further, although theories of autobiography have tended to leave Colette out, Freadman's text suggests that future work might involve not only seeing how our reading of Colette changes in the light of these theories, but also how her inclusion would change the narratives themselves.

KANSAS STATE UNIVERSITY   KATHLEEN ANTONIOLI

Time in the Philosophy of Gabriel Marcel. By HELEN TATTAM. (MHRA Texts and Dissertations, 89) London: Modern Humanities Research Association. 2013. xi+220 pp. £19.99. ISBN 978-1-907322-83-9.

Helen Tattam's *Time in the Philosophy of Gabriel Marcel* deserves to be read not only by those who find insight and inspiration in Marcel's work, but by all those interested in the question of time as well as the development of modern French philosophy. Clearly versed in Marcel's corpus, Tattam skilfully locates Marcel's achievements and shortcomings primarily in relation to modern French philosophy. Tattam engages the reader in fruitful discussions of existentialism, ontology, phenomenology, metaphysics, hermeneutics, ethics, and religious belief. These discussions highlight what is most distinctive about Tattam's efforts. She puts Marcel into conversation with a 'community' (p. 6) of philosophers with whom Marcel's work can be read productively: Derrida, Ricœur, Levinas, and Augustine are the major figures in Tattam's conversation. Given that the essence of Marcelian thought concerns his meditations on intersubjectivity, Tattam's decision to explore Marcel's work through a series of dialogues with such a community is both inspired and instructive.

While the discussion is not restricted to the question of time, time serves as the text's focal point. Tattam's interest is primarily related to the question of whether Marcel is able to remain fully engaged with time and whether Marcel's reflections on time actually undermine his philosophic devotion to lived existence. Tattam presents an image of an inconsistent Marcel. His efforts to engage fully with time were undermined by the weight of his atemporal, philosophic commitments. Yet far from voiding the importance of Marcel's thought, Tattam argues that Marcel is an important transitional figure in the French intellectual tradition, a figure whose philosophic fidelity to lived existence ultimately gave way to his privileging of eternity over time.

Tattam explores how Marcel's phenomenological analyses of experiences such as love and hope generate a Marcelian ontology that renders temporal existence not only contingent and secondary, but deficient. She rightly notes that Marcel sometimes adopts an either/or language—either one's relations are eternalized or temporality becomes a source of despair—and highlights how Marcel's use of narrative privileges eternity over time. While Marcel's use of narrative is suited to the personal nature of his philosophizing, narrative also allows the discontinuities of temporal existence to be subsumed in a unified and stable whole.

As with any thinker worthy of reflection, Marcel's position is nuanced. And, as with any scholarship worthy of attention, Tattam recognizes the complexity of her case. In exploring this complexity Tattam provides a great service to Marcel scholarship by taking his theatre seriously. Tattam considers how Marcel's theatre concentrates on characters who do not have access to a form of eternity that would grant closure and intelligibility to their lives. After recognizing certain affinities between Marcel and Augustine, Tattam notes how they diverge with regard to the separation of time and eternity. In Augustine's thought, a gulf exists between time and eternity, whereas Tattam argues that Marcel takes a more Plotinian perspective, which entails that time and eternity intermix.

While there is little to criticize in Tattam's scholarship, it should be noted that all French citations remain untranslated. For those without a working knowledge of French, a reading of Tattam's work produces an incomplete and sometimes disjointed experience. Strictly with regard to her critical scholarship, there is a question of whether Tattam overstates Marcel's privileging of eternity over time. An argument could be made, particularly with regard to Marcel's understanding of immortality, that it is precisely through an individual's complete engagement with temporal existence—and the value-laden nature of this existence—that one comes into contact with eternity. On this reading, eternity would not dilute Marcel's engagement with time, but would result from one's complete engagement with it.

Despite these reservations, Tattam's work is to be lauded. She challenges and sheds light upon a thinker deserving of greater attention. Tattam's readers will understand why such attention is merited. Her readers will gain a deeper appreciation of the philosophic significance of his contribution to modern French thought in particular and philosophic thought more generally.

NEUMANN UNIVERSITY   GEOFFREY KARABIN

Last Steps: Maurice Blanchot's Exilic Writing. By CHRISTOPHER FYNSK. New York: Fordham University Press. 2013. ix+301 pp. £19.99. ISBN 978-0-8232-5103-2.

The aim of Christopher Fynsk's book is to discover in Maurice Blanchot's writings a 'non-violent ethico-political philosophy' (pp. 18, 34, 35). In 'Toward the Question of Peace' (Chapter 1, p. 17) Fynsk explains this non-violent ethical-political philosophy through close readings of Emmanuel Levinas's *Totality and Infinity* (Dordrecht: Kluwer, 1991; originally published as *Totalité et infini: essai sur l'extériorité* (The Hague: Nijhoff, 1961)) and *Otherwise than Being* (Dordrecht:

Kluwer, 1991; originally published as *Autrement qu'être ou au-delà de l'essence* (The Hague: Nijhoff, 1974)). These two texts reveal how ethical relations should be constructed, with the answer coming from 'a sentence from Exodus that the rabbinical tradition has always used to explain the Jewish response to revelation: "We will do and we will hear"' (p. 19).

Levinas and Fynsk show that this is not a simple withdrawal from the Western idea of understanding and action, but an authentic model of ethical relation, of a non-violent ethical-political philosophy: 'the invocation of the relation to autrui' (p. 23). Fynsk consequently approaches Blanchot's exilic writing by way of Levinas's conception of the ethical as a mode of 'sabbatical existence' (p. 17), which is an ethical form of life that seeks to preserve the alterity of persons (there is no mention of animals or other forms of life) by subordinating cognition to an absolute responsibility for the other. 'Sabbatical existence' derives from the Jewish Sabbath: it is a rupture and a withdrawal from the Western conception of life. 'Sabbatical existence' as the 'ethical' way to read Blanchot is also used in the second chapter of the book, 'The Indestructible'. This is an impressive meditation on Blanchot's reading of Robert Antelme's concept of the indestructible and on Blanchot's essay 'Being Jewish' ('Être Juif', 1962). Can we discover in the first two chapters of the book the trace of a non-violent ethico-political philosophy?

The problems in answering this question are more evident when Fynsk is reading and commenting on Blanchot's political and philosophical 'refusal' (pp. 65–69). Can we explain this radical form of refusal through the Jewish acceptance of Revelation? Where is the 'step' between the idea of Blanchovian contestation and an acceptance of revelation without any choice left to the Jewish people (pp. 23–25)? Where is the 'step' between the neuter—or what Blanchot calls the 'he/it'—and the 'We will do and we will hear'? It appears that Fynsk is asking the reader to read Blanchot mainly through his particularly laudative reading of Levinas.

The last half of Fynsk's book can be described as an unimpressive reading of *Le Pas au-delà* (Paris: Gallimard, 1973) in which the author meditates upon Blanchot's obscure fragments on writing, non-identity, the fragmentary, the neuter, affliction, and the 'passion for finitude' (p. 160). However, in this section the author does not clarify the profound importance of the 'Eternal Return' in Blanchot's *Le Pas au-delà* and his continuous engagement with Nietzsche through the works of Bataille and Klossowsky. Pierre Klossowsky, despite his enormous influence on Blanchot's œuvre, is not mentioned in the whole book.

Can we find a non-violent ethico-political philosophy in Blanchot's exilic writings? We can discover it through Fynsk's astonishing meditations on Blanchot's 'refusal', but unfortunately the whole work appears contradictory in trying to link 'refusal', contestation, the neuter, and the 'Eternal Return' as 'steps' within the 'sabbatical existence'.

Not all of us will find *Last Steps: Maurice Blanchot's Exilic Writing* a pleasing and satisfying book, but the same criticism can commonly be made against Blanchot's most obscure and difficult texts.

UNIVERSITY OF STIRLING   MAURO DI LULLO

'D'un parlar ne l'altro': aspetti dell'enunciazione dal romanzo arturiano alla 'Gerusalemme liberata'. Ed. by ANNALISA IZZO. Pisa: ETS. 2013. 159 pp. €15. ISBN 978-884673401-3.

This volume brings together seven papers given in a series of sessions at the Renaissance Society of America conference at Montreal in 2011, organized by Annalisa Izzo, under the title 'Speeches by Characters (and Narrators) in the Chivalric Tradition: From the Arthurian Romance to Tasso'. Izzo's initiative arises from her own research into the stories narrated by characters within the main narrative—what she calls second-level narration or 'racconto metadiegetico' (p. 7)—in the *Orlando furioso* and the tradition from which it derives.

Richard Trachsler's opening essay on the thirteenth-century French prose romance *Guiron le courtois* is a chronological and linguistic outlier—all the other contributions are devoted to fifteenth- and sixteenth-century Italian texts in *ottave*—but thematically it is the closest to Izzo's own essay and to the specific topic on which she focuses. Noting the constraints on an author writing within a body of narrative such as the Grail cycle, where the eventual outcome and the roles played by the major characters are all predetermined, he shows how the narrative initiative is diverted away from the deeds undertaken by the protagonists to the incidental stories which they tell: 'L'Azione è stata sostituita dalla Parola' (p. 17).

The essay by Franca Strologo adds to the body of work she has carried out in recent years to disentangle the complex tradition of the fifteenth-century *Spagna in rima*. Here she examines the dialogue accompanying the duel between Orlando and Ferraù to argue that, contrary to the conventional view, it is the longer rather than the shorter version of the text which is closer to the poem's archetype.

There follow three studies which focus on two poets of the generation immediately preceding Ariosto, Matteo Maria Boiardo and Cieco da Ferrara. Annalisa Perrotta considers the topos of the hero concealing his identity, noting how this normally arises when a Christian hero appears in disguise among his 'pagan' counterparts, and how the theme therefore becomes irrelevant when, in the *Inamoramento de Orlando*, love replaces religious war as the mainspring of the action. Costantino Maeder examines the various narrative functions of soliloquies or asides to the reader in Boiardo's poem. Jane E. Everson's analysis of a lyrical episode in Cieco da Ferrara's *Mambriano* shows the poet's skilful fusion of a range of classical and contemporary sources, making the case for a higher degree of literary sophistication than has generally been attributed to him.

Annalisa Izzo's contribution looks afresh at the episodes in the *Furioso*, often labelled *novelle*, which appear to be self-contained stories with no direct bearing on the main plot, and demonstrates how on the contrary these 'second-level' narratives impinge on the story of the main character to whom they are told. Recalling the organic metaphor with which Eugène Vinaver initiated the modern study of 'entrelacement' in medieval romance (her bibliography lists Vinaver's *The Rise of Romance* (Oxford: Clarendon Press, 1971), but the key study first appeared as his MHRA Presidential Address in 1966), she shows how these so-called *novelle* 'altro non sono che germogli, piccole foglie, boccioli che fioriscono arrivando a compimento, ramificazioni a spirali e volute di uno stesso tronco. La bellezza, la complessità e soprattutto la completezza del disegno semplicemente non esisterebbe senza di esse' (pp. 137–38).

Georges Güntert examines the opening three cantos of the *Gerusalemme liberata* as they establish the antithetical 'discorsi', conventionally defined as epic and romance, which determine the 'carattere ossimorico' (p. 146) of the poem as a whole. These 'discourses' are introduced in the context of two overarching surveys of the main protagonists, from the respective viewpoints of the crusader leader Goffredo (and, implicitly, the Christian God and the poet himself) in Canto I, and of the pagan princess Erminia in Canto III.

It is a little disappointing that only the last two essays engage with the poems of Ariosto and Tasso, the undisputed big hitters of the Italian chivalric tradition. But this is still a useful volume which is well produced, with a bibliography and an abstract in English to accompany each contribution.

University of Exeter   Mark Davie

Dante's 'tenzone' with Forese Donati: The Reprehension of Vice. By Fabian Alfie. Toronto: University of Toronto Press. 2011. 240 pp. $55. ISBN 978-1-4426-4223-2.

Fabian Alfie's book on the Dante–Forese *tenzone*, notable for the courage with which it addresses a still nicely scandalous text, falls into three main parts—four if we count the introduction on Dante's and Forese's social circumstances and on the poetics of vituperation in the Duecento. First, and occupying the greater part of his discussion, comes a close reading of the poems and an account of their afterlife in Cantos xxix and xxx of the *Inferno* and Cantos xxiii and xxiv of the *Purgatorio*, Alfie's discussion thus exhibiting a welcome sense of the scope of the problem. Welcome too, and commendable for its stamina, is his struggle to make sense of it all, to unravel the knottiness of the *tenzone*, on both sides, by way of its literary allegiances and oblique social and domestic allusions. Next comes an account of the afterlife of the *tenzone*, where especially important is its presence to Boccaccio as similarly engaged in the exploration of fidelity and infidelity in marriage. And finally there is a section on the codicological situation, on the distribution and interrelationship of the manuscript sources for the *tenzone*, impressive once more for its care and precision. There is too a generous bibliography, generous in its coverage of, for example, the social and sexual mores generally of the times, all very much to the point when it comes to the Forese *tenzone*.

If there is a problem here, however, it lies, I would say, in an excess of high seriousness, in the author's at-all-costs desire to see in the *tenzone* a 'socio-political document' (p. 114) busy at the level of indictment, of scourging Florentine society generally for its reneging on every kind of civic and domestic responsibility and decency. From Rustico through to Forese and Dante it is a question, Alfie thinks, of one party to the *contentio* recalling the other to his right mind as a good citizen, the whole thing thus having about it a missionary aspect, a moral fervour both subsisting into and confirmed by its echoes in the *Commedia*. True, Alfie is careful when it comes to the Forese moment of the *Purgatorio* to insist on Dante's care in correcting his erstwhile allegations relative to Forese's marital situation, but wholly missing from his discussion is any sense of the ancient and enduring familiarity which alone accounts for, say, the 'non mi far dir mentr'io mi maraviglio, | ché mal può dir chi è pien d'altra voglia' moment of *Purg.* XXIII. 59–60 or the exquisitely tender 'Quando fia ch'io ti riveggia?' moment of XXIV. 75, testimony to something more and something other than mere indignation as the stuff of the original exchange. The argument is in this sense far too sombre, the leaden-footedness of it all being untroubled by anything making for its particular kind of humanity. A dear colleague of all English-speaking Dantists, and indeed of Dantists generally (Stephen Bemrose in *A New Life of Dante* (Exeter: University of Exeter Press, 2000), pp. 31–32), similarly struck by the ironies and paradoxes of the *tenzone* but wiser in respect of what it might all mean, had this to say about it:

Whereas some thirteenth-century *tenzoni* were on such lofty matters as the true nature of love and virtue, this one between Dante and Forese is characterized by mutual vituperation of a far from elevated kind. Dante accuses Forese of neglecting his wife (and perhaps also of impotence), of gluttony, theft and illegitimacy, Forese in turn scorns Dante's alleged humiliating and ridiculous poverty, obscurely insults his father, and accuses Dante of cowardice. Clearly the two were firm friends.

Well, maybe, maybe not. But I cannot help feeling that we are nearer the mark here.

UNIVERSITY COLLEGE LONDON   JOHN TOOK

Pastoralia. Carmina. Epigrammata. By MATTEO MARIA BOIARDO. Ed. by STEFANO CARRAI and FRANCESCO TISSONI. Novara: Centro Studi Matteo Maria Boiardo — Interlinea. 2010. 319 pp. €36. ISBN 978-88-8212-682-7.

Canzoniere Costabili. By 'AMICO DEL BOIARDO'. Ed. by GABRIELE BALDASSARI. Novara: Centro Studi Matteo Maria Boiardo — Interlinea. 2012. 899 pp. €48. ISBN 978-88-8212-888-3.

Scandiano in Emilia Romagna is the birthplace of the great Renaissance poet Matteo Maria Boiardo and the seat of the Centro Studi named after him. Since its inception in 2000, the Centro Studi has sponsored a number of worthy initiatives aimed at the exploration of the literary and artistic legacy of fifteenth-century Northern Italian courts, the world in which Boiardo cut a prominent figure. The Centre has elected among its primary objectives the publication of Boiardo's œuvre in a critical and annotated edition, planned in twelve volumes. Volume XI, the first to appear (in 2009), comprised the tragedy *Timone* edited by Mariantonietta Acocella and the anonymous *Orphei tragoedia* edited by Antonia Tissoni Benvenuti, the latter text tentatively but persuasively declared ascribable ('attribuibile') to Boiardo. A second volume, devoted to Boiardo's Latin poetry (Volume I: *Pastoralia. Carmina. Epigrammata*), was published in 2010 and is reviewed here, together with another remarkable publication promoted by the Centre, the edition of the anonymous lyric sequence known as *Canzoniere Costabili*.

The text of Boiardo's Latin poems has been critically established and provided with an Italian translation and thorough annotation by Stefano Carrai for the *Pastoralia* and the *Epigrammata*, and by Francesco Tissoni for the *Carmina in Herculem*. Carrai has authorized a reissue of his earlier edition of the *Pastoralia* (Padua: Antenore, 1996); he has also produced a concise general introduction which highlights the significance of Boiardo's Latin production in its historical and cultural context (pp. 9–15). The text of the *Pastoralia* in particular survives in two different versions. The one ultimately authorized by Boiardo is conveyed by two manuscripts (one of which bears autograph corrections and marginalia) and by the first edition (1500); it comprises ten eclogues—a patent homage to Virgil's *Bucolics*—organized, however, within a peculiar numerical grid which demands equal length (a hundred lines each) of all ten pieces. A seventeenth-century printed miscellany provides previous shorter versions for eight of the ten eclogues, the text of which is given separately in smaller type.

Both Carrai's and Tissoni's commentaries offer a lucid analysis of Boiardo's individuality as a poet. His pastoral poetry in particular draws its inspiration from Virgil, Ovid, Statius, Claudian, and even the *Corpus Theocriteum*, which in Ferrara had been popular since the middle of the fifteenth century. Further authoritative models were provided by contemporary poets active in the same city, such as Tito Vespasiano Strozzi (Boiardo's uncle), Battista Guarini, and Gaspare Tribraco. Boiardo's skilful dialogue with his sources, to which both commentaries do full justice, may be said to work like an ingeniously encoded medium conveying plentiful allusions to allegiances and rivalries of both literary and political relevance. The *Carmina in Herculem*, on the other hand, shows innovative metrical and prosodic solutions, mainly of Horatian descent but variously 'crossed' with medieval and early modern metres (notably Boethius's and Francesco Filelfo's) so as to produce unusual combinations. As Carrai had formerly observed and Tissoni is now able to argue on the basis of further evidence, inspiration for such experiments is likely to have come, at least in part, from Niccolò Perotti's influential treatises *De metris* and *De generibus metrorum quibus Horatius Flaccus et Severinus Boethius usi sunt* (pp. 184–89).

As mentioned above, the Centro Studi does not confine its activities to the demanding task of editing Boiardo's works. The *Canzoniere Costabili*, now edited by Gabriele Baldassari and sponsored by the Centre, represents a further momentous achievement for Renaissance scholarship. Thus called after the noble Ferrarese family in whose entourage the manuscript was produced, the *Canzoniere Costabili* is preserved in British Library, MS Add. 10319. A fair copy on vellum, it contains the text of a lyric sequence meticulously revised by a number of hands, the most conspicuous of which Baldassari convincingly identifies as that of the author himself. The 'canzoniere' is undoubtedly the work of a personality close to Boiardo's. As early as 1987, somewhat in the fashion of art historians' *Notnamen*, Antonia Tissoni Benvenuti had coined for the manuscript's nameless author the designation 'Amico del Boiardo', which Baldassari has unreservedly endorsed.

This unusual lyric sequence presents a complex and somewhat unfathomable story dominated by the image, or *senhal*, of the phoenix. Events and moods described in the poems involve the presence of a male narrator and at least three main female characters, as well as other 'encrypted' personalities which are likely to foreshadow those of real individuals of the Este court. These features do not surrender their meaning easily; yet Baldassari is as keen to highlight his anonymous author's poetic craft as he is to unveil the concealed identities and indistinct circumstances that give the story its distinctive charm. Albeit lyrically transfigured, words, gestures, and personal relationships appear to conform to a conduct code that must in some proportion reflect the habits and customs of the court. The social historian will find much of interest here in relation to what used to be called the civilizing process in early modern society.

There is no commentary, but the introduction offers illuminating observations on the sequence's structural features (pp. 9–86) and on selected passages and *cruces*. The palaeographical analysis of the manuscript's characteristics and the discussion of its variant readings (pp. 87–230), together with a detailed survey of the poems' language (pp 231–361), follow the painstaking deciphering of extensive erasures and marginalia, often conducted by ultraviolet light examination. The layers of successive interventions are marshalled by Baldassari into a minutely detailed textual apparatus. As a result, over and above the intrinsic value of the edited text, Baldassari's edition captures the essence of an important development in the lyric poetry of Northern Italian courts—its transition to a linguistic and stylistic model progressively dominated by Petrarch and the Tuscan vernacular.

DURHAM UNIVERSITY   CARLO CARUSO

De bello Italico. La guerra d'Italia. By BERNARDO RUCELLAI. Ed. by DONATELLA COPPINI. Foreword by RENZO MARTINELLI. (Storici e cronisti di Firenze) Florence: Firenze University Press. 2011. 180 pp. €17.90. ISBN 978-88-6453-224-0.

The *De bello Italico* of Bernardo Rucellai (1448–1514) is the first volume of a new series devoted to historians and chroniclers of Florence. This is a commendable enterprise, which will allow students of Renaissance Italy to cast their eye beyond the works of a Guicciardini or a Machiavelli and gain deeper familiarity with a seminal context for the development of modern historiography. Rucellai himself was an accomplished politician, historian, antiquarian, and patron of the arts—as well as Lorenzo de' Medici's brother-in-law. His *De bello Italico* narrates the French invasion of Italy during the biennium 1494–1495, with a coda on the sudden death of the King of France Charles VIII (7 April 1498) and the accession to the French throne of his cousin, Louis of Orléans, as Louis XII. While brought to completion some time between 1511 and 1512, the work is likely to have been conceived as early as 1495, as in that year Rucellai joined the genial and learned society which gathered in Naples under Pontano's aegis debating aims and methods of ancient and modern historiography. The text was first published in London in 1724 and reprinted only once in Florence (with the fake indication of London) in 1733. It ultimately depends on the authority of a manuscript which is believed to have been produced for Rucellai himself (Florence, Biblioteca Medicea Laurenziana, MS Plut. LXVIII 25). With only a limited number of emendations, the Laurentian manuscript essentially provides the copy-text of Coppini's edition, who has also supplied paragraph- and line-numbering, a textual apparatus, a facing-page Italian version, an introduction, and a commentary.

In the introduction to the volume Coppini illustrates Rucellai's method in the light of the ancient and modern authorities he acknowledged as such. Thucydides (in Lorenzo Valla's translation), Sallust, Cicero, and Lucian offered valuable tuition for history-writing that was meant to focus on specific situations or events (as contrasted to annalistic accounts), whereas Pontano stressed the role of the mighty forces that fashion the destiny of illustrious individuals, such as personal ambition, or Fortuna (whose nimble figure, incidentally, featured in the *impresa* of Bernardo's father Giovanni). The commentary clarifies circumstances and details of the narrated events, while appropriately highlighting Rucellai's influence over the masterpiece of early modern historiography, Francesco Guicciardini's *Storia d'Italia*. Both works are shown to share a number of distinctive features: the masterful use of direct and indirect speech in reporting orations and allocutions; sophisticated description techniques (cf. in particular the vivid account of the battle of the Taro, §§ 110–16); the thorough scrutiny of sources, both written (§ 118) and oral (§ 107). Moreover, as members of the so-called *Ottimati* or Florentine upper class, both authors display aristocratic haughtiness characteristically tempered with a pragmatic ethos of anti-monarchic (i.e. oligarchic) inspiration (for Rucellai in particular cf. §§ 16. 6–8; 150. 4–5).

For the reasons that have just been given, the importance of Coppini's contribution is beyond question. It is therefore to be lamented that editorial standards have not been given sufficient consideration. Typos, both occasional and serial, are frequent. The translation itself shows signs of hurried editorial revision (cf. e.g. §§ 6. 21–24; 12. 18–24; 20. 4–9; 25. 12–15; 26. 4–9; 32. 16; 46. 8–12; 50. 17–19; 78. 13–17; 96. 12; 102. 4–6; 122. 23), and the same should be said about the distribution of some footnote content (cf. e.g. p. 103, footnote 77; p. 135, footnote 112; pp. 155 and 157, footnotes 133 and 134). One or two points of detail in the commentary may deserve further attention. For example, *Gebenna* as a place-name in the Alps (§ 46) cannot possibly be the French Cévennes as suggested in the relevant note—it will rather be, as in Petrarch's Latin and vernacular works, the Montgenèvre Pass. In the same paragraph, *Alpes Iulias* mentioned in connection with the Piedmontese city of Asti must be a slip of Rucellai's pen, as those are in fact the *Alpes Cottiae*, while the *Iuliae* lie at the furthest eastern frontier of Italy. An Index of Names would also have been helpful. All the same, this volume represents a valuable addition to the currently available set of sources for the history of early modern Italy.

DURHAM UNIVERSITY   CARLO CARUSO

Lyric Poetry by Women of the Italian Renaissance. Ed. by VIRGINIA COX. Baltimore: Johns Hopkins University Press. 2013. xvi+455 pp. $54. ISBN 978-1-4214-0888-0.

It is impossible to overestimate the role that Virginia Cox has played in bringing to light, researching, and promoting awareness of and appreciation for writings by women in early modern Italy, since her award-winning essay 'The Single Self: Feminist Thought and the Marriage Market in Early-Modern Venice' appeared in *Renaissance Quarterly*, 48 (1995), 513–81. After her extensive monographic studies *Women's Writing in Italy, 1400–1650* (Baltimore: Johns Hopkins University Press, 2008) and *The Prodigious Muse: Women's Writing in Counter-Reformation Italy* (Baltimore: Johns Hopkins University Press, 2011), this bilingual collection of poems opens the field to countless students and researchers, as some of these texts are now available in print for the first time ever or since their sixteenth- or seventeenth-century publication.

Several features make this anthology a touchstone of the genre. The introduction (pp. 1–67) lays out the cultural, political, and spiritual contexts in which women wrote and published in early modern Italy, as well as the critical reception and printing histories of these texts. It includes a 'Note on Meter, Rhythm, and Rhyme' (pp. 46–55) that will help novices to these forms and any instructor bringing them (or Italian poetry in most periods, for that matter) to their students. This Note is complemented by a glossary towards the end of the volume (pp. 421–23) that explains key terms in prosody and style, all helpfully identified by an asterisk whenever they occur in the text. Each poem is followed by a prose translation, then by the identification of its metrical form, rhyme scheme, source, any corrections, and a concise explanation and commentary. The latter is, in some cases, a veritable tour de force of succinctness and clarity: I will single out the twelve lines Cox devotes to Tullia d'Aragona's 'Qual vaga Filomela che fuggita' (p. 88), in which she identifies the topic, connects it to its use by another woman writer, explains mythological references, ties it to a contemporary painting that d'Aragona might have seen, and mentions another scholar's reading of the same poem, all avoiding the distraction provided by numbered footnote cues.

Notable inclusions reflect Cox's revisionist approach to writings by Italian women in the Renaissance. A full eighty pages (to wit, fifty-seven poems) cover religious topics, to correct their exclusion based on 'Italian criticism's relentless secularism and its near-universal neglect of literary work written after the Council of Trent' (p. 42). Furthermore, Cox underscores the range of themes that women tackled within the stylistic boundaries of lyrical poetry by including 'Encomia of Rulers and Patrons' (pp. 287–303, ten poems), 'Verse of Friendship and Family Love' (pp. 340–53, thirteen compositions), four poems devoted to the death of people outside the family (pp. 355–58), and 'Verse of Place and Selfhood' (pp. 360–81, sixteen poems). Finally, the linguistic scope of women's poetic abilities is manifested in the portion devoted to 'Comic and Dialect Verse' (pp. 383–90, four poems) as well as in the four religiously themed compositions in Latin (three by Lorenza Strozzi, pp. 229–37, and one by Tarquinia Molza, p. 249) and in Greek (by Olimpia Morata, pp. 332–33). By emphasizing their geographical origin, Cox introduces another element that traditionally has garnered little attention, localizing poetry while connecting to pan-Italian trends.

This anthology reflects Cox's dedication to recovering texts by women authors, her encyclopedic knowledge of the literary forms and themes of early modern literature, and her superior translation abilities (evident since her work on Moderata Fonte's *The Worth of Women* (Chicago: University of Chicago Press, 1997), and Maddalena Campiglia's *Flori* (Chicago: University of Chicago Press, 2004)). It will allow the inclusion of these writers in university courses at all levels, and it will prove to be a fundamental tool to increase their study and research. Along with the scholarship carried out by other specialists in Italian literature (Elissa B. Weaver and Konrad Eisenbichler, for example), music composition and performance (such as Craig Monson, Kelley Harness, Anne MacNeil, and Colleen Reardon), and historians of culture and gender (Anne Jacobson Schutte, Gabriella Zarri, Sharon Strocchia, and Jutta Sperling, to name only a few), Cox's tireless work and elegant, timely writing continue to expand our horizon and field of enquiry. These foundational and fundamental efforts are already reshaping the discourse and, by making these texts available to the next generation, will ensure its continuity in the future.

UNIVERSITY OF MIAMI   MARIA GALLI STAMPINO

'Eunuco': un volgarizzamento anonimo in terza rima. Ed. by MATTEO FAVARETTO. (Scelta di curiosità letterarie inedite o rare dal secolo XIII al XIX. Dispensa CCCII) Bologna: Arnaldo Forni for Commissione per i testi di lingua. 2011. cx+254 pp. €32. ISBN 978-88-98096-09-1.

Translations, or rather adaptations, of classical texts for the theatre in the vernacular were quite popular in the late Quattrocento, particularly in Northern Italy, as Antonia Tissoni Benvenuti and Maria Pia Musacchi have amply demonstrated. The court of Ferrara in particular was very keen on theatrical performances long before the first Italian regular comedy, Ariosto's *Cassaria*, was represented during the carnival of 1508 (or was it *Il Formicone* at Mantua in 1503?). In 1503 Isabella Gonzaga wrote to her uncle in Ferrara to enquire about two plays by Plautus: 'Gurgulio et Ulularia [. . .] tradotte in volgare [. . .]. Del *Gurgulio* intendo di quella del Cornazano.' Antonio Cornazano, employed as 'poeta' by Ercole d'Este since 1475, died in Ferrara in February 1484, and the manuscript of his *volgarizzamento* has never been found, but Isabella's interest confirms that Plautus was more popular than Terence in the Northern Italian courts. Numerous translations, however, have come down to us in anonymous manuscripts, like the present one of Terence's *Eunuchus*, so diligently studied and lovingly edited by Favaretto. The text has reached us in a single cartaceous manuscript (Magliabechiano VII, 1304, but of Medicean Palatine provenance, previously Med. Pal. 377) which is catalogued as sixteenth-century, and is most likely to have been written in the very early 1500s. Favaretto mentions the watermark as 'bilancia in cerchio' similar to Briquet 2541, or 2537, which are found mainly in Venice *c.* 1498 and 1489–94 respectively. The only possible indication of a name, more likely to be the scribe's than the translator's, is in the capital letters at the end of the text: 'F.M. S', where the last letter could stand for 'scripsit'. However difficult and foolhardy it may be to hazard suggestions, I would venture that a possibility could be Filippo Mantovano, an author near the court of the Gonzaga who had produced *Il Formicone*, based on a story by Apuleius.

In his introduction Favaretto explains that it is virtually impossible to identify the Latin copy on which the translation is based, and quite sensibly thinks that it is likely to be a manuscript copy which has not been identified by the modern editors of Terence. The translation in *terza rima* tends to expand certain phrases and in particular some very concise repartees from the Latin text, adding colourful vernacular expressions. For example, a single-verb answer to the question of Gnatho, 'Quid agitur?' (ll. 271), given by Parmeno as 'statur', is rendered as 'Io mi sto in piè, se gli occhi tecco hai, | e son fatto al contrario de' porri | che stan col capo in giù, se tu nol sciai' (ll. 194–96). Favaretto therefore calculates that the total number of hendecasyllables is 2564 against the 1094 lines of the Latin text. The introduction proceeds, as is customary, with an accurate linguistic examination of the Italian text, with some metrical observations, and the language is labelled as 'coiné emiliano-lombardo-veneta' in which occasional dialect words confirm the Northern Italian provenance of the anonymous translator. In the phonetic analysis there is a reference to an 'iperletterario *robosto*' (p. xlv), which has been edited, quite sensibly, to *robusto*, rhyming with *cacciafrusto* and *gusto*. It seems to me that *robosto* could be a more banal scribal error, caused by attraction of the existing vowels in the first and last syllables. It is inevitable that certain choices of the editor, however well argued, cannot be wholeheartedly shared. Among those decisions I would put the editing of endings in *-ti*+vowel as *-zi-* (p. xcix) even in the *-antia*, *-entia* endings. They do look strange, especially in view of the decision to maintain forms with *-cti*+vowel (e.g. *afflictione*). Personally I believe that a preposition deriving from Latin *cum* and generally abbreviated in the manuscript as *cu-* with a *titulus* should be edited to *cum* in line with the practice of numerous fifteenth- and early sixteenth-century manuscripts, and not the hybrid *cun*, which, as stated by the editor, 'never appears *per intero*', unless one assumes the improbable existence of a nasalized pronunciation on the *-u*, which is found in some modern Emilian dialects.

But these are minor idiosyncrasies. The text is very well established and it reads well; the methodology followed seems impeccable. Unlike other volumes in the series, it is enriched by copious 'annotations' or explicatory notes (pp. 115–226) which allow the editor to make comparisons with the Latin text, and to add some discussion of the peculiar vocabulary. The last pages (227–52) are devoted to an accurate and useful *Glossario*, to which I would add at least one item: *spanto* (v. 450), which is not immediately transparent in the text and which is found in GDLI meaning 'versato, effuso'.

Overall an excellent edition and a rewarding conclusion to what has obviously been a long and painstaking period of research, as well as a worthy addition to the history of the Italian theatre.

BALLIOL COLLEGE, OXFORD   DIEGO ZANCANI

'Partenia': A Pastoral Play. By BARBARA TORELLI BENEDETTI. Ed. and trans. by LISA SAMPSON and BARBARA BURGESS-VAN AKEN. Toronto: Centre for Reformation and Renaissance Studies, University of Toronto. 2013. xiii+359 pp. $45.95. ISBN 978-0-7727-2136-5.

There are three surviving Italian pastoral plays composed by female dramatists in the 1580s. Isabella Andreini's *Mirtilla* and Maddalena Campiglia's *Flori* both have modern editions—the latter curated by Virginia Cox and Lisa Sampson, in the series 'The Other Voice in Early Modern Europe' (Chicago: Chicago University Press, 2004). That 'Other Voice' series has now moved from Chicago to Toronto, and Lisa Sampson has edited the third of these significant texts, with a new scholarly partner. *Partenia* may be the first full-length pastoral drama, in strict chronology, to have been authored by a woman.

Barbara Torelli was born in 1546, to a noble family in the Parma region. She was married to another aristocrat, Giovanni Paolo Benedetti, who died before January 1593. *Partenia* was composed around 1586: its text survives in only two manuscripts, the more important of which (now in Cremona) shows some signs of being partially edited for an unrealized printed edition. The date of Torelli's death is not known; but it is clear that she enjoyed a long respectable widowhood during which she was lauded for her literary talents by an influential circle, including the dramatist and networker Muzio Manfredi. *Partenia* was much appreciated, at least for a while, being particularly praised by Angelo Ingegneri in his influential treatise on drama of 1598. Manfredi made autograph annotations on the Cremonese manuscript, trying (patriarchally?) to impose his own linguistic and stylistic preferences: Sampson and Burgess-Van Aken have kept his interventions firmly in their meticulous textual apparatus, and presented us with what is more likely to have been Torelli's original. The play is presented with a facing-page translation in simple efficient English prose: the notes attached to this comment on those aspects of the Italian text which an anglophone reader needs to know. They also offer all the explanatory background required for a full understanding, in respect both of classical mythology and of contemporary allusions. In Appendix A the volume then includes all the supportive verse compositions by other authors which appear in the Cremonese manuscript; and in Appendix B the five verse compositions and a single prose letter which comprise Barbara Torelli's other surviving writings. All these appended texts are also accompanied by translations.

The story of *Partenia* is a simple one. The eponymous heroine is being courted by two shepherds, Leucippo and Tirsi, who are also friends: their rivalry is resolved when one of them turns out to be her long-lost brother. Partenia herself, however, has a strong inclination towards a life of virgin celibacy, expressed in terms of a devotion to the goddess Diana. In so far as she has a change of heart, we only hear it narrated, *Aminta*-style, rather than witness it on stage; and the play ends without our ever seeing the prospective bride and groom in each other's company. Much of the text is devoted to verbal exchanges between primary or secondary characters—rhetorical and moral explorations of themes such as grief, unjustified jealousy, parental authority, and the contrasting claims of love and friendship (this last being an issue frequently treated by Italian dramas of all genres in the second half of the Cinquecento). The obligatory satyr figure has lustful designs on Partenia, but is never allowed to get anywhere near her. There are allusions to the courtly and cultural environment of Parma: the play's setting is not Arcadia but Collecchio, a genuine rural estate of the Farnese dukes, and some characters on and off stage are identifiable with real people. The absentee landlord figure 'Ottinio' is probably Duke Ottavio himself, though he died in 1586 and perhaps was never able to enjoy the compliment. It is suggested that the nymph Talia, who assumes a controlling role and rescues Partenia and Tirsi from apparent death, might represent the author herself. This would be an interesting piece of meta-theatre.

The editors characterize *Partenia* as having an 'emphasis on tragic elements', an 'exclusion of traditional comic-pastoral elements', and a 'strong spiritual and specifically Christian dimension' (p. 2). Their detailed analysis underlines the Counter-Reformation spirituality displayed by the play and its author, and even notes some specifically Marian references: Partenia's submission on the one hand to an ideal of virginity, but ultimately to the overriding will of her father Ergasto, is expressed via deliberate echoes of the biblical Annunciation/*Magnificat* text.

Whether the play was ever performed, or indeed intended for performance, remains uncertain on the strength of current evidence. Lisa Sampson links it with a tendency for female-authored and female-oriented dramas to be either staged privately in 'closet' conditions, or else publicly recited without staging. Further research may one day give clearer answers to this sort of question. Meanwhile, we at least now have an impeccable edition of Barbara Torelli's full text.

University of Leeds   Richard Andrews

Comico e modernità nel 'Discorso del riso' di Basilio Paravicino. By Florinda Nardi. Lecce: Pensa Multimedia. 2010. 230 pp. €18. ISBN 978-88-8232-809-2.

This book analyses and reproduces one of the numerous albeit less-known treatises on the comic and, more specifically, on laughter, which were written in the second half of the sixteenth century. As the second element in the title suggests, Florinda Nardi's discourse is intended to demonstrate the modernity of Paravicino's ideas in this field. Therefore, she first illustrates the main theories on the comic which precede the composition (in 1574) and the later publication (by Girolamo Frova in 1595) of the *Discorso del riso*. The Renaissance debate on the comic received new stimuli from the discovery of Aristotle's *Poetics* at the end of the fifteenth century. In the following scholarly production, two different but complementary tendencies can be traced, one aiming at commentary and explanation of the Aristotelian text, the other using it as a model for the definition of comedy as well as other related literary genres (short stories, satires, and epigrams). Nardi emphasizes the crucial points of this debate: the controversial question regarding the purpose of the comic, which for some scholars (Robortello, Castelvetro) mostly lies in amusing (*delectare*) the reader/spectator, while for others (Maggi, Trissino, Piccolomini, Cinzio) in benefiting (*prodesse*) him; the interpretation of a thorny concise passage of the Aristotelian text regarding the subject of the comic, namely the imitation of 'the worst men', and its suitability; and finally, the central role played by the Academies (of the Intronati, Alterati, Umoristi, etc.) in which many of the scholars involved in such discussions operated. In the second chapter, analysing the appreciative letter by Paravicino's friend Paolo Manuzio, which accompanies the *Discorso*, as well as the proemium, Nardi highlights the original elements. Writing in Italian, Paravicino, who studied in Padua and worked as a doctor at the papal court, adopted a scientific approach to give an exhaustive explanation of the nature of laughter, which no one had attempted before him. The main points of the thirteen brief chapters comprising the treatise are subsequently examined. Referring to the Aristotelian method, Paravicino defines laughter through the description of its effects and argues that its main purpose is to relieve tension in the mind. As a specific characteristic of human beings, true laughter (not laughter simulated or induced by tickling) is a passion of the sensitive soul which is excited by unexpected cheerfulness (*allegrezza*). This element, which shows many similarities with the idea of wonder (*admiratio*) introduced by Maggi in his *De ridiculis* (1550), is not a manifestation of ignorance, but rather a means of acquiring knowledge (though such a question is not analysed systematically by Paravicino). Laughter is provoked by the spectacle of unseemly things that according to tradition are related either to body or to mind, whereas those related to external circumstances are omitted as not necessary. A physiological explanation of laughter, based on the ancient models (Galen) rather than contemporary new scientific achievements, is illustrated through the theory of the vital spirits which depart from the heart once it is cheered, to reach the other parts of the body. With a penchant for classification that will be more evident in baroque writers, Paravicino distinguishes four professions of men to whom exciting laughter is suitable: witty poets, comics, orators, and courtiers. In particular, the inclusion of comic actors, who, however, must avoid obscene and scornful behaviour, is in opposition to the strict attitude of the Counter-Reformation towards comedy. Nardi's analysis is followed by biographical and bibliographical information regarding Paravicino, the reprint of the text of the *Discorso* contained in a miscellany kept at the Biblioteca Centrale of Rome, and a bibliography including treatises on the subject published in Italy in the sixteenth and seventeenth centuries.

Nardi's work is of great interest because it provides access to an important document in the study of Renaissance discussions on the comic. Unfortunately, the start of the thirteenth and final chapter is missing in the edition of Paravicino's text, while the second part of the previous chapter (p. 48) is reproduced twice. Two main aspects of this commendable volume are questionable, the first concerning the originality of Paravicino's work. Before him, a similar Aristotelian approach to the subject is shown by Maggi, who, in the third part of *De ridiculis*, illustrates the questions about laughter omitted by Cicero in *De oratore* (II. 58). Maggi defines unintentional laughter as the wonder one feels in the face of harmless unseemly things, the purpose being to give the mind respite from the process of reasoning. It is explained as a dilation of the heart causing the vital spirits to be released and the face to contract. Secondly, it seems to me that a treatment of the comic should also include the contemporary (negative) reception of Aristophanes' model, which might explain the patchy diffusion of Aristophanic texts. Although the Greek comedian was not completely unknown to Tuscan authors in the first half of the fifteenth century (Leonardo Bruni, Rinuccio Aretino), the *editio princeps* of all his plays was printed by Aldo Manuzio only in 1498. In the treatises by Vittore Fausto (*De comoedia libellus*, 1511) and Robortello (*Explicationes de satyra, de epigrammate, de comoedia, de salibus*, 1548), both containing references to the three phases of Greek comedy, the satirical function and scornful language of Aristophanes' plays are clearly rejected in favour of the Latin model (Terence). Not surprisingly, this type of theatre was not considered in line with the idea of the comic deriving from Cicero and Aristotle.

ROYAL HOLLOWAY, UNIVERSITY OF LONDON   MATTEO FAVARETTO

Aesthetic Modernism and Masculinity in Fascist Italy. By JOHN CHAMPAGNE. London and New York: Routledge. 2013. viii+221 pp. £85. ISBN 978-0-415-52862-7.

This study takes as its complex subject the evolving vocabularies of aesthetic modernism and the queer representation of masculinities in Italian art, music, and literature. Supplementing works such as Barbara Spackman's *Fascist Virilities: Rhetoric, Ideology and Social Fantasy in Italy* (Minneapolis and London: University of Minnesota Press, 1996), Lorenzo Benadusi's *Il nemico dell'uomo nuovo: l'omosessualità nell'esperimento totalitario fascista* (Milan: Feltrinelli, 2005; trans. by Suzanne Dingee and Jennifer Pudney as *The Enemy of the New Man: Homosexuality in Fascist Italy* (Madison: University of Wisconsin Press, 2012)), and Derek Duncan's *Reading and Writing Italian Homosexuality: A Case of Possible Difference* (Aldershot: Ashgate, 2006), in often productive and striking ways, it extends critical debate on the construction and representation of masculinities, and on the role that different artistic media played as spaces in which some of the contradictions of the Fascist project were articulated and exposed. The study is also concerned with the relationship between Fascism and global capitalism, and poses some searching questions:

How can we square the fascist regime's overt critique of American-style consumerism with its desire to compete in a world economy that was itself being significantly restructured by that consumerism? How do Italian fascist representations of masculinity respond to the competing demands of nationalism and the early twentieth-century's 'insertion' of the Western male subject 'into the new circuits of commodity culture and consumer desire', with their contradictory understanding of maleness? (p. 10)

John Champagne's analysis strives to move beyond facile labels of art or its creators as Fascist/anti-Fascist, homo/heterosexual, but instead identifies and explores the queer aspects of a range of texts, from different disciplines, which, taken together, indicate the presence of a discourse on masculinity that troubled dominant Fascist narratives, and revealed their inherent inconsistencies.

After an engaging introduction, Champagne provides a helpful overview of scholarship on the tensions inherent in and between Fascism, modernism, and capitalism; this is followed by four further chapters which analyse works which were either produced during the Fascist regime or set in the *ventennio*. He devotes one chapter to Luigi Pirandello's plays, showing how they reveal a 'masculinity in crisis' that, if not overtly anti-Fascist, certainly disrupted its narratives (p. 45); in the next he discusses visual art, focusing on homoeroticism in paintings by Filippo de Pisis, Carlo Carrà, Mario Maffai, Alberto Ziveri, Giuseppe Capogrossi, and Guglielmo Janni, which seem to tread a fine line between illustrating and subverting Fascist ideals of masculinity. He then turns to music, and the Jewish composer Mario Castelnuovo-Tedesco, who was first acclaimed by the Regime and then driven to emigrate to America by the 1938 Racial Laws. Champagne analyses Castelnuovo-Tedesco's 1936 unpublished and unrecorded setting to music of Walt Whitman's 'Calamus' songs, which, he suggests, can be seen to deploy Whitman's verses in such a way that they both mimic Fascist aesthetics and function as a 'coded insurgency' against the Regime (p. 147). Finally, he considers Giorgio Bassani's novels, arguing that their narrators are neither homosexual nor heterosexual but queer, and exploring the relationship between non-normative masculinity and Jewish identity.

Champagne's study constitutes an important contribution to debate in several respects: it amplifies discussion in innovative, interdisciplinary ways, bringing some striking and, in some cases, largely forgotten works and artists to our attention; it traces discourses of masculinity across different media, while providing insights into their specific, formal idioms; it engages with a broad range of critical debates, developing them or showing, crucially, how even relatively recent studies may either remain blind to questions of homosexuality or else take a problematic view of its representation; it uses queer theory productively to complicate binary understandings of masculinity, desire, and political sympathies; it brings a critical sensitivity to issues of race and class. The theoretical range of reference is broad and variegated, including queer theory, cultural studies, psychoanalysis, and historical materialism, which Champagne handles deftly on the whole, although at times his prose is a little dense. The ambitious scope of the book means that it does occasionally strain slightly at the seams. Despite the author's best intentions, the link between the earlier contextualizing chapter on capitalism and Fascism, and the textual analysis, is not always clear, as Champagne himself obliquely acknowledges (p. 150). This is particularly evident in the conclusion, which seems to pull in several different directions. However, on the whole this is a compelling, rich, and provocative study that provides plenty of food for thought and invites further investigation in this vein.

UNIVERSITY OF BIRMINGHAM   CHARLOTTE ROSS

German Colour Terms: A Study in their Historical Evolution from Earliest Times to the Present. By WILLIAM JERVIS JONES. (Studies in the History of the Language Sciences, 119) Amsterdam and Philadelphia: Benjamins. 2013. xiv+663 pp. €110; $165. ISBN 978-90-272-4610-3.

This monograph concerns the way in which colour terms in the history of German relate to cultural factors and word-formation processes. It draws on material collected in the author's five-volume *Historisches Lexikon deutscher Farbbezeichnungen* (Berlin: Akademie Verlag), which also appeared in 2013. *German Colour Terms* is a work of the highest quality: it is clearly written and laid out, meticulously researched, and it represents a successful attempt to organize and interpret the material assembled in the *Lexikon*. The work also helps to fill a major gap in the literature.

Part 1, 'Colour Linguistics from a German Perspective', summarizes the three main schools of thought in colour nomenclature. The now discarded evolutionary view put forward by, among others, William Ewart Gladstone in his work on Homer is that simplistic colour terms in early cultures bear witness to an underdeveloped colour perception. The relativist approach, in line with the work of Edward Sapir and Benjamin Lee Whorf in the first half of the twentieth century, holds that colour perception is partly conditioned by natural language, and so varies from one language to another. The third main school, universalism, maintains that colour perception is innate and common to all, and universalists have argued that languages consistently encode certain colours first; these basic colours have abstract names (terms such as *red*), as opposed to object-bound terms such as *orange*. Universalists have also tried to demonstrate that the focal points of basic colour terms are constant and universal. In recent work on colour nomenclature, attempts have been made to integrate relativist and universalist approaches, and the author seems to sympathize with a balanced viewpoint, adopting an 'open theoretical framework' (p. 44). In Part 1 we are also introduced to key concepts in colour theory: the distinction between chromatic values (or 'hues'), e.g. red, green, blue, and achromatic values, i.e. black, white, and grey (both sets are considered in colour theory); and two other dimensions of colour: saturation, i.e. the degree to which a hue differs from grey, and brightness. As a survey of approaches to the relationship between colour terms and colour perception, Part 1 is important scene-setting for what is to come, but most of the rest of the book is in fact devoted to the relationship between colour terms on the one hand, and cultural factors and morphological processes on the other.

Part 2, 'Cultural Aspects of Colour Naming and Inventorisation in German', gives an account of colour nomenclatures used in practical applications (e.g. astronomy/ astrology, medicine, the human body, cosmetics, painting, dyeing, fashion). It also charts the principal approaches to the theoretical classification of colour from Greek and Roman times to the present. The sections on the seventeenth century and the Enlightenment are especially detailed. The seventeenth century marks a significant shift towards the systematic classification of colours. However, the basis on which writers constructed their systems could vary considerably. For Schottel, writing in the middle of the seventeenth century, the basis was morphological: the distinction between 'Haubtfarben' and other colours corresponded to that between, on the one hand, simplex words, e.g. *roht*, *weiß*, and, on the other hand, word formations, e.g. *flachsfärbig*, for which, he believed, German was uniquely well equipped. For Schottel's contemporary Harsdörffer, on the other hand, the distinction between basic and other colour terms had a more scientific foundation: he distinguished five colours as basic—white, black, yellow, red, and blue—because other colours could be mixed from them. Enlightenment theories continued the scientific approach to colour, but they were shaped by new discoveries, notably Newton's prismatic analysis of white light into coloured beams. Enlightenment theorists also sought to establish correspondences between colour systems and systems in other fields, for example those of musical scales or of the vocalic systems of language. One section in Part 2 shows how Goethe objected to Newton's purely objective analysis of colour, and paid particular attention to the interaction between colour and perception, which led him to devise a number of (not always consistent) colour categorizations. Part 2 is an excellent guide to the development of colour systems in the German-speaking world. It will be valuable for specialists from other disciplines, including cultural and art historians; and for anyone interested in the relationship between colour theories and the wider intellectual movements in which they were formulated, this account will provide an outstanding foundation.

Part 3, 'Linguistic Aspects of German Colour Lexis', is 'the core of the present work' (p. 529). It opens with a review of recent classificatory systems for German colour terms, before offering a diachronic account of the main simplex colour words (as opposed to compounds or derivations) in each of the standard segments of the history and prehistory of German: Proto-Indo-European (PIE), Proto-Germanic (PGmc), Old High German (OHG), Middle High German (MHG), Early New High German (ENHG), and New High German (NHG). Reconstructions for the PIE period are used to test the universalist hypothesis that the basic colour terms are encoded first, but the evidence is inconclusive. It is true that the roots that have been reconstructed for PIE denote some of the colours expected by universalists to be encoded first. However, for black and white, which are among the most basic terms in universalism, there are no consistent PIE roots. The analysis of colour names after PIE begins with the PGmc antecedents of terms which were to become prominent in German: *blank, blau, bleich, braun, fahl, gelb, grau, greis, grün, rot, schwarz,* and *weiß.* Among these, the PGmc terms for chromatic values (as opposed to achromatic values or brightness) are likely to have had a wider denotational range than their later counterparts, and two of these stand out for other reasons: the PGmc antecedent of *braun,* linked etymologically to a verb meaning 'to burn', denotes both hue and brightness, and the antecedent of *grün,* probably an adjective from the verb meaning 'to grow', denotes not only hue, but also vitality. After PGmc, the development of colour vocabulary places emphasis increasingly on chromatic distinctions. Thus, *braun* and *grün* lose their other senses, while new words, largely borrowings originally denoting colour vectors, are recruited to enlarge the set of simplex terms; these include *lila, orange, pink, purpur, rosa, scharlach, türkis,* and *violett.* In this section Jones supplements evidence from secondary sources with abundant material from his own database.

The next section of Part 3 analyses transferred (symbolic and connotative) uses of the main colour names, and their hyponyms, across all periods. The older abstract terms each show a greater range of transferred meanings than the object-bound younger ones. For example, in the field of human moods and qualities alone, *rot* has been associated with joy, grief, anger, sickness, injury, shame, love, falsehood, among others. The transferred uses for *orange,* by contrast, are limited to a national marker in the Netherlands, and the political independence movement in Ukraine in the early twenty-first century. In this section the author demonstrates how unstable the transferred uses of the principal colour terms are, and he acknowledges that 'all-embracing semantic classifications have not yet been devised' (p. 406)—a clear challenge to future researchers.

Having provided a history of simplex colour terms in German, Part 3 proceeds to an analysis of colour word formations. Adjectival compounds are grouped by semantic function, with a diachronic treatment within each category: additive (e.g. MHG *rôtgrüene*), causal/temporal (e.g. *fiebergelb, winterweiß*), comparative (e.g. OHG *bluotrôt*), intensifying (e.g. *kohlpechschwarz*), and modificative (e.g. *scharfblau*). At this point Jones discusses exocentric compounds, both those which form adjectives of the type [adj+noun=adj], such as MHG *valevahs* 'fair-haired' (along the lines of NHG *barfuß* or Modern English *barefoot*), and those which form nouns of the type [adj+noun=noun], such as *Rothaar* (used of a person). Next, adjective derivations are grouped by affix, i.e. morphologically rather than semantically. Some affixes, such as *hoch-, voll-,* and *-haft(ig)* are widely used in word formation across all semantic fields, while others, such as *hell-, knall-,* are found particularly in colour formations. The author uses the term 'affixoid' as a label for morphemes, such as *Knall/knall-,* which are in a transitional state between compound constituent and affix (*Knall* as a free morpheme means 'bang, crack', but in colour word formations *knall-* means 'bright'). In fact, the author classes some formations both as compounds and as derivations (e.g. *knallblau* on pages 420 and 431), and further research might explore where, or at least how, to draw the line between compound constituents and affixoids in colour vocabulary. Jones comments on noun compounds and derivations only briefly. As he writes of noun compounds, '[t]he material is infinite' (p. 450), and it is clear that a detailed discussion of nominal word formation would have taken the work to unmanageable lengths. However, this is fertile ground for future research: the relationship between types of nominal word formation and their denotative and connotative functions is one possible line of enquiry.

The final main section of the book concerns verb word formation. Verbs predicate not only states, but also changes, of colour, and Jones begins this section by distinguishing between the various *Aktionsarten* (or 'lexical aspects') of verbs (stative, inchoative, terminative, etc.). Many colour verbs are unprefixed conversions from colour adjectives (e.g. MHG *brûn* → *briunen*, *rôt* → *rœten*), and they may be assigned to a number of different *Aktionsart* categories unless disambiguated in context. Thus, *rœten* may be factitive-causative ('to make red'), durative-stative ('to be red') or inchoative-evolutive ('to become (more) red'). Here the author draws on his own *Lexikon* to provide valuable detail about the *Aktionsart* of such verbs, including the finding that it is rarely possible to define them unambiguously as durative-stative. This may reflect the existence of competing expressions combining the verb 'to be' with colour adjectives (*ist rôt* etc.), which are always durative-stative. Indeed, there is an illuminating section 'Verbal vs. Adjectival Exponence of Colour', in which the author discusses the view, associated with the twentieth-century German relativist Leo Weisgerber and others, that the use of verbs (as opposed to adjectives) to denote colour coincides with the perception that colour emanates dynamically from objects. Colour verbs with prefixes (*an-*, *be-*, *durch-*, *er-*, *ge-*, *ver-*, etc.) are also surveyed, but there is no clear evidence that the semantic and syntactic function of these prefixes in colour words is different from their functions generally.

German Colour Terms is an exemplary piece of scholarship. Colour classification is a highly complex topic, which involves the interaction between the perception, interpretation, and lexicalization of referents (colours) which themselves combine a number of dimensions (hue, saturation, and brightness). A diachronic approach introduces further complication, and yet the author has brought order to this almost chaotic semantic field, and done so with clarity and rigour. Given its subject matter the book could have done with some colour plates, or links to a companion website with colour illustrations, but this is a minor quibble about what is a major contribution to the historical lexicology of German. As Jones points out, his work raises questions for future researchers, and it is to be hoped that he and the publishers of the *Lexikon* make his database available. Some specific lines of enquiry have been mentioned above, but there is also a broader research opportunity, which bears on the relativist–universalist debate. It is clear, in the light of the material assembled in this book, that cultural and historical factors affect colour nomenclature—dyeing is just one example—and neither relativists nor universalists would contest this. The real bone of contention between the two schools concerns the relationship between the perception of colour and colour terms. In his concluding remarks Jones sees 'no reason [. . .] to doubt the co-existence in colour perception of neurophysically determined universals *and* relativistic effects' (p. 530). Although this conclusion appears justified in the light of the material assembled, further research might allow us to measure the contribution of these two effects more precisely. For example, to test systematically whether the main colours are encoded in the history of German in the order which the universalists expect, we might use linguistic proxies for the 'basicness' of colour terms, such as their freedom to inflect fully, their readiness to form comparatives and superlatives, and their availability to take part in word formation (all characteristics which the author mentions in passing). Or, in order to situate the focal points of basic colour terms, which universalists expect to be constant, we might analyse the names used at different times for referents whose colour is likely to have remained stable (e.g. objects in the natural world). This would be a major undertaking, but if anyone attempted such a study, *German Colour Terms*, and the author's *Historisches Lexikon deutscher Farbbezeichnungen*, would be indispensable resources.

KEBLE COLLEGE   HOWARD JONES

Diskurslinguistik im Spannungsfeld von Deskription und Kritik. Ed. by ULRIKE HANNA MEINHOF, MARTIN REISIGL, and INGO H. WARNKE. (Diskursmuster — Discourse Patterns) Berlin: Akademie Verlag. 2013. 430 pp. €99.80. ISBN 978-3-05-005843-6.

Since the pragmatic turn in the 1970s, the study of discourse has become a major endeavour in Germanic Linguistics, leading to the development of new research fields, most notably Discourse Linguistics (DL) and Critical Discourse Analysis (CDA). While both aim at a better understanding of how discourse reflects and constitutes social practice, they seem to approach the issue with diverging methodological and analytical paradigms. Whereas DL is concerned with the description of language use and tends to refrain from critical and/or prescriptive opinions, CDA takes examples of language usage as a means to explicitly critique socio-political reality. This has led to an understanding that DL and CDA are two opposing camps that 'cannot talk to each other'. As the editors of the present volume argue, this is a serious misconception that does not reflect the intellectual endeavours which underpin much of the work undertaken in both fields. The primary aims of this volume are, therefore, to demonstrate that description and critique are mutually dependent research components and that both DL and CDA share more similarities than differences.

The collection, which consists of sixteen articles, begins with an introduction that reassesses the binary opposition between description and critique, culminating in seven statements at the end that summarize the futility of such an opposition. Assessing discursive constructions of the financial crises in press discourse, Martin Wengeler then takes as an example a case study of dominant topoi in the constructions of the financial crises of 1982 and 2003 in *Der Spiegel*. The analysis reveals that media representations share a number of topoi, especially that of 'gloom' in present times, but that the topos of 'incompetent politicians', which dominates the discourse of the 2003 crisis, is absent in 1982. Nina Janich and Anne Simmerling focus specifically on the discursive representations of *Nichtwissen* in decisions about the implementation of a highly controversial environmental experiment, carefully analysing lexical patterns in a range of media, academic, governmental, and non-governmental texts. In the third essay, by looking at the media discourse surrounding the PISA study, Ina Karg demonstrates how the notion of *Bildung* is highly instrumentalized and ultimately dominated by cost–benefit analysis. Investigating an area traditionally in the domain of CDA research, in his 'Graswurzelanalyse' entitled 'Kritische Diskursgrammatik?' Marcus Müller studies the relationship between power and language, basing his analysis on a systematic, corpus-based description of a smaller language feature such as the possessive determiner in the first-person plural in the context of a bioethics debate.

Noah Bubenhofer and Joachim Scharloth explore the potential for Corpus Linguistics methodology to analyse discourse, illustrating the advantages of corpus methods by examining key words, complex n-grams and visualizations of language data in a diachronic corpus of texts on Alpine mountaineering: the visualization aspect provides a new perspective on how corpus data could be used to depict connections that are not immediately visible to the naked eye. Philipp Dreesen's essay, 'Kritik als Erkenntnismodus', draws on Kant's Doctrine of Method and Horkheimer's critical theory to support the preservation of the opposition between critique and description by simultaneously offering four ways of how critique can be integrated into DL. Gesine Lenore Schiewer, in 'Discourse and the City', gives welcome attention to a neglected area of Discourse Analysis, suggesting that the inequalities and fragmentation implied by the rise of global cities call for a critical approach (and a linguistic description of the dominant discourses) to expose power relations and patterns of domination and injustice.

The contribution by Helga Kotthoff, 'Mario Barths Späße rund um Geschlechterstereotypen', discusses the role of gender ideology as a factor in comedy. By drawing on CDA and Conversational Analysis, she examines stand-up by the comedian Mario Barth, demonstrating that his performances draw heavily on clichéd images of femininity and masculinity, and that by employing excessive stylization, he perpetuates existing asymmetries. In another very different paper on humour later in the volume, Silvia Bonacchi undertakes an analysis of a satirical text published in *Die Tageszeitung* in 2006 describing a former Polish president as a potato, triggering diplomatic tensions in its Polish translation. By adopting the DIMEAN model, Bonacchi shows how the satirical and ironic tone of the *TAZ* article is lost in the translated version, which instead foregrounds taboo words and topics. Andreas Rothenhöfer calls for more research into the historical and contextual factors determining the meaning of key words and phrases in political discourse. By drawing on the iconic and indexical function of linguistic signs, he highlights the role of context and co-text in the change of lexical meanings, demonstrated by looking at four examples: capitalism, democracy, *Stunde Null*, and triplet forms in slogans.

Friedemann Vogel's 'Linguistische Diskursanalyse als engagierte Wissenschaft' starts with the observation that there are two types of criticism practised by DL and

CDA, language critique (DL) and social critique (CDA), suggesting that it is the latter form that DL needs to consider as a form of engagement with social practice. In the wake of Bourdieu, he proposes a rethinking of DL as a theory of practice as practice. Following the approach of *histoire de mentalités*, Simon Meier attempts to reconstruct the normative conceptions that have shaped the concept of *Gespräch* since 1945, using key linguistic and philosophical texts to show how *Gespräch* was gradually constructed as a form of symbolic talk associated with empathy and reconciliation, and as a force binding a community together. It is not a coincidence that such normative conceptions occurred after 1945, mostly in opposition to the dominant Anglo-American communication form of discussion. This study provides a good example of earlier claims that even supposedly neutral linguistic terms such as *Gespräch* are discursive constructs embedded in historical and social contexts and shaped by dominant norms and values. Outlining key theoretical and methodological principles of Contrastive Discourse Linguistics, Waldemar Czachur then argues that comparative descriptions are inherently critical in that they juxtapose different norms and means of expressing meanings. Critique here is understood as a means of raising awareness of linguistic strategies used to construct social phenomena. In 'Stil im Diskurs' Stefan Meier combines a number of semiotic and linguistic concepts such as those developed by the Oldenburg School, calling for a stronger consideration of the poststructuralist critical theories, especially the claim for *Alternativdenken*. This perspective is then adopted by examining different forms of stylization in fragments of online discourse. By drawing on Functional Pragmatics, Stephanie Risse explores the role of the nominal phrase 'das Land' in public discourse in South Tyrol. Her critical analysis highlights a whole range of political and social meanings with which the phrase is associated in this region, and that a purely descriptive approach would not reveal. The final contribution, Tina Deist's 'Intra- und interkultureller Wissenstransfer im Menschenrechtsdiskurs', points to problems in conveying the supposedly universal claims of human rights to lay audiences, and by analysing various digests of human rights, she reveals the transformation undertaken in these intertexts. In the second part of her article she turns to issues emerging in the intercultural reception of human rights by comparing the Arab Charter on Human Rights with the Universal Declaration of Human Rights.

This substantial volume tackles methodological and analytical issues of real significance and that have seen a two-way split in discourse studies in the German-speaking context. It brings together an impressive selection of papers that demonstrate the potential of integrating both description and critique in studying discourse. In so doing, each paper—some more overtly than others—builds bridges between DL and CDA and points to synergies that arise when the opposition between description and critique is suspended. To help the reader to navigate through this diverse selection, it might have been more helpful to have divided the volume into sections and to have edited the essays to promote more cross-referencing. These minor concerns aside, the volume is an inspiring contribution to anyone interested in discourse studies irrespective of their leaning towards CDA or DL.

UNIVERSITY OF READING   SYLVIA JAWORSKA

The Faustian Century: German Literature and Culture in the Age of Luther and Faustus. Ed. by J. M. VAN DER LAAN and ANDREW WEEKS. (Studies in German Literature, Linguistics, and Culture) Rochester, NY: Camden House. 2013. xi+399 pp. £60. ISBN 978-1-57113-552-0.

A welcome addition even to the existing enormous body of literature on the Faust theme, this volume comprises thirteen essays, written by an international team of highly respected scholars, focusing chiefly on the anonymous 1587 Faust Book, *Historia von D. Johann Fausten, dem weitbeschreyten Zauberer und Schwartzkünstler* [...], published by Johann Spies at Frankfurt am Main, and related contemporary texts (the Wolfenbüttel manuscript dating from between 1572 and 1585, the *Wagnerbuch* of 1593, and so on). Above all, the contributors are concerned to locate the text amid the tensions of what they call 'the Faustian century' and to examine it as it were with sixteenth-century eyes, rather than from a post-Enlightenment, post-Goethean, modern perspective. 'Does Faustus signify the rebellion of the new sciences against religious authority or the rejection of Renaissance humanism, the obscurantism of the Reformation or the latent nihilism of the dawning modern age?' (p. 17) are some of the questions Andrew Weeks poses in the first essay, which surveys the dimensions of 'the Faustian century'. Each of the contributors addresses such issues in his or her own way; no consensus is achieved, but as a whole the volume represents a stimulating contribution to the ongoing scholarly debate.

Three of the contributions discuss the origins of the Faust figure and the early growth of the Faust myth. Frank Baron revisits the familiar ground of the various references to a historical Faust, showing how there is reason to believe that an original Georg(ius)/Jörg Helmstetter from Helmstadt (postcode 74921, near Heidelberg, not 97264 Helmstadt near Würzburg), first attested at Heidelberg university in 1483, came to be credited with additional, mostly unsavoury characteristics during the early decades of the sixteenth century, thanks not least to Abbot Johannes Trithemius (1462-1516) and the Würzburg canon Daniel Stiebar (1503-1555), as well as Luther, Melanchthon, and others. Against such a background, the 1587 Faust Book came to be written 'by an ardent Lutheran who opposed the prominence of Melanchthon, whom many at this time had considered a traitor to Luther's cause' (p. 55). In an addendum (pp. 62-64) Baron firmly—and surely rightly—rebuts the claim, promoted principally by Günther Mahal, former director of the Faust Museum at Knittlingen, that Faustus hailed from that town (near Melanchthon's birthplace, Bretten), which today steadfastly describes itself on its official website as 'Fauststadt im Herzen des Naturparks Stromberg-Heuchelberg'. The next two chapters, covering less familiar ground, are especially valuable. First, Michael Keefer investigates the relevance of the controversial occultist Agrippa of

Nettesheim (1486–1535) for the evolution of the Faust story, showing how he and his ideas slotted into the broader cultural climate of the 'Faustian century'; then Urs Gantenbein examines how the association of the contemporary figures of Paracelsus (1493–1541) and Trithemius with magical practices intertwined and blended with existing knowledge of Faustus to help shape the legend. Of ancillary interest is the discussion of how the image of Paracelsus was lastingly shaped by the views of his critics, Thomas Erastus, the printer Johannes Oporinus, Heinrich Bullinger, and Conrad Gesner (pp. 105–13).

J. M. van der Laan is less concerned with historical figures—he is pretty dismissive of the case advanced for Georg Helmstetter, saying that Faust is 'more sign and symbol than historical person' (p. 130). His interest is in the early growth of the fictionalized life of Faustus. *En passant*, it is worth noting that van der Laan points out that the earliest attestation of the name Mephistophiles in connection with Faustus is to be found in the *Praxis Magica FaustiAna* (Weimar, Herzogin Anna Amalia Bibliothek, MS Q 455), which he firmly believes to have been written in or soon after 1527, whereas Hans Henning in his *Faust-Bibliographie* (Berlin and Weimar: Aufbau, 1966), I, 434, held it to be an eighteenth-century product.

The next three essays deal with what may be loosely called theological aspects of the story. In seeking to identify the aesthetic merits of the Faust Book which many earlier scholars have found utterly elusive, Marguerite de Huszar Allen revisits the long-held thesis that Faustus is a kind of anti-saint (an idea that can be traced back at least to an article by Susan Snyder on Marlowe's *Doctor Faustus* in 1966). His story is the antithesis of a saint's legend of the kind included in Jacobus de Voragine's *Legenda aurea*. Whereas Catholic legends depicted saints who, through God's mercy, triumph over all tribulations and gain salvation, in the Faust Book the focus shifts from saint to sinner, God to the Devil, faith to despair, from salvation to damnation. Such an inversion ties in with Luther's rejection of saints' legends. An especially valuable contribution is that by Kresten Thue Andersen, who analyses theological elements in the Faust Book, notably repentance and faith, in relation to the Augsburg Confession of 1530. Particularly interesting is the distinction he makes between the narrator's and the protagonist's horizons of expectation in regard to Faustus's situation and ultimate fate. Another important theme in the Faust Book is marriage; indeed, as Paul Ernst Meyer notes, it serves as 'a structural lynchpin' (p. 208; he means 'linchpin' of course) in the text. Contrasting with Bettina Mathes's interpretation of the work, in an article published in 2000, as a heterosexual pornographic fantasy, Meyer offers a sober assessment of the representation of marriage and sex in the Faust Book, examining them in the context of changing attitudes in the Reformation period. In what is arguably the most stimulating essay in the whole volume, Andrew Weeks sees the Faust Book as set against a climate of anticlericalism and the rejection of educational elitism, usefully comparing it with Valentin Weigel's *Dialogus de Christianismo* (1584) and indeed with Jacob Bidermann's *Cenodoxus* (1602) too.

The final four essays focus on various aspects of the problem of knowledge. Helen Watanabe-O'Kelly investigates Faustus's engagement with magic, alchemy, and astrology, setting these concerns in the context of real-life interest in such disciplines among sixteenth-century contemporaries (not least at Rudolph II's court at Prague as well as the Elector of Saxony's at Dresden). No book on Faust would be complete without a thorough consideration of the Devil, through whom Faustus seeks to acquire knowledge. For Luther and others the Devil was a concrete reality. Albrecht Classen gives a wide-ranging review of the Devil in late medieval and early modern writing, from the fourteenth-century Innsbruck Easter Play via the so-called 'devil books' of the sixteenth century to Johan Riemer's *Erz-Verläumder und Ehe-Teuffel von Schottland* (1679). Whereas Classen adds relatively little to our understanding of the 1587 text and the 1593 *Wagnerbuch*, Günther Bonheim's discussion of the nature and role of the Devil in the Faust Book is helpfully illuminated by analysis of writings by Jacob Böhme (1575–1624), notably his *Aurora* and his *Trost-Spiegel*, in which the Devil serves to illustrate the idea that evil is the essential opposite of good. In the final essay (previously published in German), Karl Guthke confronts 'the puzzling geographical backwardness of the *Faustbuch*' (p. 325), compared with the *Wagnerbuch*. Faustus sets out to explore 'the whole world', yet—nearly a century after Columbus—this still excluded America. One explanation may be sought in the anonymous author's sources: after all, Faustus's bizarre itinerary reflects the author's use of Hartmann Schedel's *Weltchronik* (Nuremberg, 1493), which lists the towns in question in chronological order of their supposed foundation dates. But Guthke offers a more satisfying intellectual, theological explanation for the absence of the New World: some contemporaries saw the new discoveries of the conquistadors as revelation of God's creation through 'blessed men' (p. 330), so Faustus could hardly be shown as one of these.

The book ends with a substantial chronological listing of relevant world events (from the birth of Luther in 1483 to the outbreak of the Thirty Years War in 1618) printed in a parallel column with key dates relating to Faust (from his putative birth in 1466 to the first performance of a Faust play by the Englische Komödianten at Graz in 1608). This is followed by a select bibliography, a list of contributors, and a good index. Disregarding a few minor misprints, the book is well edited, though the openings of several of the contributions tend to be somewhat repetitive in rehearsing the background and publishing history of the Faust Book. It is curious, however, that the editors did not consider the convenience of their readers and insist on contributors citing the same edition of the Spies text and referencing it in a uniform way. Most of them have used the excellent critical edition by Stephan Füssel and Hans-Joachim Kreutzer published by Reclam in 1988, but Weeks refers to it with *Historia*, van der Laan calls it S[*pies*], Watanabe-O'Kelly and Guthke call it F[*austbuch*] (or F[üssel], perhaps?), Meyer and Bonheim call it H[*istoria*], while Classen uses this abbreviation to cite J. D. Müller's Deutsche Klassiker edition (Frankfurt a.M., 1990).

INSTITUTE OF MODERN LANGUAGES RESEARCH, LONDON   JOHN L. FLOOD

Aufklärung bis zum Himmel: Emanuel Swedenborg im Kontext der Theologie des 18. Jahrhunderts. By FRIEDEMANN STENGEL. (Beiträge zur historischen Theologie, 161) Tübingen: Mohr Siebeck. 2011. xvi+802 pp. €134. ISBN 978-3-16-150965-0.

'To high heavens' is a curious collocation to use with the noun 'Enlightenment', since it is usually used with verbs of olfaction rather than intellection. Yet this paradoxical title is, in its way, entirely appropriate for a work on the complex figure of Emanuel Swedenborg, who belongs among the pantheon of eighteenth-century European intellectuals. Or at least that is where he was placed by Ernst Benz, the theologian and ecclesiastical historian whose 1948 monograph has hitherto dominated discussion of Swedenborg. In 1931 Benz had received his *Habilitation* at the University of Halle, and as it happens this new monograph by Friedemann Stengel arises from work conducted as part of a larger research project at Halle, based in its Interdisciplinary Centre for European Enlightenment Studies, into the Enlightenment in the context of modern esotericism. With *his* monograph, Stengel has moved research into Swedenborg substantially forward—and a second volume, dealing with the reception of Swedenborg at the turn of the eighteenth into the nineteenth century, is promised.

The focus of this study, however, is firmly on the reception of Swedenborg's ideas in the theological and philosophical discourses of the eighteenth century (to this extent, it might even be seen as a paradigm of impact studies…), and it will surely become the standard work in the field. In his opening chapter Stengel gives a comprehensive account of Swedenborg's professional, intellectual, and religious development, from his career as an engineer and scientist to a theologian and a seer, whose writings provided the foundation of the New Church established by followers fifteen years after Swedenborg's death. In Swedenborg's biography a turning-point is formed by his spiritual experiences of 1743–45, after which he believed he had a new (and divine) calling. Stengel explicitly refrains from any kind of evaluation, be it epistemological, systematic-theological, or psycho-historical, of the allegedly revelatory nature of Swedenborg's conversion or his claim to have acquired knowledge of a higher world; indeed, this rigorous abstention licenses a scholarly approach to Swedenborg's œuvre, without at the same time emptying it of its significance. That significance is shown to reside essentially in the reception of those writings, hence Stengel's focus on the reactions and responses of Swedenborg's immediate contemporaries—who turn out to be a surprisingly large constituency.

In the next chapter Stengel examines Swedenborg's early scientific writings, in which one can already discern the gradual formation of a *Naturphilosophie*, inasmuch as speculative principles came to play an increasingly important role amid empirical observation. As well as being interested in how to determine longitude while at sea, Swedenborg is curious about the relation between matter and mind (or between body and soul); his bullular hypothesis postulated that, within particles of water, motion was created by the *materia subtilis* between them. Following criticism of his first great theoretical works of 1721–22, Swedenborg did not publish anything further for the next twelve years: but his publications of the 1730s and 1740s demonstrate—against the contemporary background of Wolffianism, deism, and materialism—an intensification of his interest in the body–soul problem. After a lucid exposition of his subject's theological system, Stengel turns to a consideration of Swedenborg's intellectual sources, before undertaking an exhaustive analysis of the reception of his theological ideas. Among these recipients, F. C. Oetinger and Kant stand out as the most prominent, and the responses of both are discussed in detail. Oetinger, with his connections to Böhme, to Kabbalah, and to J. A. Bengel, mediates Schellingian ideas and Swabian Pietism as well as Swedenborgian thought to the esoteric tradition of the nineteenth century. In the case of Kant, the complex relation between, on the one hand, the explicit rejection of Swedenborg in *Träume eines Geistersehers* on epistemological grounds and, on the other, the adoption in Kant's lectures and in *Das Ende aller Dinge* of positions entirely compatible with Swedenborg's eschatology points to the 'subcutaneous' reception of Swedenborg in the critical philosophy. Even if Swedenborg is not exactly Kant's 'twin brother', neither is he Kant's shadowy, irrational 'other'.

The key to this monograph's success—aside from its detailed references to sources, both primary and secondary—is Stengel's shrewd methodological decision to focus on the historical, textual aspects of Swedenborg's 'spiritual world' and of contemporary accounts of his supernatural gifts. This *Literarizität* provides the basis for Stengel's rich, analytical description of Swedenborg's achievement: its context, its intellectual sources and debts. Of the many pointers for future research arising from (and, in fact, made possible by) Stengel's work, surely one of the most potentially fruitful is the issue of Swedenborg's relation to Neoplatonism. In *Oeconomia regni animalis* (1740–41)—that is, before his visionary experiences—a paradigm shift in Swedenborg's thinking can be observed, in which his Cartesian dualism is modified by a Neoplatonic conception of an *influxus* of divine life (cf. pp. 141, 154). Swedenborg's view of the soul shows the influence of Neoplatonism, inasmuch as the tradition is reflected in the medieval *Liber de spiritu et anima* (mistakenly attributed to St Augustine) and the so-called *Theology of Aristotle*, a paraphrase of extracts from Plotinus's sixth Ennead, both of which Swedenborg knew (p. 139). And in his *De commercio animae et corporis* (1769) the threefold model of the soul (as purposefulness, causality, and activity) constitutes a further example of how Swedenborg's thought was informed by Neoplatonism (p. 234). Yet Stengel also questions the view that reading Leibniz had been responsible for Swedenborg's shift from a mechanistic world-view to a more Neoplatonic one (p. 185), and he puts a further question mark over this 'Neoplatonic turn' in relation to Swedenborg's traducionist conception of the soul as something propagated by the father (p. 240), while noting that Swedenborg never seems to have noticed the connection between the *Theology of Aristotle* and the Plotinus he had read in 1705 in Marsilio Ficino's edition of 1580 (p. 345). Further on, Stengel expresses a more general scepticism about the alleged influence of Christian Kabbalah, Philo of Alexandria, Pico della Mirandola, as well as Origen, Paracelsus, and Böhme, regarding any claims of influence as based on 'phenomenological' comparisons, rather than founded on evidence of an actual textual reception (p. 406). After all, when contemporary commentators drew these comparisons, it was largely because Kabbalah and Renaissance Neoplatonism functioned as defamatory labels or markers of disapprobation (p. 417). Thus what emerges from these pages is not so much a *prophetic* Swedenborg, as a *textual* Swedenborg.

In a vision recorded in *Vera Christiana religio* (1771), Swedenborg saw the New Church as a magnificent temple, over a pearly door to which was affixed the inscription 'Nunc licet', which he interpreted as meaning 'it is permitted to enter understandingly into the mysteries of faith' (§ 508). The limitations of this programme were all too clear to Swedenborg himself: thanks to Stengel's scrupulous scholarship, we can also become aware of the limitations of those limitations, and gain a finer appreciation of Swedenborg's contribution to the theological debates of the Enlightenment period.

UNIVERSITY OF GLASGOW   PAUL BISHOP

Querdenker der Aufklärung: Studien zu Johann Georg Hamann. By SVEN-AAGE JØRGENSEN. Göttingen: Wallstein. 2013. 223 pp. €34.90. ISBN 978-3-8353-1232-6.

All thirteen of the essays in this volume have been published before, over the half-century or so spanned by Sven-Aage Jørgensen's distinguished career as a Hamann scholar. The earliest, a seminal account in English of Hamann's reception of Francis Bacon, first appeared in 1961; the most recent, a compelling examination of some of the similarities but also differences between Hamann's metacritical practice and the processes of Derridean deconstruction, was first published in 2005. In so far as the essays have contributed to the fundamental change in our image of the 'Magus im Norden' (before, an obscure irrationalist—now, an incisive metacritic), Jørgensen argues '[daß] eine Auswahlpublikation, und zwar in der ursprünglichen Gestalt, sinnvoll erschien' (p. 7).

This book is helpful for anyone trying to plot a path through Hamann's polyhistoric writings. In addition to a 'Vorwort' that usefully outlines the problems treated in the essays, Jørgensen sketches the shape of his book by organizing his selection under three headings: 'Der Polyhistor' (pp. 15–80); 'Der Hermeneutiker' (pp. 81–129); and 'Der Metakritiker' (pp. 131–219). While it is impossible to do justice to all of the 'Studien' here, I would note that common to each of them is the careful presentation of a writer and thinker who, while insisting on the transitory nature of philosophical systems, remains engrossed in the intellectual traditions of his time: rooted Socrates-wise in the fragmentary nature of human knowledge, Hamann's thinking and argumentation are nonetheless 'coherent and cogent' (p. 35).

The appreciation of such coherence and cogency is no small challenge to readers of Hamann, many of whose writings are fiendishly difficult. It is therefore appropriate that the first essay is devoted to a study of the style of the Magus. While exposing some of the inadequacies of older critical commonplaces (p. 18), Jørgensen stresses both the classical rhetorical tradition in which Hamann was steeped (focusing specifically on the *Aesthetica in nuce*, 1762) and his near-epiphanic encounter with Augustine's thoughts on Mosaic and scriptural writing style in general. A biblically inspired stylistic mixture of *genus sublime* and *genus humile* is found to be at the heart of Hamann's aesthetic programme (p. 23) and informs many of the arguments presented elsewhere in this book; it is how Hamann expresses his experience of man's corporality and of God's condescension in assuming corporeal form.

Hamann's adoption of this tradition of biblical realism is traced persuasively to his reading of James Hervey, a representative of condescension theology in England and a committed subscriber to typological exegesis. In Hamann, a similar commitment becomes an 'allgemeine[s] Auslegungsprinzip' (p. 105): typological structure is applicable not just to biblical narrative, but to all of human history. An example, as Jørgensen explains, is Hamann's identification in Socrates of a prefiguration of Christ. Furthermore, the significance of that narrative and history—God's 'text'—is fully realized only in our application of its meaning to our own lives. Thus, in one of two essays that question the extent of the affinities between Herder and Hamann, Jørgensen discovers a distinctiveness in the latter's questioning not just the 'wann, wo und wie' of history but also the 'wozu' (p. 178).

All such existential analysis for Hamann must begin with our fundamental dependence on the other, on God, and on our neighbour. In an important letter to Kant he writes: 'ich glaube wie Socrates alles, was der andere glaubt — und geh nur darauf aus, andere in ihrem Glauben zu stöhren' (cited on page 117). So, when responding to Moses Mendelssohn's criticism of *La Nouvelle Héloïse*, he is not primarily set on defending Rousseau but rather on uncovering the weaknesses in Mendelssohn's argument. By a similar token, in *Schriftsteller und Kunstrichter* (1762), Hamann calls not for the moral reform of what he describes as 'die Anarchie in der gelehrten Welt' (cited on page 156), but instead, according to Jørgensen, for a kind of satirical solidarity, based on the model of divine humility. How fitting, then, that the volume's final essay, on the neglected topic of Hamann's humour, highlights 'superbia' (p. 217) as the original sin that, failing to acknowledge our God-willed corporality, becomes the target for much of the Magus's metacritical satire.

WITTENBERG UNIVERSITY   DAVID BARRY

Gotthold Ephraim Lessing: His Life, Works, and Thought. By HUGH BARR NISBET. Oxford: Oxford University Press. 2013. xiv+734 pp. £85. ISBN 978-0-19-967947-8.

There are various reasons why a monograph on Lessing's life, work, and thought was highly desirable. Even though Lessing is a key player in various areas of German *Aufklärung*, the over seventy biographies that have appeared since Lessing's death are either not comprehensive, or outdated, or inaccurate, or a combination of all. With over 700 pages, stretching from Lessing's childhood to an outline of his reception after death, H. B. Nisbet's monograph is not only hugely comprehensive but also draws on the most up-to-date research in order to fashion an accurate picture of this author and his work in all phases of his life. Emphasis is put on the 'reciprocal interaction' (p. 5) of life and work: that is, biographical information is not only provided but also employed to discuss Lessing's writings. Moreover, the notion of life is not restricted to Lessing's 'immediate personal experience' but also incorporates the 'intellectual, social, and cultural climate of his age' (p. 6). This agenda leads to a multifaceted picture not only of Lessing's diverse life and versatile work, but also of a whole range of places and institutions in which he worked (e.g. Leipzig, Berlin, Hamburg, Wolfenbüttel) as well as of important figures with or against whom he collaborated (e.g. Gottsched, Mendelssohn, Nicolai, Ewald von Kleist, Gleim). In other words, this book on Lessing also serves as a well-informed guide to the German *Aufklärung*.

Most of the twenty-two chapters follow a similar pattern. Each opens with a concise outline of the place where Lessing spent a certain period of his life, and introduces figures who played a major role for Lessing at that time; moreover, we learn about Lessing's motives for moving to a given place, and the opportunities and problems he encountered there. In this biographical outline Nisbet resists the attempt to impose a *Bildungsroman*-style development onto a life that does not in truth show such a development; instead Lessing's biography appears as 'rather an episodic series of actions and impulses, of sudden departures and impromptu responses to situations or opinions which arouse his enthusiasm—or more often, his opposition' (p. 4). Embedded in these sometimes rapidly changing contexts are thorough explorations of the writings that came into being in a particular phase of Lessing's life. This is the point where Nisbet's study outgrows a biographical concept in the narrow sense; by leading from life to work, the biography becomes a 'reference work on Lessing's achievement as a whole' (p. 6).

The publication of Lessing's *Life, Works, and Thought* is highly desirable for yet another reason. British interest in the age of Enlightenment tends to focus on home-grown and French authors. Nisbet's excellent account of Lessing as 'the central and most representative literary figure of the German *Aufklärung*' (p. 2) will help to broaden this horizon. In fact, Lessing is the best starting point for such an endeavour, not least because he was one of the most important promoters of British literature and philosophy in German culture. His most innovative ideas on drama were influenced by up-to-date developments in British literature, his ethics were informed by English and Scottish moral philosophy, and being one of only few German authors at the time who were able to read English, he also translated a great deal into German. Lessing would have loved the idea that an outstanding English biography on him was first published in German translation (*Lessing: Eine Biographie* (Munich: Beck, 2008); reviewed in *MLR*, 104 (2009), 902–03). We should appreciate the fact that this important book is now also available in English.

DURHAM UNIVERSITY   THOMAS MARTINEC

German Freedom and the Greek Ideal: The Cultural Legacy from Goethe to Mann. By WILLIAM J. MCGRATH. Ed. by CELIA APPLEGATE, STEPHANIE FRONTZ, and SUZANNE MARCHAND. (Palgrave Studies in Cultural and Intellectual History) New York: Palgrave Macmillan. 2013. xxxv+236 pp. $95. ISBN 978-1-137-36947-5.

The intellectual historian William J. McGrath, who died in 2008 aged 71, was well known as the author of two important books, *Dionysian Art and Popular Politics in Austria* (New Haven: Yale University Press, 1974) and *Freud's Discovery of Psychoanalysis: The Politics of Hysteria* (Ithaca, NY: Cornell University Press, 1986). By the time of his death he had virtually completed a manuscript on a very different subject—the specifically German conception of freedom, illustrated from Goethe's *Faust II*, the neoclassical architecture of Gottfried Semper, Wagner's *Ring*, and the works of Nietzsche and Thomas Mann.

By contrast with an Anglo-American notion of freedom as unbridled activity in the outer world, the German conception, for which McGrath refers especially to Kant, stresses the self-mastery and autonomy of the individual. 'Der moralisch gebildete Mensch, und nur dieser, ist ganz frei', says Schiller in *Über das Erhabene*. This autonomy is compatible with considerable external restrictions. Thus Kant tells us in 'Was ist Aufklärung?' that enlightened freedom is unimpaired by the need to obey Frederick the Great. Such a conception produces interesting tensions when it encounters a revolutionary demand for freedom from external constraint, and McGrath focuses on a series of such tensions.

In *Faust II* the protagonist gradually gains self-mastery through the experience of beauty (Helena), culminating in his final vision of a future free society. Along the way, Goethe responds with qualified sympathy to the Greek independence movement, to which he alludes in the difficult passage beginning 'Welche dies Land gebar' (*Faust*, l. 9843). McGrath tells how Goethe mocked the theoretical philhellenism of the London Greek Committee, which thought British liberal institutions could be transferred wholesale to Greece, and sympathized instead with the revolutionary aristocrat Lord Byron. However, in the self-destructive figure of Euphorion, Goethe associated Byron with the wild, directionless search for freedom that he deplored in the Greeks. McGrath's account of *Faust* enables one to understand better the conception of disciplined freedom formulated in the lines: 'Nur der verdient sich Freiheit wie das Leben, | Der täglich sie erobern muß' (11575–76).

McGrath then shows compellingly how a similar balance between freedom and discipline governs the architectural theories of Gottfried Semper and, especially, his decorative programme for the Kunsthistorisches Museum in Vienna. Although Semper sympathized with the revolutions of 1830 and 1848, his views about political freedom are not explored. As a friend of Wagner, however, he provides a bridge to the long chapter on Wagner's *Ring* and the 1848 revolutions, which forms the heart of the book. Here McGrath combines literary and musical analysis to trace the composition of the *Ring* in detail, showing how Wagner initially hoped that the 1848 revolutions would lead to a free state of autonomous citizens on the ancient Greek model. Wagner's distrust of modern democracy found expression in *Götterdämmerung*, the first part of the *Ring* cycle to be planned, where Siegfried is enmeshed in shabby intrigues which Wagner considered 'the political perversion of freedom' (p. 124). Thereafter, inspired by Feuerbach, he increasingly turned his thoughts to redemption through love. This careful analysis deserves the attention of everyone fascinated by the complexities of the *Ring*.

The Wagner and Nietzsche chapters are linked by the Aeschylean figure of Prometheus, a prototype for both Siegfried and Zarathustra. Besides showing how the ideal of self-mastery is expressed in the underrated essay 'Schopenhauer als Erzieher', McGrath sheds much new light on *Die Geburt der Tragödie*. By examining Nietzsche's preparatory notes, he reveals the importance of Semper, a figure absent from standard studies of Nietzsche: in Semper's argument that Greek statues were originally coloured, Nietzsche found an encouraging parallel to his thesis that Greek tragedy was originally musical. Finally we arrive at Thomas Mann, who in *Buddenbrooks* gently satirizes democratic revolutionaries (Morten Schwarzkopf, 'Corl Smolt') but also reveals the ideal of self-mastery, in Thomas Buddenbrook and later in Aschenbach, to be fragile and perhaps illusory. Although he shored up the German concept of freedom in *Betrachtungen eines Unpolitischen* (which McGrath enables us to read with more sympathetic understanding), post-war turmoil compelled him to engage with democratic politics. Though McGrath has not space to argue this, Mann's masterpiece, *Der Zauberberg*, can now be read as Hans Castorp's journey, via the tutelage of Settembrini and Naphta, to self-command and autonomy.

This is a small book on a big subject. McGrath illuminates every author he discusses, and suggests many further reflections. One—not explored here—must be that the German image of Greece was hopelessly idealistic. Burckhardt in *Griechische Kulturgeschichte* gave a horribly plausible picture of Periclean and later Athens as enslaved to demagogy. Another is that the German ideal of freedom has a longer ancestry, including the neo-Stoic ideal of self-control and the conception of a republic of responsible citizens that goes back to Machiavelli's *Discorsi*. McGrath's impressive book should both improve historical understanding and inspire much further research.

THE QUEEN'S COLLEGE, OXFORD   RITCHIE ROBERTSON

Goethe's Visual World. By PAMELA CURRIE. (Germanic Literatures, 3) London: Legenda. 2013. ix+166 pp. £45. ISBN 978-1-907975-89-9.

With *Goethe's Visual World*, Pamela Currie has made a contribution of exemplary sophistication and clarity to an ever-expanding field of Goethe studies. By virtue of its status as a collection of essays published over a number of years, the book's approach to its subject matter is non-linear; but this makes it all the more effective as a guide through the 'visual world' of the polymath. Indeed, one of Goethe's favourite developmental models, the spiral, would be apposite here too: each essay, though self-sufficient, builds on the previous one, turning related questions over from different angles, and steadily advancing our understanding of the field as a whole. The reader is expertly led from prose and poetry, through optics, to aesthetics and art history. After an introduction by T. J. Reed, the collection opens with an essay on 'Goethe's Mental Images', which serves to announce the major themes of the study as a whole: vision and imagination, science and art, theory and literature. The second essay uses the concept of the 'Gestalt shift' to offer a shrewd reading of *Wilhelm Meisters Lehrjahre* and its 'ambiguous figures'. Next, there is an interesting and useful interlude in the form of a response to David Wellbery's seminal study *The Specular Moment* (Stanford, CA: Stanford University Press, 1996). From here, the focus shifts to Goethe's *Farbenlehre*, with an essay on boundary colours, and then to his theories on painting, with the last four chapters devoted to different aspects of his intellectual collaboration with Heinrich Meyer.

The book, then, moves gracefully round the reaches of this 'visual world'. The early chapters combine insights in the tradition of some of the very best Goethe scholarship with an approach informed by more recent developments in neuroscience and cognitive psychology. Elizabeth Wilkinson, seeking in 1962 to nuance the ingrained perception of Goethe as an 'objective' poet, suggested that 'subject-objectivity' would be a more useful notion, arguing that 'the essence of "Gegenständlichkeit" [is] not that the observer, the subject, should be ruled out, but that he should not project on to the object' ('Goethe's Poetry', in Elizabeth M. Wilkinson and L. A. Willoughby, *Goethe: Poet and Thinker* (London: Arnold, 1962), p. 28). In an inverse but strikingly similar manœuvre, Currie pre-empts the charge that Goethe falls prey to 'ocularcentric subjectivism' (p. 15) by highlighting the continuity of his thought with cognitive neuroscience: just as '[Goethe's] objective seeing is a form of perception in which we are filled with objects' (p. 15), so 'recent neuroscientific theory [. . .] suggests that the mind can have knowledge only by training itself through exposure to the world of objects' (p. 12). This is consistent with a concern elsewhere in the book to emphasize the prescience of Goethe's understanding of vision and of colour, in spite of its shortcomings. Colour theory forms the arc from science to aesthetics in the study, and three out of the four chapters on Goethe and Meyer are concerned with colour and harmony in painting. The final essay refreshes tired notions of classicism by highlighting the 'alternative antiquity' represented in the decorative work of Giulio Romano, admired by Goethe and Meyer, and so different from 'the Winckelmannian equation of antiquity with classical Greek sculpture' (p. 136).

Pamela Currie's arguments never fail to challenge the reader, but are crafted with a lightness of touch, and display a sustained resistance to theoretical excess. The book works across genres and disciplines—and it works beautifully. It is a fitting way to remember a much-respected scholar, who died as the book was in preparation.

MURRAY EDWARDS COLLEGE, CAMBRIDGE   CHARLOTTE LEE

Zwischen Eros und Mitteilung: Die Frühromantik im Symposion der 'Athenaeums-Fragmente'. By MAY MERGENTHALER. (Schlegel-Studien, 6) Paderborn: Schöningh. 2012. 344 pp. €39.90. ISBN 978-3-506-77360-9.

Alarcos: Ein Trauerspiel. Historisch-kritische Edition mit Dokumenten. By FRIEDRICH SCHLEGEL. Ed. by MARK-GEORG DEHRMANN with NILS GELKER. Hanover: Wehrhahn. 2013. 232 pp. €28. ISBN 978-3-86525-292-0.

These two very different studies demonstrate the continuing critical interest in every aspect of Friedrich Schlegel's life and works. May Mergenthaler's book is based on her dissertation, and under those conventions there is a fifty-page introductory section dealing generally with Friedrich Schlegel's notions of irony, fragment, and discourse ('Gespräch') and their reception in the various schools of modern critical theory, including among others deconstruction, system theory, performance theory, and 'dialogicity'. This leads into a long discussion of Plato's *Symposium*, its nature, the individual participants, and the significance of the Socratic/Platonic form for Schlegel himself. With this we come to the main thesis itself: that the collection of fragments published in 1798 in the periodical *Athenaeum* is in effect Schlegel's own recreation and sympathetic reception of the Socratic colloquy. We know that the *Fragmente* contain contributions by August Wilhelm Schlegel and Friedrich Schleiermacher, as well as by Friedrich Schlegel himself, and also that they contain individual fragments by the author of the other great collection in the same volume, its second item, Novalis's *Blüthenstaub*.

Of course in the *Athenaeum* interlocution and collocution ('Gespräche') stand in a kind of dialectic relationship to the other main form of discourse, namely proclamatory statement, challenging articulation, homiletic insistence. The Schlegel brothers announced this in their joint foreword (itself an echo of the 'Unterhaltung' that Schiller's preface to *Die Horen* promised—and failed to deliver). Friedrich Schlegel's *Gespräch über die Poesie* (1800) and August Wilhelm's *Die Gemählde* (1799) are thus but the two best-known examples of 'Gespräche' that occur in various forms throughout the three volumes from 1798 to 1800.

Whereas *Blüthenstaub* challenges readers with its uncompromising aphoristic stance and through the deliberate and consciously self-contained 'Igel' (to use Friedrich Schlegel's term) of each fragment, the *Fragmente*, because of their joint authorship and identifiable individual voices—identified, that is, by twentieth-century editors, not necessarily by eighteenth-century readers—lend themselves to a 'Socratic' reading. This is (to simplify a closely argued and complex thesis) the kernel of Mergenthaler's study. In her terms, the Jena Symposium would consist of the Schlegel brothers themselves (with Friedrich as a kind of Socratic moderator), their partners Caroline Schlegel and Dorothea Veit, Friedrich von Hardenberg (Novalis), Friedrich Schleiermacher, and Caroline's daughter, Auguste Böhmer. It would unite as a Socratic parley a constellation never present together in real terms but only on the printed page.

I have no objection to seeing August Wilhelm Schlegel as a kind of Alcibiades, representing what in Plato would be poetic vision, Hardenberg as a kind of philosophical or religious Diotima, Schleiermacher representing moral virtue, or Dorothea love ('Eros') but also 'Witz'. All this is compatible with the evidence and can be adduced from the fragments they actually wrote or extrapolated from other contexts (such as Dorothea's remarks on Jean Paul). Caroline Schlegel seems to me altogether more problematic in this constellation. Friedrich Schlegel certainly asked her for fragments (which she did not provide), but while she is in one respect very present in the *Athenaeum* (as Louise in *Die Gemählde*), she is otherwise never mentioned by name—nor for that matter is Dorothea. I cannot see any sound evidence for Auguste Böhmer's inclusion (despite her step-uncle Friedrich's adulation of her childlike qualities and her wit) and it seems that an element of the wishful enters the argument when she is mentioned on an equal basis with the adults. The idea of a Socratic role distribution transferred to the *Fragmente* is certainly both challenging and stimulating, reinforcing the existing multiform discourse of the *Athenaeum*, but readers must judge whether they are prepared to accept all the correspondences and the details that go with them, and they must be ready to enter into the complexities of the arguments that Mergenthaler adduces in their favour.

With *Alarcos: Ein Trauerspiel* we meet the other Friedrich Schlegel. This play has already been edited in the *Kritische Ausgabe*: is there a good case for going over the same ground again? One reason cited is that Hans Eichner, the first editor, did not have all the relevant source material at his disposal, whereas Dehrmann and Gelker do. They also make as strong a case as they can for taking seriously this ill-starred tragedy—indeed 'Schlegel poeta' as a whole. It was, as Schlegel announced, an 'antique tragedy in modern costume' (pp. 194–95), in the lineage of Goethe's *Iphigenie*, Schiller's *Die Braut von Messina*, and his own brother's (similarly ill-starred) *Ion*. That is to say, it enshrined a Greek view of fate as absolute necessity, together with modern, political, reflective culture as a counterweight (in the Spanish notion of honour). Having discovered the language and literature of Spain, Schlegel was concerned to introduce into the severe pronouncements of 'Schicksal' a lyrical, Christian tone, taking particular pains over the versification and its variations. All would have been fine—the play would have remained a literary curiosity, perhaps—had not Goethe, heedless of Schiller's advice, agreed to have *Alarcos* performed in Weimar in 1802. The scandal it produced was of the same order as that accompanying August Wilhelm's *Ion* in 1801. The riot, set up by August von Kotzebue and his associates, compromised Goethe, not to speak of Schlegel himself, and contributed to Schlegel's departure for Paris later in the same year. Goethe's favour towards the Romantics virtually ended. Everything that can be said for or against this tragedy, including sentiments expressed at the time, is contained in this excellently documented edition. It will, one hopes, encourage readers to examine the text itself, not just its unfortunate reputation, and to form judgements that are not based simply on the prejudices of two centuries.

TRINITY COLLEGE, CAMBRIDGE   ROGER PAULIN

Sprechzeiten: Rhythmus und Takt in Hölderlins Elegien. By ANITA-MATHILDE SCHRUMPF. Göttingen: Wallstein. 2011. 368 pp. €38. ISBN 978-3-8353-0968-5.

More than any other German poet and for reasons that are not far to seek, Hölderlin continues to inspire scholarship in which questions of prosody play a prominent role. Where, in the case of any other representative of the modern German lyric, such matters tend to remain in the background, books on Hölderlin invariably—and justifiably—feel the need to make them a strong part of the argument. Winfried Menninghaus's *Hälfte des Lebens: Versuch über Hölderlins Poetik* (Frankfurt a.M.: Suhrkamp, 2005) is a good example, and studies of more protracted but still modern vintage, such as David Constantine's *Hölderlin* (Oxford: Clarendon Press, 1988)—pre-eminent as a general account in English—have devoted considerable attention, as part of their efforts of interpretation, to the technicalities of Alcaic and Asclepiadic ode forms, to the precise prosodic contours of the Pindaric inheritance, and not least to the question of elegy. Among Hölderlin's contributions to the latter genre, 'Menons Klagen um Diotima' and 'Brod und Wein' stand out as pinnacles in the lonely tragic air that Hölderlin created and which large stretches of the nineteenth- and twentieth-century European lyric continue to breathe.

For Anita-Mathilde Schrumpf in her study of rhythm in Hölderlin's elegies, these considerations have an a priori status as self-evident and therefore not requiring generalized exposition with reference either to eighteenth-century classicizing obsessions or to the existential concerns of the modern lyric, though both of these are alluded to. Schrumpf's book, which in scope if not necessarily in theme recalls older, specialized treatments of Hölderlin's poetics such as Lawrence Ryan's *Hölderlins Lehre vom Wechsel der Töne* (Stuttgart: Kohlhammer, 1960), has a twofold purpose: to integrate Hölderlin's elegiac prosody into the context of German discussions of rhythm from around 1600, and to account for the unique dynamism of Hölderlin's elegiac mode through a metrics defined by Schrumpf's central—and, as she shows, historically warranted—concept of the musical 'bar' ('Takt') which is analogous to but not identical with the metrical 'foot'. One must conclude that she succeeds in both endeavours, though the first is likely to make her book of more lasting use than the second, which is probably the reverse of what she intends.

Avoiding excessive jargon (the exceptional culprits being in any case more quaint than irritating, at least for the English-speaking reader: 'statement', 'interplay', 'Untersuchungsdesign'), Schrumpf shows clearly how concern with 'Takt'—the musical, which is to say temporal, rather than just formal, or rhythmical, dimension of prosody—was a fundamental particularity of German poetics from the middle of the eighteenth century. It was at the centre of competing and overlapping conceptions of poetic rhythm and musico-literary interaction, and gave rise to such questions as the appropriate 'time signature' in which the elements of the elegiac distich—hexameter and pentameter—should be scanned. Engaging with 'Takt' also means, for example, understanding acoustic elements of poetic language not as extrinsic to formal metrical patterns but as interwoven with them. Schrumpf's comprehensiveness and capacity for historical synthesis in delineating the notion of 'Takt'—which (undeservedly, she argues) fell from favour because of the dubious political ends to which it was put by its major twentieth-century exponent, Andreas Heusler—are highly impressive and provide a useful conspectus for less specialized scholars of Hölderlin. No less impressive, in many respects, are her minute analyses of the mechanisms of 'Takt' in Hölderlin's elegies, where her argument is determined by such detailed considerations (derived from her prosodic framework) as how often Hölderlin replaces the dactyl (the primal rhythmic unit of elegy) with either a spondee or a trochee. Nonetheless, however much the pursuit of such questions may be consequent on Schrumpf's established terms, it is difficult to extract from them substantial interpretative force. To a large extent Schrumpf wants to absolve her study from any duty to provide interpretative readings, but it is uncertain how helpful these minutiae will be for others who do want to do just that. She does argue, however, that the temporal dimension of 'Takt' opens onto the question of memory in Hölderlin's elegiac mode, and that her findings show 'Erinnerung' at work in the way poetic sound recollects in its utterance what it has been. This is an attractive and very plausible claim, even if Schrumpf's huge philological efforts in arriving at it are likely to feature at best in the footnotes of those who wish to talk about what the poems actually say.

UNIVERSITY OF KENT   IAN COOPER

Brentano in Wien: Clemens Brentano, die Poesie und die Zeitgeschichte 1813/14. By DIETMAR PRAVIDA. (Frankfurter Beiträge zur Germanistik, 52) Heidelberg: Winter. 2013. 427 pp. €46. ISBN 978-3-8253-6143-3.

Dietmar Pravida presents a comprehensive study of Clemens Brentano's stay in Vienna in 1813–14, where the German Romantic poet attempted to gain a financial foothold and pursued ambitions both as a reviewer and as a playwright. The extensive collation of available sources and documents on Brentano's time in the Austrian capital—which is one of the overt aims of this monograph—has allowed Pravida to anchor Brentano's Vienna writings in their spatio-historical context and in so doing to cast useful light on the specificities of his literary work.

The volume offers first an introductory account of Brentano's time in Bohemia from 1811 to 1813 (immediately preceding his visit to Vienna), and proceeds to a prosopography of contemporary social and intellectual circles in Vienna and a thorough analysis of the manuscripts, publications, and transmission of Brentano's Viennese works. After these preliminary explorations, Pravida embarks on a detailed examination of Brentano's views on war poetry in Austria, informed by the Prussian circles in which he previously moved: for various reasons, war poetry played a more marginal role in Austria, although this did not prevent Brentano from employing the same ground rules and perspectives he had assimilated from the 'deutsche Tischgesellschaft', founded in Berlin by Achim von Arnim and Adam Heinrich Müller, and Luise Voß's 'Berliner Salon'. Since much of Brentano's political occasional poetry remained unpublished at that time, however, Pravida highlights the difficulties in assessing the precise intentions of these patriotic contributions. Pravida here scrupulously analyses the materials Brentano worked with and the changes he saw fit to make in view of the anticipated audience reception. In a chapter on the Brentano's drama *Victoria*, Pravida's detailed approach yields many interesting insights with respect to the genesis of the play, to the theatrical scene in Vienna, and to Brentano's intention to publish a book version of the text. Brentano struggled with the inherently contemporary character of the play, which had ultimately lost all of its appeal when the book finally came out in 1816–17.

The analytical part of the monograph concludes with Brentano's ambitions for success at the Hofburgtheater. Pravida lays out a complex scenario in which Brentano's Viennese theatre reviews had prepared the ground for an ironic and hostile reception of the play *Valeria* by his fellow reviewers in Vienna, who proved to be fundamentally alienated by Brentano's Romantic style. The harsh rejection of his plays also refuted Brentano's assumption that a quick and superficial 'Verwienerung' of selected plays would provide him with an instant income. Furthermore, Pravida shows that Brentano's attempt to secure a post at the Burgtheater had always been futile, since he was perceived as too closely associated with Arnim (whose hapless confrontation with Moritz Itzig—in the so-called 'Itzig-Affäre'—caused quite a stir) and with the anti-Semitism of the 'Tischgesellschaft', which did not sit well with the theatre management. With such contextual precision, this monograph therefore suggests a more complex explanation for Brentano's failure as a playwright than is offered by the almost ritually repeated view that Brentano's plays defied staging *per se*.

In a supplement to this volume, Pravida collates pertinent materials, including reviews of *Valeria* and letters (among them letters to Beethoven). This documentation rounds off a thorough and perspicacious analysis of the Viennese period in Brentano's life and writing.

DURHAM UNIVERSITY   CLAUDIA NITSCHKE

Korrespondenzen und Transformationen: Neue Perspektiven auf Adalbert von Chamisso. Ed. by MARIE-THERES FEDERHOFER and JUTTA WEBER. Göttingen: V&R unipress. 2013. 311 pp. €49.99. ISBN 978-3-8471-0010-2.

The natural scientist, ethnographer, world traveller, poet, and, as this volume reveals anew, prolific letter-writer Adalbert von Chamisso was a fascinating figure who bridged the science–literature divide to an even greater extent than better-known contemporaries (one thinks of Goethe's colour theory, or von Hardenberg's management of a salt mine). This collection of fourteen essays therefore attempts to re-examine Chamisso in his various guises, emphasizing his pioneering scientific research as well as his influential status as a man of letters. More than a straightforward study of the man and his work, the volume reflects the interdisciplinary connections resulting from engagement with this work and its reception in changing historical and social contexts.

The volume is usefully divided into three sections that guide the reader through Chamisso's discoveries as the botanist on the *Rurik*, explain his attempts to carve out a place for himself in Berlin's literary circles, and finally examine 'transformations' of Chamisso's literary work. The aim set out in the introduction, to illuminate Chamisso as 'Naturforscher und Zeichner, Ethnologer und Weltreisender, Korrespondenzpartner und "Generator" von Übersetzungen und Vertonungen' (pp. 14–15), is clearly achieved, in many cases via painstaking study of hitherto overlooked papers in the Staatsbibliothek in Berlin. Michael Bienert's chapter on the notebooks Chamisso filled during the *Rurik* voyage, for example, brings Chamisso's many talents into relief, affording an insight into his development as a scientist, his efforts at mastering Hawaiian dialects, and his skill at sketching.

Most interesting are the connections to be traced between the sections of the book. A recurring theme is the notion of Chamisso as a progressive thinker. Harry Liebersohn's chapter on Chamisso's official 1821 voyage account reveals that the self-reflexive style so typical of the Romantics resulted in a suitably empirical journal that nevertheless imaginatively allows for the possibility of foreign perspectives. Long before postcolonialism, Chamisso records how the gaze of the other is turned on the observer. Both Matthias Glaubrecht and Michael Schmidt, meanwhile, position Chamisso at the forefront of developments in science and scientific reporting. The former discusses Chamisso's ground-breaking discovery of the principle of alteration of generations, while the latter reveals his willingness to experiment with modern printing techniques to communicate new findings in the natural sciences. Moving beyond scientific innovation, Rufus Hallmark calls for a re-examination of Chamisso's *Frauenliebe und -Leben* (1830), seeking to revise the dominant view of the song cycle as misogynistic with a discussion of Chamisso's interest in promoting women's voices in literature. The cycle *Thränen* (also written in 1830), furthermore, is read as a counterweight to the portrayal of the satisfied wife in *Frauenliebe*, evidencing Chamisso's sympathetic attitude to the plight of women coerced into less than happy marriages. As Sharon Krebs points out, radical elements of the *Thränen* cycle proved problematic for nineteenth-century composers wishing to adapt the work.

Throughout the collection, Chamisso emerges as adept in the art of self-fashioning. His professional and literary development is presented as the result not only of talent, but also of a determined effort to make his name. Johannes Görbert compares Chamisso's two travel reports of his time on the *Rurik* (the 1821 *Bermerkungen und Ansichten* and the revised 1836 *Tagebuch*), charting his growing confidence and development from an official subordinate of Otto von Kotzebue to an established botanist keen to secure an independent position in his field. Both Monika Sproll and Selma Jahnke consider the implications of the young poet's active decision to write in his adopted German rather than his native French. In this respect his correspondence comes into its own: Chamisso wrote to both Goethe and Schiller on the eve of publication of the 1804 *Musenalmanach*, in Sproll's view an attempt to become part of a German tradition; the 1810 correspondence between Chamisso and his lover Helmina von Chézy, meanwhile, contained Lieder, a formal choice in which Jahnke reads Chamisso's ultimate achievement of a distinctively German voice. Marie-Theres Federhofer is less interested in the struggles of a foreign poet than in his professionalism in expanding the readership of the *Musenalmanach* by savvy networking. In a similar vein, Nikolas Immer examines Chamisso and Karl Varnhagen von Ense's employment of literary modes as an editorial strategy in their attempt to establish the journal between 1803 and 1806.

This volume also invites further research. Anna Busch's close comparison of Chamisso's original letters with those edited and published by Julius Eduard Hitzig in 1839 makes a convincing case for a new edition of Chamisso's correspondence, while Sarah Michaelis's study of Grimmelshausen's influence proves that even the well-known *Peter Schlemihl* (1814) can benefit from new approaches. Finally, Kjetil Berg Henjum uses the broad cross-cultural appeal of *Peter Schlemihl* as a springboard from which to illuminate modern theories in Translation Studies. Taking into account one Danish, one English, and three Norwegian versions, Henjum examines the issues surrounding the situation of translated texts for a culturally or temporally distant readership.

It is left to the reader to make these links, however, and the smooth translation of conference papers into a coherent volume remains at times incomplete. The choice of French for the opening word of welcome is somewhat jarring in an otherwise bilingual German–English collection. Several contributors are prone to anecdotal style or conjecture, and now and again risk overstating the significance of their findings in Chamisso's papers. Nevertheless this enthusiastic and informed volume opens up new areas of enquiry and should encourage yet more scholarly consideration of an often neglected Renaissance man.

WADHAM COLLEGE, OXFORD   JOANNA NEILLY

Geschichte und Wesen des Urheberrechts, vol. I. By ECKHARD HÖFFNER. Rev. edn. Munich: Verlag Europäische Wirtschaft. 2011. 518+10 pp. €48. ISBN 978-3-930893-18-8.

Before tackling a book of such denseness and specialized discourse, it might be useful to take an item down from one's own shelves that illustrates concretely the problems this volume discusses: *Gellerts moralische Vorlesungen*, in the series 'Sammlung der besten deutschen prosaischen Schriftsteller und Dichter', published in 1774 in Karlsruhe by Christian Gottlieb Schmieder, 'Mit allerhöchst-gnädigst Kayserlichem Privilegio'. This is a speaking title-page, telling us that the works of Gellert, who had not long since died, are free to be published in Karlsruhe under imperial privilege. It is a reprint, and only the Emperor's permit makes it legal. Gellert made little out of publishing during his lifetime (p. 127), despite being one of Germany's most read authors. Anyone who has worked on areas in German literature involving readership and publishing will recognize patterns here: few rights for the author even during his/her lifetime, and those acquired often after a tussle, little security as a writer before about 1790 (usually, like Gellert, dependent on another profession for a livelihood), and always the threat of pirate publishers. Wieland, Klopstock, Goethe, Schiller, Jean Paul, and many others would have been familiar with these conditions and the mechanisms needed to survive under them (see the very revealing table of royalty payments to German authors on page 334). The non-specialist (non-legal) reader will seek such familiar territory in a book as highly technical as this one.

Eckhard Höffner's volume is concerned with these issues, but under the general head of a history of copyright in the German lands, with a comparative look over borders to examine conditions in France and Britain. The latter need not detain us long—William St Clair's *The Reading Nation in the Romantic Period* (Cambridge: Cambridge University Press, 2004) tells us all that we need to know about Britain— except in its function as a point of reference, showing that Germany, in its attitudes to publishing rights, also had its own 'Sonderweg'. Whereas for a large part of the period under discussion publishers elsewhere were subject to the regulations of guilds (England up to 1694) or directly controlled by the state (pre-1789 France), in Germany neither force held sway. We learn in the process much about book production and distribution, about privileges, about censorship, about payments to authors.

The different thing about Germany was that it was not a unified or centralized state entity like France or England; it was not physically concentrated and had no capital city as focus of the book trade. From the earliest beginnings of book production, printing, with its attached privileges and restrictions, was centred in places as geographically scattered as Strasbourg, Frankfurt, Nuremberg, Wittenberg, Leipzig, and elsewhere. Until Leipzig established itself as the hub of the book trade (in the Protestant centre and north), it had to share a book fair with Frankfurt. Officially, privileges, such as sole publishing rights, were in the gift of the Holy Roman Emperor and continued to be granted well into the eighteenth century, as the case of Gellert cited above illustrates. Imperial jurisdiction did not, however, extend to the individual states: during the eighteenth century books could be banned in Austria or Bavaria (and most were) that were freely available in Prussia or Saxony and elsewhere. Despite these factors, Vienna was the centre of the pirate book trade, as most major authors up to 1815 knew to their chagrin (and cost). On the one hand, this system might seem repressive or capricious (think of the Saxon authorities banning Fichte and setting the 'Atheismusstreit' in train); on the other, it did mean that all but the most tendentious or subversive of texts were available somewhere in the German lands. Who says that *Werther* was not read in Vienna or in other Catholic territories just because it was banned there? I feel that the advantages accruing to the author's reputation (if not to his wallet) might have been stressed more than they are here, where the question of authors' privileges is more to the fore. Nonetheless, there was no binding legislation on copyright or piracy effectively until 1837, and after various enactments in the individual states (see the table on page 368), definitively in 1871. Censorship could be blanket (as with the Carlsbad Decrees of 1819) or subject to local enforcement.

Under the circumstances set out, there was no chance of founding a unified publishers' guild because there were no national privileges. It did not, however, prevent an energetic debate, notably in the latter half of the eighteenth century, on what constituted 'geistiges Eigentum' and thus publishers' or authorial copyright. The arguments adduced by Locke and later by Diderot, the growing status of intellectual property and originality, the question, based on reason and logic, of whether a book was an author's 'property': all these factors are discussed by Höffner. The philosophical questions of individual rights (Kant, Fichte) are balanced against the findings of academic jurists based on Roman law, natural law, or the 'historische Rechtsschule'.

Very often, especially in the later eighteenth century, it was a question of an author's relationship with his/her publisher that established questions of 'property', the bond of trust that, say, Wieland eventually built up with Weigand, or Goethe and Schiller with Cotta, the Romantics with Reimer. The realities of reading also played their part: there was little incentive to piracy—pirates did not come cheaply—if a publisher brought out a 'wohlfeile Ausgabe' that was within the purchasing power of a wider range of potential readers. This book is technical and is primarily intended for a legally trained readership, but it does have a historical narrative as its base, and it may serve as a useful book of reference on more specialized matters.

TRINITY COLLEGE, CAMBRIDGE   ROGER PAULIN

Realism and Romanticism in German Literature/Realismus und Romantik in der deutschsprachigen Literatur. Ed. by DIRK GÖTTSCHE and NICHOLAS SAUL. Bielefeld: Aisthesis. 2013. 468 pp. €58. ISBN 978-3-89528-995-8.

This stout volume, the proceedings of a conference at the IRGS in London in 2011, treats a central issue of German nineteenth-century literature: the presence of Romanticism in Realism, a movement itself contemporary with, sharing in, overlapping with, eliding into, the general critique of Romanticism that began with the Young Germans, took off with the Young Hegelians, and became a kind of doctrine with the Programmatic Realists. Of course this critique also served as a reminder of what Romanticism had once been. For this period was also in real terms a kind of 'Schwundstufe' for the reputations of many (the Schlegel brothers, for instance); the works of some leading Romantics on the market had notable omissions (no *Lucinde*, no *Godwi*). Tieck was maintaining an ironic distance from his early beginnings (see Rainer Hillenbrand's detailed discussion in this volume of Tieck's late story 'Waldeinsamkeit'). Friedrich Schlegel and Brentano had been annexed by Catholic and conservative circles. One could go on.

This volume, although sometimes sorely tempted to do so, does not essay a definition of Romanticism as such, sagely concluding that the 'talk of 'Romanticism' as a self-contained epoch defined as an internally consistent singular body of thought and cultural strategy' is probably illusory (p. 11). Similarly, there is no attempt to make 'the often rather crude politics of Realist theory' (p. 17) fit the literary production of the day, which was so much more nuanced and graduated, crucially, more aesthetically pleasing, and, as the volume stresses at many turnings, is now perceived as part of a Modernist discourse.

Inevitably, in a volume of essays loosely united around one central theme, 'Romanticism', will depend on what 'Romantic' elements are discerned in the literary works of Realism. Or indeed even 'romantic'. For one does wonder whether 'romantisch' is not sometimes just a catch-all for anything sentimental, 'empfindsam', or just plain mawkish—whether, for instance, the reference to *Werther* in Storm's *Immensee* almost says all that needs to be said (despite Magdolna Orosz's useful analysis of that novella), or if Heinrich Lee's landscape in *Der grüne Heinrich* (cited in Martin Swales's finely crafted piece on the European novel of Realism) does not owe just as much to Matthisson and his descendants in Biedermeier almanacs as to anything consciously Romantic.

The borders are fluid: Berthold Auerbach's 'Dorfgeschichten' stand back from a perceived Romantic aestheticism, only to embrace notions of 'Volk' that Romanticism engendered; by contrast, the genre is expanded by others to accommodate the requirements of a Realist aesthetic (in the contributions by Jesko Reiling and Gert Vonhoff on this narrative form). Similarly, the novel of Realism, as exemplified by Gustav Freytag, identifies Romantic tropes in order to invalidate them for the needs of a new and self-conscious age (Benedict Schofield). Theodor Storm, a very selective recipient of Romanticism, takes what he needs from that source in order to create a symbolism that is essentially his own (Magdolna Orosz).

These are primarily reactions to a literary tradition. What happens when Romantic 'science'—in its widest sense—is involved? Or with notions of Romanticism as the dark, unhealthy, uncanny side of nature? Romantic medicine is the subject of Martina King's fascinating contribution on the relationship between Stifter's *Die Mappe meines Urgroßvaters* and the holistic theory and therapeutics represented by Carl Gustav Carus. Deliberate use of anachronistic narrative overlaying enables Stifter, in a story set in the eighteenth century, to advance a critique of the nineteenth century's less intuitively based diagnostic methods. With its dialogue between narrative experiment (the technique of reminiscence) and actual scientific practice, King's essay is a model of how the stated relationship between Romanticism and Realism comes alive. Christiane Arndt, on the other hand, draws on the darker side of Romanticism (Goethe's 'das Kranke'), as the Realist generation perceived it, in her analysis of novellas by Storm and Raabe and their symbolism of insalubrity. Christian Begemann and Philip Ajouri explore the ghost story of Realism and its legitimacy, one (Fontane's *Unterm Birnbaum*) in its relationship to forensics, the other (Keller's *Der Geisterseher*) as a retelling of Hoffmann that owes its allegiance neither to that Romantic source nor to contemporary theories of 'real life'. Nicholas Saul examines Raabe's *Vom alten Proteus* for its presentation—often ironical and self-referential—of spiritualism. Martina Süess returns to more familiar territory in her examination of Fontane's *Effi Briest*, extending the discussion to the fundamental question of reality and illusion.

A third group of essays takes as its theme 'memory, art, and history'. Dirk Göttsche chooses a group of chronologically scattered stories, by Roquette, Raabe, and Jensen, to examine post-1848 attitudes to the Wars of Liberation, a significant moment in both Romantic and general national consciousness. Martin Swales illustrates how Keller's *Der grüne Heinrich* (with glances at other traditions) still adheres to the regenerative power of the imagination. Ralf Simon undertakes in a historical broad sweep a survey of notions of history and the individual (with a welcome and useful reference to Tieck's neglected novel *Der Aufruhr in den Cevennen*) and extends it in an analysis of Raabe's negative historical narrative. Russell A. Berman's essay looks at Storm's relationship between 'Enge' and 'Weite', his cultivation of personal integrity in the face of shifting values, and combines it with a general critique of contemporary (twenty-first-century) institutions, political and cultural, which is not an inappropriate note on which to end the whole volume.

This collection covers a wide range of authors and expands the 'canon' of those writers considered to be serious representatives of Realism. One notes all the same that Ebner-Eschenbach, Liliencron, and Saar are missing altogether, and Gotthelf, Sealsfield, and Spielhagen are merely touched on. It is also a collection about nineteenth-century German prose and moves within those terms of reference. Would the inclusion of lyrical poetry or even verse narrative have challenged its findings? It is worth thinking about.

TRINITY COLLEGE, CAMBRIDGE   ROGER PAULIN

Out of Place: German Realism, Displacement and Modernity. By JOHN B. LYON. (New Directions in German Studies, 7) London: Bloomsbury. 2013. 241 pp. £60. ISBN 978-1-4411-3340-3.

The aim of this book is to offer an alternative reading of German Realism as a whole, arguing that the movement is modern in its understanding of the meaning of place in the empirical world, and close to Modernism in its representations of spatial experience in the imaginative world of literary texts. Lyon proposes an interpretation of nineteenth-century Germany's urban and industrial development, arguing that this resulted in a sense of displacement, which is understood as a shift from rootedness in a coherent, meaningful, and stable milieu to a relationship with the environment which is characterized by the latter's commodification and fluidity. On this basis, Lyon presents readings of texts by three Realists (Raabe, Fontane, and Keller), demonstrating that the representations of place in these novels can be read as reactions to the process of displacement, and that these texts ultimately point forward to the spatial turn in twentieth-century critical thought.

Lyon introduces his study with a survey of theoretical approaches to place, differentiating phenomenological approaches (Heidegger) from political ones (Foucault, Lefebvre). The nineteenth century sees a gradual evolution from the phenomenological understanding of place, focused on dwelling, to the political understanding of space as impersonal and determined by outside forces: 'A sense of place gives way to space' (p. 6). Lyon rejects Marxist assessments of German Realism, arguing that, whatever their settings, Realist texts explore the 'struggle between the two extremes of being in place and being out of place' (p. 19): 'authors recognize place as a social construct that provides both meaning and identity, but [. . .] they perceive it as threatened' (p. 28). Realists are therefore 'on the cusp of a discursive shift [. . .] towards modernist conceptions of place and space' (p. 14). A chapter on nineteenth-century Berlin demonstrates that several factors created this feeling of displacement: population growth, agrarian reform, housing and planning policy, especially the development of the *Mietskaserne*, and the process of unification.

The chapter on Raabe considers *Die Chronik der Sperlingsgasse* and *Die Akten des Vogelsangs*: an exposition on the metropolis and dwelling (Heidegger, Gurlitt, Simmel) leads to a reading of the Sperlingsgasse as an embedded and protected locus, a refuge no longer possible in the later *Akten*, which is read as the relinquishing of a desire to preserve ties to significant home environments. The chapter on Fontane analyses *Irrungen Wirrungen* through Deleuze, Guattari, and Edward Casey, arguing that characters' ideal imaginings of place as static are contrasted with pragmatic experiences in which place emerges as dynamic. Importantly, Lyon demonstrates that apparently stable oppositions—such as town/country—emerge as confused and conflicting. The final reading, of Keller's *Martin Salander*, begins with a historical overview of urbanization in Zurich, and the proposal of Benjamin's concept of allegory as a way of reading place in the text. Lyon presents place in the novel as broken, diffuse, and full of unresolved tension, preparing the way for German Modernism.

The book is well argued, although with two introductory chapters and theoretical underpinnings for each reading, it does tend to repetition. Essentially, Lyon situates Realism within critical discourses on place, rather than offering a broad study of Realism itself. This is not necessarily a weakness, and even if the metaphor of displacement does appear stretched at times, the readings emerge as interesting and differentiated. Many readers will disagree with the ultimate conclusion, that for late Realists 'place was no longer linked to individual experience and meaning' (p. 214), and certainly the indication that in Fontane's *Stechlin* place and experience are 'wholly separate' is difficult to follow (p. 218). Nevertheless, the argument that German Realism prefigures twentieth-century critical concerns is both persuasive and welcome.

UNIVERSITY OF ST ANDREWS   MICHAEL WHITE

Dekadenz: Studien zu einer großen Erzählung der frühen Moderne. By CAROLINE PROSS. Göttingen: Wallstein. 2013. 436 pp. €34.90. ISBN 978-3-8353-1201-2.

Readers misled by the title of this book who expect to plunge into a fragrant pool of literary decadence will soon learn that they must first slog through a hundred-page swamp of theory before reaching the refreshing waters of text and analysis. When will German publishers learn that the wider academic public is not interested in the preliminary material included by candidates hoping to impress the evaluators of their *Habilitationsschriften*—not to mention the voluminous footnotes that take up almost half of the book? Caroline Pross's *Habilitationsschrift* (St. Gallen, 2009) consists substantively of extensive and detailed analyses of five novels that she assigns to the genre of the German *Dekadenzroman*, which flourished from the late 1880s to the end of the First World War. After making our way through a hundred pages of 'Begriffsbildung', 'Narrativität', and 'Diskursbeziehungen', we learn that 'decadence' refers etymologically to a decline, that a decline occurs temporally, that temporal discourse requires a narrative form, and that this metanarrative form is exemplified by Zola in his Rougon-Macquart cycle. What Pross repeatedly terms 'Dekadenz (in) der Moderne' (in all its ambiguity) thereby becomes a 'diskursives Ereignis' (p. 12).

A first substantive chapter entitled 'Übersetzungen' is devoted to Max Nordau, who—prior to his well-known 'popular-scientific' work, *Entartung* (1892)—published a novel entitled *Die Krankheit des Jahrhunderts* (1887). Using Bénédicte Morel's *Traité des dégénérescences* (1857), which emphasized the negative aspects of nineteenth-century progress, Nordau 'translated' Zola's *décadence* into a distinctly German theory of *Dekadenz*. With this novel, and more generally with his study of *Entartung* and its literary-cultural effects, Nordau initially shaped the German discourse on decadence, warning against the fashionable notion that 'brilliant degenerates constitute a driving force of progress of humanity' (p. 161).

Following a brief look at Hedwig Dohm's *Sibilla Dalmar* (1896), a novel unknown today outside German gender studies, the author moves on to 'Umwertungen', which are represented principally by the father of Rilke's dedicatee for the *Sonette an Orpheus*, Gerhard Ouckama Knoop and his novel *Die Dekadenten* (1898). Here Pross introduces the work of the French psychopathologist Valentin Magnan, who advanced a theory of 'dégénérés supérieurs' in his *Psychiatrische Vorlesungen* (1892–94). Unlike Morel and Nordau, who saw society as a whole as caught in a process of decadence, but following Magnan, Knoop focused in his novel on that group of 'superior degenerates' whose 'sensibility is excessively developed' (p. 202). The 'model readers' projected here are those 'concerned with an approach through reading to the thought-, experiential-, and linguistic worlds of exceptional individuals [whose existence] points proleptically to the future' (p. 241).

To exemplify 'Ambiguierungen' Pross takes up *Buddenbrooks* (1901), where Thomas Mann employs the 'paradigm of the German-language *Dekadenzroman*' (p. 243) established by his predecessors, but his narrative modelling of the existing theory of German *Dekadenz* also adapts George Miller Beard's theory of neurasthenia (from *Die Nervenschwäche*, 1881) and Nietzsche's view of Wagner's 'Stil der décadence' (p. 284). Mann's ambiguity does not deny the negative effects of decadence on society as a whole, but he finds the neurasthenically afflicted cultural elite most interesting for several reasons. Because their neurasthenia intensifies from generation to generation, it fits the 'longue durée' of the new metanarratives, and to the extent that it produces an enhanced sensibility this decadence can be presented positively; and because of the close connection with 'Geistesarbeiter' and the cultivated elite, it enhances the status and influence of reading and literature.

Accordingly, because of its enormous success (its 'performative Verstärkereffekte', p. 307), Mann's novel can be viewed also as a symptom of the society attracted to the work: hence 'Dekadenz (in) der Moderne'.

'Generalisierungen' appear in the fictions of Eduard von Keyserling, which incorporate a 'Kulturtheorie' embracing widespread popular-scientific ideas about 'the nervous age' (p. 324) and represent decadence as the inevitable flipside of progress. Keyserling sees this situation best illustrated in the palaces and country houses that provide the setting for his novel *Abendliche Häuser* (1914) and other 'Schloßgeschichten'. Here 'evening' symbolizes the decline of the families in their 'longue durée'—a decline in which love is reduced to sympathy (which Nietzsche called the 'virtue of the décadents') and family members die young. Escape is possible only by a radical break with the past and its reverence for the culture of decadence (p. 350).

With 'Historisierungen' Pross returns to Thomas Mann, whose *Der Zauberberg* (1924) she presents as an 'archival' novel recapitulating the 'discourse universe of "Dekadenz (in) der Moderne"' (p. 410). Instead of the action in historical time that characterized the earlier novels, meaning is communicated by the discourse of the figures in the timeless atmosphere of their Alpine sanatorium, notably by Settembrini, whose critique of decadence and praise of progress reflect Nordau's position while Naphta expresses Spengler's sense of the inevitability of decline. As the author's mouthpiece, Hofrat Behrens assumes the role of the onlooking physicians featured in many of the earlier works. The outbreak of the First World War exemplifies the final coincidence of the life of the cultivated neurasthenics 'up here' and reality 'down below' (p. 379). Accordingly, Pross concludes, Mann's novel is a 'book of departure' not only from the standpoint of discourse history but also in its 'aesthetics of effect' (p. 410).

Pross has provided a persuasive history of a phenomenon, a period, and a literary genre that have received, for almost a century, considerable critical and scholarly attention. Presented as a two-hundred-page book in readable prose, her provocative ideas might well have attracted a sizeable audience. Unfortunately, only a few specialists will have the will and energy to plough through the theory-laden language and over-footnoted text of her unrevised *Habilitationsschrift*, which would have benefited from judicious editing.

PRINCETON UNIVERSITY   THEODORE ZIOLKOWSKI

Walter Benjamins anthropologisches Denken. Ed. by CAROLIN DUTTLINGER, BEN MORGAN, and ANTHONY PHELAN. Freiburg i.Br.: Rombach. 2012. 370 pp. €54. ISBN 978-3-7930-9688-7.

Walter Benjamins anthropologisches Denken is based on a conference held in Oxford in 2009. Each of the essays is based on a close reading of Benjamin's texts while at the same time being concerned with the ideas and practices that were generated within the intellectual and artistic avant-gardes of Europe from the turn of the twentieth century. The editors' introduction boldly recruits Benjamin for a particular theoretical trend, an alleged 'anthropological turn' in the twentieth century, and the volume's overall intention is to reconstruct the anthropological foundation of Benjamin's thought, its development in later writings, and its connections with that of many other thinkers and writers, since nowhere did Benjamin elaborate systematically what he meant by materialist anthropology or anthropological materialism. As the editors rightly point out, thinking in this direction was giving expression to a persistent theoretical concern that moved him to the extent of dispersing anthropological reflections throughout his critical articles and larger projects. One of the major outcomes of this book is, therefore, to demonstrate the continuities in Benjamin's thought despite its many intellectual turns.

Duttlinger, Morgan, and Phelan state early on that Benjamin's pursuit of anthropological themes meant that he was able to discover a row of ancestors in nineteenth-century German and French literature: Büchner, Hebel, Lautréamont, and Rimbaud; Nietzsche was never far away and Marx came to loom very large from the late 1920s onwards. These figures were joined by the proponents of French surrealism, whom Benjamin admired because he saw in them the attempt to make art into a direct instrument of revolutionary political action. That meant that he believed he had found the possibility of intellectual labour not just as an explicatory system for present-day reality but as a direct lever for changing social reality by working alongside the most avant-garde positions within it. However, these perspectives on Benjamin's labours only appear with any clarity in the 1930s. Archival faithfulness to Benjamin's texts, involving research into the entirety of his unpublished notes in the now accessible materials of the *Nachlass*, obliges the editor-authors to introduce a great number of qualifications. They find themselves confronted with an evident continuity of attention given by Benjamin to aspects of anthropology, including a strange diagram from 1918 that suggests he had a fully worked-out model in mind that would allow deeper insight into what it is to be human. The ambiguities of this model with a multidetermined notion of the individual at its centre only prove that the materialist anthropology, if at this stage it can be called such, is but a tentative complex of ideas in Benjamin's restless search in a variety of directions to find meaning and commitment to what a writer could do. The deeper the editors' hermeneutic efforts penetrate Benjamin's thinking, the more definitely—even if perhaps involuntarily—the impression is conveyed that that thinking is inspired by many other theoretical approaches in which a materialist anthropology is but one trajectory. They take great care to point out that the individual gains self-consciousness only via the senses and actions of the human body. The animal heritage provides the basis for the explorations that give human beings, individually and collectively, reminiscences of happiness and horror, reflection and alienation.

It is impossible to do full justice here to the fourteen essays that follow the ambitious claims contained in the introductory one. Michael Jennings traces the development of what he calls Benjamin's 'theological politics' by going into his remarkable intellectual biography in the 1910s and 1920s, which encompasses close relationships with Gustav Wyneken, Ernst Bloch, Erich Unger, Martin Buber, Karl Barth, and others. Jennings shows why Benjamin longed for an experimental poverty to make possible the emergence into eschatological perspectives. Uwe Steiner establishes the importance of Edmund Husserl's phenomenology for Benjamin's conception of language, although he also acknowledges the influence of Hamann and hence also connections to a critique of the Enlightenment. Ben Morgan's attempt to construct a perceptual similarity between Heidegger, Benjamin, and the film-maker Helmut Käutner is extremely problematic, because the presentation of the everyday by these figures is carried out from different vantage points that resist integration into a common anthropology. Gustav Frank establishes the context of anthropological thought in the lectures and publications of Max Scheler, Helmut Plessner, and Arnold Gehlen, and also the background of the growing social sciences (Leopold von Wiese, the Frankfurt Institute for Social Research, Karl Korsch, Georg Lukács, Siegfried Kracauer, and others) in the 1920s. The question of the nature of modernity in general, and the meaning of technology in particular, is further elaborated in the complex contribution by Sami Kathib on 'trans-materialist materialism', which tries to shed light on Benjamin's ideas of *Bildraum* and *Leibraum* and their importance for the conception of truth. The enormous breadth of Benjamin's inspirations is made explicit: he drew not just on anthropological studies but also on psychoanalytical, theological, sociological, literary, and art-historical reflections in order to reach a new terrain of intellectual perception. To what extent that includes a significant break with Hegelian Marxism (particularly with the thought of Adorno) must remain a matter for further investigation, particularly since it is quite possible to detect strong influences of philosophical idealism in Benjamin's writings. Also, whether it is helpful to designate his thinking as trans-materialist must remain questionable, especially since in the same breath it is perhaps more aptly referred to as a 'new materialism' in which nature and technology enter an evolving contemporary constellation.

The next section of the book addresses important questions of language, childhood, mimesis, socialization, education, and memory. It is followed by one with a very broad title, 'Literatur, Medien, Materialismus', but which in fact concentrates once more on fundamental problems of theory. Sabine Müller analyses the method of the *Passagenarbeit* as one that is to allow insights into the nature of modernity in the nineteenth century and at the same time might reveal futures in the twentieth, opening up the involvement of intellectuals in the historical process. Anthony Phelan follows with a densely argued piece on the importance of gesture in Benjamin's thinking. Phelan is surely right to say that in describing *Eduard Fuchs, der Sammler und der Historiker* Benjamin is defining his own contemporary situation as that of the epochal evolution of historical materialism itself. Gesture is seen as a primal form of communication and explored first in respect of Kant's anthropology and then in relation to Benjamin's interpretation of Karl Kraus, Bertolt Brecht, and Franz Kafka. Phelan speaks several times of gesture that points to or reveals 'powers', but cannot break through the ambiguities in Benjamin's texts to explain how precisely these might work. Similarly, Gerhard Neumann makes a lucid attempt to establish first of all Benjamin's inspiration by Kant's anthropology, then to go on to its fundamental modification through his reading of Kafka, only to end in a narrative of guilt that appears to have lost all connection with Benjamin's search for possible intervention in a modernity which challenges the writer to find the point of engagement with social praxis. Benjamin's closeness to figures critically fired by Marxism, socialism, and the perspective of communism is entirely lost in this essay to the extent that it is not discussed as such but replaced by an anthropology solely constructed out of an exposition of Kafka, which in itself is extremely well informed intertextually. In the penultimate essay of this volume Philip Ross Bullock considers that some of the propositions of the *Kunstwerk* essay can be reversed: counter to Benjamin's assertions that collective identity could not be imparted by the bourgeois painter, Bullock shows that Nicolai Leskov's observations in his story *The Sealed Angel* prove the effect of traditional Russian icons to be precisely to furnish a sense of collective uniqueness. Mareike Stoll's essay, with which the volume finishes, proves the usefulness of Benjamin's analysis of photography by applying it to Michael Schmidt's book *Berlin nach 45*. Here photographs of waste ground and the Berlin Wall teach their own political messages.

It is regrettable that there is no index, especially in view of the range of persons that played a role in Benjamin's intellectual orbit or the polysemy of his ideas. In what sense Benjamin was right to believe that he stood within a time of the epiphany of historical materialism and to what extent he was successful in developing that concept further, remain matters for further investigation. In particular, his interpretation of European Fascism has to be scrutinized since he appears to have looked at it as a 'Sklavenaufstand der Technik'. Did he think that the revolutionary productive forces were led astray by retarded, bourgeois, idealistically distorted relations of production and that the aestheticization of politics gave Fascism the possibility of sweeping up the masses into its ranks? Was a concept like 'false consciousness' therefore redundant or misleading? And did Marx's critique of political economy have to be rethought in terms of a secular Messianic concept of history where the process of modernity provided the sudden moment of mankind's emancipation from enfetterment to destruction? Some of these questions are of course raised in the discussions of Benjamin's anthropological thinking, and one can only concur with the editors when they say that this volume documents 'die fortdauernde Bedeutung von Benjamins anthropologischem Denken für eine kritische Analyse der Gegenwart — innerhalb der dialektischen Tradition oder aber über diese hinausgehend' (p. 38).

UNIVERSITY OF BIRMINGHAM   WILFRIED VAN DER WILL

Letzte Worte. By ERNST JÜNGER. Ed. by JÖRG MAGENAU. Stuttgart: Klett-Cotta. 2013. 245 pp. €22.95. ISBN 978-3-608-93949-1.

Atlantische Fahrt: 'Rio: Residenz des Weltgeistes'. By ERNST JÜNGER. Ed. by DETLEV SCHÖTTKER. Stuttgart: Klett-Cotta. 2013. 207 pp. €19.95. ISBN 978-3-608-93952-1.

Feldpostbriefe an die Familie: 1915–1918; mit ausgewählten Antwortbriefen der Eltern und Friedrich Georg Jüngers. By ERNST JÜNGER. Ed. by HEIMO SCHWILK. Stuttgart: Klett-Cotta. 2014. 133 pp. €19.95. ISBN 978-3-608-93950-7.

Ernst Jünger, the writer, warrior, and entomologist who died aged 102 in February 1998, was one of less than a handful of German authors who published two editions of their collected works during their lifetimes. Comprising travel, war, and home diaries, novels and stories, speeches, memoirs, and essays on a range of issues rivalled by few, the twenty-two volumes of Jünger's second collection amount to no fewer than 12,000 pages. And yet Jünger is not only one of the most dramatically under-researched of German writers but—as became evident when his private manuscript collection arrived at the Deutsches Literaturarchiv in Marbach am Neckar—also one whose published output is dwarfed by what has so far remained unpublished. There are letters to and from Jünger (many of which survive in more than one version), galley proofs, typescripts, manuscripts of works published and unpublished, notebooks, diaries, and photographs. While some of Jünger's books carry an air of monumental closure, the basic premise of their explicit poetics is rather humble: Jünger liked to think of his writings as 'Annäherungen', inconclusive gestures towards a perfect world that cannot be attained in this life, and not through words. Based on this view, Jünger felt obliged to edit or even rewrite many of his works, often over several decades. The two most striking examples of this process are his First World War diary *In Stahlgewittern* (originally published in 1920, and available in a critical edition by Helmuth Kiesel since 2013), and the two versions of *Das abenteuerliche Herz* (1929 and 1938), which bear little resemblance to each other. It is in a similar vein that many of the manuscripts, typescripts, and notes held at the DLA can be seen as versions in their own right. The fact that the author himself did not prepare them for publication does not make them categorically different from his published output.

Together, the three volumes reviewed here indicate the variety of ways in which previously unpublished materials enrich our view of Jünger. *Letzte Worte*—a particularly handsomely produced volume—contains a substantial number of statements made on the brink of death or, in Jünger's view, on the threshold between two worlds, which, as Jünger hoped, would appear in a new light through his collection. Both an unfinished draft for an essay on the subject and Jörg Magenau's afterword indicate, however, that he abandoned his project because last words only make sense in the context of last scenes—and these are rarely known. Detlev Schöttker's edition of *Atlantische Fahrt* sheds new light on Jünger's 1936 cruise to Brazil through letters sent by Jünger to his brother Friedrich Georg from Brazil and letters sent by fellow travellers to Jünger after his return to Germany. *Atlantische Fahrt*, highly selective in its perspective and radically different from other contemporary European accounts of this multi-racial country, is one of the milestones in Jünger's development from war writer to world writer, and Schöttker's afterword conveys a sense of the feeling of liberation that the journey instilled in Jünger.

It is Jünger's writings on the First World War, however, that still dominate his public image. Adding to the *Stahlgewitter* edition mentioned above and an earlier edition of Jünger's wartime notebooks, Heimo Schwilk's edition of the letters exchanged between Jünger, his parents, and Friedrich Georg between 1915 and 1918 provides further insight into the author's experience of trench warfare. These are some of the earliest texts Jünger addressed to an audience (however small it may have been), and Schwilk carefully traces the influence of various family members on Jünger's early years. Like the materials contained in the other two volumes, parerga like these indicate the fragility of any presumed boundary between life and œuvre.

UNIVERSITY OF BRISTOL   CHRISTOPHE FRICKER

Iris Murdoch and Elias Canetti: Intellectual Allies. By ELAINE MORLEY. London: Legenda. 2013. x+162 pp. £45. ISBN 978–1–90975–74–5.

The relationship between the British author Iris Murdoch and the Bulgarian-born Nobel Prize winner Elias Canetti has been the topic of several biographical and literary critical enquiries. As Elaine Morley aptly observes in her exciting and innovative book, the majority of publications foreground personality and relationship issues but allow little room for discussion of the creative affinity between the two authors or their continued intellectual interchange and intellectual curiosity, if not attraction, for each other's writings. The much-needed shift of focus from the personal to the literary and philosophical in Morley's analysis of Murdoch and Canetti as intellectual allies is path-breaking. It sheds new light on other relationships Canetti had with British authors and members of extensive circles of exiles from Nazi-controlled Europe in Britain. It also allows Murdoch, whom Canetti scholars have often portrayed as little more than the adept of the overpowering guru-like Canetti, to emerge as a creative force in her own right.

Morley argues that, rather than configuring and reconfiguring Elias-Canetti-the-person in her novels as a tyrant and power-seeker, Murdoch, like Canetti himself, was grappling with the big questions confronting their world during and after National Socialism and the Second World War. Aware of the threat residing in the distorted views of humanity that foster global destruction, Morley argues that Murdoch's approach, in a search for goodness, allows for a more optimistic outlook than Canetti's. In her rigorous comparative analysis of the two authors' literary expression, Morley addresses historical and cultural aspects shaping their works as well as generational differences (Canetti began publishing in Vienna during the inter-war period, for example, while Murdoch did so in the post-war era). These and other circumstances set their points of view apart while intertextualities and mutual contacts provide transcontinental connections.

Central to Morley's study is Canetti's novel *Die Blendung* (1935). She examines the work's central motifs, such as the metaphors of blindness and vision, and identifies these motifs in major texts by Murdoch, beginning with *The Flight from the Enchanter* (1956). She establishes similarities in the authors' representational modes, common motifs, and characters with similar traits, thus tracing intertextualities and complementary critical trajectories. For example, Morley argues that, rather than representing Canetti as a person, Murdoch's character Peter Seward serves as a response to critical concepts embedded in Canetti's Peter Kien. Morley's close analyses of female characters in Canetti and Murdoch culminate in a revision of an earlier view, according to which Canetti's female characters reveal misogynistic views and are derivatives of Viennese misogyny as exemplified by Weininger, Freud, and Kraus. Instead, Morley concludes, these figures are part of a far-reaching critique of social and philosophical tendencies in the twentieth century, and she identifies similar female figures in Murdoch. The 'power figures' in Canetti and Murdoch, according to Morley (p. 140), are part of the author's critical spectrum of post-Enlightenment representations of the human being, including, notably, Western man. They illuminate the solipsism and megalomania characteristic of the modern age and as models are applicable to psychopaths (such as Daniel Paul Schreber) and dictators alike. Morley maintains that Canetti and Murdoch perceive power as it expresses itself in the intimate as well as the political arena as a world problem, and as such it is of utmost concern in both writers.

Such shared intellectual concerns are what ultimately motivate the relationship between Canetti and Murdoch. Supporting her claims with careful documentation, Morley describes this relationship as a give-and-take that did not end, even though the intimate part of the relationship did not endure. Her analysis calls to mind the kind of intellectual-literary relationships that Canetti maintained with other intellectuals and artists, many of them women. A closer look at his network of creative minds reveals a model of collaborative productivity that resembles Bertolt Brecht's mode of production, especially while in exile. In Canetti's case, as in Brecht's, critics have described the relationships supporting their creative work as one-sided or even exploitative. As far as Canetti is concerned, negative stereotypes about him abound, and one such is his image as a god-monster, which certainly originated with Murdoch (Elias Canetti, *Party in the Blitz: The English Years* (New York: New Directions, 2003), p. 232). Energetically separating ideas and publications from personalities and rumours, however, Morley's study redirects the focus of attention to Canetti and Murdoch's œuvre, to their remarkable contributions to the world of literature and thought, and it invites future scholarship on Canetti's other creative affinities.

University of Illinois at Chicago   Dagmar C. G. Lorenz

Crisis and Form in the Later Writing of Ingeborg Bachmann: An Aesthetic Examination of the Poetic Drafts of the 1960s. By ÁINE MCMURTRY. (Bithell Series of Dissertations, 39) London: Modern Humanities Research Association. 2012. ix+250 pp. £19.99. ISBN 978-1-907322-39-6.

Love died in 1962 and experimental poetry began, at least as far as Ingeborg Bachmann was concerned. Much has been written about her sparsely documented relationship with Max Frisch, by whom she felt at the end bitterly betrayed and emotionally wounded—see most recently Ingeborg Gleichauf, *Ingeborg Bachmann und Max Frisch: Eine Liebe zwischen Intimität und Öffentlichkeit* (Munich: Piper, 2013). In the absence of their correspondence, which will not be available until 2025, speculation about the 'true nature' of this relationship remains rife. It all began in 1958, following Bachmann's separation from Paul Celan, and ended in 1962, when a traumatized Bachmann, in November that year, admitted herself to the Bircher-Brenner clinic in Zurich followed by more such hospitalizations in clinics and sanatoriums.

Frisch's subsequent prose, in particular *Mein Name sei Gantenbein*, *Der Mensch erscheint im Holozän*, and *Montauk*, reflects a writer very much in charge of his subject matter and language even though it considers the trauma of failure in love, too. But his prose appears seemingly less troubled than in Bachmann's *Malina* and *Der Fall Franza*, let alone her growing 'disillusion with lyric forms, culminating [...] in the lyric farewell to lyric poetry "Keine Delikatessen"'(p. 1). In both cases, however, this failure was a catalyst for literary production.

Tracing Bachmann's profound disillusionment as an expression of personal and artistic crisis is the object of Áine McMurtry's impressive study. In fact, *Crisis and Form in the Later Writings of Ingeborg Bachmann* is the first attempt in English to develop a comprehensive approach to Bachmann's poetic fragments, which are rich in poetological significance, as the author is able to demonstrate convincingly. It offers a detailed and helpfully contextualizing analysis of the poetess's 'poetic drafts of the 1960s' together with her few published poems of that period. It could be argued that McMurtry considers mainly the 'crisis *of* form', which would have been a more poignant title for this aesthetic investigation that draws on biographical material only if it cannot be helped, particularly in the chapter that deals with Bachmann's 'Berlin Writings' (pp. 86–133). Appropriately, the draft, the abandoned poem, and Bachmann's abortive attempts to keep her lyrical options open take centre stage in this landmark study.

There is precious little in McMurtry's approach and textual interpretation that invites criticism. In fact, one so often feels compelled to applaud the subtlety of these examinations, the comprehensiveness of argument, and sheer erudition of the author. If pressed, one point of criticism could be made: just occasionally there is a slight mismatch between quotations of primary material and its discursive evaluation. In analytic terms, more could be made of Bachmann's point that first attempts to write prose derive from the 'Zustand des Gedichteschreibens. Es sind noch viele Versuche darin, den Satz so hochzutreiben, daß kein Erzählen mehr möglich ist'

(p. 53). This self-comment is particularly telling given Bachmann's later remark, quoted but not sufficiently analysed as regards its poetologcial implications by McMurtry, 'und ich habe deswegen meine ersten Geschichten in mancher Hinsicht verfehlt, weil ich immer noch gemeint habe, jeden Satz hinaufheben zu müssen, zum Äußersten treiben zu müssen' (p. 223).

But this shortcoming is more than compensated by intriguing findings presented in the third and fourth chapters: McMurtry's discussion of the 'Gaspara Stampa' motif and the significance of Wagner's *Tristan und Isolde* in Bachmann's 'Reflexive Aesthetic' are genuinely rewarding. Whether we regard these motifs as hyper-, inter-, or subtexts in Bachmann's late writings is perhaps less important than the recognition of the fact that she treated these texts as materials, or verbal textures. At the same time, she needed musical structures as terms of reference for writing. A particular strength of McMurtry's own 'writing techniques' is the elegant way in which she integrates secondary material into her argument, for instance her appropriately critical literature survey on Bachmann's 'musical poetics' (pp. 190–92). With this study McMurtry has positioned herself in the forefront of contemporary Bachmann scholarship. It would not be surprising to find that *Crisis and Form* will serve one day as a prelude to a desirable comprehensive study by the same author on the development of Bachmann's poetics. Its starting point can be derived from the present examination in that we begin to see the *Todesarten* project, in effect, also as the result of experimenting with 'Schreibarten'—a poetological conception that seemed to have been present in Bachman's writings from her very beginning.

QUEEN MARY UNIVERSITY OF LONDON/UNIVERSITY OF SALZBURG

RÜDIGER GÖRNER

German Text Crimes: Writers Accused, from the 1950s to the 2000s. Ed. by TOM CHEESMAN. (German Monitor, 77) Amsterdam and New York: Rodopi. 2013. 242 pp. €52. ISBN 978–94–012–0949–6.

The term 'text crime' does not feature in the *Oxford English Dictionary*. This provides the editor with the opportunity to propose a broad but productive definition of the guiding concept of the present volume: All literary texts that are, or could be perceived as, incriminating in any way raise the question whether they are somehow 'justiceable', that is, whether they could potentially become the subject of the conventional tools of the justice system. In his introduction Tom Cheesman cites the plagiarism allegation against Feridun Zaimoğlu, who in his novel *Leyla* (2006) used motifs, imagery, and configurations reminiscent of Emine Sevgi Özdamar's *Das Leben ist eine Karawanserei* (1992), as an example of the grey zone which exists between outright plagiarism and the depiction of similar experiences in a similar register—with devastating consequences for the violated party. He further deploys the case of Maxim Biller's novel *Esra* (2003), where complainants were able to achieve a ruling forcing the publisher to blank out text that might identify the characters' real-life models (to somewhat ridiculous effect) so as to highlight how intervention by the courts defies rather than supports its intended purpose. Some of the other articles concern cases where literary texts of various genres (including travelogues) have caused public outrage or heated media reaction, that is, became 'justiceable' in the court of public opinion, and they explain the reasons behind these reactions, the historical and cultural backgrounds against which such debates gain meaning, and also put the validity of the arguments to a test, mostly by close textual and contextual analysis. Examples include Elfriede Jelinek's *Lust* and Charlotte Roche's *Feuchtgebiete* (both found guilty of violating the boundaries of sexual decency), Martin Walser's *Tod eines Kritikers* (accused of literary anti-Semitism), Peter Handke's *Eine winterliche Reise* [. . .] *oder Gerechtigkeit für Serbien* (deemed to understate the extent and severity of Serbian war crimes), Bernhard Schlink's *Der Vorleser* (accused of historical relativism), and three instances where violence against representatives of rampant capitalism appears to be treated sympathetically (Franz-Maria Sonner's *Die Bibliothek des Attentäters*, Thomas Weiss's *Tod eines Trüffelschweins*, and Rolf Hochhuth's *McKinsey kommt*). Further contributions describe Hochhuth's attempts to defend the presumed integrity of his own text against objectionable productions by proponents of *Regietheater*, the treatment of Wolf Biermann and the cabaret duo Hans-Eckhardt Wenzel and Steffen Mensching at the hands of the GDR authorities as examples of different consequences for similar offences, and the criticism of members of Ingeborg Bachmann's family for doing the author's memory a disservice by releasing a volume of drafts and notes under the title *Ich weiß keine bessere Welt* (Munich: Piper, 2000).

The chapters thus highlight some of the most notorious controversies surrounding the publication of literary texts of the post-war era. All of them offer considered and thoroughly readable reconstructions of the 'cases' and debates, explanations for the 'incriminating' reception or notoriety that certain publications have achieved, and explanations of the reasons and specifically German or Austrian conditions that created a sense of offence—from the sensitivities arising from historical experience and the alleged tarnishing of good names to the conflation of moral and aesthetic criteria. All the cases have in common the ways in which the debates transcended the realm of the literary, or, more specifically, they show what happens when non-literary criteria are applied to literary production—it is indeed this very phenomenon that constitutes a 'text crime' in the first place and potentially makes a text subject to legal proceedings or trial by media. The volume opens, however, with the study of an instance of productive intra-literary engagement with an incriminated object, namely Tom Paulin's nuanced and imaginary poetic reflection on Heidegger's dubious role during the Nazi period. This illustrates a refreshing alternative to factitious (and often self-righteous) media outrage or recourse to the authorities of civic society. While legal proceedings and public accusations polarize and defame, this creative form of reaction sensitizes and engages.

NATIONAL UNIVERSITY OF IRELAND MAYNOOTH   FLORIAN KROBB

Aging and Old-Age Style in Günter Grass, Ruth Klüger, Christa Wolf, and Martin Walser: The Mannerism of a Late Period. By STUART TABERNER. Rochester, NY: Camden House. 2013. viii+258 pp. £60. ISBN 978-1-57113-578-0.

Stuart Taberner's *Aging and Old-Age Style* deals not with life review or autobiography in a general sense, but with the '*past-oriented* works of literary life review' of four prominent writers, and how these relate to a 'not-too-distant *future* that they will not inhabit and that will look very different [. . .] from the postwar world they describe in their books' (p. 210). This work sets out from the incontrovertible fact that societies are getting older. While critical studies have treated the representation of ageing in contemporary culture (pp. 10–14, 193–94; the bibliography provides several examples), Taberner sets out primarily to examine style. His interest lies in the '*aesthetic* strategies' (p. 194) used by writers in conducting narrative life review. The term 'life review'—'a form of storytelling which selects from the remembered past, reworks events, and narrates meaning' (p. 20)—appears to liberate the discussion of conventionally termed 'autobiographical' or 'auto-fictional' texts and allows Taberner's focus to remain on his chosen topic without having to dwell on excessively rehearsed genre designations and distinctions. His intention is to read such works 'within the literary-theoretical frameworks of old-age style and late style, while drawing on psychological and gerontological understandings of life review and the sociological discussion of "the aging society" in order to demonstrate their wider relevance' (p. viii). A number of more general literary questions underpin the study, as well as those pertaining to the German context: how does a writer at the end of his/her life review the preceding events? What conventions are associated with old-age style and how do writers confirm, subvert, or reject them? Can old-age style 'function as *late* style', and how does this relate to the 'post-postwar era'? (pp. vii–viii).

The introduction ('Old-Age Societies—Old-Age Style') begins with a thorough set of demographics and statistics which demonstrate that populations are ageing—both globally, and specifically in Germany (and as Taberner shows, this is a particularly German problem, pp. 5–7)—and provides an overview of ageing in German culture (film, television, and literature) which establishes a useful context, and addresses some of the theoretical issues associated with 'old-age style': for example, how does 'intentionality' (p. 23) affect our reading of these works? To what extent is old age *performed* (p. 25)? Taberner subsequently explores the issues outlined above using four case studies: Günter Grass, Ruth Klüger, Christa Wolf, and Martin Walser—literary giants, or literary dinosaurs, to use an image upon which both Grass and Wolf draw (pp. 41, 97). The experiences of growing up of these four authors, born between 1927 and 1931, have been, to varying degrees, the subject of their texts and of public and academic discussion. It is thus refreshing to encounter this differentiated analysis of their works. In the first chapter ('Old-Age Style and Self-Monumentalization') Taberner focuses on Grass's 'late works', from *Beim Häuten der Zwiebel* to *Die Box*, and *Grimms Wörter*, concluding with a discussion of Grass's controversial 2012 poem 'Was gesagt werden muss'. According to Taberner,

Grass stridently proclaims his senescence and impotence, yet this self-presentation as the relic of a bygone public intellectual tradition may not be enough to 'convince readers of his "late" relevance' (p. 203).

In 'Old-Age Style and Self-Healing' Taberner explores works by Klüger and Wolf. These two writers have been shown elsewhere to bear comparison despite their contrasting formative experiences and perspectives (see Caroline Schaumann, *Memory Matters: Generational Responses to Germany's Nazi Past in Recent Women's Literature* (Berlin: de Gruyter, 2008)). The issue of how gender might be seen to affect style is explicitly tackled, and Klüger's focus on 'the gendered social construction of aging' (p. 101) lends itself to the discussion. Wolf's old-age style is treated largely with reference to *Stadt der Engel oder The Overcoat of Dr. Freud*, the last of her works to be published before her death in 2011. While Grass condemns the effects of his own 'lateness', but nonetheless refuses to relinquish his position in shaping public discourse, Wolf challenges the reader to understand that what they took to be universals are no longer so, and consequently to come to see him/herself as 'a "late" subject butting up against the assumptions, or presumptions, of Western modernity' (p. 206). The final case study, in Chapter 3 ('Old-Age Style and Self-Transcendence'), explores Martin Walser's 'old-age trilogy'—*Der Augenblick der Liebe*, *Angstblüte*, and *Ein liebender Mann*—and in his 2011 novel *Muttersohn*. Especially in the last of these, Walser's presentation of his characters' final rejection of absolute dominance and independence might well take us beyond such a modern illusion to an understanding and acceptance of 'our essential interdependence with all others [which] might *liberate* us of Western modernity's self-delusions' (p. 210).

Each of the three chapters is clearly delineated with the focus on the writer at hand, yet Taberner repeatedly draws thematic and formal links as he goes along, which makes for a rich and engaging study. A thread one might discern throughout is the way in which Taberner views Grass as an example of how not to go about being 'late', Wolf leads the reader to recognize his/her own lateness, and Walser offers an attitudinal stance in relation to that lateness. In addition, although Taberner focuses on a few specific texts in each of his case studies, he also makes reference to a significant range of works, which ought to lend this study a broad appeal.

In the introduction Taberner pointed out that old-age style and late style are not synonymous, although they may 'occasionally overlap' (p. 23). In the conclusion ('Old-Age Style as Late Style?') he deftly draws together the various strands of his argument and takes it a stage further, namely in his consideration of how we might read the old-age style of Grass, Wolf, and Walser as late style. The close reading and analysis of the three preceding chapters are utilized to support the argument and to demonstrate how the works can be viewed as 'an *intervention* in today's "new" lateness' (p. 210). On the last page Taberner claims that it 'falls to the reader to judge' the success of his project (p. 211). This reader is more than satisfied: Taberner's book is characteristically well written and will appeal to scholars in the field, as well as students, who will greatly benefit from this refreshing take on well-known and widely discussed writers. Yet, as Taberner points out, there is more work to be done (p. 211), and one of the many strengths of this rich and complex text is that, far from granting him the last word, it opens up exciting possibilities for further research.

ST EDMUND HALL, OXFORD   ALEXANDRA LLOYD

Medialität der Kunst: Rolf Dieter Brinkmann in der Moderne. Ed. by MARKUS FAUSER. Bielefeld: transcript. 2011. 290 pp. €31. ISBN 978-3-8376-1559-3.
Rainald Goetz. Ed. by HEINZ LUDWIG ARNOLD with CHARIS GOER and STEFAN GREIF. Göttingen: text+kritik. 2011. 117 pp. €19. ISBN 978-3-86916-108-2.

Rolf Dieter Brinkmann and Rainald Goetz are two of the best-known figures of German pop literature. With his programmatic references to brands and bands, his insistence on the mundanity of the 'here and now', and his sustained critique of 'high' literary culture, Brinkmann (1940–1975) initiated this literary movement in West Germany in the late 1960s. His aesthetic techniques of cutting, mixing, and experimenting in multiple written, audio, and visual media have lived on in the work of Rainald Goetz (b. 1954). Both authors deliberately place themselves at the avant-garde end of pop literature, both programmatically rail against the literary industry, and yet both remain reliant on this industry's critical apparatus to articulate their wider cultural value.

This is nowhere more evident than in the way both of them pulled off stunts with their own authorial person—Goetz by cutting open his own forehead while reading at the Ingeborg Bachmann competition in 1983 and Brinkmann by making a rhetorical death threat to Marcel Reich-Ranicki during the course of a public meeting at the Academy of Arts in Berlin in 1968. As Jochen Bonz and Dirk Niefanger both show in their chapters on each author's self-aware literary aesthetics, these performances were not only planned for maximum media exposure, but also demonstrate the central importance of 'mediality' for the authors' work. Brinkmann and Goetz are both driven by a concern with process, and the radical aesthetic innovations that define their work are designed to shine a light on the linguistic and visual structures that shape our perception of the world. This is not so much a case of 'the medium is the message' as a programmatically developed belief, held by both these authors and their acolytes, that the juxtaposition of multiple media and creative-performative practices is the only way we can hope to stand outside of discourse in order to see its normative messages being formed.

So far, so compelling; but can this insight alone sustain a literary career, never mind a whole literary practice over fifty years? The principal achievement of Markus Fauser's edited volume of fifteen essays is to suggest that Brinkmann's literary finesse is in fact a lot more indebted to established styles and structures than the author would have us believe. Moritz Baßler shows us a Brinkmann whose characters have psychological depth and whose plots owe a considerable deal to realism, despite the author's professed obsession with surface. Dirk Niefanger writes interestingly on his authoritative authorial stance, despite or perhaps precisely because of the autonomous tendencies vaunted by his texts. Sascha Seiler and Eckhard Schumacher explore the problems that Brinkmann will experience as the rebellious pop music that inspired him sells out to the market and he catches himself acting as the very kind of tourist his writing set out to undermine. This gentle wrong-footing of the posturing author opens up his writing in more interesting ways than the chapters that explore his deliberately self-referential aesthetic technique can do—although Stefan Greif on hybrid art, and Heinz Drügh and Stephanie Schmitt on consumer goods and the boundary between high and low culture, are also insightful. Fauser's volume both explores how Brinkmann's work underpins the German pop literature movement and suggests new ways of looking at the wider literary context of this phenomenon. It is an important and well-produced work, but it is crying out for an index and a bibliography to fulfil its potential as a lasting reference work.

Meanwhile, the slim text+kritik volume on Goetz guest-edited by Charis Goer and Stefan Greif represents the first collection of academic essays to engage systematically with all of Goetz's major works; critical discussion to date has been largely confined to isolated, often comparative articles and a notable preponderance of journalistic pieces, as the useful bibliography indicates. Essays by Jochen Bonz, Stefan Greif, Andreas Wicke, and Charis Goer explain the author's aesthetic indebtedness to punk, rave, and techno and offer close readings that show how his texts enact an assault on the senses in order to encourage more complex political and aesthetic debate within the left-wing cultural milieu. Norbert Otto Eke, Mirko F. Schmidt, and Lutz Hagestedt investigate Goetz's ongoing engagement with audio, visual, and social media as a further attempt both to reach out to and to challenge his audience. The way Goetz blurs fact and fiction and plays with his own author person is addressed directly by Eckhard Schumacher, but these tropes also cut across the volume as a whole. Characteristically, Goetz's own contribution is an extract from a recent publication where, reflecting on an invitation to be the subject of a text+kritik volume, he speculates on producing work that would contain its own critical apparatus and be 'text+kritik' in one. This would render redundant interviews and other paratextual engagement with the author—although, as the bibliography shows, this very media interest is what has carried Goetz's career to date.

Such disingenuous circling around himself as a player in the literary scene brings us back to the posturing author. Only one or two essays in this volume attempt to probe the success of such posing. Instead, the emphasis is on explaining it through poststructuralist theory: Niklas Luhmann's systems theory is a repeated point of reference, and some essays risk overwhelming the reader with references to cultural critics. While it is entirely appropriate to consider experimental writing of the 1980s and 1990s through the lens of the cultural theory that was on the ascendant at that time, from an 'after theory' standpoint in 2011 the resulting essays can appear too caught up in that late twentieth-century cultural moment.

So how can critics analysing pop literature get beyond explaining its game-playing and the self-reflexivity of the hybrid media it employs in order to reach a more durable evaluation of these authors and their works—especially when the authors programmatically set out to say and do it all themselves? These volumes have no ready answers, although Fauser's cultivates more critical distance to its subject (easier, of course, when the querulous author is dead). Versed in the language of literary and cultural theory and demanding readers rich in cultural capital, both Brinkmann and Goetz are thoroughly convincing subjects of the serious academic study represented in these volumes. And that is perhaps the real death knell for these kings of pop. The one should be turning in his grave and the other ferociously wielding his shovel.

Lancaster University   Rebecca Braun

Ilija Trojanow. Ed. by Julian Preece. (Contemporary German Writers and Filmmakers, 2) Oxford: Peter Lang. 2013. 209 pp. £42. ISBN 978-3-0343-0894-6.

This volume offers an overview of an author who is becoming increasingly visible both within and beyond Germany. Indeed, Ilija Trojanow is establishing himself at the vanguard of a renewed tradition of socially committed writing in Germany, with a growing corpus of literary texts but also polemical interventions, essays, and speeches on a wide range of issues of pressing contemporary importance, most notably the global electronic and telephonic mass surveillance operations carried out by America's National Security Agency over recent years. Indeed, in early September 2013 Trojanow was barred from entering the United States to attend a seminar series organized by the author of this review at the German Studies Association annual conference. No reason was given but it is difficult not to draw the conclusion that this decision must be linked to Trojanow's publication in 2009, with his colleague Juli Zeh, of *Angriff auf die Freiheit: Sicherheitswahn, Überwachungsstaat und der Abbau bürgerlicher Rechte*, a polemic aimed, in part, at the NSA operations.

Julian Preece has assembled a strong team of scholars, who together cover the most important aspects of Trojanow's work: his social commitment; engagement with world religions, especially Islam; environmentalism; and cosmopolitan vision. The nine essays (plus a preface) in the volume also deal well with the aesthetic dimensions to his literary work, with a particular focus on multiperspectivality, hybridity, and epic scope. There is also an interview with the author, conducted by Preece, and an essay by Trojanow, 'Weltbürgertum heute: Rede zu einer kosmpolitischen Kultur', although these, unfortunately, have the feel of a 'missed opportunity'. The first remains somewhat general (Trojanow is a subtle and articulate interlocutor, but the interview is perhaps too genteel to provoke this), whereas the second is not an original piece (although one recognizes, of course, that authors cannot be required to write original pieces for companion volumes such as this).

The critical essays are of a uniformly high standard. It is particularly pleasing to see an essay devoted to Trojanow's dramatic work (*EisTau*), though Preece's careful analysis perhaps betrays that the author is indeed better in prose, and to see a discussion of less-known texts such as *Autopol* (Cornelius Partsch), *Die Welt ist groß und Rettung lauert überall* (Eva Knopp), and *Nomade auf vier Kontinenten* (Christina Kraenzle). Partsch is helpful on the Internet novel *Autopol*, though perhaps a little descriptive; Knopp draws out the humour in the author's work well and offers interesting insights into his use of the 'transcultural trickster figure' (p. 105) to undermine stereotypes and cultural assumptions, and Kraenzle provides a thoughtful discussion of Trojanow's travelogues as an engagement with the genre's origins in, or close connection with, European colonialism. This essay points forward nicely to Preece's chapter (his second in the volume) on the author's extensive reportage and journalism.

The majority of the essays, however, either wholly or mostly, are concerned with Trojanow's best-known (and probably best) work, *Der Weltensammler*. Here there are some real gems. Caitríona Ní Dhúill gives a compelling account of Trojanow's novel as a form of metabiography, showing how the author deconstructs the genre of the biography in order to show how (national and individual) stereotypes are constructed and circulate. Ernest Schonfield sets *Zu den heiligen Quellen des Islam*, the author's account of his research for *Der Weltensammler* (and of his own pilgrimage to Mecca), and *Der Weltensammler* itself alongside their 'original' source material, Sir Richard Francis Burton's *Personal Narrative of a Pilgrimage*, to great (and revealing) effect. And Ben Morgan—in perhaps the most stimulating if quirky essay of the volume—discusses Trojanow's engagement with religion in *Der Weltensammler* (and elsewhere) in the context of St Augustine, Kierkegaard, and Heidegger. Morgan's contextualization of Trojanow with these thinkers on religion is at times a little forced—he comes close to saying that Trojanow 'fails' because he has a different concept of inner life from theirs (why should he share it?)—but he is fascinating on Trojanow's insistence on the unknowability of others, and on unknowability as an invitation to communicate across cultures in the hope of empathy and understanding. This is a very good volume, which will be of great use to scholars and students alike. It is tightly edited, well conceived, and does a great service in making this important writer better known to readers and academics in the anglophone world.

UNIVERSITY OF LEEDS   STUART TABERNER

Religion in Contemporary German Drama. By SINÉAD CROWE. Rochester, NY: Camden House. 2013. 178 pp. £50. ISBN 978-1-5711-3549-0.

Sinéad Crowe's study explores the claim that, at the beginning of the twenty-first century, religion has made a comeback on the German-language stage. The volume therefore belongs in the context of worldwide debates about whether we are in the midst of a religious revival—illustrated most notoriously by the rise of fundamentalism—or whether the current interest in religiosity is merely part of an individualist desire for a 'feeling of faith' to counterbalance the rationality of high-tech, consumer capitalism. Crowe's book is therefore a timely publication, offering an alternative to scholarly treatments of German-language drama founded in theories of the post-dramatic or cultural memory.

The first of seven chapters offers an overview of the relationship between theatre and ritual, drawing attention to the complex and often blurred boundary between

Judaeo-Christian rites and theatrical practice. It thus links the question of religion with two key concerns in twentieth- and twenty-first-century theatre, namely the transformative, educational potential of the contemporary stage and the desire to counter a secularized, rational world in staged 're-ritualizations'. The second chapter identifies four ways in which twentieth-century European theatre is informed by religion: aestheticized religiosity, the quest for spiritual renewal, the notion of ritualistic 'holy' theatre, and the dramatization of the absence of religious meaning. Crowe illustrates these trends with reference to key movements and figures: Symbolism, Expressionism (Georg Kaiser, Ernst Toller), August Strindberg, Antonin Artaud, Jerzi Grotowski, and Samuel Beckett. Although this discussion confines itself to the twentieth century and covers territory that will be familiar to scholars working in the field, it nevertheless offers a useful starting point for the student interested in questions of spirituality and ritual on the European stage.

Chapters 3–7 look in turn at plays by Botho Strauß (*Groß und Klein*, 1979; *Die Eine und die Andere*, 2005), George Tabori (*Mein Kampf*, 1996), Werner Fritsch (*Wondreber Totentanz: Traumspiel*, 1999; *Aller Seelen: Traumspiel*, 2000), and Lukas Bärfuss (*Der Bus: Das Zeug einer Heiligen*, 2005). A central concern is whether these works are able genuinely to engage with spirituality, thereby progressing beyond a postmodern impasse in which religion is merely an empty, aesthetic resource. The perspective throughout is critical and the discussion draws on a range of interesting textual examples. The momentum of the debate is a little uneven, which may be a consequence of the 'one-author-per-chapter' approach. Some of the analysis suggests, unsurprisingly, that traditional religious forms are shown to be inadequate to contemporary needs and that religious motifs and themes continue to be deployed to highlight the moral bankruptcy of society. Rather more interesting, however, are Crowe's critical reflections on claims that theatre can offer an alternative spiritual space. Her analyses of the work of Werner Fritsch offer an important critique of his complex and contradictory claims about the value and function of theatre. Her discussions of plays by Botho Strauß and Lukas Bärfuss are particularly fruitful, showing that treatments of religion may be able to extend beyond social critique or the creation of an 'Ersatz religion' on stage: Crowe argues that these dramatists employ questions of religion to challenge 'complacent secularity' and to explore contemporary attitudes to belief. It is, however, a shame that Ulrich Seidl (and in particular *Vater Unser*, 2010), whom Crowe identifies as interesting in this regard, could not be included in this study.

The relevance and appeal of this volume are beyond doubt. It is elegantly written and offers a readable and accessible introduction that will be particularly useful to university students of German and Drama Studies. Nevertheless, Crowe's restricted focus on plays invoking the Judaeo-Christian tradition—bracketing out, therefore, recent work engaging with questions of fundamentalism and the implication of questions of religiosity in multicultural societies—while acknowledged and justified by the author, does somewhat undermine the potential of this study to contribute to broader social and cultural debates.

UNIVERSITY COLLEGE DUBLIN   GILLIAN PYE

Modern German Literature. By MICHAEL MINDEN. Cambridge: Polity. 2011. 253 pp. £17.99. ISBN 978-0-7456-2920-9.

The trend in recent histories of German literature has been about finding new ways to tell an old story. From the monumental—David Wellbery's compendium *A New History of German Literature* (Cambridge, MA, and London: Belknap Press of Harvard University Press, 2004)—to the miniature—Nicholas Boyle's *German Literature: A Very Short Introduction* (Oxford and New York: Oxford University Press, 2008)—scholars have striven for fresh perspectives on a familiar body of material. Wellbery's contributors focus on datable 'encounters', Boyle on the defining duopoly of *Beamter* and *Bürger*. Michael Minden's approach differs not only in its concentration on the 'modern', but also in its insistence on returning texts to their original contexts. Appearing in a series on the 'Cultural History of Literature', Minden's study seeks to rescue canonical works from the straitjacket of posterity, placing a particular emphasis on how they were actually read at the time, rather than on how they have subsequently been received. Both in style and in substance, this approach has much to offer.

Minden begins with a brief methodological introduction, in which he stakes a claim for the ground between literary criticism and literary history. His chief contention is intriguing: that the idealism (with both lower and upper cases) that drove the Romantic flowering of German literature also covered it up again, in as much as the pragmatism of nineteenth-century nation-building looked to extract *ideas* from texts rather than to engage with the specificity of the texts themselves. Minden's stated aim is accordingly to 'correct' the characteristically German imposition of philosophy on literature, and to replace it with the lived experience of literature within its changing cultural contexts. It comes down, he suggests, to a question of narrative.

If this narrative can be said to commence in the manner in which it will continue, it is because the very first adjective employed is 'best-selling' (p. 4). Time and again over the course of his study, Minden returns to sales figures as 'one of the few clues to what a modern public [. . .] is actually thinking or feeling' (p. 87). This method offers refreshing attention to what is actually being read at any given moment—as opposed to what critical posterity has decided *should* have been read—and throws a welcome light on a range of minor figures; what Minden calls 'serious popular writers' (p. 55) emerge as a recurring theme of the book. Nonetheless, the emphasis also throws up some questionable decisions of weighting: eyebrows may be raised, for instance, at the inclusion of three pages on Max Kretzer, Gustav Frenssen, and Bernhard Kellermann, and at the exclusion of almost any sustained discussion of *Faust*. Criticizing omissions in a study of this impressive breadth is perhaps facile, but sales figures can surely hide a multitude of whims.

This is not to say that Minden is not a stylish and sure-footed guide to the loftier peaks of German literature, however contentious some of his emphases may be. Beginning from the Gottscheds' creation of modern German drama as a normative institution, he traces the twin senses of writing as both private and public enterprise with verve and erudition. A key early moment is Karl Philipp Moritz's theorization, in the 1780s, of the 'autonomy' of art. Given Minden's insistence on the context of the 'modern book market' (p. 47), the self-conscious autonomy of literature emerges as a pivotal concept in his narrative. Indeed, beyond its inevitable periodization of literary history—Enlightenment to Romanticism, nineteenth-century Realism, Wilhelmine Germany, the two world wars and the Weimar Republic, the Third Reich and the GDR, and the post-war capitalist era—Minden's account of German literature can be understood as tracing the precise calibrations of its supposed autonomy. One of the more enlightening ways in which he questions this quintessentially Germanic presupposition—aside from highlighting the paradox of promoting 'autonomous' art as a sellable commodity—is to view German literature as a series of sublimations. Winckelmann's *Gedancken über die Nachahmung der griechischen Wercke in der Mahlerei und Bildhauer-Kunst* 'must be the most influential piece of sublimation in art history' (p. 22), he suggests; much of Goethe and indeed Classical-Romantic literature as a whole can be read as 'an act of sublimation' (p. 52); and Stifter, perhaps most memorably of all, emerges as nothing less than 'the Shakespeare of repression' (p. 73). Autonomy, then, is in the eye of the beholder.

In keeping with this emphasis on the cultural preconditions of aesthetics, Minden's later chapters swing from the literature of 'negation' to that of 'affirmation'. Reading modernism as an expression of resistance to modernity, he argues that serious literature creates the conditions for 'silence' in a society of spectacle (p. 207), whether that society be the pre-Second World War Weimar Republic or the post-war Federal Republic. In the former, Minden considers the various political inflections of literature in the period, from the implicit ideological Fascism of Jünger (p. 127) to the explicit communism of Brecht, as the legacy of the First World War; in the latter, he views 'Literature in Democratic Capitalism' as an expression of what Peter Sloterdijk calls 'enlightened false consciousness' (p. 180). His section on the two non-democratic regimes of the Third Reich and the GDR, meanwhile, focuses on the instrumentalization of literature and how (at least some) writers find ways to affirm not just the political status quo, but also their own aesthetic autonomy.

Minden's conclusion—at the end not only of this book, perhaps, but of a long and distinguished teaching career—is that literature has had to come to terms with its increasing marginalization. He does, however, find room for optimism: after a period of aesthetic stagnation as the two Germanies played out their sibling rivalry, he sees the *Wende* as having brought 'a powerful new impetus' (p. 229) to German literature, and he closes accordingly with one writer who has sought to redeem the false consciousness of late modernity. It is striking how rapidly W. G. Sebald has become the acknowledged endpoint of German literature in recent (English-language) accounts: both Wellbery's and Boyle's narratives finish with the same focus, and the preternatural poise of Sebald's prose provides a fitting conclusion to Minden's thought-provoking study. Despite its inevitable omissions and compressions, as an account of the *Sonderweg* of modern German literature within its complex cultural context this is a rich and rewarding book.

UNIVERSITY OF KENT   BEN HUTCHINSON

The Englishman From Lebedian'—A Life of Evgeny Zamiatin (1884–1937). By J. A. E. CURTIS. Boston. Academic Studies Press. 2013. 394 pp. $75. ISBN 978-1-618112-80-4.

In his recollections Andrei Levinson painted the following word portrait of his friend Evgeny Zamiatin:

His influence is exceptionally powerful: for those who know only the small stack of his books, it is at times rather mysterious. His power is personal, it is the direct emanation of a hardened will. The whole of Zamiatin is of a harmonious cut; everything in him is precisely fitted... His hair is parted, there's a mocking smile on his lips, and at the corner of his smile there's a pipe... He is an Englishman out of Leskov; a coloniser in a white helmet; Mister Zamiatin; Zamiatin Effendi; a gentleman.

This assessment of Zamiatin (quoted by Julie Curtis on pages 108–09 of the volume under review) corresponds closely to the image of him that appears in many photographs and sketches, not least in the cartoon by Nikolai Radlov reproduced on the front cover. Yet as compelling as such portraits are, they can also mislead if they suggest someone who was a detached and ironic bystander. For throughout this compelling new biography we are struck above all by Zamiatin's multifaceted personality and extraordinary vitality. From the moment he came of age to his final years of exile in Paris he was caught up in a whirlpool of professional commitments, constantly struggling to establish and maintain his position as a central figure in the literary world. The fact that throughout this period he was, in one way or another, politically suspect only serves to emphasize the unusual force of his presence and influence. Remarkably, this intense activity was hardly to diminish even after the fateful day in late August 1929 when he was subjected, together with Boris Pil'niak, to a vicious attack by the press, the start of a campaign that, within two years, was to lead to exile in Paris. And even in Paris, unlike the majority of his émigré colleagues whose right-wing ideological stance he was unwilling to share, he remained deeply concerned with the state of Soviet literature.

Among the most intriguing aspects of Zamiatin's life is the complex nature of his relationships with his literary colleagues. Although Maksim Gor'ky was subsequently to become a more distant figure, we see him playing a highly significant and generally positive role in Zamiatin's life. Figures such as Boris Grigor'ev, Aleksandr Krolenko, Alexei Remizov, and Iury Annenkov were especially supportive. There are some surprises: on the one hand we see someone such as Konstantin

Fedin emerging as a friend and confidant of Zamiatin; on the other, we find Kornei Chukovsky making unexpectedly snide remarks, claiming that Zamiatin knew 'strikingly little about English literature and life' (p. 119); and, even more devastatingly, apropos *We*, that 'in one line of Dostoevsky there is more intelligence and anger than in the whole of Zamiatin's novel' (p. 137).

Publishers' claims for their authors are often marred by hyperbole, but in this case their praise for Curtis's work is fully justified. Their comment, however, that Zamiatin is revealed as someone who 'negotiated the political dilemmas of his day—including his relationship with Stalin—with great shrewdness' is questionable. Zamiatin may well have dealt shrewdly with others in all kinds of ways, but Stalin was not someone who was open to 'negotiation' in any rational sense. As much as any other Soviet citizen during those terrifyingly arbitrary years, Zamiatin was subject to the whims of a paranoid dictator and therefore as powerless when it came to deciding his own fate. In this connection there are still some unanswered questions. Why, for example, was Zamiatin allowed to leave the Soviet Union whereas his great friend Mikhail Bulgakov was refused permission? Both wrote letters to members of the government and to Stalin himself using very similar phraseology. Was it a direct result of Gor′ky's intercession on Zamiatin's behalf, or were there other factors involved? And how likely was it that Stalin would ever have granted Zamiatin's often expressed wish to return from France to the Soviet Union?

Curtis naturally pays a lot of attention to Zamiatin's voluminous creative output, but this is not her primary focus here. Drawing on all available sources, she provides the reader with a detailed account of Zamiatin's life, covering the tribulations and successes of his literary career, his professional life as a designer of icebreakers including his time in England, his prolific correspondence, his surprisingly few moments of relaxation on holiday, his frequent bouts of ill health (besides other afflictions, he suffered from chronic colitis), and his sometimes uneasy relationship with his wife Liudmila Nikolaevna. The sheer amount of detail could have become overwhelming, but Curtis never allows it to stifle a narrative that brilliantly illuminates the life of one of the most talented figures in twentieth-century Russian life and letters.

UNIVERSITY OF EXETER   ROGER COCKRELL

When Pigs Could Fly and Bears Could Dance: A History of the Soviet Circus. By MIRIAM NEIRICK. Madison: University of Wisconsin Press. 2012. xix+287 pp. $29.95. ISBN 978-0-299-28764-1.

In her informative history of the Soviet circus, Miriam Neirick sets out to address 'what the circus meant to so many who loved it and why the circus came to mean so much in the Soviet Union' (p. 13). Noting that it seems paradoxical for a state with 'an admitted interest in using cultural objects to propagate transparent, monosemic, and didactic messages' to promote such a fluid cultural form (p. 14), Neirick argues that the circus's indeterminacy was the key to its popularity with and significance for the Soviet state and Soviet audiences alike.

Against a familiar periodization of Soviet political history, the book's six main chapters analyse specific circus acts, official rhetoric about the circus, and popular responses to it, drawing on a wide range of archival documents, first-hand accounts, and secondary sources. The first chapter examines the 'revolutionizing' of the circus (involving 'revolutionary pantomimes', for example) between 1918 and 1920 and of rhetoric about the circus between 1921 and 1929. The second chapter focuses on the early Stalin period (1929–39), when the circus was celebrated for its ability to transform viewers into 'future Soviet men and women' (p. 66) through elaborate spectacles showcasing human physical perfection; and then, after 1935, to 'ma[k]e audiences happy by showing them how happy they already were' (p. 80), with clowning routines featuring personae such as Mikhail Rumiantsev's 'young, cheerful, heroic' Karandash, who ostensibly 'represented the ordinary Soviet individual' (pp. 87, 84). The third chapter discusses the mobilization of the circus during the Second World War to maintain audiences' morale and alleviate their fears, tasks addressed through 'politically tendentious clowning' (p. 94) and various acts of daring (animal acts, clowns' 'William Tell routines') that heightened fear and then delivered cathartic release. The fourth and fifth chapters address the immediate post-war and Cold War period, surveying a dizzyingly broad range of issues that the circus addressed: from the scarcity and poor quality of material goods (satirized in clowning routines); to presentation of the 'Western menace' (demonized in clowning routines); to interethnic relations in the Soviet Union and multinational friendships abroad (demonstrated through multiethnic, multinational circus troupes themselves). The sixth chapter focuses on the late Soviet period, examining clowning as a medium through which 'individual expression and collective labor' were presented as 'complementary sources of renewal' for Soviet society (p. 191). While the Soviet circus's 'indeterminate, flexible, and polyvalent' nature and its use as an ideological instrument are hardly novel, Neirick concludes, the Soviet circus was unique in its ability to satisfy both state and society precisely because it remained 'an indeterminate, flexible, and polyvalent form of art that constantly propagated political messages, ideological lessons, and legitimating myths' (p. 216).

Neirick's interesting and well-researched history will appeal to scholars of the circus and of Soviet popular culture and cultural politics more generally. However, a significant emphasis on clowning comes at the expense of other acts (gymnastic and aerial routines, animal acts, illusionists, jugglers, and others are all accorded far less attention); thus, arguably, a full sense of the breadth and variety of the Soviet circus is lacking. Additionally, the indeterminacy and uniqueness of the Soviet circus are noted frequently, but little attempt is made to draw parallels between the circus and other (potentially) ambivalent cultural forms and practices such as popular song; as a result, the Soviet circus's uniqueness is compellingly asserted but not unequivocally proven. These criticisms notwithstanding, Neirick's book is a welcome and much-needed analysis of the Soviet circus and its repeated transformations within a shifting political and ideological landscape.

UNIVERSITY OF MANCHESTER   RACHEL S. PLATONOV

Moscow Prime Time: How the Soviet Union Built the Media Empire that Lost the Cultural Cold War. By KRISTIN ROTH-EY. Ithaca, NY, and London: Cornell University Press. 2011. 320 pp. $39.95. ISBN 978-0-8014-4874-4.

This monograph is a useful contribution to our understanding of Soviet media and culture in the post-war period, a period that remains under-researched because for a long time researchers had limited access to Soviet archives. Kristin Roth-Ey's book draws on a wealth of archival materials which she collected in ten different archives in Russia, Ukraine, and Hungary. The book presents many new facts and materials. For example, the Western reader is for the first time invited to engage in a discussion of Soviet viewing culture in the Khrushchev and Brezhnev eras.

The book is divided into five chapters, with an introduction and an epilogue. The first chapter is dedicated to the Soviet film industry, focusing on the production and distribution of films and on post-war changes in the film industry. Roth-Ey gives many specific examples of films which demonstrate both the successes and failures of the Soviet film industry. For example, the discussion of the reception of two contrasting films, *Ivan's Childhood* (Andrei Tarkovskii, 1962) and the first Soviet blockbuster *Amphibian Man* (Vladimir Chebotarev and Gennadii Kazanskii, 1962), is illuminating. Roth-Ey goes on to examine the impact of Western films and popular culture on post-war Russian culture. She discusses the effect of the popularity of such Western films as *The Woman of My Dreams* (*Die Frau meiner Traüme*: Georg Jacoby, 1944), the *Tarzan* films, and *The Magnificent Seven* (John Sturges, 1960), among others. To mirror this discussion, Roth-Ey also examines the impact of Soviet films on Western culture and cinema by looking at which films actually made it to Western cinemas at the time. She offers her understanding of how the Soviets defined and redefined the success of their film industry: in terms of *tirazh* (the number of copies produced) and profit (second only to the production of vodka!).

The chapter on Soviet film culture focuses on the Golden Age of Soviet film-going: between 1950 and 1970. This chapter is rich in facts and interesting figures. For example, in the 1960s a Soviet person went to the cinema on average twenty times a year. Roth-Ey proceeds to discuss the rapid growth in numbers of cinema theatres and then turns to some fascinating cultural aspects related to film-going, such as popular taste, glamour, cinema festivals, fandom, and popular literature about film, with the focus on Soviet journals about film such as *The Art of Cinema* and *The Soviet Screen*.

A considerable section of the chapter on radio is dedicated to how foreign radio stations were jammed. Roth-Ey also analyses the consequences of Soviet electrification, which led to an expansion of coverage of the Soviet radio stations across the Soviet Union. Her analysis of the scheduling of radio programmes yields some interesting facts about radio production and consumption. For example, news programmes were not specifically scheduled at particular times; airtime was dominated by music programmes. Interestingly, the Soviets made an effort to maintain active audience participation by requesting listeners to write to them with their feedback on radio programmes and suggestions. The impact of radio on the Soviet citizen's daily life is exemplified by a case study focusing on the Maiak radio station.

Chapter 5 focuses on the spread of television in the USSR. Both the number of television stations and the quantity of TV sets acquired by individual households rocketed in post-war Russia. Roth-Ey is not the first to describe the incredible pace at which television became ubiquitous throughout the whole of the USSR. Ellen Mickiewicz wrote about it in her well-regarded volumes about Soviet television: *Split Signals: Television and Politics in the Soviet Union* (New York: Oxford University Press, 1988) and *Changing Channels: Television and the Struggle for Power in Russia* (New York: Oxford University Press, 1997). Surprisingly Roth-Ey does not refer to these books; however, she contributes a new and refreshing discussion of Soviet television culture not covered by Mickiewicz. Roth-Ey examines everyday television viewing and how it was perceived, as reflected in popular cartoons and magazines as well as through the lens of the Soviet hierarchy of arts, which was translated into television viewing. At the end of the chapter, she also examines the role of leading figures in the development of Soviet television, in particular Sergei Liapin, Gosteleradio chairman from 1970 until the time of perestroika. Chapter 6 continues to discuss television: it examines scheduling, focuses on some specific programmes, and sheds light on television production by presenting some curious facts about technical failures.

This is a book which covers a lot of new and interesting material which will undoubtedly be useful to those interested in Soviet and Russian film, media, history, and culture, and should be added to students' reading lists. However, I do have one reservation, concerning the framework for the discussion of all the fascinating material the author has collected. The framework for the argument, presented in the introduction, is very much based on the binaries entrenched by the Cold War; this is also obvious from the title. The development of the Soviet media is seen through the lens of losers and winners within the Western academic tradition of 'binary historiography': 'The Soviet culture formation was a most successful failure. It was very good at being bad' (p. 23). Of course, Roth-Ey is writing about the period during which duality and binary representations of the relationship between the Soviet Union and the West were ingrained, but it seems to me that it would be more productive to go against the grain and frame the discussion of Soviet post-war media differently, for example by exploring the relationship between technological development and ideology. In their introduction to *Russian Cultural Studies: An Introduction* (Oxford: Oxford University Press, 1998), the editors Catriona Kelly, David Shepherd, and Vadim Volkov traced the origins of the tradition to which Roth-Ey's argument may be said to belong—the tradition of looking at Russia as the West's most significant other. Although they point out that 'dualism in propaganda, literature, and texts of all kinds is ubiquitous and overt' and that 'dualistic analysis is not without a foundation' (p. 2), they go on to say that 'it is perhaps time to recognize that Russian history is neither more nor less complex and illogical than histories of European countries' and that 'causative' processes 'cannot be subsumed into easy conflicts between', in this case, the West and the Soviets (p. 3). The current political leadership in Russia is only too keen to blame the West and Western scholarship for taking dualistic approaches when researching Russia; it might be worth reflecting on how our work may inadvertently help to reinforce their assumptions.

UNIVERSITY OF BIRMINGHAM   NATASHA RULYOVA

ABSTRACTS

The Disenchantment/Re-enchantment of the World: Aesthetics, Secularization, and the Gods of Greece from Friedrich Schiller to Walter Pater   by Sara Lyons

This article charts part of the literary genealogy of **Max Weber**'s claim that modernity is defined by the '**disenchantment** of the world'. It clarifies the relationship between Weber's disenchantment diagnosis and the **gods-in-exile** theme as variously rendered by **Friedrich Schiller**, **Heinrich Heine**, and **Walter Pater**. It also sheds light on current debates about **secularization**, particularly on the extent to which the concepts of the 'pagan' and the 'aesthetic' tend by turns to enable and to destabilize secularization narratives.

Problematic Realisms: German Poetic Realism and Michel Butor's *Portrait de l'artiste en jeune singe*   by Michael J. White

This essay has two purposes: it proposes a reading of **Michel Butor**'s *Portrait de l'artiste en jeune singe* (1967) through the interpretative lens of **German** nineteenth-century **Realism**; in so doing, it argues that **Poetic Realism** is relevant to prose writing beyond Germany and beyond the nineteenth century. It outlines the major interpretative difficulties posed by Realism, before suggesting an analysis of Realist poetics, the characteristics of which are seen as strategies of **indirectness**. This analysis forms the basis for the reading of Butor's *Portrait*, which uncovers not only remarkable formal affinities but also a shared problematization of subjective **representation**.

Science in Three Dimensions: Werner Herzog's *Cave of Forgotten Dreams*   by Christopher Johnson

Filmed in 3-D, *Cave of Forgotten Dreams* is not only about the prehistoric site of **Chauvet** but also the community of researchers who create meaning around it. This article approaches **Herzog**'s **documentary** as a work of **science communication** which combines explanation of the scientific facts with more reflexive testimonies regarding Chauvet's possible meanings. While critical preconceptions about Herzog's cinematic 'vision' might suggest a metaphysical bias, it is argued that his highly structured staging of the protagonists produces a play of perspectives in which evolutionary-materialist explanations are juxtaposed with more spiritualist interpretations. The result is a fascinating insight into the **human science** of **prehistory** in the twenty-first century.

Gower *Agonistes* and Chaucer on Ovid (and Virgil)   by David R. Carlson

Gower was emulous and rivalrous: he set himself to master and overcome other poets whose work he knew; **Ovid** principally, though also his contemporary **Chaucer** and, later, his own younger self. Examination of Gower's uses of the Ovidian tale of Ceyx and Alcione, over a twenty-year period, in three languages, compared with Chaucer's use of the same matter, establishes that Gower learnt emulation from Ovid and used what he learnt to castigate Chaucer. An atypical resort to **Virgil** in Gower, again in castigation of Chaucer, confirms that, despite Chaucer's knowledge of **Boethius**, Gower's mastery of the Latin writers was greater.

Royal Self-Assertion and the Revision of Chivalry: *The Entertainment at Kenilworth* (1575), Jonson's *Masque of Owls* (1624), and *The King's Entertainment at Welbeck* (1633)   by Lesley Mickel

This article examines the **self-assertion** of **Queen Elizabeth I** in conjunction with analysis of the thematic and linguistic connections between *The Entertainment at Kenilworth* (1575), *The Masque of Owls* (1624), and *The King's Entertainment at Welbeck* (1633). The Queen's rejection of Leicester's neo-chivalric script is linked with a radical revision of traditional chivalry. Discussion of texts authored by **Laneham** and **Gascoigne** recording events at **Kenilworth** reveals a reimagining of chivalry in democratic terms; and the article shows how **Ben Jonson** co-opted this radical rethinking in his entertainments into a defence of country sports, and the rights of poet and patron.

ABSTRACTS 1163

'Il n'y a presque pas de ces génies grandioses qui étonnent le monde': Unveiling Genius in David d'Angers's *Paganini* by Vivienne Suvini-Hand

This article examines the bronze **portrait bust** of the Italian virtuoso violinist and composer **Niccolò Paganini** by **David d'Angers**, a major innovator in **French sculpture** of the 1830s. The bust is analysed in the light of David's own observations about the violinist, recorded in his *Carnets*, published posthumously in Paris in 1858. The focal point of David's prose, which alludes to a range of French, German, and English writers, as well as to **phrenological theories** of the **Romantic** period, is Paganini's **genius**, and it is this concept that is most pronounced in the sculptured effigy of the violinist.

Maupassant's *Bel-Ami* and the Secrets of *Actualité* by Edmund Birch

This article takes as its subject **Maupassant's** *Bel-Ami*, tracing the connections between politics, finance, and the **media** which lie at the heart of this 1885 **novel of journalism**. Identifying such thematic concerns in contemporary debates about the **1881 occupation of Tunisia**, it is argued here that the novel probes the sense of complicity uniting journalist and politician under the **French Third Republic**. Drawing on **Marc Angenot**'s concept of social discourse, the article explores the ways in which Maupassant's writing (both fictional and journalistic) interrogates the very notion of *actualité*, outlining the various vested interests which underpin the news.

Gil y Zárate and *Carlos II el hechizado* by Jorge Avilés Diz

Carlos II el hechizado (1837) enjoyed an enormous success in its time, and was regarded up to the end of the nineteenth century as a symbol of **liberal ideas** in Spain. Although the play was traditionally seen as an example of **Antonio Gil y Zárate**'s **eclecticism**, in fact the author tried from the very conception of his work to write a play which imitated the subversive **Romantic dramas** of the 1830s. This article discusses the extent to which Gil y Zárate attained his objective.

Home and Homelessness in Works by Novalis, Dorothea Schlegel, and Tieck by Charlotte Lee

The article addresses the question of **ontological security** in three texts from the Early **Romantic** period by **Novalis, Dorothea Schlegel**, and Ludwig **Tieck** which offer related, yet divergent, accounts of attempts by individuals to establish a sense of continuity and order. In Novalis's *Heinrich von Ofterdingen* Heinrich's development is smooth and is aided by a constant, if evolving, parental presence; but in Dorothea Schlegel's *Florentin* the hero is caught between murky origins and a blurred destination, and struggles both to find and to establish a home, and Tieck's Christian in *Der Runenberg* oscillates between commitment to and rejection of his father's world.

THE
MODERN LANGUAGE REVIEW

VOLUME 109

2014

THE MODERN LANGUAGE REVIEW

Edited by

D. CONNON   A. HISCOCK
A. WILLIAMS   J. EVERSON
D. FLITTER   K. KOHL/R. VILAIN   K. HODGSON

VOLUME 109
2014

Modern Humanities Research Association

The Modern Language Review

is published by

THE MODERN HUMANITIES RESEARCH ASSOCIATION

and may be ordered from JSTOR (http://about.jstor.org/csp)

ISSN 0026-7937 (Print)
ISSN 2222-4319 (Online)

© 2014 THE MODERN HUMANITIES RESEARCH ASSOCIATION

All rights reserved. No part of this publication may be reproduced in any material form (including photocopying or storing it in any medium by electronic means) without the prior written permission of the copyright owner, except in accordance with the provisions of the Copyright, Designs and Patents Act 1988, or under the terms of a licence permitting restricted copying issued in the UK by the Copyright Licensing Agency Ltd, Saffron House, 6–10 Kirby Street, London EC1N 8TS, England, or in the USA by the Copyright Clearance Centre, 222 Rosewood Drive, Danvers, Mass. 01923. Application for the written permission of the copyright owner to reproduce any part of this publication must be made to the General Editor.

DISCLAIMER

Statements of fact and opinion in the content of the *Modern Language Review* are those of the respective authors and contributors and not of the journal editors or of the Modern Humanities Research Association (MHRA). MHRA makes no representation, express or implied, in respect of the accuracy of the material in this journal and cannot accept any legal responsibility or liability for any errors or omissions that may be made.

TYPESET BY JOHN WAŚ, OXFORD

CONTENTS

ALIX-NICOLAÏ, FLORIAN, Ruins and Visions: Stephen Spender in Occupied Germany 54
AUGHTERSON, KATE, The Courtesan and the Bed: Successful Tricking in Middleton's *A Mad World, my Masters* 333
AVILÉS DIZ, JORGE, Gil y Zárate and *Carlos II el hechizado* 1013
BATCHELOR, JOHN, 'Why don't you write a play?' Kipling the Poet in Full . . 663
BIRCH, EDMUND, Maupassant's *Bel-Ami* and the Secrets of *Actualité* 996
BOLLIG, BEN, What Do We Say When We Say 'Juan Gelman'? On Pseudonyms and Polemics in Recent Argentine Poetry 121
CARLSON, DAVID R., Gower *Agonistes* and Chaucer on Ovid (and Virgil) . . 931
CHATSIOU, OURANIA, Lord Byron: Paratext and Poetics 640
DALTON-BROWN, SALLY, Looking for the Creator: Pelevin and the Impotent Writer in *T* (2009) and *Ananasnaia voda dlia prekrasnoi damy* (2011) . 199
DAVIES, PETER, 'Die Juden schießen!' Translations by Hermann Adler and Wolf Biermann of Yitzhak Katzenelson's Epic Poem of the Warsaw Ghetto . 708
DREYER, NICOLAS, Freedom and Captivity in the Works of Vladimir Sorokin and Vladimir Tuchkov 749
FUCHS, ANNE, After the *Flâneur*: Temporality and Connectivity in Wilhelm Genazino's *Belebung der toten Winkel* and *Das Glück in glücksfernen Zeiten* 431
GILLESPIE, DAVID, Evgenii Popov: A New Gogol' for a New Russia? 447
HUGHES, EDWARD J., Lacunary Knowledge in Sebald and Proust 15
JOHNSON, CHRISTOPHER, Science in Three Dimensions: Werner Herzog's *Cave of Forgotten Dreams* 915
KHAIROV, SHAMIL, Writers' Linguistic Observations and Creating Myths about Languages: Czesław Miłosz and Joseph Brodsky in Search of the 'Slavonic Genius of Language' 726
LEE, CHARLOTTE, Home and Homelessness in Works by Novalis, Dorothea Schlegel, and Tieck 1030
LEWIS, CHARLES, Hölderlin on Tragedy and Paradox: 'Die Bedeutung der Tragödien [. . .]' 139
LYONS, SARA, The Disenchantment/Re-enchantment of the World: Aesthetics, Secularization, and the Gods of Greece from Friedrich Schiller to Walter Pater 873
MENDOLA, T. S., Mediterranean Mediations: Language and Cultural (Ex)change in BnF, MS fr. 19152 375
MEYER, JÜRGEN, An Unthinkable *History of King Richard the Third*: Thomas More's Fragment and his Answer to Lucian's *Tyrannicide* 629
MICKEL, LESLEY, Royal Self-Assertion and the Revision of Chivalry: *The Entertainment at Kenilworth* (1575), Jonson's *Masque of Owls* (1624), and *The King's Entertainment at Welbeck* (1633) 953
MORAN, DOMINIC, Vallejo and González Prada: A Note on *Trilce* XIX . . . 689
PARISI, LUCIANO, Narratives of Child Sexual Abuse in Cristina Comencini's Novel *La bestia nel cuore* 674

ARTICLES (cont.) PAGE

Ponnou-Delaffon, Erin Tremblay, Filming the Silent (Br)Other: Levinasian Ethics and Aesthetic Faith in Patrick Drevet's *Les Gardiens des pierres* and Philip Gröning's *Die große Stille* 617
Purssell, Andrew, 'The Senses of Primitive Man': Joseph Conrad, W. H. R. Rivers, and Representing the Other in 'The End of the Tether' 357
Sanson, Helena, 'Simplicité, clarté et précision': Grammars of Italian 'pour les Dames' and Other Learners in Eighteenth- and Early Nineteenth-Century France 593
Schmid, Marion, Henri-Georges Clouzot's *L'Enfer*: Modern Cinema at the Crossroads of the Arts 75
Seeber, Stefan, Medieval Humour? Wolfram's *Parzival* and the Concept of the Comic in Middle High German Romances 417
Stańczyk, Ewa, 'Long Live Poland!': Representing the Past in Polish Comic Books 178
Stoll, Jessica, Petrarch's *De vita solitaria*: Samuel Daniel's Translation c. 1610 313
Suvini-Hand, Vivienne, 'Il n'y a presque pas de ces génies grandioses qui étonnent le monde': Unveiling Genius in David d'Angers's *Paganini* . . 977
Terry, Richard, 'P.S.': The Dangerous Logic of the Postscript in Eighteenth-Century Literature 35
Wampole, Christy, Michel Tournier and the Virtual Essay 96
Weisl-Shaw, Andreea, The Power of Woman's Words, the Power of Woman's Silence: How the *Madrastra* Speaks in the Thirteenth-Century Castilian *Sendebar* 110
White, Michael J., Problematic Realisms: German Poetic Realism and Michel Butor's *Portrait de l'artiste en jeune singe* 896
Wood, Gareth J., Galdós, Shakespeare, and What to Make of *Tormento* . . 392
Wood, Michael, 'Das Land, in dem das Proletariat [nur] genannt werden darf': The Language of Participation in Heiner Müller's *Der Lohndrücker* 160
Zaharchenko, Tanya, Thesaurus of the Unspeakable: *Thanatopraxis* in Kharkiv's Tales of Trauma 462
Ziolkowski, Theodore, 'Tolle lege': Epiphanies of the Book 1

REVIEWS

[AA.VV.], Adam Max Cohen, *Wonder in Shakespeare* (Peter Sillitoe) . . 781
[AA.VV.], Procès de Jacques d'Armagnac: édition critique du ms. 2000 de la Bibliothèque Sainte-Geneviève, ed. by Joël Blanchard (Irène Fabry-Tehranchi) 800
[AA.VV.], The Fabliaux: A New Verse Translation, trans. by Nathaniel Dubin, intro. by R. Howard Bloch (Glyn S. Burgess) 509
[Anon.] ('Amico del Boiardo'), Canzoniere Costabili, ed. by Gabriele Baldassari (Carlo Caruso) 1094
[Anon.], Les Paroles Salomun, ed. by Tony Hunt (Maureen Boulton) . . 798
[Anon.], The Song of Roland, trans. by John DuVal, intro. by David Staines (Luke Sunderland) 795
[Anon.], Eunuco: un volgarizzamento anonimo in terza rima, ed. by Matteo Favaretto (Diego Zancani) 1099
Abravanel, Genevieve, Americanizing Britain: The Rise of Modernism in the Age of the Entertainment Empire (Arin Keeble) 1074

Contents

REVIEWS (*cont.*) PAGE

Adam, Wolfgang, and Siegrid Westphal, eds, Handbuch kultureller Zentren der Frühen Neuzeit: Städte und Residenzen im alten deutschen Sprachraum (JOHN L. FLOOD) 537
Agazzi, Elena, ed., Tropen und Metaphern im Gelehrtendiskurs des 18. Jahrhunderts (ORSOLYA KISS) 224
Albert, Georg, Innovative Schriftlichkeit in digitalen Texten: Syntaktische Variation und stilistische Differenzierung in Chat und Forum (ALAN SCOTT) 523
Alfie, Fabian, Dante's *tenzone* with Forese Donati: The Reprehension of Vice (JOHN TOOK) 1093
Amberson, Deborah, Giraffes in the Garden of Italian Literature: Modernist Embodiment in Italo Svevo, Federigo Tozzi and Carlo Emilio Gadda (GIUSEPPE STELLARDI) 828
Anderson, Lisa Marie, German Expressionism and the Messianism of a Generation (CAITRÍONA NÍ DHÚILL) 562
Andrew, Lucy, and Catherine Phelps, eds, Capital Crimes: Crime Fiction in the City (KATHARINA HALL) 1056
Applegate, Celia, and others, eds, William J. McGrath, *German Freedom and the Greek Ideal: The Cultural Legacy from Goethe to Mann* (RITCHIE ROBERTSON) 1121
Armenteros, Carolina, The French Idea of History: Joseph de Maistre and his Heirs, 1794–1854 (FRANCESCO MANZINI) 515
Arnold, Heinz Ludwig, and others, eds, Rainald Goetz (REBECCA BRAUN) . 1149
Ashton, Rosemary, Victorian Bloomsbury (ROSALIND CRONE) 786
Augeron, Mickaël, and Olivier Caudron, eds, La Rochelle, l'Aunis et la Saintonge face à l'esclavage (ROGER LITTLE) 252
Aurnhammer, Achim, and Hanna Klessinger, eds, Johann Peter Hebel und die Moderne (ROBERT GILLETT) 552
Bacigalupo, Massimo, and Luisa Villa, eds, The Politics and Poetics of Displacement: Modernism off the Beaten Track (PAUL POPLAWSKI) 1072
Baker, Robert, In Dark Again in Wonder: The Poetry of René Char and George Oppen (MICHAEL KINDELLAN) 492
Baldassari, Gabriele, ed., 'Amico del Boiardo', *Canzoniere Costabili* (CARLO CARUSO) 1094
Balzac, Honoré de, 'The Girl with the Golden Eyes' and Other Stories, trans. by Peter Collier, intro. by Patrick Coleman (ANDREW WATTS) 807
Banerjee, Anindita, We Modern People: Science Fiction and the Making of Russian Modernity (ERIC LAURSEN) 867
Barker, Andrew, Fictions from an Orphan State: Literary Reflections between Habsburg and Hitler (DAVID MIDGLEY) 857
Bassin, Mark, and Catriona Kelly, eds, Soviet and Post-Soviet Identities (VICTORIA DONOVAN) 307
Bay, Hansjörg, and Wolfgang Struck, eds, Literarische Entdeckungsreisen: Vorfahren — Nachfahren — Revisionen (DIRK GÖTTSCHE) 528
Bayle, Pierre, Correspondance de Pierre Bayle, X: Avril 1696–juillet 1697. Lettres 1100–1280, ed. by Elisabeth Labrousse and Antony McKenna (JOHN CHRISTIAN LAURSEN) 805
Bearden, Elizabeth B., The Emblematics of the Self: Ekphrasis and Identity in Renaissance Imitations of Greek Romance (STEVEN MENTZ) 777

Contents

REVIEWS (cont.)   PAGE

Becher, Peter, and others, eds, Kafka und Prag: Literatur-, kultur-, sozial- und sprachhistorische Kontexte (JEREMY ADLER)   853

Becker, Karina, Der andere Goethe: Die literarischen Fragmente im Kontext des Gesamtwerks (OSMAN DURRANI)   544

Becker, Sabine, Literatur im Jahrhundert des Auges: Realismus und Fotografie im bürgerlichen Zeitalter (J. J. LONG)   554

Beckett, Samuel: The Letters of Samuel Beckett 1941–1956, ed. by George Craig and others (DERVAL TUBRIDY)   1076

Behrens, Franz Richard, Mein bester Freund — Hamlet: Drehbücher, Kinotexte, Filmkritiken, ed. by Gerhard Rühm and Monika Lichtenfeld (JEREMY ADLER)   850

Behrens, Franz Richard, Todlob: Feldtagebuchgedichte 1915/16, ed. by Michael Lentz (JEREMY ADLER)   850

Belletto, Steven, No Accident, Comrade: Chance and Design in Cold War American Narratives (DAVID SEED)   506

Benhaïm, André, and Aymeric Glacet, eds, Albert Camus au quotidien (MARK ORME)   816

Benson, Richard V., and others, eds, Literary Studies and the Pursuits of Reading (JOHANNES ENDRES)   776

Bergfelder, Tim, and Hans-Michael Bock, eds, The Concise CineGraph: Encyclopaedia of German Cinema (ERICA CARTER)   577

Berghahn, Cord-Friedrich, and Till Kinzel, eds, Johann Joachim Eschenburg und die Künste und Wissenschaften zwischen Aufklärung und Romantik: Netzwerke und Kulturen des Wissens (ROGER PAULIN)   268

Bernaerts, Lars, and others, eds, Stories and Minds: Cognitive Approaches to Literary Narrative (RICHARD WALSH)   775

Bernini, Cornelia, and others, eds, Thomas Mann, Briefe, III: 1924–1932 (RITCHIE ROBERTSON)   287

Bischof, Anja, Funktion und Bedeutung von Erinnerung im erzählerischen Werk Johannes Urzidils (RITCHIE ROBERTSON)   860

Bischoff, Doerte, Poetischer Fetischismus: Der Kult der Dinge im 19. Jahrhundert (FLORIAN KROBB)   532

Bivort, Olivier, ed., La Littérature symboliste et la Langue (SAM BOOTLE) . .   810

Blacker, Jean, and others, ed. and trans., Wace, The Hagiographical Works: The 'Conception Nostre Dame' and the Lives of St Margaret and St Nicholas (HUW GRANGE)   796

Blanchard, Joël, ed., 1511–2011, Philippe de Commynes: droit, écriture. Deux piliers de la souveraineté (JELLE HAEMERS)   510

Blanchard, Joël, ed., Procès de Jacques d'Armagnac: édition critique du ms. 2000 de la Bibliothèque Sainte-Geneviève (IRÈNE FABRY-TEHRANCHI) .   800

Bloch, R. Howard, intro., The Fabliaux: A New Verse Translation, trans. by Nathaniel Dubin (GLYN S. BURGESS)   509

Bock, Hans-Michael, and Tim Bergfelder, eds, The Concise CineGraph: Encyclopaedia of German Cinema (ERICA CARTER)   577

Boes, Tobias, Formative Fictions: Nationalism, Cosmopolitanism, and the Bildungsroman (MICHAEL MINDEN)   484

Boiardo, Matteo Maria, Pastoralia. Carmina. Epigrammata, ed. by Stefano Carrai and Francesco Tissoni (CARLO CARUSO)   1094

Contents

REVIEWS (cont.)   PAGE

Bowden, Sarah, Bridal-Quest Epics in Medieval Germany: A Revisionary Approach (ANNETTE VOLFING) 534

Bradley, Laura, and Karen Leeder, eds, Brecht and the GDR: Politics, Culture, Posterity (IAN WALLACE) 571

Brockes, Barthold Heinrich, Werke, I: Selbstbiographie, Verdeutschter Bethlemitischer Kinder-Mord, Gelegenheitsgedichte, Aufsätze, ed. by Jürgen Rathje (KEVIN HILLIARD) 840

Broomhall, Susan, and Jennifer Spinks, Early Modern Women in the Low Countries: Feminizing Sources and Interpretations of the Past (JANE FENOULHET) 301

Brown, Hilary, Luise Gottsched the Translator (JOHN L. FLOOD) 269

Burgess, Glyn S., and others, ed. and trans., Wace, The Hagiographical Works: The 'Conception Nostre Dame' and the Lives of St Margaret and St Nicholas (HUW GRANGE) 796

Burgess-Van Aken, Barbara, and Lisa Sampson, eds and trans., Barbara Torelli Benedetti, 'Partenia': A Pastoral Play (RICHARD ANDREWS) 1101

Burns, Jennifer, and others, eds, The Printed Media in Fin-de-Siècle Italy: Publishers, Writers, and Readers (URSULA J. FANNING) 824

Bussmann, Monica, and Thomas Sprecher, eds, Thomas Mann, Bekenntnisse des Hochstaplers Felix Krull: Der Memoiren erster Teil (RITCHIE ROBERTSON) 287

Butler, Erik, trans., Hans Ulrich Gumbrecht, Atmosphere, Mood, Stimmung: On a Hidden Potential of Literature (PIERPAOLO ANTONELLO) 231

Caesar, Ann Hallamore, and others, eds, The Printed Media in Fin-de-Siècle Italy: Publishers, Writers, and Readers (URSULA J. FANNING) 824

Carrai, Stefano, and Francesco Tissoni, eds, Matteo Maria Boiardo, Pastoralia. Carmina. Epigrammata (CARLO CARUSO) 1094

Carù, Carlo, ed., Idee su Dante: esperimenti danteschi 2012. Atti del Convegno, Milano, 9–10 maggio 2012 (PAOLO DE VENTURA) 822

Caudron, Olivier, and Mickaël Augeron, eds, La Rochelle, l'Aunis et la Saintonge face à l'esclavage (ROGER LITTLE) 252

Caudron, Olivier, and others, Être noir en France au XVIIIe siècle (1685–1805) (ROGER LITTLE) 252

Champagne, John, Aesthetic Modernism and Masculinity in Fascist Italy (CHARLOTTE ROSS) 1104

Cheesman, Tom, ed., German Text Crimes: Writers Accused, from the 1950s to the 2000s (FLORIAN KROBB) 1145

Chevillot, Frédérique, and Colette Trout, eds, Rebelles et criminelles chez les écrivaines d'expression française (NATHALIE MORELLO) 819

Class, Monika, Coleridge and Kantian Ideas in England, 1796–1817: Coleridge's Responses to German Philosophy (PHILIPP HUNNEKUHL) 780

Cohen, Adam Max, Wonder in Shakespeare (PETER SILLITOE) 781

Cohen, Lara Langer, and Jordan Alexander Stein, eds, Early African American Print Culture (KATY L. CHILES) 783

Coleman, Patrick, intro., Honoré de Balzac, 'The Girl with the Golden Eyes' and Other Stories, trans. by Peter Collier (ANDREW WATTS) 807

Collier, Peter, trans., Honoré de Balzac, 'The Girl with the Golden Eyes' and Other Stories, intro. by Patrick Coleman (ANDREW WATTS) 807

Contents

REVIEWS (cont.)   PAGE

Cooke, Paul, and Chris Homewood, eds, *New Directions in German Cinema*
  (Seán Allan) 298
Cooper, Barbara T., ed., Charles Lafont and Charles Desnoyer, *Le Tremblement
  de Terre de la Martinique: drame en cinq actes, suivi de documents inédits*
  (M. Lynn Weiss) 1086
Coppini, Donatella, ed., Bernardo Rucellai, *De bello Italico. La guerra d'Italia*,
  foreword by Renzo Martinelli (Carlo Caruso) 1096
Corbett, George, *Dante and Epicurus: A Dualist Vision of Secular and Spiritual
  Fulfilment* (Jennifer Rushworth) 821
Corkhill, Alan, *Spaces for Happiness in the Twentieth-Century German Novel:
  Mann, Kafka, Hesse, Jünger* (Ingo Cornils) 565
Corneille, *Cinna*, in *Corneille, Molière, Racine: Four French Plays. 'Cinna', 'The
  Misanthrope', 'Andromache', 'Phaedra'*, trans. by John Edmunds, intro. by
  Joseph Harris (Tim Chilcott) 802
Corngold, Stanley, and Ruth V. Gross, eds, *Kafka for the Twenty-First Century*
  (Julian Preece) 568
Cosgrove, Mary, and Anna Richards, eds, *Sadness and Melancholy in German-
  Language Literature and Culture* (Ingo Cornils) 839
Cottom, Daniel, *International Bohemia: Scenes of Nineteenth-Century Life*
  (Andrew J. Counter) 486
Cox, Virginia, ed., *Lyric Poetry by Women of the Italian Renaissance* (Maria
  Galli Stampino) 1098
Craig, George, and others, eds, *The Letters of Samuel Beckett 1941–1956*
  (Derval Tubridy) 1076
Crowe, Sinéad, *Religion in Contemporary German Drama* (Gillian Pye) . 1152
Currie, Pamela, *Goethe's Visual World* (Charlotte Lee) 1122
Curtis, J. A. E., *The Englishman From Lebedian'—A Life of Evgeny Zamiatin
  (1884–1937)* (Roger Cockrell) 1156
Cusack, Andrew, and Barry Murnane, eds, *Popular Revenants: The German
  Gothic and its International Reception 1800–2000* (Michael Minden) 531
D[oolittle], H[ilda], *Bid Me to Live: A Madrigal*, ed. by Caroline Zilboorg
  (Alice Kelly) 243
Dafgård Norén, Sigun, ed., Friedrich Melchior Grimm, *Correspondance lit-
  téraire*, VII: *1760* (Derek Connon) 253
Dalmas, Davide, *Il saggio, il gusto e il cliché: per un'interpretazione di Mario
  Praz* (Ilaria Mallozzi) 262
Darlow, Mark, *Dissonance in the Republic of Letters: The Querelle des Glu-
  ckistes et des Piccinnistes* (Derek Connon) 513
De Geest, Dirk, and others, eds, *Stories and Minds: Cognitive Approaches to
  Literary Narrative* (Richard Walsh) 775
Dehrmann, Mark-Georg, with Nils Gelker, eds, Friedrich Schlegel, *Alarcos:
  Ein Trauerspiel. Historisch-kritische Edition mit Dokumenten* (Roger
  Paulin) 1124
Delogu, C. Jon, trans., Georges Vigarello, *The Metamorphoses of Fat: A History
  of Obesity* (Anna Jenkin) 482
Delsaux, Olivier, *Manuscrits et pratiques autographes chez les écrivains
  français de la fin du moyen âge: l'exemple de Christine de Pizan* (Angus
  J. Kennedy) 1082

Contents

REVIEWS (*cont.*)   PAGE

Desnoyer, Charles, and Charles Lafont, *Le Tremblement de Terre de la Martinique: drame en cinq actes, suivi de documents inédits*, ed. by Barbara T. Cooper (M. LYNN WEISS) 1086
Deutsch, Helen, and Mary Terrall, eds, *Vital Matters: Eighteenth-Century Views of Conception, Life, and Death* (ANDREW WELLS) 223
Dietschy, Beat, and others, eds, *Bloch-Wörterbuch: Leitbegriffe der Philosophie Ernst Blochs* (CATHERINE MOIR) 292
Dinega Gillespie, Alyssa, ed., *Taboo Pushkin: Topics, Texts, Interpretations* (JAMES RANN) 584
Donahue, William Collins, and Martha B. Helfer, eds, *Nexus: Essays in Jewish Studies*, vol. 1 (ANDREA REITER) 558
Downing, Eric, and others, eds, *Literary Studies and the Pursuits of Reading* (JOHANNES ENDRES) 776
Dubin, Nathaniel, trans., *The Fabliaux: A New Verse Translation* (GLYN S. BURGESS) 509
Duttlinger, Carolin, and others, eds, *Walter Benjamins anthropologisches Denken* (WILFRIED VAN DER WILL) 1137
DuVal, John, trans., *The Song of Roland*, intro. by David Staines (LUKE SUNDERLAND) 795
Eagleton, Terry, *How to Read Literature* (ADAM WATT) 1048
Easterlin, Nancy, *A Biocultural Approach to Literary Theory and Interpretation* (GAVIN MILLER) 239
Edmiston, William F., *Sade: Queer Theorist* (PETER CRYLE) 806
Edmunds, John, trans., Corneille, Molière, Racine: *Four French Plays. Cinna, The Misanthrope, Andromache, Phaedra*, intro. by Joseph Harris (TIM CHILCOTT) 802
Eichel-Lojkine, Patricia, *Contes en réseaux: l'émergence du conte sur la scène littéraire européenne* (MARIE-CLAUDE CANOVA-GREEN) 779
Engel, Manfred, and Ritchie Robertson, eds, *Kafka und die kleine Prosa der Moderne/Kafka and Short Modernist Prose* (RONALD SPEIRS) 282
Engel, Manfred, and Ritchie Robertson, eds, *Kafka, Prag und der Erste Weltkrieg/Kafka, Prague and the First World War* (JEREMY ADLER) . . 853
Engel, William F., *Early Modern Poetics in Melville and Poe: Memory, Melancholy and the Emblematic Tradition* (DAVID E. E. SLOANE) 501
Englund, Axel, *Still Songs: Music in and around the Poetry of Paul Celan* (ANNJA NEUMANN) 862
Estraikh, Gennady, and others, eds, *Translating Sholem Aleichem: History, Politics, and Art* (LEAH GARRETT) 299
Evdokimova, Svetlana, *Pushkin's Historical Imagination* (JAMES RANN) . . 584
Fauser, Markus, ed., *Medialität der Kunst: Rolf Dieter Brinkmann in der Moderne* (REBECCA BRAUN) 1149
Favaretto, Matteo, ed., *Eunuco*: un volgarizzamento anonimo in terza rima (DIEGO ZANCANI) 1099
Federhofer, Marie-Theres, and Jutta Weber, eds, *Korrespondenzen und Transformationen: Neue Perspektiven auf Adalbert von Chamisso* (JOANNA NEILLY) 1128
Fehsenfeld, Martha Dow, and others, eds, *The Letters of Samuel Beckett 1941–1956* (DERVAL TUBRIDY) 1076

REVIEWS (cont.) PAGE

Feilla, Cecilia, The Sentimental Theater of the French Revolution (CATRIN FRANCIS) 514
Félibien, André, Les Fêtes de Versailles, ed. by Michel Jeanneret (MARIE-CLAUDE CANOVA-GREEN) 803
ffytche, Matt, The Foundation of the Unconscious: Schelling, Freud and the Birth of the Modern Psyche (MARTIN LIEBSCHER) 848
Finkin, Jordan, and others, eds, Translating Sholem Aleichem: History, Politics, and Art (LEAH GARRETT) 299
Fischer, Mary, trans., The Chronicle of Prussia by Nicolaus von Jeroschin: A History of the Teutonic Knights in Prussia, 1190–1331 (ALASTAIR MATTHEWS) 535
Flower, John, Historical Dictionary of French Literature (NICHOLAS HAMMOND) 1080
Ford, John, The Collected Works of John Ford, vol. I, ed. by Gilles Monsarrat and others (LESEL DAWSON) 235
Ford, Philip, and Neil Kenny, eds, La Librairie de Montaigne: Proceedings of the Tenth Cambridge French Renaissance Colloquium, 2–4 September 2008 (JEAN BRAYBROOK) 249
Fraser, Jennifer Margaret, Be a Good Soldier: Children's Grief in English Modernist Novels (ANEESH BARAI) 1075
Fraser, Robert, Night Thoughts: The Surreal Life of the Poet David Gascoyne (NEIL ROBERTS) 790
Freadman, Anna, The Livres-Souvenirs of Colette: Genre and the Telling of Time (KATHLEEN ANTONIOLI) 1088
Fronius, Helen, and Anna Richards, eds, German Women's Writing of the Eighteenth and Nineteenth Centuries: Future Directions in Feminist Criticism (ROBERT GILLETT) 547
Frontz, Stephanie, and others, eds, William J. McGrath, German Freedom and the Greek Ideal: The Cultural Legacy from Goethe to Mann (RITCHIE ROBERTSON) 1121
Fynsk, Christopher, Last Steps: Maurice Blanchot's Exilic Writing (MAURO DI LULLO) 1090
Gainot, Bernard, and others, Être noir en France au XVIIIe siècle (1685–1805) (ROGER LITTLE) 252
Gąsiorek, Andrzej, and others, eds, Wyndham Lewis and the Cultures of Modernity (RANDALL STEVENSON) 505
Gelker, Nils, and Mark-Georg Dehrmann, eds, Friedrich Schlegel, Alarcos: Ein Trauerspiel. Historisch-kritische Edition mit Dokumenten (ROGER PAULIN) 1124
Georganta, Konstantina, Conversing Identities: Encounters between British, Irish and Greek Poetry, 1922–1952 (GONDA VAN STEEN) 494
Geulen, Eva, and Stephan Kraft, eds, Grenzen im Raum — Grenzen in der Literatur (TOM CHEESMAN) 837
Ginzburg, Lydia, Lydia Ginzburg's Alternative Literary Identities: A Collection of Articles and New Translations, ed. by Emily Van Buskirk and Andrei Zorin (SARAH PRATT) 305
Gisi, Lucas Marco, and others, eds, Schreiben und Streichen: Zu einem Moment produktiver Negativität (ANDREAS KRAMER) 525

Contents

REVIEWS (cont.) — PAGE

Glacet, Aymeric, and André Benhaïm, eds, Albert Camus au quotidien (MARK ORME) — 816
Gladfelder, Hal, Fanny Hill in Bombay: The Making & Unmaking of John Cleland (CAROLYN D. WILLIAMS) — 238
Goer, Charis, and others, eds, Rainald Goetz (REBECCA BRAUN) — 1149
Goodman, Nan, Banished: Common Law and the Rhetoric of Social Exclusion in Early New England (PHILIP MAJOR) — 1066
Gorrara, Claire, French Crime Fiction and the Second World War: Past Crimes, Present Memories (ANGELA KIMYONGÜR) — 817
Goßens, Peter, Weltliteratur: Modelle transnationaler Literaturwahrnehmung im 19. Jahrhundert (ANNA GUILLEMIN) — 274
Göttsche, Dirk, and Nicholas Saul, eds, Realism and Romanticism in German Literature/Realismus und Romantik in der deutschsprachigen Literatur (ROGER PAULIN) — 1132
Gouraud, Julie, Les Deux Enfants de Saint-Domingue, ed. and intro. by Roger Little (JARROD HAYES) — 813
Gouriou, Catherine, Du fatum au divin: le mythe dans l'œuvre d'Alfred Döblin (1935–1957) (DAVID MIDGLEY) — 285
Gragnolati, Manuel, and others, eds, Desire in Dante and the Middle Ages (RUTH CHESTER) — 221
Greif, Stefan, and others, eds, Rainald Goetz (REBECCA BRAUN) — 1149
Griffiths, Kate, and Andrew Watts, Adapting Nineteenth-Century France: Literature in Film, Theatre, Television, Radio and Print (BRADLEY STEPHENS) — 815
Grill, Genese, The World as Metaphor in Robert Musil's The Man without Qualities: Possibility as Reality (DANIEL STEUER) — 851
Grimm, Friedrich Melchior, Correspondance littéraire, VII: 1760, ed. by Sigun Dafgård Norén (DEREK CONNON) — 253
Gross, Ruth V., and Stanley Corngold, eds, Kafka for the Twenty-First Century (JULIAN PREECE) — 568
Grossman, Jonathan H., Charles Dickens's Networks: Public Transport and the Novel (PAUL YOUNG) — 1069
Gumbrecht, Hans Ulrich, Atmosphere, Mood, Stimmung: On a Hidden Potential of Literature (PIERPAOLO ANTONELLO) — 231
Gunn, Dan, and others, eds, The Letters of Samuel Beckett 1941–1956 (DERVAL TUBRIDY) — 1076
Hadfield, Andrew, Edmund Spenser: A Life (ELIZABETH HEALE) — 497
Haralson, Eric, and John Carlos Rowe, eds, A Historical Guide to Henry James (RICHARD SALMON) — 503
Harris, Joseph, intro., Corneille, Molière, Racine: Four French Plays. Cinna, The Misanthrope, Andromache, Phaedra, trans. by John Edmunds (TIM CHILCOTT) — 802
Harrow, Susan, and Andrew Watts, eds, Mapping Memory in Nineteenth-Century French Literature and Culture (ANDREW J. COUNTER) — 517
Hayes, Kevin J., A Journey through American Literature (MICHAEL J. COLLINS) — 242
Helfer, Martha B., and William Collins Donahue, eds, Nexus: Essays in Jewish Studies, vol. 1 (ANDREA REITER) — 558

REVIEWS (cont.)

Helgason, Jon, Schriften des Herzens: Briefkultur des 18. Jahrhunderts im Briefwechsel zwischen Anna Louisa Karsch und Johann Wilhelm Ludwig Gleim, trans. by Jana Mohnike (K. F. HILLIARD) 543
Heller-Andrist, Simone, The Friction of the Frame: Derrida's *Parergon* in Literature (K. M. NEWTON) 1061
Herman, Luc, and others, eds, Stories and Minds: Cognitive Approaches to Literary Narrative (RICHARD WALSH) 775
Herzog, Hillary Hope, Vienna is Different: Jewish Writers in Austria from the *fin de siècle* to the Present (ANDREA REITER) 558
Hess, Jonathan M., and others, eds, Literary Studies and the Pursuits of Reading (JOHANNES ENDRES) 776
High, Jeffrey L., and others, eds, Who Is This Schiller Now? Essays on his Reception and Significance (OSMAN DURRANI) 545
Hill, Colin, Modern Realism in English-Canadian Fiction (MICHELLE SMITH) 789
Hillebrandt, Claudia, Das emotionale Wirkungspotenzial von Erzähltexten: Mit Fallstudien zu Kafka, Perutz und Werfel (ERNEST SCHONFIELD) . . 280
Hinton, Thomas, The *Conte du Graal* Cycle: Chrétien de Troyes's *Perceval*, the Continuations and French Arthurian Romance (AD PUTTER) 246
Höffner, Eckhard, Geschichte und Wesen des Urheberrechts, vol. I, rev. edn (ROGER PAULIN) 1130
Hofmann, Gert, and others, eds, German and European Poetics after the Holocaust: Crisis and Creativity (KIRSTIN GWYER) 296
Hoge, Kerstin, and others, eds, Translating Sholem Aleichem: History, Politics, and Art (LEAH GARRETT) 299
Höhne, Steffen, and others, eds, Kafka und Prag: Literatur-, kultur-, sozial- und sprachhistorische Kontexte (JEREMY ADLER) 853
Holmes, John, ed., Science in Modern Poetry: New Directions (PAUL WRIGHT) 787
Homewood, Chris, and Paul Cooke, eds, New Directions in German Cinema (SEÁN ALLAN) 298
Horton, David, Thomas Mann in English: A Study in Literary Translation (RITCHIE ROBERTSON) 563
Howard, Henry, A Critical Edition of the Complete Poems of Henry Howard, Earl of Surrey, ed. by William McGaw (ANDREW HISCOCK) 495
Howells, Christina, Mortal Subjects: Passions of the Soul in Late Twentieth-Century French Thought (JAMES WILLIAMS) 818
Hughes-Edwards, Mari, Reading Medieval Anchoritism: Ideology and Spiritual Practices (REBECCA PINNER) 234
Hume, Kathryn, Aggressive Fictions: Reading the Contemporary American Novel (BRIAN JARVIS) 508
Hunt, Tony, ed., *Les Paroles Salomun* (MAUREEN BOULTON) 798
Ireton, Sean, and Caroline Schaumann, eds, Heights of Reflection: Mountains in the German Imagination from the Middle Ages to the Twenty-First Century (THEODORE ZIOLKOWSKI) 526
Izzo, Annalisa, ed., 'D'un parlar ne l'altro': aspetti dell'enunciazione dal romanzo arturiano alla *Gerusalemme liberata* (MARK DAVIE) 1092
Jeanneret, Michel, ed., André Félibien, *Les Fêtes de Versailles* (MARIE-CLAUDE CANOVA-GREEN) 803
Jeanneret, Michel, Versailles, ordre et chaos (MARIE-CLAUDE CANOVA-GREEN) 803

REVIEWS (cont.)

	PAGE
Jens, Inge, and Uwe Naumann, eds, Klaus Mann, 'Lieber und verehrter Onkel Heinrich' (KARINA VON LINDEINER-STRÁSKÝ)	290
Joeres, Yvonne, Die Don-Quijote-Rezeption Friedrich Schlegels und Heinrich Heines im Kontext des europäischen Kulturtransfers: Ein Narr als Angelpunkt transnationaler Denkansätze (CLAUDIA NITSCHKE)	845
Johnson, Christopher D., Memory, Metaphor, and Aby Warburg's Atlas of Images (RITCHIE ROBERTSON)	279
Jones, Sara, Complicity, Censorship and Criticism: Negotiating Space in the GDR Literary Sphere (KAREN LEEDER)	572
Jones, William Jervis, German Colour Terms: A Study in their Historical Evolution from Earliest Times to the Present (HOWARD JONES)	1106
Jörg Magenau, ed., Ernst Jünger, Letzte Worte (CHRISTOPHE FRICKER)	1141
Jørgensen, Sven-Aage, Querdenker der Aufklärung: Studien zu Johann Georg Hamann (DAVID BARRY)	1118
Jullien, Benoît, Un commerce pour gens ordinaires? La Rochelle et la traite négrière au XVIIIe siècle (ROGER LITTLE)	252
Jünger, Ernst, Atlantische Fahrt: 'Rio: Residenz des Weltgeistes', ed. by Detlev Schöttker (CHRISTOPHE FRICKER)	1141
Jünger, Ernst, Feldpostbriefe an die Familie: 1915–1918; mit ausgewählten Antwortbriefen der Eltern und Friedrich Georg Jüngers, ed. by Heimo Schwilk (CHRISTOPHE FRICKER)	1141
Jünger, Ernst, Letzte Worte, ed. by Jörg Magenau (CHRISTOPHE FRICKER)	1141
Jüngers, Friedrich Georg, in Ernst Jünger, Feldpostbriefe an die Familie: 1915–1918; mit ausgewählten Antwortbriefen der Eltern und Friedrich Georg Jüngers (CHRISTOPHE FRICKER)	1141
Kapczynski, Jennifer M., and Michael D. Richardson, eds, A New History of German Cinema (MARTIN BRADY)	865
Kay, Tristan, and others, eds, Desire in Dante and the Middle Ages (RUTH CHESTER)	221
Kelly, Catriona, and Mark Bassin, eds, Soviet and Post-Soviet Identities (VICTORIA DONOVAN)	307
Kenny, Neil, and Philip Ford, eds, La Librairie de Montaigne: Proceedings of the Tenth Cambridge French Renaissance Colloquium, 2–4 September 2008 (JEAN BRAYBROOK)	249
Kindt, Tom, Literatur und Komik: Zur Theorie literarischer Komik und zur deutschen Komödie im 18. Jahrhundert (THOMAS MARTINEC)	844
Kinzel, Till, and Cord-Friedrich Berghahn, eds, Johann Joachim Eschenburg und die Künste und Wissenschaften zwischen Aufklärung und Romantik: Netzwerke und Kulturen des Wissens (ROGER PAULIN)	268
Kipling, Rudyard, The Cambridge Edition of the Poems of Rudyard Kipling, ed. by Thomas Pinney (JOHN BATCHELOR)	663
Kleiman, Irit Ruth, Philippe de Commynes: Memory, Betrayal, Text (CATHERINE EMERSON)	801
Klessinger, Hanna, and Achim Aurnhammer, eds, Johann Peter Hebel und die Moderne (ROBERT GILLETT)	552
Kozlov, Denis, The Readers of Novyi mir: Coming to Terms with the Stalinist Past (CLAIRE SHAW)	868

REVIEWS (cont.)

	PAGE
Kraft, Stephan, and Eva Geulen, eds, Grenzen im Raum — Grenzen in der Literatur (TOM CHEESMAN)	837
Kraft, Stephan, Zum Ende der Komödie: Eine Theoriegeschichte des Happyends (THOMAS MARTINEC)	836
Krämer, Thomas, Die Poetik des Gedenkens: Zu den autobiographischen Romanen H. G. Adlers (HELEN FINCH)	295
Kroll, Frank-Lothar, and Rüdiger von Voss, eds, Schriftsteller und Widerstand: Facetten und Probleme der inneren Emigration (WILLIAM J. DODD)	570
Kruks, Sonia, Simone de Beauvoir and the Politics of Ambiguity (CATHERINE RODGERS)	519
Krutikov, Mikhail, and others, eds, Translating Sholem Aleichem: History, Politics, and Art (LEAH GARRETT)	299
Kuxhausen, Anna, From the Womb to the Body Politic: Raising the Nation in Enlightenment Russia (URSULA STOHLER)	582
Kwakkel, Erik, and Stephen Partridge, eds, Author, Reader, Book: Medieval Authorship in Theory and Practice (VENETIA BRIDGES)	219
Labère, Nelly, ed., Texte et contre-texte pour la période pré-moderne (JONATHAN PATTERSON)	799
Labrousse, Elisabeth, and Antony McKenna, eds, *Correspondance de Pierre Bayle*, X: *Avril 1696–juillet 1697. Lettres 1100–1280* (JOHN CHRISTIAN LAURSEN)	805
Lafont, Charles, and Charles Desnoyer, Le Tremblement de Terre de la Martinique: drame en cinq actes, suivi de documents inédits, ed. by Barbara T. Cooper (M. LYNN WEISS)	1086
Lane, Melissa S., and Martin A. Ruehl, eds, A Poet's Reich: Politics and Culture in the George Circle (CHRISTOPHE FRICKER)	560
Laursen, Eric, Toxic Voices: The Villain from Early Soviet Literature to Socialist Realism (MAX ANLEY)	588
Leake, Elizabeth, After Words: Suicide and Authorship in Twentieth-Century Italy (ROBERT S. C. GORDON)	826
Leeder, Karen, and Laura Bradley, eds, Brecht and the GDR: Politics, Culture, Posterity (IAN WALLACE)	571
Legault, Marianne, Female Intimacies in Seventeenth-Century French Literature (EMILIA WILTON-GODBERFFORDE)	1083
Lentz, Michael, ed., Franz Richard Behrens, *Todlob: Feldtagebuchgedichte 1915/16* (JEREMY ADLER)	850
Lichtenfeld, Monika, and Gerhard Rühm, eds, Franz Richard Behrens, *Mein bester Freund — Hamlet: Drehbücher, Kinotexte, Filmkritiken* (JEREMY ADLER)	850
Lifschitz, Avi, Language and Enlightenment: The Berlin Debates of the Eighteenth Century (H. B. NISBET)	539
Little, Roger, ed. and intro., Alfred Séguin, *Le Robinson noir* (JARROD HAYES)	813
Little, Roger, ed. and intro., Julie Gouraud, *Les Deux Enfants de Saint-Domingue* (JARROD HAYES)	813
Little, Roger, ed. and intro., Michel Möring, *L'Esclave de Saint-Domingue* (JARROD HAYES)	813
Lobsien, Verena O., Jenseitsästhetik: Literarische Räume letzter Dinge (THEODORE ZIOLKOWSKI)	1049

Contents

REVIEWS (*cont.*) PAGE

Lochert, Véronique, and Zoé Schweitzer, eds, Philologie et théâtre: traduire, commenter, interpréter le théâtre antique en Europe (xve–xviiie siècle) (EDWARD FORMAN) 1052

Lombardi, Elena, and others, eds, Desire in Dante and the Middle Ages (RUTH CHESTER) 221

Lozier, Claire, De l'abject et du sublime: Georges Bataille, Jean Genet, Samuel Beckett (DAVID HOUSTON JONES) 256

Lughofer, Johann Georg, and Mira Miladinović Zalaznik, eds, Joseph Roth: Europäisch-jüdischer Schriftsteller und österreichischer Universalist (ANDREW BARKER) 286

Lützeler, Paul Michael, Hermann Broch und die Moderne: Roman, Menschenrecht, Biografie (DARIA SANTINI) 856

Lynall, Gregory, Swift and Science: The Satire, Politics, and Theology of Natural Knowledge, 1690–1730 (BREAN S. HAMMOND) 499

Lyon, John B., Out of Place: German Realism, Displacement and Modernity (MICHAEL J. WHITE) 1134

McGaw, William, ed., A Critical Edition of the Complete Poems of Henry Howard, Earl of Surrey (ANDREW HISCOCK) 495

McGrath, William J., German Freedom and the Greek Ideal: The Cultural Legacy from Goethe to Mann, ed. by Celia Applegate and others (RITCHIE ROBERTSON) 1121

McKenna, Antony, and Elisabeth Labrousse, eds, *Correspondance de Pierre Bayle*, x: *Avril 1696–juillet 1697. Lettres 1100–1280* (JOHN CHRISTIAN LAURSEN) 805

McLelland, Nicola, J. G. Schottelius's *Ausführliche Arbeit von der Teutschen HaubtSprache* (1663) and its Place in Early Modern European Vernacular Language Study (DAVID N. YEANDLE) 829

McMurtry, Áine, Crisis and Form in the Later Writing of Ingeborg Bachmann: An Aesthetic Examination of the Poetic Drafts of the 1960s (RÜDIGER GÖRNER) 1144

McPeak, Rick, and Donna Tussing Orwin, eds, Tolstoy on War: Narrative Art and Historical Truth in *War and Peace* (W. GARETH JONES) 304

MagShamhráin, Rachel, and others, eds, German and European Poetics after the Holocaust: Crisis and Creativity (KIRSTIN GWYER) 296

Maguire, Muireann, Stalin's Ghosts: Gothic Themes in Early Soviet Literature (ROGER COCKRELL) 586

Mandel, Miriam, ed., Hemingway in Africa (WILLIAM BLAZEK) 240

Mann, Klaus, 'Lieber und verehrter Onkel Heinrich', ed. by Inge Jens and Uwe Naumann (KARINA VON LINDEINER-STRÁSKÝ) 290

Mann, Thomas, Bekenntnisse des Hochstaplers Felix Krull: Der Memoiren erster Teil, ed. by Thomas Sprecher and Monica Bussmann (RITCHIE ROBERTSON) 287

Mann, Thomas, Briefe, III: 1924–1932, ed. by Thomas Sprecher and others (RITCHIE ROBERTSON) 287

Manzini, Francesco, The Fevered Novel from Balzac to Bernanos: Frenetic Catholicism in Crisis, Delirium and Revolution (OWEN HEATHCOTE) . 808

REVIEWS (cont.)

Marchand, Suzanne, and others, eds, William J. McGrath, *German Freedom and the Greek Ideal: The Cultural Legacy from Goethe to Mann* (RITCHIE ROBERTSON) 1121

Martin, Nicholas, and others, eds, *Who Is This Schiller Now? Essays on his Reception and Significance* (OSMAN DURRANI) 545

Martinelli, Renzo, foreword to Bernardo Rucellai, *De bello Italico. La guerra d'Italia*, ed. by Donatella Coppini (CARLO CARUSO) 1096

Matthes, Frauke, *Writing and Muslim Identity: Representations of Islam in German and English Transcultural Literature, 1990–2006* (TOM CHEESMAN) 575

Mavor, Carol, *Black and Blue: The Bruising Passion of 'Camera Lucida', 'La Jetée', 'Sans soleil', and 'Hiroshima mon amour'* (CATHERINE RODGERS) 520

Mehtonen, P. M., and Matti Savolainen, eds, *Gothic Topographies: Language, Nation Building and 'Race'* (KATHARINA HALL) 1056

Meinhof, Ulrike Hanna, and others, eds, *Diskurslinguistik im Spannungsfeld von Deskription und Kritik* (SYLVIA JAWORSKA) 1110

Melzer, Sara E., *Colonizer or Colonized: The Hidden Stories of Early Modern French Culture* (MICHAEL HARRIGAN) 248

Mergenthaler, May, *Zwischen Eros und Mitteilung: Die Frühromantik im Symposion der Athenaeums-Fragmente* (ROGER PAULIN) 1124

Meyer-Sickendiek, Burkhard, *Lyrisches Gespür: Vom geheimen Sensorium moderner Poesie* (RÜDIGER GÖRNER) 834

Miladinović Zalaznik, Mira, and Johann Georg Lughofer, eds, *Joseph Roth: Europäisch-jüdischer Schriftsteller und österreichischer Universalist* (ANDREW BARKER) 286

Minden, Michael, *Modern German Literature* (BEN HUTCHINSON) 1154

Mohnike, Jana, trans., Jon Helgason, *Schriften des Herzens: Briefkultur des 18. Jahrhunderts im Briefwechsel zwischen Anna Louisa Karsch und Johann Wilhelm Ludwig Gleim* (K. F. HILLIARD) 543

Molière, Le Misanthrope, in *Corneille, Molière, Racine: Four French Plays. 'Cinna', 'The Misanthrope', 'Andromache', 'Phaedra'*, trans. by John Edmunds, intro. by Joseph Harris (TIM CHILCOTT) 802

Monsarrat, Gilles, and others, eds, *The Collected Works of John Ford*, vol. I (LESEL DAWSON) 235

Montemaggi, Vittorio, and Matthew Traherne, eds, *Dante's Commedia: Theology as Poetry* (JULIA BOLTON HOLLOWAY) 261

Morgan, Ben, and others, eds, *Walter Benjamins anthropologisches Denken* (WILFRIED VAN DER WILL) 1137

Möring, Michel, *L'Esclave de Saint-Domingue*, ed. and intro. by Roger Little (JARROD HAYES) 813

Morley, Elaine, *Iris Murdoch and Elias Canetti: Intellectual Allies* (DAGMAR C. G. LORENZ) 1142

Mucignat, Rosa, *Realism and Space in the Novel, 1795–1869: Imagined Geographies* (ARI J. BLATT) 228

Müller, Jan, and E. Theodor Voss, eds, Gottlieb Wilhelm Rabener, *Briefwechsel und Gespräche* (K. F. HILLIARD) 540

Murnane, Barry, and Andrew Cusack, eds, *Popular Revenants: The German Gothic and its International Reception 1800–2000* (MICHAEL MINDEN) 531

Contents

REVIEWS (cont.)

	PAGE
Nardi, Florinda, Comico e modernità nel *Discorso del riso* di Basilio Paravicino (MATTEO FAVARETTO)	1102
Naumann, Uwe, and Inge Jens, eds, Klaus Mann, *'Lieber und verehrter Onkel Heinrich'* (KARINA VON LINDEINER-STRÁSKÝ)	290
Neirick, Miriam, When Pigs Could Fly and Bears Could Dance: A History of the Soviet Circus (RACHEL S. PLATONOV)	1157
Nekula, Marek, and others, eds, Kafka und Prag: Literatur-, kultur-, sozial- und sprachhistorische Kontexte (JEREMY ADLER)	853
Nelson, Cary, ed., The Oxford Handbook of Modern and Contemporary American Poetry (STEPHEN FREDMAN)	791
Newton, K. M., Modernizing George Eliot: The Writer as Artist, Intellectual, Proto-Modernist, Cultural Critic (JOSIE BILLINGTON)	502
Nicolaus von Jeroschin, *The Chronicle of Prussia* by Nicolaus von Jeroschin: A History of the Teutonic Knights in Prussia, 1190–1331, trans. by Mary Fischer (ALASTAIR MATTHEWS)	535
Nielaba, Daniel Müller, and others, eds, 'Man will werden, nicht gewesen sein': Zur Aktualität Max Frischs (HANS J. HAHN)	861
Nisbet, Hugh Barr, Gotthold Ephraim Lessing: His Life, Works, and Thought (THOMAS MARTINEC)	1119
Niven, Bill, and Chloe Paver, eds, Memorialization in Germany since 1945 (DORA OSBORNE)	293
Noël, Erick, and others, Être noir en France au XVIIIe siècle (1685–1805) (ROGER LITTLE)	252
Notter, Annick, and others, Être noir en France au XVIIIe siècle (1685–1805) (ROGER LITTLE)	252
Novak, Julia, Live Poetry: An Integrated Approach to Poetry in Performance (SAMUEL ROGERS)	794
Oellers, Norbert, and others, eds, Who Is This Schiller Now? Essays on his Reception and Significance (OSMAN DURRANI)	545
Ogden, Amy V., and others, ed. and trans., Wace, *The Hagiographical Works: The 'Conception Nostre Dame' and the Lives of St Margaret and St Nicholas* (HUW GRANGE)	796
Orwin, Donna Tussing, and Rick McPeak, eds, Tolstoy on War: Narrative Art and Historical Truth in *War and Peace* (W. GARETH JONES)	304
O'Sullivan, Daniel E., and Laurie Shepard, eds, Shaping Courtliness in Medieval France: Essays in Honor of Matilda Tomaryn Bruckner (CATHERINE LEGLU)	1081
Oswald von Wolkenstein: Die Lebenszeugnisse Oswalds von Wolkenstein: Edition und Kommentar, IV: 1438–1442, Nr. 277–386, ed. by Anton Schwob and Ute Monika Schwob (ALMUT SUERBAUM)	266
Overbeck, Lois More, and others, eds, *The Letters of Samuel Beckett 1941–1956* (DERVAL TUBRIDY)	1076
Page, Michael R., The Literary Imagination from Erasmus Darwin to H. G. Wells: Science, Evolution, and Ecology (KEITH WILLIAMS)	784
Pajević, Marko, and others, eds, German and European Poetics after the Holocaust: Crisis and Creativity (KIRSTIN GWYER)	296
Palumbo-Liu, David, The Deliverance of Others: Reading Literature in a Global Age (LOUIS LO)	229

REVIEWS (cont.)

Partridge, Stephen, and Erik Kwakkel, eds, Author, Reader, Book: Medieval Authorship in Theory and Practice (VENETIA BRIDGES) 219
Paschoud, Adrien, and Nathalie Vuillemin, eds, Penser l'ordre naturel, 1680–1810 (NICK TREUHERZ) 250
Paul, Verena, 'Schreiben mit gespaltener Feder': Peter Rühmkorfs ästhetisch-politisches Doppelengagement (RÜDIGER GÖRNER) 574
Paver, Chloe, and Bill Niven, eds, Memorialization in Germany since 1945 (DORA OSBORNE) 293
Peschio, Joe, The Poetics of Impudence and Intimacy in the Age of Pushkin (JAMES RANN) 584
Pfitzinger, Elke, Die Aufklärung ist weiblich: Frauenrollen im Drama um 1800 (STEFFAN DAVIES) 271
Phelan, Anthony, and others, eds, Walter Benjamins anthropologisches Denken (WILFRIED VAN DER WILL) 1137
Phelps, Catherine, and Lucy Andrew, eds, Capital Crimes: Crime Fiction in the City (KATHARINA HALL) 1056
Pinney, Thomas, ed., The Cambridge Edition of the Poems of Rudyard Kipling (JOHN BATCHELOR) 663
Pirholt, Mattias, Metamimesis: Imitation in Goethe's *Wilhelm Meisters Lehrjahre* and Early German Romanticism (MARTIN SWALES) 548
Platten, David, The Pleasures of Crime: Reading Modern French Crime Fiction (LUCY O'MEARA) 257
Ponomareff, Constantin V., The Time before Death: Twentieth-Century Memoirs (SCOTT FREER) 1057
Potolsky, Matthew, The Decadent Republic of Letters: Taste, Politics, and Cosmopolitan Community from Baudelaire to Beardsley (RICHARD HIBBITT) 487
Powell, Manushag N., Performing Authorship in Eighteenth-Century English Periodicals (DANIEL COOK) 1068
Pravida, Dietmar, Brentano in Wien: Clemens Brentano, die Poesie und die Zeitgeschichte 1813/14 (CLAUDIA NITSCHKE) 1127
Preece, Julian, ed., Ilija Trojanow (STUART TABERNER) 1151
Pross, Caroline, Dekadenz: Studien zu einer großen Erzählung der frühen Moderne (THEODORE ZIOLKOWSKI) 1135
Qian, Zhaoming, ed., Modernism and the Orient (SHUANGYI LI) 489
Rabener, Gottlieb Wilhelm, Briefwechsel und Gespräche, ed. by E. Theodor Voss with Jan Müller (K. F. HILLIARD) 540
Racine, Andromache; Phaedra, in *Corneille, Molière, Racine: Four French Plays*. 'Cinna', 'The Misanthrope', 'Andromache', 'Phaedra', trans. by John Edmunds, intro. by Joseph Harris (TIM CHILCOTT) 802
Rash, Felicity, German Images of the Self and the Other: Nationalist, Colonialist and Anti-Semitic Discourse, 1871–1918 (FLORIAN KROBB) 832
Rathje, Jürgen, ed., Barthold Heinrich Brockes, *Werke*, I: *Selbstbiographie, Verdeutschter Bethlemitischer Kinder-Mord, Gelegenheitsgedichte, Aufsätze* (KEVIN HILLIARD) 840
Reeve-Tucker, Alice, and others, eds, Wyndham Lewis and the Cultures of Modernity (RANDALL STEVENSON) 505
Reinhard, Nadja, Moral und Ironie bei Gottlieb Wilhelm Rabener: Paratext und Palimpsest in den Satyrischen Schriften (K. F. HILLIARD) 842

REVIEWS (cont.)

Reisigl, Martin, and others, eds, Diskurslinguistik im Spannungsfeld von Deskription und Kritik (SYLVIA JAWORSKA) 1110
Reuß, Roland, 'Im Freien?' Kleist-Versuche (K. F. HILLIARD) 550
Riccobono, Rossella M., ed., The Poetics of the Margins: Mapping Europe from the Interstices (SILVIA ROSS) 1059
Richards, Anna, and Helen Fronius, eds, German Women's Writing of the Eighteenth and Nineteenth Centuries: Future Directions in Feminist Criticism (ROBERT GILLETT) 547
Richards, Anna, and Mary Cosgrove, eds, Sadness and Melancholy in German-Language Literature and Culture (INGO CORNILS) 839
Richardson, Michael D., and Jennifer M. Kapczynski, eds, A New History of German Cinema (MARTIN BRADY) 865
Robertson, Ritchie, and Manfred Engel, eds, Kafka und die kleine Prosa der Moderne/Kafka and Short Modernist Prose (RONALD SPEIRS) 282
Robertson, Ritchie, and Manfred Engel, eds, Kafka, Prag und der Erste Weltkrieg/Kafka, Prague and the First World War (JEREMY ADLER) . . 853
Robinson, Alan, Narrating the Past: Historiography, Memory and the Contemporary Novel (DAVID JAMES) 245
Rogowski, Christian, ed., The Many Faces of Weimar Cinema: Rediscovering Germany's Filmic Legacy (ERICA CARTER) 579
Romani, Gabriella, and others, eds, The Printed Media in Fin-de-Siècle Italy: Publishers, Writers, and Readers (URSULA J. FANNING) 824
Roth-Ey, Kristin, Moscow Prime Time: How the Soviet Union Built the Media Empire that Lost the Cultural Cold War (NATASHA RULYOVA) 1159
Rowe, John Carlos, and Eric Haralson, eds, A Historical Guide to Henry James (RICHARD SALMON) 503
Rucellai, Bernardo, De bello Italico. La guerra d'Italia, ed. by Donatella Coppini, foreword by Renzo Martinelli (CARLO CARUSO) 1096
Ruehl, Martin A., and Melissa S. Lane, eds, A Poet's Reich: Politics and Culture in the George Circle (CHRISTOPHE FRICKER) 560
Rühm, Gerhard, and Monika Lichtenfeld, eds, Franz Richard Behrens, Mein bester Freund — Hamlet: Drehbücher, Kinotexte, Filmkritiken (JEREMY ADLER) 850
Ryan, Judith, The Cambridge Introduction to German Poetry (IAN COOPER) 265
Salmons, Joseph, A History of German: What the Past Reveals about Today's Language (MARTIN DURRELL) 522
Sampson, Lisa, and Barbara Burgess-Van Aken, eds and trans., Barbara Torelli Benedetti, 'Partenia': A Pastoral Play (RICHARD ANDREWS) 1101
Sanson, Helena, Women, Language and Grammar in Italy, 1500–1900 (FRANCESCO SBERLATI) 258
Saul, Nicholas, and Dirk Göttsche, eds, Realism and Romanticism in German Literature/Realismus und Romantik in der deutschsprachigen Literatur (ROGER PAULIN) 1132
Savolainen, Matti, and P. M. Mehtonen, eds, Gothic Topographies: Language, Nation Building and 'Race' (SARAH ILOTT) 1054
Schaumann, Caroline, and Sean Ireton, eds, Heights of Reflection: Mountains in the German Imagination from the Middle Ages to the Twenty-First Century (THEODORE ZIOLKOWSKI) 526

REVIEWS (cont.)

	PAGE
Schlegel, Friedrich, Alarcos: Ein Trauerspiel. Historisch-kritische Edition mit Dokumenten, ed. by Mark-Georg Dehrmann with Nils Gelker (ROGER PAULIN)	1124
Schofield, Benedict, and Charlotte Woodford, eds, The German Bestseller in the Late Nineteenth Century (DIRK GÖTTSCHE)	555
Schofield, Benedict, Private Lives and Collective Destinies: Class, Nation and the Folk in the Works of Gustav Freytag (FLORIAN KROBB)	556
Scholar, Richard, and Alexis Tadié, eds, Fiction and the Frontiers of Knowledge in Europe, 1500–1800 (SÍOFRA PIERSE)	511
Schossböck, Judith, Letzte Menschen: Postapokalyptische Narrative und Identitäten in der Neueren Literatur nach 1945 (ROBERT WENINGER)	863
Schöttker, Detlev, ed., Ernst Jünger, Atlantische Fahrt: 'Rio: Residenz des Weltgeistes' (CHRISTOPHE FRICKER)	1141
Schrumpf, Anita-Mathilde, Sprechzeiten: Rhythmus und Takt in Hölderlins Elegien (IAN COOPER)	1126
Schumacher, Yves, and others, eds, 'Man will werden, nicht gewesen sein': Zur Aktualität Max Frischs (HANS J. HAHN)	861
Schur, Anna, Wages of Evil: Dostoevsky and Punishment (SARAH J. YOUNG)	302
Schuster, Matthias, Franz Kafkas Handschrift zum Schloss (RITCHIE ROBERTSON)	567
Schweitzer, Zoé, and Véronique Lochert, eds, Philologie et théâtre: traduire, commenter, interpréter le théâtre antique en Europe (xve–xviiie siècle) (EDWARD FORMAN)	1052
Schwilk, Heimo, ed., Ernst Jünger, Feldpostbriefe an die Familie: 1915–1918; mit ausgewählten Antwortbriefen der Eltern und Friedrich Georg Jüngers (CHRISTOPHE FRICKER)	1141
Schwilk, Heimo, Hermann Hesse: Das Leben des Glasperlenspielers (OSMAN DURRANI)	283
Schwob, Anton, and Ute Monika Schwob, eds, Die Lebenszeugnisse Oswalds von Wolkenstein: Edition und Kommentar, IV: 1438–1442, Nr. 277–386 (ALMUT SUERBAUM)	266
Schwob, Ute Monika, and Anton Schwob, eds, Die Lebenszeugnisse Oswalds von Wolkenstein: Edition und Kommentar, IV: 1438–1442, Nr. 277–386 (ALMUT SUERBAUM)	266
Scott, Maria C., Stendhal's Less-Loved Heroines: Fiction, Freedom, and the Female (SUSANNAH WILSON)	1084
Séguin, Alfred, Le Robinson noir, ed. and intro. by Roger Little (JARROD HAYES)	813
Sell, Roger D., Communicational Criticism: Studies in Literature as Dialogue (JONATHAN BALDO)	1062
Sell, Roger D., ed., Literary Community-Making: The Dialogicality of English Texts from the Seventeenth Century to the Present (RENZO D'AGNILLO)	236
Sessions, William A., foreword to A Critical Edition of the Complete Poems of Henry Howard, Earl of Surrey, ed. by William McGaw (ANDREW HISCOCK)	495
Sheckels, Theodore F., The Political in Margaret Atwood's Fiction: The Writing on the Wall of the Tent (KIRIAKI MASSOURA)	1078
Shepard, Laurie, and Daniel E. O'Sullivan, eds, Shaping Courtliness in Medieval France: Essays in Honor of Matilda Tomaryn Bruckner (CATHERINE LEGLU)	1081

REVIEWS (*cont.*)

Shields, Michael, and others, eds, German and European Poetics after the Holocaust: Crisis and Creativity (KIRSTIN GWYER)   296
Shoemaker, Peter William, ed., Jean Donneau de Visé, *Les Costeaux; ou, Les Marquis frians* (DEREK CONNON)   513
Sipe, Daniel, Text, Image, and the Problem with Perfection in Nineteenth-Century France: Utopia and its Afterlives (GREG KERR)   518
Smith, Nicole D., Sartorial Strategies: Outfitting Aristocrats and Fashioning Conduct in Late Medieval Literature (SARAH L. PEVERLEY)   1065
Socarides, Alexandra, Dickinson Unbound: Paper, Process, Poetics (PÁRAIC FINNERTY)   1070
Sohrabi, Naghmeh, Taken for Wonder: Nineteenth-Century Travel Accounts from Iran to Europe (REBECCA BUTLER)   1053
Southerden, Francesca, and others, eds, Desire in Dante and the Middle Ages (RUTH CHESTER)   221
Spinks, Jennifer, Early Modern Women in the Low Countries: Feminizing Sources and Interpretations of the Past (JANE FENOULHET)   301
Sprecher, Thomas, and Monica Bussmann, eds, Thomas Mann, *Bekenntnisse des Hochstaplers Felix Krull: Der Memoiren erster Teil* (RITCHIE ROBERTSON)   287
Sprecher, Thomas, and others, eds, Thomas Mann, *Briefe*, III: *1924–1932* (RITCHIE ROBERTSON)   287
Staines, David, intro., *The Song of Roland*, trans. by John DuVal (LUKE SUNDERLAND)   795
Steier, Christoph, and others, eds, 'Man will werden, nicht gewesen sein': Zur Aktualität Max Frischs (HANS J. HAHN)   861
Stein, Jordan Alexander, and Lara Langer Cohen, eds, Early African American Print Culture (KATY L. CHILES)   783
Stengel, Friedemann, Aufklärung bis zum Himmel: Emanuel Swedenborg im Kontext der Theologie des 18. Jahrhunderts (PAUL BISHOP)   1116
Stockinger, Claudia, and Stefan Scherer, eds, Ludwig Tieck: Leben — Werk — Wirkung (BRIAN HAMAN)   273
Struck, Wolfgang, and Hansjörg Bay, eds, Literarische Entdeckungsreisen: Vorfahren — Nachfahrten — Revisionen (DIRK GÖTTSCHE)   528
Szmurlo, Karyna, ed., Germaine de Staël: Forging a Politics of Mediation (JOANNE WILKES)   254
Taberner, Stuart, Aging and Old-Age Style in Günter Grass, Ruth Klüger, Christa Wolf, and Martin Walser: The Mannerism of a Late Period (ALEXANDRA LLOYD)   1147
Tadié, Alexis, and Richard Scholar, eds, Fiction and the Frontiers of Knowledge in Europe, 1500–1800 (SÍOFRA PIERSE)   511
Tambling, Jeremy, Literature and Psychoanalysis (LUCIANO PARISI)   491
Tattam, Helen, Time in the Philosophy of Gabriel Marcel (GEOFFREY KARABIN)   1089
Terence, Eunuco: un volgarizzamento anonimo in terza rima, ed. by Matteo Favaretto (DIEGO ZANCANI)   1099
Terrall, Mary, and Helen Deutsch, eds, Vital Matters: Eighteenth-Century Views of Conception, Life, and Death (ANDREW WELLS)   223
Thakkar, Amit, The Fiction of Juan Rulfo: Irony, Revolution and Postcolonialism (OLIVIA VÁZQUEZ-MEDINA)   264
Thiher, Allen, Understanding Marcel Proust (JENNIFER RUSHWORTH) . . .   812

REVIEWS (cont.)

	PAGE
Thompson, Hannah, Taboo: Corporeal Secrets in Nineteenth-Century France (Françoise Grauby)	809
Thüring, Hubert, and others, eds, Schreiben und Streichen: Zu einem Moment produktiver Negativität (Andreas Kramer)	525
Tissoni, Francesco, and Stefano Carrai, eds, Matteo Maria Boiardo, *Pastoralia. Carmina. Epigrammata* (Carlo Caruso)	1094
Torelli Benedetti, Barbara, Partenia: A Pastoral Play, ed. and trans. by Lisa Sampson and Barbara Burgess-Van Aken (Richard Andrews)	1101
Tracy, Larissa, Torture and Brutality in Medieval Literature: Negotiations of National Identity (David Matthews)	220
Traherne, Matthew, and Vittorio Montemaggi, eds, Dante's *Commedia*: Theology as Poetry (Julia Bolton Holloway)	261
Trout, Colette, and Frédérique Chevillot, eds, Rebelles et criminelles chez les écrivaines d'expression française (Nathalie Morello)	819
Vaget, Hans R., and others, eds, Thomas Mann, *Briefe*, III: *1924–1932* (Ritchie Robertson)	287
Van Buskirk, Emily, and Andrei Zorin, eds, Lydia Ginzburg's Alternative Literary Identities: A Collection of Articles and New Translations (Sarah Pratt)	305
Van der Laan, J. M., and Andrew Weeks, eds, The Faustian Century: German Literature and Culture in the Age of Luther and Faustus (John L. Flood)	1113
Van der Steeg, Christian, Wissenskunst: Adalbert Stifter und Naturforscher auf Weltreise (Michael Minden)	846
Vasset, Sophie, ed., Medicine and Narration in the Eighteenth Century (Clark Lawlor)	483
Vervaeck, Bart, and others, eds, Stories and Minds: Cognitive Approaches to Literary Narrative (Richard Walsh)	775
Vickers, Brian, and others, eds, *The Collected Works of John Ford*, vol. I (Lesel Dawson)	235
Vigarello, Georges, The Metamorphoses of Fat: A History of Obesity, trans. by C. Jon Delogu (Anna Jenkin)	482
Villa, Luisa, and Massimo Bacigalupo, eds, The Politics and Poetics of Displacement: Modernism off the Beaten Track (Paul Poplawski)	1072
Villani, Stefano, George Frederick Nott (1768–1841): un ecclesiastico anglicano tra teologia, letteratura, arte, archeologia, bibliofilia e collezionismo (Fabio Camilletti)	226
Visé, Jean Donneau de, Les Costeaux; ou, Les Marquis frians, ed. by Peter William Shoemaker (Derek Connon)	513
Voss, E. Theodor, with Jan Müller, eds, Gottlieb Wilhelm Rabener, *Briefwechsel und Gespräche* (K. F. Hilliard)	540
Voss, Rüdiger von, and Frank-Lothar Kroll, eds, Schriftsteller und Widerstand: Facetten und Probleme der inneren Emigration (William J. Dodd)	570
Vuillemin, Nathalie, and Adrien Paschoud, eds, Penser l'ordre naturel, 1680–1810 (Nick Treuherz)	250
Wace, The Hagiographical Works: The *Conception Nostre Dame* and the Lives of St Margaret and St Nicholas, ed. and trans. by Jean Blacker and others (Huw Grange)	796

Contents

REVIEWS (cont.)   PAGE

Wadell, Nathan, and others, eds, Wyndham Lewis and the Cultures of Modernity (RANDALL STEVENSON)   505

Walker, John, The Truth of Realism: A Reassessment of the German Novel 1830–1900 (DIRK GÖTTSCHE)   847

Warnke, Ingo H., and others, eds, Diskurslinguistik im Spannungsfeld von Deskription und Kritik (SYLVIA JAWORSKA)   1110

Watt, R. J. C., and others, eds, *The Collected Works of John Ford*, vol. I (LESEL DAWSON)   235

Watts, Andrew, and Kate Griffiths, Adapting Nineteenth-Century France: Literature in Film, Theatre, Television, Radio and Print (BRADLEY STEPHENS)   815

Watts, Andrew, and Susan Harrow, eds, Mapping Memory in Nineteenth-Century French Literature and Culture (ANDREW J. COUNTER)   517

Weber, Jutta, and Marie-Theres Federhofer, eds, Korrespondenzen und Transformationen: Neue Perspektiven auf Adalbert von Chamisso (JOANNA NEILLY)   1128

Weeks, Andrew, and J. M. van der Laan, eds, The Faustian Century: German Literature and Culture in the Age of Luther and Faustus (JOHN L. FLOOD)   1113

Weninger, Robert K., The German Joyce (DAVID MIDGLEY)   858

Westphal, Siegrid, and Wolfgang Adam, eds, Handbuch kultureller Zentren der Frühen Neuzeit: Städte und Residenzen im alten deutschen Sprachraum (JOHN L. FLOOD)   537

White, Michael James, Space in Theodor Fontane's Works: Theme and Poetic Function (JEFFREY L. SAMMONS)   277

White, Nicholas, French Divorce Fiction from the Revolution to the First World War (PHOEBE MALTZ BOVY)   1086

Wiggins, Martin, Drama and the Transfer of Power in Renaissance England (NICHOLAS GRENE)   498

Wirtz, Irmgard M., and others, eds, Schreiben und Streichen: Zu einem Moment produktiver Negativität (ANDREAS KRAMER)   525

Woodford, Charlotte, and Benedict Schofield, eds, The German Bestseller in the Late Nineteenth Century (DIRK GÖTTSCHE)   555

Zeilinger, Doris, and others, eds, Bloch-Wörterbuch: Leitbegriffe der Philosophie Ernst Blochs (CATHERINE MOIR)   292

Zilboorg, Caroline, ed., H.D., *Bid Me to Live: A Madrigal* (ALICE KELLY) . .   243

Zimmermann, Rainer, and others, eds, Bloch-Wörterbuch: Leitbegriffe der Philosophie Ernst Blochs (CATHERINE MOIR)   292

Zorin, Andrei, and Emily Van Buskirk, eds, Lydia Ginzburg's Alternative Literary Identities: A Collection of Articles and New Translations (SARAH PRATT)   305

Abstracts of Articles, Vol. 109, Part 1 (January 2014)   309
Abstracts of Articles, Vol. 109, Part 2 (April 2014)   590
Abstracts of Articles, Vol. 109, Part 3 (July 2014)   870
Abstracts of Articles, Vol. 109, Part 4 (October 2014)   1162

www.ingramcontent.com/pod-product-compliance
Lightning Source LLC
Chambersburg PA
CBHW072122290426
44111CB00012B/1747